POINTS OF VIEW FOR COLLEGE STUDENTS

BY

PAUL KAUFMAN, Ph.D.

PROFESSOR OF ENGLISH LITERATURE,
AMERICAN UNIVERSITY

GARDEN CITY NEW YORK
DOUBLEDAY, DORAN & COMPANY, Inc.
1931

PR
928
K21P

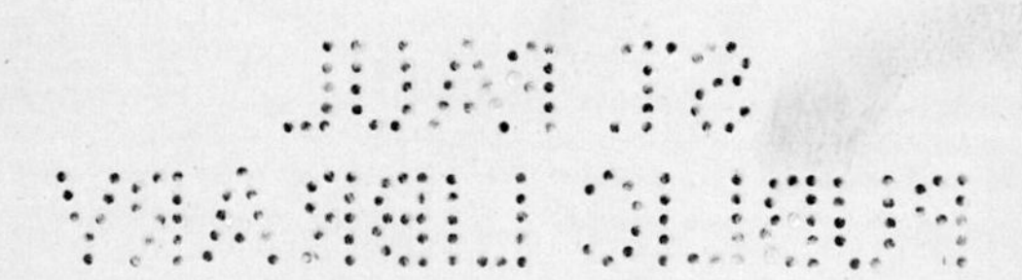

FOREWORD

"Mankind has struck its tents and is on the march." It is not only one race or one nation which is moving on from its camping-ground of tradition but throughout the world all peoples seem, as never before in history, to be in the confusion of a spiritual migration. The pace is fast and the scenery is too often blurred by conflicting road signs. Within the few short years since the dawn of the twentieth century, and particularly within the last decade, horizons have been almost unbelievably widened. But between us and new goals for human achievement lie yet vaster stretches of uncharted lands. Beyond

Hills peep o'er hills, and Alps on Alps arise.

The college is, or should be, a genuine center of information for travelers,—equipped with the latest guidebooks, with maps of the surrounding country, and of the good and bad roads ahead: it should prove itself the modern "House of the Interpreter" along the path of the present-day Pilgrim's Progress. It should be a school of human engineering able to train leaders who can go forth to find and to make roads through the unknown.

Happily the American college has recognized this obligation to the present age. It has realized that to pass on our heritage and to develop a lively appreciation of current problems are tasks not to be wholly prepared for through a succession of the traditional separate courses. It has begun to learn the necessity of correlating the various branches of knowledge as they are actually related in human experience. And it has finally realized that the student should be given the opportunity to acquire, at the very beginning of his college career, a comprehensive background of human experience.

To this end, general introductory courses in "orientation"—"turning towards the light," or finding our bearings—have met with widespread favor. Freshman English also is now becoming recognized as essentially orientation. The prime purpose of this course—training in effective expression—should not be abandoned, but in providing ideas as the basis for such expression we can do much better than limit the student to such subjects as "Impressions of My First Day at College," "The Big Game," and "Sunset from a College Window." Particularly in that momentous epoch in the student's career, the first semester, when exposition is the form of writing most commonly stressed, the models for study may profitably present the background for the solution of contemporary human problems—and a sort of panorama of cultural horizons.

This panorama I have tried to construct in the present volume of readings. The essays have been selected to give the student an intelligent point of view, and they have been classified under the very divisions of human culture listed in any college catalogue: Literature, Art, Science, Philosophy, and Social Science. The student can thus determine, at least to some extent, at the beginning of his course, what subjects he will find most appealing to him as he faces the problem of making his choice among the riches of the curriculum; and he can construct a comprehensive view of the whole range of human thought.

In the character of the selections this book marks a departure from its predecessors. I have felt that our objective in this course should be not to impart information but to present points of view, and to afford breadth of view. I have, therefore, striven particularly to choose the general rather than the particular and to include those essays which, individually, reveal wide and intimate relationships among human interests.

The concentration is upon contemporary problems, but it would be an unfortunate limitation to exclude from a book of Freshman readings all of the great utterances of the nineteenth century, and I have consequently included something from Carlyle, Ruskin, Huxley, Stevenson, and Emerson. All of these fit logically into an orientation program; and Emerson's "American Scholar," particularly, may be regarded as the peculiar birthright of every American student; it could come into his possession never more opportunely than in his Freshman year.

To my colleague, Dean George B. Woods, I must express deep gratitude for continual aid in making difficult choices among selections. I have also to thank Professor Odell Shepard for valuable suggestions. To my wife must be given the credit not only for intelligent, painstaking preparation of manuscript but also for constant counsel in the make-up of the entire volume. To all the publishers, particularly Harper & Brothers, and Harcourt, Brace and Co., who have generously permitted use of material, I owe my best thanks. For permission to use the poem "Attainment" by Madison Cawein I am indebted to Small, Maynard and Co. Detailed credit for the use of copyright works is given in the footnotes.

PAUL KAUFMAN

WASHINGTON, D. C.
May, 1926

CONTENTS

PIONEERS! O PIONEERS![1]

WALT WHITMAN

COME my tan-faced children,
Follow well in order, get your weapons ready,
Have you your pistols? have you your sharp-edged axes?
Pioneers! O pioneers!

For we cannot tarry here,
We must march my darlings, we must bear the brunt of danger,
We the youthful sinewy races, all the rest on us depend,
Pioneers! O pioneers!

O you youths, Western youths,
So impatient, full of action, full of manly pride and friendship,
Plain I see you Western youths, see you tramping with the foremost,
Pioneers! O pioneers!

Have the elder races halted?
Do they droop and end their lesson, wearied over there beyond the sea?
We take up the task eternal, and the burden and the lesson,
Pioneers! O pioneers!

[1] From *Drum Taps*, 1865.

All the past we leave behind,
We debouch upon a newer mightier world, varied world,
Fresh and strong the world we seize, world of labor and the march,
Pioneers! O pioneers!

We detachments steady throwing,
Down the edges, through the passes, up the mountain steep,
Conquering, holding, daring, venturing as we go the unknown ways,
Pioneers! O pioneers!

We primeval forests felling,
We the rivers stemming, vexing we and piercing deep the mines within,
We the surface broad surveying, we the virgin soil upheaving,
Pioneers! O pioneers!

Colorado men are we,
From the peaks gigantic, from the great sierras and the high plateaus,
From the mine and from the gully, from the hunting trail we come,
Pioneers! O pioneers!

From Nebraska, from Arkansas,
Central inland race are we, from Missouri, with the continental blood intervein'd,

All the hands of comrades clasping, all the Southern, all
the Northern,
Pioneers! O pioneers!

O resistless, restless race!
O beloved race in all! O my breast aches with tender
love for all!
O I mourn and yet exult, I am rapt with love for all,
Pioneers! O pioneers!

Raise the mighty mother mistress,
Waving high the delicate mistress, over all the starry mis-
tress (bend your heads all),
Raise the fang'd and warlike mistress, stern, impassive,
weapon'd mistress,
Pioneers! O pioneers!

See my children, resolute children,
By those swarms upon our rear we must never yield or
falter,
Ages back in ghostly millions frowning there behind us
urging,
Pioneers! O pioneers!

On and on the compact ranks,
With accessions ever waiting, with the places of the dead
quickly fill'd,
Through the battle, through defeat, moving yet and never
stopping,
Pioneers! O pioneers!

O to die advancing on!
Are there some of us to droop and die? has the hour
come?
Then upon the march we fittest die, soon and sure the gap
is fill'd,
Pioneers! O pioneers!

All the pulses of the world,
Falling in they beat for us, with the Western movement
beat,
Holding single or together, steady moving to the front,
all for us,
Pioneers! O pioneers!

Life's involv'd and varied pageants,
All the forms and shows, all the workmen at their work,
All the seamen and the landsmen, all the masters with
their slaves,
Pioneers! O pioneers!

All the hapless silent lovers,
All the prisoners in the prisons, all the righteous and the
wicked,
All the joyous, all the sorrowing, all the living, all the
dying,
Pioneers! O pioneers!

I too with my soul and body,
We, a curious trio, picking, wandering on our way,
Through these shores amid the shadows, with the appari-
tions pressing,
Pioneers! O pioneers!

Lo, the darting bowling orb!
Lo, the brother orbs around, all the clustering suns and planets,
All the dazzling days, all the mystic nights with dreams,
Pioneers! O pioneers!

These are of us, they are with us,
All for primal needed work, while the followers there in embryo wait behind,
We to-day's procession heading, we the route for travel clearing,
Pioneers! O pioneers!

O you daughters of the West!
O you young and elder daughters! O you mothers and you wives!
Never must you be divided, in our ranks you move united,
Pioneers! O pioneers!

Minstrels latent on the prairies!
(Shrouded bards of other lands, you may rest, you have done your work),
Soon I hear you coming warbling, soon you rise and tramp amid us,
Pioneers! O pioneers!

Not for delectations sweet,
Not the cushion and the slipper, not the peaceful and the studious,
Not the riches safe and palling, not for us the tame enjoyment,
Pioneers! O pioneers!

Do the feasters gluttonous feast?
Do the corpulent sleepers sleep? Have they lock'd and bolted doors?
Still be ours the diet hard, and the blanket on the ground,
Pioneers! O pioneers!

Has the night descended?
Was the road of late so toilsome? did we stop discouraged nodding on our way?
Yet a passing hour I yield you in your tracks to pause oblivious,
Pioneers! O pioneers!

Till with sound of trumpet,
Far, far off the daybreak call—hark! how loud and clear I hear it wind,
Swift! to the head of the army!—swift! spring to your places,
Pioneers! O pioneers!

EDUCATION

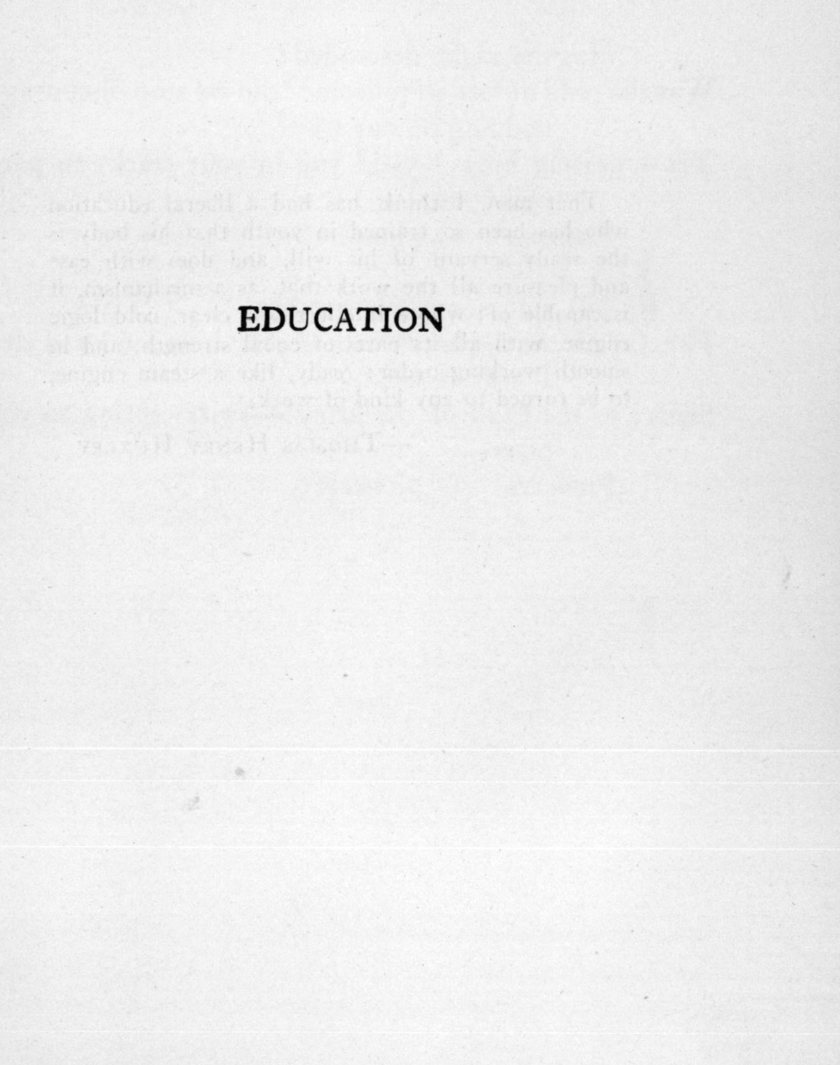

That man, I think, has had a liberal education who has been so trained in youth that his body is the ready servant of his will, and does with ease and pleasure all the work that, as a mechanism, it is capable of; whose intellect is a clear, cold logic engine, with all its parts of equal strength, and in smooth working order; ready, like a steam engine, to be turned to any kind of work.

—Thomas Henry Huxley

POINTS OF VIEW FOR COLLEGE STUDENTS

FOUR KINDS OF THINKING[1]

JAMES HARVEY ROBINSON

[James Harvey Robinson was born in Bloomington, Illinois, in 1863. He is a graduate of Harvard and received his Ph.D. from the University of Freiberg. From 1892 to 1919 he was professor of history at Columbia and from 1919 to 1921 he lectured at the New School of Social Research, New York, of which he was one of the founders. He is the author of standard text-books of European history. The widespread influence which he has recently exerted upon changing thought may be partly inferred from the titles of his recent books, *The Mind in the Making* and *The Humanizing of Knowledge*.]

WE do not think enough about thinking, and much of our confusion is the result of current illusions in regard to it. Let us forget for the moment any impressions we may have derived from the philosophers, and see what seems to happen in ourselves. The first thing that we notice is that our thought moves with such incredible rapidity that it is almost impossible to arrest any specimen of it long enough to have a look at it. When we are offered a penny for our thoughts we always find that we have recently had so many things

[1] From *The Mind in the Making*. Copyright, 1921, by Harper and Brothers. Reprinted by permission of the publishers.

in mind that we can easily make a selection which will not compromise us too nakedly. On inspection we shall find that even if we are not downright ashamed of a great part of our spontaneous thinking it is far too intimate, personal, ignoble or trivial to permit us to reveal more than a small part of it. I believe this must be true of everyone. We do not, of course, know what goes on in other people's heads. They tell us very little and we tell them very little. The spigot of speech, rarely fully opened, could never emit more than driblets of the ever renewed hogshead of thought—*noch grösser wie's Heidelberger Fass.* We find it hard to believe that other people's thoughts are as silly as our own, but they probably are.

We all appear to ourselves to be thinking all the time during our waking hours, and most of us are aware that we go on thinking while we are asleep, even more foolishly than when awake. When uninterrupted by some practical issue we are engaged in what is now known as a *reverie.* This is our spontaneous and favorite kind of thinking. We allow our ideas to take their own course and this course is determined by our hopes and fears, our spontaneous desires, their fulfillment or frustration; by our likes and dislikes, our loves and hates and resentments. There is nothing else anything like so interesting to ourselves as ourselves. All thought that is not more or less laboriously controlled and directed will inevitably circle about the beloved Ego. It is amusing and pathetic to observe this tendency in ourselves and in others. We learn politely and generously to overlook this truth, but if we dare to think of it, it blazes forth like the noontide sun.

The reverie or "free association of ideas" has of late become the subject of scientific research. While investigators are not yet agreed on the results, or at least on the proper interpretation to be given to them, there can be no doubt that our reveries form the chief index to our fundamental character. They are a reflection of our nature as modified by often hidden and forgotten experiences. We need not go into the matter further here, for it is only necessary to observe that the reverie is at all times a potent and in many cases an omnipotent rival to every other kind of thinking. It doubtless influences all our speculations in its persistent tendency to self-magnification and self-justification, which are its chief preoccupations, but it is the last thing to make directly or indirectly for honest increase of knowledge. Philosophers usually talk as if such thinking did not exist or were in some way negligible. This is what makes their speculations so unreal and often worthless.

The reverie, as any of us can see for himself, is frequently broken and interrupted by the necessity of a second kind of thinking. We have to make practical decisions. Shall we write a letter or no? Shall we take the subway or a bus? Shall we have dinner at seven or half-past? Shall we buy U. S. Rubber or a Liberty Bond? Decisions are easily distinguishable from the free flow of reverie. Sometimes they demand a good deal of careful pondering and the recollection of pertinent facts; often, however, they are made impulsively. They are a more difficult and laborious thing than the reverie, and we resent having to "make up our mind" when we are tired, or absorbed in a congenial reverie. Weighing a decision, it should be noted, does not necessarily add anything to our knowledge, although we may, of course, seek further information before making it.

A third kind of thinking is stimulated when anyone questions our belief and opinions. We sometimes find ourselves changing our minds without any resistance or heavy emotion, but if we are told that we are wrong we resent the imputation and harden our hearts. We are incredibly heedless in the formation of our beliefs, but find ourselves filled with an illicit passion for them when anyone proposes to rob us of their companionship. It is obviously not the ideas themselves that are dear to us, but our self-esteem, which is threatened. We are by nature stubbornly pledged to defend our own from attack, whether it be our person, our family, our property, or our opinion. A United States Senator once remarked to a friend of mine that God Almighty could not make him change his mind on our Latin-American policy. We may surrender, but rarely confess ourselves vanquished. In the intellectual world at least peace is without victory.

Few of us take the pains to study the origin of our cherished convictions; indeed, we have a natural repugnance to so doing. We like to continue to believe what we have been accustomed to accept as true, and the resentment aroused when doubt is cast upon any of our assumptions leads us to seek every manner of excuse for clinging to them. *The result is that most of our so-called reasoning consists in finding arguments for going on believing as we already do.*

I remember years ago attending a public dinner to which the Governor of the state was bidden. The chairman explained that His Excellency could not be present for certain "good" reasons; what the "real" reasons were the presiding officer said he would leave us to conjecture. This distinction between "good" and "real" reasons is one of the most clarifying and essential in the whole realm of thought. We can readily give what seem to us "good" reasons for being a Catholic or a Mason, a Republican or a Democrat, an adherent or opponent of the League of Nations. But the "real" reasons are usually on quite a different plane. Of course the importance of this distinction is popularly, if somewhat obscurely, recognized. The Baptist missionary is ready enough to see that the Buddhist is not such because his doctrines would bear careful inspection, but because he happened to be born in a Buddhist family in Tokio. But it would be treason to his faith to acknowledge that his own partiality for certain doctrines is due to the fact that his mother was a member of the First Baptist Church of Oak Ridge. A savage can give all sorts of reasons for his belief that it is dangerous to step on a man's shadow, and a newspaper editor can advance plenty of arguments against the Bolsheviki. But neither of them may realize why he happens to be defending his particular opinion.

The "real" reasons for our beliefs are concealed from ourselves as well as from others. As we grow up we simply adopt the ideas presented to us in regard to such matters as religion, family relations, property, business, our country, and the state. We unconsciously absorb them from our environment. They are persistently whispered in our ear by the group in which we happen to live. Moreover, as Mr. Trotter has pointed out, these judgments, being the product of suggestion and not of reasoning, have the quality of perfect obviousness, so that to question them

. . . is to the believer to carry skepticism to an insane degree, and will be met by contempt, disapproval, or condemnation, according to the nature of the belief in question. When, therefore, we find ourselves entertaining an opinion about the basis of which there is a quality of feeling which tells us that to inquire into it would be absurd, obviously unnecessary, unprofitable, undesirable, bad form, or wicked, we may know that that opinion is a non-rational one, and probably, therefore, founded upon inadequate evidence.[1]

Opinions, on the other hand, which are the result of experience or of honest reasoning do not have this quality of "primary certitude." I remember when as a youth I heard a group of business men discussing the question of the immortality of the soul, I was outraged by the sentiment of doubt expressed by one of the party. As I look back now I see that I had at the time no interest in the matter, and certainly no least argument to urge in favor of the belief in which I had been reared. But neither my personal indifference to the issue, nor the fact that I had previously given it no attention, served to prevent an angry resentment when I heard *my* ideas questioned.

This spontaneous and loyal support of our preconceptions—this process of finding "good" reasons to justify our routine beliefs—is known to modern psychologists as "rationalizing"—clearly only a new name for a very ancient thing. Our "good" reasons ordinarily have no value in promoting honest enlightenment, because, no matter how solemnly they may be marshaled, they are at bottom the result of personal preference or prejudice, and not of an honest desire to seek or accept new knowledge.

In our reveries we are frequently engaged in self-

[1] *Instincts of the Herd,* p. 44.

justification, for we cannot bear to think ourselves wrong, and yet have constant illustrations of our weaknesses and mistakes. So we spend much time finding fault with circumstances and the conduct of others, and shifting on to them with great ingenuity the onus of our own failures and disappointments. *Rationalizing is the self-exculpation which occurs when we feel ourselves, or our group, accused of misapprehension or error.*

The little word *my* is the most important one in all human affairs, and properly to reckon with it is the beginning of wisdom. It has the same force whether it is *my* dinner, *my* dog, and *my* house, or *my* faith, *my* country, and *my* God. We not only resent the imputation that our watch is wrong, or our car shabby, but that our conception of the canals of Mars, of the pronunciation of "Epictetus," of the medicinal value of salicine, or the date of Sargon I, are subject to revision.

Philosophers, scholars, and men of science exhibit a common sensitiveness in all decisions in which their *amour propre* is involved. Thousands of argumentative works have been written to vent a grudge. However stately their reasoning, it may be nothing but rationalizing, stimulated by the most commonplace of all motives. A history of philosophy and theology could be written in terms of grouches, wounded pride, and aversions, and it would be far more instructive than the usual treatments of these themes. Sometimes, under Providence, the lowly impulse of resentment leads to great achievements. Milton wrote his treatise on divorce as a result of his troubles with his seventeen-year-old wife, and when he was accused of being the leading spirit in a new sect, the Divorcers, he wrote his noble *Areopagitica* to prove his right to say what he thought fit, and incidentally to establish the advantage of a free press in the promotion of Truth.

All mankind, high and low, thinks in all the ways which have been described. The reverie goes on all the time not only in the mind of the mill hand and the Broadway flapper, but equally in weighty judges and godly bishops. It has gone on in all the philosophers, scientists, poets, and theologians that have ever lived. Aristotle's most abstruse speculations were doubtless tempered by highly irrelevant reflections. He is reported to have had very thin legs and small eyes, for which he doubtless had to find excuses, and he was wont to indulge in very conspicuous dress and rings and was accustomed to arrange his hair carefully.[1] Diogenes the Cynic exhibited the impudence of a touchy soul. His tub was his distinction. Tennyson in beginning his "Maud" could not forget his chagrin over losing his patrimony years before as the result of an unhappy investment in the Patent Decorative Carving Company. These facts are not recalled here as a gratuitous disparagement of the truly great, but to insure a full realization of the tremendous competition which all really exacting thought has to face, even in the minds of the most highly endowed mortals.

And now the astonishing and perturbing suspicion emerges that perhaps almost all that had passed for social science, political economy, politics, and ethics in the past may be brushed aside by future generations as mainly rationalizing. John Dewey has already reached this conclusion in regard to philosophy.[2] Veblen [3] and other

[1] Diogenes Laertius, Book V.
[2] *Reconstruction in Philosophy.*
[3] *The Place of Science in Modern Civilization.*

writers have revealed the various unperceived presuppositions of the traditional political economy, and now comes an Italian sociologist, Vilfredo Pareto, who, in his huge treatise on general sociology, devotes hundreds of pages to substantiating a similar thesis affecting all the social sciences.[1] This conclusion may be ranked by students of a hundred years hence as one of the several great discoveries of our age. It is by no means fully worked out, and it is so opposed to nature that it will be very slowly accepted by the great mass of those who consider themselves thoughtful. As a historical student I am personally fully reconciled to this newer view. Indeed, it seems to me inevitable that just as the various sciences of nature were, before the opening of the seventeenth century, largely masses of rationalizations to suit the religious sentiments of the period, so the social sciences have continued even to our own day to be rationalizations of uncritically accepted beliefs and customs.

It will become apparent as we proceed that the fact that an idea is ancient and that it has been widely received is no argument in its favor, but should immediately suggest the necessity of carefully testing it as a probable instance of rationalization.

This brings us to another kind of thought which can fairly easily be distinguished from the three kinds described above. It has not the usual qualities of the reverie, for it does not hover about our personal com-

[1] *Traité de Sociologie Générale, passim.* The author's term *"derivations"* seems to be his precise way of expressing what we have called the "good" reasons, and his *"residus"* correspond to the "real" reasons. He well says, *"L'homme éprouve le besoin de raisonner, et en outre d'étendre une voile sur ses instincts et sur ses sentiments"*—hence, rationalization. (p. 788.) His aim is to reduce sociology to the "real" reasons. (p. 791.)

placencies and humiliations. It is not made up of the homely decisions forced upon us by everyday needs, when we review our little stock of existing information, consult our conventional preferences and obligations, and make a choice of action. It is not the defense of our own cherished beliefs and prejudices just because they are our own—mere plausible excuses for remaining of the same mind. On the contrary, it is that peculiar species of thought which leads us to *change* our mind.

It is this kind of thought that has raised man from his pristine, subsavage ignorance and squalor to the degree of knowledge and comfort which he now possesses. On his capacity to continue and greatly extend this kind of thinking depends his chance of groping his way out of the plight in which the most highly civilized peoples of the world now find themselves. In the past this type of thinking has been called Reason. But so many misapprehensions have grown up around the word that some of us have become very suspicious of it. I suggest, therefore, that we substitute a recent name and speak of "creative thought" rather than of Reason. *For this kind of meditation begets knowledge, and knowledge is really creative inasmuch as it makes things look different from what they seemed before and may indeed work for their reconstruction.*

In certain moods some of us realize that we are observing things or making reflections with a seeming disregard of our personal preoccupations. We are not preening or defending ourselves; we are not faced by the necessity of any practical decision, nor are we apologizing for believing this or that. We are just wondering and looking and mayhap seeing what we never perceived before.

Curiosity is as clear and definite as any of our urges. We wonder what is in a sealed telegram or in a letter in which some one else is absorbed, or what is being said in the telephone booth or in low conversation. This inquisitiveness is vastly stimulated by jealousy, suspicion, or any hint that we ourselves are directly or indirectly involved. But there appears to be a fair amount of personal interest in other people's affairs even when they do not concern us except as a mystery to be unraveled or a tale to be told. The reports of a divorce suit will have "news value" for many weeks. They constitute a story, like a novel or play or moving picture. This is not an example of pure curiosity, however, since we readily identify ourselves with others, and their joys and despair then become our own.

We also take note of or "observe," as Sherlock Holmes says, things which have nothing to do with our personal interests and make no personal appeal either direct or by way of sympathy. This is what Veblen so well calls "idle curiosity." And it is usually idle enough. Some of us when we face the line of people opposite us in a subway train impulsively consider them in detail and engage in rabid inferences and form theories in regard to them. On entering a room there are those who will perceive at a glance the degree of preciousness of the rugs, the character of the pictures, and the personality revealed by the books. But there are many, it would seem, who are so absorbed in their personal reverie or in some definite purpose that they have no bright-eyed energy for idle curiosity. The tendency to miscellaneous observation we come by honestly enough, for we note it in many of our animal relatives.

Veblen, however, uses the term "idle curiosity" somewhat ironically, as is his wont. It is idle only to those who fail to realize that it may be a very rare and indispensable thing from which almost all distinguished human achievement proceeds since it may lead to systematic examination and seeking for things hitherto undiscovered. For research is but diligent search which enjoys the high flavor of primitive hunting. Occasionally and fitfully, idle curiosity thus leads to creative thought, which alters and broadens our own views and aspirations and may in turn, under highly favorable circumstances, affect the views and lives of others, even for generations to follow. An example or two will make this unique human process clear.

Galileo was a thoughtful youth and doubtless carried on a rich and varied reverie. He had artistic ability and might have turned out to be a musician or painter. When he had dwelt among the monks at Vallombrosa he had been tempted to lead the life of a religious. As a boy he busied himself with toy machines and he inherited a fondness for mathematics. All these facts are of record. We may safely assume also that, along with many other subjects of contemplation, the Pisan maidens found a vivid place in his thoughts.

One day when seventeen years old he wandered into the cathedral of his native town. In the midst of his reverie he looked up at the lamps hanging by long chains from the high ceiling of the church. Then something very difficult to explain occurred. He found himself no longer thinking of the building, worshipers, or the services; of his artistic or religious interests; of his reluctance to become a physician as his father wished. He forgot the question of a career and even the *graziosissime donne.* As he watched the swinging lamps he was suddenly wondering if mayhap their oscillations, whether long or short, did not occupy the same time. Then he tested this hypothesis by counting his pulse, for that was the only timepiece he had with him.

This observation, however remarkable in itself, was not enough to produce a really creative thought. Others may have noticed the same thing and yet nothing came of it. Most of our observations have no assignable results. Galileo may have seen that the warts on a peasant's face formed a perfect isosceles triangle, or he may have noticed with boyish glee that just as the officiating priest was uttering the solemn words, *Ecce agnus Dei,* a fly lit on the end of his nose. To be really creative, ideas have to be worked up and then "put over," so that they become a part of man's social heritage. The highly accurate pendulum clock was one of the later results of Galileo's discovery. He himself was led to reconsider and successfully to refute the old notions of falling bodies. It remained for Newton to prove that the moon was falling, and presumably all the heavenly bodies. This quite upset all the consecrated views of the heavens as managed by angelic engineers. The universality of the laws of gravitation stimulated the attempt to seek other and equally important natural laws and cast grave doubts on the miracles in which mankind had hitherto believed. In short, those who dared to include in their thought the discoveries of Galileo and his successors found themselves in a new earth surrounded by new heavens.

On the 28th of October, 1831, two hundred and fifty years after Galileo had noticed the isochronous vibrations of the lamps, creative thought and its currency had so far increased that Faraday was wondering what would happen if he mounted a disk of copper between the poles of a horsehoe magnet. As the disk revolved an electric current was produced. This would doubtless have seemed the idlest kind of experiment to the stanch business men of the time, who, it happened, were just then denouncing the child-labor bills in their anxiety to avail themselves to the full of the results of earlier idle curiosity. But should the dynamos and motors which have come into being as the outcome of Faraday's experiment be stopped this evening, the business man of to-day, agitated over labor troubles, might, as he trudged home past lines of "dead" cars, through dark streets to an unlighted house, engage in a little creative thought of his own and perceive that he and his laborers would have no modern factories and mines to quarrel about if it had not been for the strange practical effects of the idle curiosity of scientists, inventors, and engineers.

The examples of creative intelligence given above belong to the realm of modern scientific achievement, which furnishes the most striking instances of the effects of scrupulous, objective thinking. But there are, of course, other great realms in which the recording and embodiment of acute observation and insight have wrought themselves into the higher life of man. The great poets and dramatists and our modern story-tellers have found themselves engaged in productive reveries, noting and artistically presenting their discoveries for the delight and instruction of those who have the ability to appreciate them.

The process by which a fresh and original poem or drama comes into being is doubtless analogous to that which originates and elaborates so-called scientific discoveries; but there is clearly a temperamental difference. The genesis and advance of painting, sculpture, and music offer still other problems. We really as yet know shockingly little about these matters, and indeed very few people have the least curiosity about them.[1] Nevertheless, creative intelligence in its various forms is what makes man. Were it not for its slow, painful, and constantly discouraged operations through the ages man would be no more than a species of primate living on seeds, fruit, roots, and uncooked flesh, and wandering naked through the woods and over the plains like a chimpanzee.

The origin and progress and future promotion of civilization are ill understood and misconceived. These should be made the chief theme of education, but much hard work is necessary before we can construct our ideas of man and his capacities and free ourselves from innumerable persistent misapprehensions. There have been obstructionists in all times, not merely the lethargic masses, but the moralists, the rationalizing theologians, and most of the philosophers, all busily if unconsciously engaged in ratifying existing ignorance and mistakes and discouraging creative thought. Naturally, those who

[1] Recently a re-examination of creative thought has begun as a result of new knowledge which discredits many of the notions formerly held about "reason." See, for example, *Creative Intelligence*, by a group of American philosophic thinkers: John Dewey, *Essays in Experimental Logic* (both pretty hard books): and Veblen, *The Place of Science in Modern Civilization*. Easier than these and very stimulating are Dewey, *Reconstruction in Philosophy*, and Woodworth, *Dynamic Psychology*.

reassure us seem worthy of honor and respect. Equally naturaliy those who puzzle us with disturbing criticisms and invite us to change our ways are objects of suspicion and readily discredited. Our personal discontent does not ordinarily extend to any critical questioning of the general situation in which we find ourselves. In every age the prevailing conditions of civilization have appeared quite natural and inevitable to those who grew up in them. The cow asks no questions as to how it happens to have a dry stall and a supply of hay. The kitten laps its warm milk from a china saucer, without knowing anything about porcelain; the dog nestles in the corner of a divan with no sense of obligation to the inventors of upholstery and the manufacturers of down pillows. So we humans accept our breakfasts, our trains and telephones and orchestras and movies, our national Constitution, or moral code and standards of manners, with the simplicity and innocence of a pet rabbit. We have absolutely inexhaustible capacities for appropriating what others do for us with no thought of a "thank you." We do not feel called upon to make any least contribution to the merry game ourselves. Indeed, we are usually quite unaware that a game is being played at all.

We have now examined the various classes of thinking which we can readily observe in ourselves and which we have plenty of reasons to believe go on, and always have been going on, in our fellow-men. We can sometimes get quite pure and sparkling examples of all four kinds, but commonly they are so confused and intermingled in our reverie as not to be readily distinguishable. The reverie is a reflection of our longings, exultations, and complacencies, our fears, suspicions, and disappointments. We are chiefly engaged in struggling to maintain our self-respect and in asserting that supremacy which we all crave and which seems to us our natural prerogative. It is not strange, but rather quite inevitable, that our beliefs about what is true and false, good and bad, right and wrong, should be mixed up with the reverie and be influenced by the same considerations which determine its character and course. We resent criticisms of our views exactly as we do of anything else connected with ourselves. Our notions of life and its ideals seem to us to be *our own* and as such necessarily true and right, to be defended at all costs.

We very rarely consider, however, the process by which we gained our convictions. If we did so, we could hardly fail to see that there was usually little ground for our confidence in them. Here and there, in this department of knowledge or that, some one of us might make a fair claim to have taken some trouble to get correct ideas of, let us say, the situation in Russia, the sources of our food supply, the origin of the Constitution, the revision of the tariff, the policy of the Holy Roman Apostolic Church, modern business organization, trade unions, birth control, socialism, the League of Nations, the excess-profits tax, preparedness, advertising in its social bearings; but only a very exceptional person would be entitled to opinions on all of even these few matters. And yet most of us have opinions on all these, and on many other questions of equal importance, of which we may know even less. We feel compelled, as self-respecting persons, to take sides when they come up for discussion. We even surprise ourselves by our omniscience. Without taking thought we see in a flash that it is most righteous and expedient to discourage birth control by legislative enactment, or that one who decries intervention in Mexico is clearly wrong, or that big advertising is essential to big business and that big business is the pride of the land. As godlike beings why should we not rejoice in our omniscience?

It is clear in any case, that our convictions on important matters are not the result of knowledge or critical thought, nor, it may be added, are they often dictated by supposed self-interest. Most of them are *pure prejudices* in the proper sense of that word. We do not form them ourselves. They are the whispering of "the voice of the herd." We have in the last analysis no responsibility for them and need assume none. They are not really our own ideas, but those of others no more well informed or inspired than ourselves, who have got them in the same humiliating manner as we. It should be our pride to revise our ideas and not to adhere to what passes for respectable opinion, for such opinion can frequently be shown to be not respectable at all. We should, in view of the considerations that have been mentioned, resent our supine credulity. As an English writer has remarked:

> If we feared the entertaining of an unverifiable opinion with the warmth with which we fear using the wrong implement at the dinner table, if the thought of holding a prejudice disgusted us as does a foul disease, then the dangers of man's susceptibility would be turned into advantages.[1]

[1] Trotter, *Instincts of the Herd*, p. 45.

THINKING FOR ONESELF[1]

ARTHUR SCHOPENHAUER

[Arthur Schopenhauer (1788–1860) was born at Danzig, Germany, and educated at Göttingen. From 1820 to 1825 he lectured at Berlin on the philosophical subjects to which he devoted his life. He is considered the most eminent pessimistic thinker of the 19th century. While we may not accept his results, we must accept the ideal of independence and sincerity in the process of thinking, as held up in the following essay. It is interesting to note the similarity between his ideas and those developed in the selections (found in this book) from Carlyle and Emerson.]

A LIBRARY may be very large; but if it is in disorder, it is not so useful as one that is small but well arranged. In the same way, a man may have a great mass of knowledge, but if he has not worked it up by thinking it over for himself, it has much less value than a far smaller amount which he has thoroughly pondered. For it is only when a man looks at his knowledge from all sides, and combines the things he knows by comparing truth with truth, that he obtains a complete hold over it and gets it into his power. A man cannot turn over anything in his mind unless he knows it; he should, therefore, learn something; but it is only when he has turned it over that he can be said to know it.

Reading and learning are things that any one can do of his own free will; but not so thinking. Thinking must be

[1] From *Parerga und Paralipomena* (Berlin, 1851), translated as *Chips and Scraps*. The essay is entitled "Selbstdenken."

kindled, like a fire, by a draught; it must be sustained by some interest in the matter in hand. This interest may be of purely objective kind, or merely subjective. The latter comes into play only in things that concern us personally. Objective interest is confined to heads that think by nature, to whom thinking is as natural as breathing; and they are very rare. This is why most men of learning show so little of it.

It is incredible what a different effect is produced upon the mind by thinking for oneself as compared with reading. It carries on and intensifies that original difference in the nature of two minds which leads the one to think and the other to read. What I mean is that reading forces alien thoughts upon the mind—thoughts which are as foreign to the drift and temper in which it may be for the moment, as the seal is to the wax on which it stamps its imprint. The mind is thus entirely under compulsion from without; it is driven to think this or that, though for the moment it may not have the slightest impulse or inclination to do so.

But when a man thinks for himself, he follows the impulse of his own mind, which is determined for him at the time, either by his environment or some particular recollection. The visible world of a man's surroundings does not, as reading does, impress a single definite thought upon his mind, but merely gives the matter and occasion which lead him to think what is appropriate to his nature and present temper. So it is that much reading deprives the mind of all elasticity; it is like keeping a spring continually under pressure. The safest way of having no thoughts of one's own is to take up a book every moment one has nothing else to do. It is this practice which explains why erudition makes most men more stupid and silly than they are by nature, and prevents their writings obtaining any measure of success. They remain, in Pope's words:

> Forever reading, never to be read!

Men of learning are those who have done their reading in the pages of a book. Thinkers and men of genius are those who have gone straight to the book of nature; it is they who have enlightened the world and carried humanity further on its way.

If a man's thoughts are to have truth and life in them, they must, after all, be his own fundamental thoughts; for these are the only ones that he can fully and wholly understand. To read another's thoughts is like taking the leavings of a meal to which we have not been invited, or putting on the clothes which some unknown visitor has laid aside.

The thought we read is related to the thought which springs up in ourselves, as the fossil-impress of some prehistoric plant to a plant as it buds forth in springtime.

Reading is nothing more than a substitute for thought of one's own. It means putting the mind into leading-strings. The multitude of books serves only to show how many false paths there are, and how widely astray a man may wander if he follows any of them. But he who is guided by his genius, he who thinks for himself, who thinks spontaneously and exactly, possesses the only compass by which he can steer aright. A man should read only when his own thoughts stagnate at their source, which will happen often enough even with the best of minds. On the other hand, to take up a book for the purpose of scaring away one's own original thoughts is sin against the Holy Spirit. It is like running away from nature to look at a museum of dried plants or gaze at a landscape in copper-plate.

A man may have discovered some portion of truth or wisdom, after spending a great deal of time and trouble in thinking it over for himself and adding thought to thought; and it may sometimes happen that he could have found it all ready to hand in a book and spared himself the trouble. But even so, it is a hundred times more valuable if he has acquired it by thinking it out for himself. For it is only when we gain our knowledge in this way that it enters as an integral part, a living member into the whole system of our thought; that it stands in complete and firm relation with what we know; that it is understood with all that underlies it and follows from it; that it wears the color, the precise shade, the distinguishing mark of our own way of thinking; that it comes exactly at the right time, just as we felt the necessity for it; that it stands fast and cannot be forgotten. This is the perfect application, nay, the interpretation, of Goethe's advice to earn our inheritance for ourselves so that we may really possess it:

Was du ererbt von deinen Vätern hast,
Erwirb es, um es zu besitzen.[1]

The man who thinks for himself forms his own opinions and learns the authorities for them only later on, when they serve but to strengthen his belief in them and in himself. But the book-philosopher starts from the

[1] "What you from your fathers have inherited,
Earn it, in order to possess it."

authorities. He reads other people's books, collects their opinions, and so forms a whole for himself, which resembles an automaton made up of anything but flesh and blood. Contrarily, he who thinks for himself creates a work like a living man as made by Nature. For the work comes into being as a man does; the thinking mind is impregnated from without and it then forms and bears its child!

Truth that has been merely learned is like an artificial limb, a false tooth, a waxen nose; at best, like a nose made out of another's flesh; it adheres to us only because it is put on. But truth acquired by thinking of our own is like a natural limb; it alone really belongs to us. This is the fundamental difference between the thinker and the mere man of learning. The intellectual attainments of a man who thinks for himself resemble a fine painting, where the light and shade are correct, the tone sustained, the color perfectly harmonized; it is true to life. On the other hand, the intellectual attainments of the mere man of learning are like a large palette, full of all sorts of colors, which at most are systematically arranged, but devoid of harmony, connection, and meaning.

Reading is thinking with some one else's head instead of one's own. To think with one's own head is always to aim at developing a coherent whole—a system, even though it be not a strictly complete one; and nothing hinders this so much as too strong a current of others' thoughts, such as comes of continual reading. These thoughts, springing every one of them from different minds, belonging to different systems, and tinged with different colors, never of themselves flow together into an intellectual whole; they never form a unity of knowledge, or insight, or conviction; but, rather, fill the head with a Babylonian confusion of tongues. The mind that is over-loaded with alien thought is thus deprived of all clear insight, and so well-nigh disorganized. This is a state of things observable in many men of learning; and it makes them inferior in sound sense, correct judgment, and practical tact, to many illiterate persons, who, after obtaining a little knowledge from without by means of experience, intercourse with others, and a small amount of reading, have always subordinated it to, and embodied it with, their own thought.

The really scientific *thinker* does the same thing as these illiterate persons, but on a larger scale. Although he has need of much knowledge, and so must read a great deal, his mind is nevertheless strong enough to master it all, to assimilate and incorporate it with the system of his thoughts, and so to make it fit in with the organic unity of his insight, which, though vast, is always growing. And in the process, his own thought, like the bass in an organ, always dominates everything, and is never drowned by other tones, as happens with minds which are full of mere antiquarian lore; where shreds of music, as it were, in every key, mingle confusedly, and no fundamental note is heard at all.

Those who have spent their lives in reading, and taken their wisdom from books, are like people who have obtained precise information about a country from the descriptions of many travelers. Such people can tell a great deal about it; but, after all, they have no connected, clear, and profound knowledge of its real condition. But those who have spent their lives in thinking resemble the travelers themselves; they alone really know what they are talking about; they are acquainted with the actual state of affairs, and are quite at home in the subject.

The thinker stands in the same relation to the ordinary book-philosopher as an eye-witness does to the historian; he speaks from direct knowledge of his own. That is why all those who think for themselves come, at bottom, to much the same conclusion. The differences they present are due to their different points of view; and when these do not affect the matter, they all speak alike. They merely express the result of their own objective perception of things. There are many passages in my works which I have given to the public only after some hesitation, because of their paradoxical nature; and afterward I have experienced a pleasant surprise in finding the same opinion recorded in the works of great men who lived long ago.

The book-philosopher merely reports what one person has said and another meant, or the objections raised by a third, and so on. He compares different opinions, ponders, criticizes, and tries to get at the truth of the matter; herein on a par with the critical historian. For instance, he will set out to inquire whether Leibnitz was not for some time a follower of Spinoza, and questions of a like nature. The curious student of such matters may find conspicuous examples of what I mean in Herbart's *Analytical Elucidation of Morality and Natural Right,* and in the same author's *Letters on Freedom.* Surprise may be felt that a man of the kind should put himself to so much trouble; for, on the face of it, if he would only examine the matter for himself, he would speedily attain his object by the exercise of a little thought. But there is a small difficulty in the way. It does not depend upon his own will. A man can always sit down and read, but not—think. It is with thoughts as with men: they cannot always be summoned at pleasure; we must wait for them to come. Thought about a subject must appear of itself, by a happy and harmonious combination of external stimulus with mental temper and attention; and it is just that which never seems to come to these people.

This truth may be illustrated by what happens in the case of matters affecting our own personal interest. When it is necessary to come to some resolution in a matter of that kind, we cannot well sit down at any given moment and think over the merits of the case and make up our mind; for, if we try to do so, we often find ourselves unable at that particular moment to keep our mind fixed upon the subject; it wanders off to other things. Aversion to the matter in question is sometimes to blame for this. In such a case we should not use force, but wait for the proper frame of mind to come of itself. It often comes unexpectedly and returns again and again; and the variety of temper in which we approach it at different moments puts the matter always in a fresh light. It is this long process which is understood by the term *a ripe resolution.* For the work of coming to a resolution must be distributed; and in the process much that is overlooked at one moment occurs to us at another; and the repugnance vanishes when we find, as we usually do, on a closer inspection, that things are not so bad as they seemed.

This rule applies to the life of the intellect as well as to matters of practice. A man must wait for the right moment. Not even the greatest mind is capable of thinking for itself at all times. Hence a great mind does well to spend its leisure in reading, which, as I have said, is a substitute for thought; it brings stuff to the mind by letting another person do the thinking; although that is always done in a manner not our own. Therefore, a man should not read too much, in order that his mind may not become accustomed to the substitute and thereby forget the reality; that it may not form the habit of walking in well-worn paths; nor by following an alien course of thought grow a stranger to its own. Least of all should a man quite withdraw his gaze from the real world for the mere sake of reading; as the impulse and the temper which prompt to thought of one's own come far oftener from the world of reality than from the world of books. The real life that a man sees before him is the natural subject of thought; and in its strength as the primary element of existence, it can more easily than anything else rouse and influence the thinking mind.

After these considerations, it will not be matter for surprise that a man who thinks for himself can easily be distinguished from the book-philosopher by the very way in which he talks, by his marked earnestness, and the originality, directness, and personal conviction that stamp all his thought and expressions. The book-philosopher, on the other hand, lets it be seen that everything he has is secondhand; that his ideas are like the lumber and trash of an old furniture-shop, collected together from all quarters. Mentally, he is dull and pointless—a copy of a copy. His literary style is made up of conventional, nay, vulgar phrases, and terms that happen to be current; in this respect much like a small state where all the money that circulates is foreign, because it has no coinage of its own.

Mere experience can as little as reading supply the place

of thought. It stands to thinking in the same relation in which eating stands to digestion and assimilation. When experience boasts that to its discoveries alone is due the advancement of the human race, it is as though the mouth were to claim the whole credit of maintaining the body in health.

The works of all truly capable minds are distinguished by a character of decision and definiteness, which means that they are clear and free from obscurity. A truly capable mind always knows definitely and clearly what it is that it wants to express, whether its medium is prose, verse, or music. Other minds are not decisive and not definite; and by this they may be known for what they are.

The characteristic sign of a mind of the highest order is that it always judges at first hand. Everything it advances is the result of thinking for itself; and this is everywhere evident by the way in which it gives its thoughts utterance. Such a mind is like a prince. In the realm of intellect its authority is imperial, whereas the authority of minds of a lower order is delegated only; as may be seen in their style, which has no independent stamp of its own.

Everyone who really thinks for himself is so far like a monarch. His position is undelegated and supreme. His judgments, like royal decrees, spring from his own sovereign power and proceed directly from himself. He acknowledges authority as little as a monarch admits a command; he subscribes to nothing but what he has himself authorized. The multitude of common minds, laboring under all sorts of current opinions, authorities, prejudices, is like the people, which silently obeys the law and accepts orders from above.

Those who are so zealous and eager to settle debated questions by citing authorities, are really glad when they are able to put the understanding and the insight of others into the field in place of their own, which are wanting. Their number is legion. For, as Seneca says, there is no man but prefers belief to the exercise of judgment—*unusquisque mavult credere quam judicare.* In their controversies such people make a promiscuous use of the weapon of authority, and strike out at one another with it. If any one chances to become involved in such a contest, he will do well not to try reason and argument as a mode of defense; for against a weapon of that kind these people are like Siegfrieds, with a skin of horn, and dipped in the flood of incapacity for thinking and judging. They will meet his attack by bringing up their authorities as a way of abashing him—*argumentum ad verecundiam,* and then cry out that they have won the battle.

In the real world, be it never so fair, favorable, and pleasant, we always live subject to the law of gravity, which we have to be constantly overcoming. But in the world of intellect we are disembodied spirits, held in bondage to no such law, and free from penury and distress. Thus it is that there exists no happiness on earth like that which, at the auspicious moment, a fine and fruitful mind finds in itself.

The presence of a thought is like the presence of a woman we love. We fancy we shall never forget the thought nor become indifferent to the dear one. But out of sight, out of mind! The finest thought runs the risk of being irrevocably forgotten if we do not write it down, and the darling of being deserted if we do not marry her.

There are plenty of thoughts which are valuable to the man who thinks them; but only a few of them which have enough strength to produce repercussive or reflex action —I mean, to win the reader's sympathy after they have been put on paper.

But still it must not be forgotten that a true value attaches only to what a man has thought in the first instance for his own case. Thinkers may be classed according as they think chiefly for their own case or for that of others. The former are the genuine independent thinkers; they really think and are really independent; they are the true *philosophers;* they alone are in earnest. The pleasure and the happiness of their existence consist in thinking. The others are the *sophists;* they want to seem that which they are not, and seek their happiness in what they hope to get from the world. They are in earnest about nothing else. To which of these two classes a man belongs may be seen by his whole style and manner. Lichtenberg is an example of the former class; Herder, there can be no doubt, belongs to the second.

When one considers how vast and how close to us is the problem of existence—this equivocal, tortured, fleeting, dream-like existence of ours—so vast and so close that a man no sooner discovers it than it overshadows and obscures all other problems and aims; and when one sees how all men, with very rare exceptions, have no clear consciousness of the problem, nay, seem to be quite unaware of its presence, but busy themselves with everything rather than with this, and live on, taking no thought but for the passing day and the hardly longer span of their own personal future, either expressly discarding the problem or else overready to come to terms with it by adopting some system of popular metaphysics and letting it satisfy them; when, I say, one takes all this to heart, one may come to the opinion that man may be said to be *a thinking being* only in a very remote sense, and henceforth feel no special surprise at any trait of human thoughtlessness or folly; but know, rather, that the normal man's intellectual range of vision does indeed extend beyond that of the brute, whose whole existence is, as it were, a continual present, with no consciousness of the past or the future, but not such an immeasurable distance as is generally supposed.

This is, in fact, corroborated by the way in which most men converse; where their thoughts are found to be chopped up fine, like chaff, so that for them to spin out a discourse of any length is impossible.

If this world were peopled by really thinking beings, it could never be that noise of every kind would be allowed such generous limits, as is the case with the most horrible and at the same time aimless form of it. If nature had meant man to think, she would not have given him ears; or, at any rate, she would have furnished them with airtight flaps, such as are the enviable possession of the bat. But, in truth, man is a poor animal like the rest, and his powers are meant only to maintain him in the struggle for existence; so he must needs keep his ears always open, to announce of themselves, by night as by day, the approach of the pursuer.

LEARN WHILE YOU SLEEP[1]

From *The New Republic*

A REVOLUTIONARY discovery was recently announced in the newspapers. It appears that the radio has uses far beyond the dreams of its inventors. An unnamed victim, presumably of the male sex, was put to bed with a head-set over his ears. In a very short time, in spite of the obvious discomfort, he was sound asleep. He slept for the customary eight hours, during which time he was, unwittingly, the recipient, via the radio head-set, of considerable educational matter, all of which, upon waking up in the morning, he turned out to have learned by heart. From eleven at night until seven the next morning, his plastic unconscious mind was assaulted by an explanation of the binomial theorem, the story of Washington's crossing the Delaware, an original proposition in plane geometry—with diagrams, select passages from Hiawatha, and the irregular French verb meaning to pay a debt, or debts, or some, but not all, debts. At seven an alarm clock, broadcasted from Buffalo (the victim was in Terre Haute) woke him up. After a hearty breakfast (for study, even in sleep, induces hunger) he recited upon the matter which had just been pumped into his subconscious, and was pronounced 60 percent correct. This is unbelievably high. It is high

[1] From *The New Republic* of Nov. 25, 1925. Reprinted by permission of the editors.

enough to get anyone through any college. But the victim was not a particularly promising specimen. He was a replacer of defective parts in tractor transmissions, and had never been in high school. Therefore the results are all the more astonishing.

It is curious that this discovery was not made earlier. Of course, science has known for a long time that the mind in a somnolent, or even a somnolescent state, is peculiarly receptive to suggestion and even information. The psychological basis of the phenomenon is perfectly simple. The consciousness may go to sleep, but the mind never does. While the body rests, and the throat snores, the mind, like a racing engine in a motionless automobile, performs wonder of fantastic narrative. These are called dreams. The nonsensical intricacy of dreams is useless except for the purpose of deceiving a certain school of psychologists—some of whom are called gypsies, others, more colloquially, Freudians. Dreams, since they serve no better purpose, must go. The space they now occupy must be filled. The fact that the dream-gap has never before been filled is a blot on the escutcheon of human intelligence.

In the wakeful state, the powers of the human mind to resist information and guidance are prodigious. In sleep, these powers are no longer exerted. Professors, unfortunately, have never recognized this obvious fact, and resent even the simulation of sleep in their classes, whereas, on the contrary, they ought to encourage it. But since nothing we can say will ever change the prejudices of the professors, we must turn to this newest development of the radio for the fulfilment of the nation's greatest need, education.

The prospect opened up by the experiment upon the man from Terre Haute is exhilarating. We are a nation of workers, Florida to the contrary notwithstanding. We hate to give up our work even in order to get educated. Several hundred thousand of us over the working age of eighteen are at college. These boys and girls will never give up the things that colleges are famous for, football, junior proms, sororities, pocket flasks, raccoon coats and glee clubs, in exchange for mere education. Many of them indeed can only study in their painfully acquired spare time. To all such, and to the great American public athirst for culture, the radio which teaches while you sleep will be an epoch-making blessing. People will at last have their cake and eat it too. Even the cake-eaters.

Taking a jump into the future, we can imagine the life of the average citizen immeasurably enriched by the discovery that knowledge can enter into him, as it were, via the Ostermoor. Within a year or two, nine thirty-five will find Mr. John Gutz, citizen and monkey-wrench merchant, at his desk on the ninth floor of the Consolidated Asset and Liability Building. The day will pass in dictating letters, evading callers and biting the ends off ten-cent cigars. Mr. Gutz will go to lunch with a big customer, and tell him the story of the girl from Duluth. After lunch his routine will be varied by a personal call from the representative of the Learn-o-Radio Company, and Mr. Gutz will sign up for a six weeks General Culture Course. When he gets home, he will find the head-set hanging by the head of his bed. He will go to bed earlier than usual, but, being in a state of some excitement, will remember nothing, even though he heard it, of the first half-hour on the history of bee-keeping. Eventually, under the influence of a discourse on vital statistics among the janitors of Atlantis, he will fall asleep. From that point on he will begin to learn. By learning we do not mean that he will be training his mind, which has never been the serious purpose of education, but that he will remember, not in substance or in part, but in toto, everything which has been imparted to him over the radio. He will wake up the next morning to recall, with literal accuracy: the multiplication table up to forty-nine times forty-nine (which will help him in his business); the full names, addresses and positions of all state and county officers (which will make him interested in self-government); the principal parts of speech in Swedish (which will go far toward solving the servant question); the Gettysburg address (for possible use on the Fourth of July); a list of all paintings by Rubens, the size thereof, the subject, and where now located (which will give him an insight into the world of art); and the name, price, and major specifications of every passenger automobile manufactured in the U. S. A. (which will increase his powers of conversation in the world of men). All at a moderate charge, without the slightest contribution of effort on his part.

Night after night knowledge (or information—they are much the same) will pour in upon him. Mr. Gutz will astound his customers by his familiarity with the populations of their native towns, and his miraculous grasp of the principal names in Persian literature will compel other monkey-wrench merchants to elect him President of their Association. But gradually he will find that the efforts of the radio company cause other men to creep up on him. Some of them, by sleeping late Sunday morning, will even manage to surpass his knowledge of famous burial grounds in Missouri. But the radio people are ready for Mr. Gutz, and switch him, at a slight increase in price, to the Advanced Course. Which is the same as the elementary course, only backwards. So that Mr. Gutz, if the monkey-wrench field isn't productive, can make a little money in the two-a-day reciting the Declaration of Independence from the signatures back to the thunderous culminating Whereas.

After Mr. Gutz and all his fellow citizens and his sisters and his cousins and his aunts have been playing Addison Sims forwards and backwards for a number of years, they will find happily filled up in their minds those chinks formerly occupied by thought—too much of which never did anybody any good anyway.

IDOLS OF OUR EDUCATION[1]

CHARLES MILLS GAYLEY

[Charles Mills Gayley was born in Shanghai, China, in 1858 and was educated at the University of Michigan and in Germany. For nearly thirty-five years he was professor of English and for a time dean of the faculties in the University of California. He is the author and editor of many books which aim to bring out the human interests of literature. In 1924–25 he served as director of the American University Union in London.]

THE world of learning was never better worth preparing for. Why is it, then, that from every university in the land, and from every serious journal, there goes up the cry, "Our young people were never more indifferent."

How many nights a week does the student spend in pursuits non-academic; how great a proportion of his days? What with so-called "college activities," by which he must prove his allegiance to the university, and social functions by which he must recreate his jaded soul, no margin is left for the one and only college activity—which is study. Class meetings, business meetings, committee meetings, editorial meetings, football rallies, baseball rallies, pyjama rallies, vicarious athletics on the bleachers, garrulous athletics in the dining-room and parlor and on the porch, rehearsals of the glee club, rehearsals of the mandolin club and of the banjo, rehearsals for dramatics

[1] Reprinted from *Idols* with the permission of Doubleday, Page and Co.

(a word to stand the hair on end), college dances and class banquets, fraternity dances and suppers, preparations for the dances and banquets, more committees for the preparations; a running up and down the campus for ephemeral items for ephemeral articles in ephemeral papers, a soliciting of advertisements, a running up and down for subscriptions to the dances and the dinners, and the papers and the clubs; a running up and down in college politics, making tickets, pulling wires, adjusting combinations, canvassing for votes—canvassing the girls for votes, spending hours at sorority houses for votes—spending hours at sorority houses for sentiment; talking rubbish unceasingly, thinking rubbish, revamping rubbish—rubbish about high jinks, rubbish about low, rubbish about rallies, rubbish about pseudo-civic honor, rubbish about girls;—what margin of leisure is left for the one activity of the college, which is study?

In Oxford and Cambridge, than which no universities have turned out finer, cleaner, more manly, more highly cultivated, and more practically trained scholars, statesmen, empire builders, or more generous enthusiasts for general athletics and clean sport—in Oxford and Cambridge the purpose is study, and the honors are paid to the scholar. There are no undergraduate newspapers, no class meetings, no college politics, no football rallies, no business managers, no claque for organized applause, no yell leaders, no dances, no social functions of the mass. Social intercourse during term between the sexes is strictly forbidden; and it is a matter of college loyalty to live up to the rule. Of non-academic activities there are but two—athletics and conversation. They are not a function but a recreation; nor are they limited to specialists whose reputation is professed. Young Oxonians, in general, lead a serene and undistracted, but rich and wholesome life. They cultivate athletics because each is an active devotee of some form of sport. And conversation—in junior commons, in the informal clubs, in study or in tutor's rooms—it is an education, a passion, an art.

The Bandar-log

A foreigner, attending, in an American university, an assembly of student speakers, will be justified in concluding that the university exists for nothing but so-called "student activities." The real purpose of the university will not be mentioned, for usually our undergraduates live two lives—distinct; one utterly non-academic. The non-academic is for them the real; the scholarly an encroachment. The student who regards the scholarly as paramount is deficient in "allegiance to his university."

Athletics, meanwhile, which should play a necessary part in the physical, and therefore spiritual, development of all students, are relegated to ten per cent of the students. The rest assist—on the bleachers. The ninety per cent are killing two birds with one stone. They are taking second-hand exercise; and, by their grotesque and infantile applause, they are displaying what they call their "loyalty."

Those *noctes cœnæque deum* of history and poetry and philosophical discourse, to the memory of which the older generation reverts with rapture, have faded in this light of common day. In the hurry of mundane pursuit the student rarely halts to read, rarely to consider; rarely to discuss the concerns of the larger life.

President Schurman has recently said that there has been no decline of scholarship in the people's universities; but only in the older institutions of the East, to which rich parents send their sons with the view to the advantages of social position; and that in the people's universities the social standing of students has never cut so much figure as scholarship. The assurance is comfortable; but it obscures the issue. If by "social standing" the president of Cornell means position in the coteries of wealth, fashion, conviviality, it may be that "social standing" bulks larger in the older university than in the university of the state. But the fact is that, in student esteem, East and West, social standing means no such thing: it means the position achieved by prominence in non-academic or "campus" activities. And in student esteem such prominence cuts a far more important figure than that of either wealth or scholarship. Such prominence has been gaining ground for fifteen years. So long as the social pressure of the university is toward mundane pursuits, it will be vain to expect the student to achieve distinction in that for which the university stands.

This false standard of prominence, with its feigned allegiance to the interests of the university, has produced that class of student which, adapting from the *Jungle Book,* I call the "Bandar-log."

Mowgli had never seen an Indian city before, and though this was almost a heap of ruins it seemed very wonderful and splendid. Some king had built it long ago on a little hill. . . . The Bandar-logs called the place their city, and pretended to despise the jungle people because they lived in the forest. And yet they never knew what the buildings were made for nor how to use them. They would sit in circles in the hall of the King's council-chamber and scratch for fleas and pretend to be men; or they would run in and out of the roofless houses and collect pieces of plaster and old bricks in the corner and forget where they had hidden them, and fight and cry in scuffling crowds, and then break off to play up and down the terraces of the King's garden, where they would shake the rose-trees and the oranges in sport to see the fruit and flowers fall. They explored all the passages and dark tunnels in the palace, and the hundreds of little dark rooms, but they never remembered what they had seen and what they had not, and so drifted about in ones and twos or crowds, telling one another that they were doing as men did—or shouting "there are none in the jungle so wise and good and clever and strong and gentle as the Bandar-log." Then they would tire and seek the treetop, hoping the jungle people would notice them . . . and then they joined hands and danced about and sang their foolish songs. "They have no law," said Mowgli to himself, "no hunting call and no leaders." . . . And he could not help laughing when they cried, "We are great, we are free, we are wonderful . . . we all say so, and so it must be true . . . you shall carry our words back to the jungle people that they may notice us in future."

The Bandar-log is with us. Busy to no purpose, imitative, aimless; boastful but unreliant; inquisitive but quickly losing his interest; fitful, inconsequential, platitudinous, forgetful; noisy, sudden, ineffectual.—The Bandar-log must go.

Because it is the spirit of the American university to prove the things that are new, to hold fast that which is good; to face abuses boldly and to reform them; because I am the son of an American university, and have grown in her teaching, and in my observation of many universities and many schools, to regard the evil as transitory and abuses as remediable, I have ventured in this essay to set down simply, and with a frankness that I trust may not be misconstrued, some of the vagaries of our educational system at the present time, and some of the reasons for their existence. For I am sure that in the recognition of the cause is to be found the means of cure.

The Man of Argos

Another class also of students makes, though unconsciously, for the wane of general scholarship—the class of the prematurely vocational. It is not futile, like that of the Bandar-log, but earnest, and with a definite end in view. Still, unwisely guided to immature choice and hasty study of a profession, it not only misses the liberal equipment necessary for the ultimate mastery of life, but indirectly diverts the general scope of education from its true ideals.

The spirit of the Renaissance, says a modern historian of poetry, is portrayed in a picture by Moretto. It is of a young Venetian noble. "The face is that of one in the full prime of life and of great physical strength; very handsome, heavy and yet tremulously sensitive, the large eyes gazing at some thing unseen, and seeming to dream of vastness. On his bonnet is a golden plaque with three words of Greek inscribed on it—*ἰοὺ λίαν ποθῶ*—"Oh, but I am consumed, with excess of desire."

If this be the motto of the Renaissance, what shall we say is the motto of to-day? Not *ἰοὺ λίαν ποθῶ*; no creed of vague insatiable yearning, but rather the *πάντα αὐτίκα ποθῶ*—the lust for immediate and universal possession: as who should cry,

> I want no little here below,
> I want it all, and quick.

In one of his odes, Pindar, lauding the older times when the Muse had not yet learned to work for hire, breaks off "but now she biddeth us observe the saying of the Man of Argos, 'Money maketh man'"—*χρήματα,* χρήματ' ἀνήρ. If not money, then sudden success—that is the criterion of the Man of Argos to-day.

The Bandar-log and the Argive retard the advance of scholarship in the university; and not the university alone is responsible for their presence, but the elementary school as well.

[NOTE.—There follow here two sections treating of the lax conditions in our secondary schools consequent on the overwhelming demand for education. This "advance of democracy," a splendid sign itself, creates new ideals, but it also sets up certain idols in the university.]

Idols of the Tribe

Roger Bacon, long ago, and after him, Francis, in their quest of truth, perceived that there were four grounds of human error. Of these the first is "the false appearances that are imposed upon us by the general nature of the mind" of man. The mind is always prone to accept the affirmative or active as proof rather than the negative; so that if you hit the mark a few times you forget the many that you missed it. You worship Neptune for the numerous pictures in his temple of those that escaped shipwreck, but you omit to ask: "Where are the pictures of those that were drowned?" And because you are mentally equipped to seek uniformity, you ascribe to "Nature a greater equality and uniformity than is, in truth." In this refractory mind of man "the beams of things" do not "reflect according to their true incidence"; hence our fundamental superstitions, fallacies which Francis Bacon calls the Idols, or delusions, of the Race, or Tribe.

In matters of education the dearest delusion of our Tribe to-day is *that the university should reflect the pub-*

lic. This is the idol of the Popular Voice. Once the university is joined to this idol, it is joined to all the idols of that Pantheon. It accepts the fallacy that our sons and daughters are equally gifted and zealous, and hence that each must profit by the higher education. This is the idol of Inevitable Grace; that is, of grace innate and irresistible by which every youth is predestinated to intellectual life, "without any foresight of faith or good works, or perseverance in either of them, or any other thing in the creature, as conditions or causes moving him thereunto," or anything in the tutor. No Calvinistic favor this, by which some are chosen while others are ordained to ignorance and sloth; but a favor not contemplated in the Westminster Confession, by which all are elect and all, in due season, effectually called to learning, and quickened and renewed by the Spirit of Zeal, and so enabled to answer this call and embrace the Grace offered and conveyed in it. The university is then joined to the idol of Numbers. And of these worships the shibboleth is "mediocrity": for to raise the standard of university requirement is to discriminate between candidates, and to doubt Inevitable Grace; while to decrease the bloated registration is a sacrilege which Numbers will avenge with curtailment of prosperity. And the ritual march is by lock-step: for tests, competition, and awards are alien to the American spirit thus misrepresented—save athletic competition: that is a divine exception.

The university is next joined to the idol of Quick Returns. It accepts the fallacy of utilitarian purpose; and hence, that a profession must be chosen prematurely and immaturely entered; and hence that studies are not for discipline or intrinsic worth, but from the primary school to the Ph.D., for purely vocational value; and hence that every incipient vocation from making toy boats and paper mats to making tariffs and balloons must find its place in every school and in every grade for every man or woman child. And since the man or woman child may find perchance a vocation in the liberal arts, the child must bestride both horses, though with the usual aërial result.

And our students—they worship the idol of Incidental Issues: the fallacy that the aim of the university is deliberately to make character. As if character were worth anything without mind, and were any other, as President Wilson has wisely said, than the by-product of duty performed; or that the duty of the student were any other than to study. They accept the fallacy that the gauge of studentship is popularity, and that popularity during academic years is to be won by hasty achievement and the babbling strenuous life, by allegiance to a perverted image of the Alma Mater, by gregariousness, by playing at citizenship. Of this popularity the outward and visible index is mundane prominence and the lightly proffered laurel of the campus.

I said that the dearest delusion of the Tribe was that the university should reflect the public. But this delusion requires also *that our universities be continually figuring in the public eye.* So far as such activity is necessary to the building up of schools, and to the education of a community to an understanding of the ideals and the needs of higher education, it is not only legitimate but laudable. But when, under the name of university extension, our universities undertake the higher education of the periphery, in dilettantism or methods of research, they run the risk of university attenuation and simulation. When, not dispassionately, they figure in public issues, they lay themselves open to the charge of partisanship. Time was when academic etiquette forbade the university professor to participate in political contests. Now there are who dare to inject the university into prejudiced affairs; even into criminal cases pending in the courts. They have joined themselves to the idol of Parade.

To this same false policy of figuring in the public eye our universities bow when they sanction amphitheatrical spectacles, at some of which money enough passes hands to build a battleship. Football is a most desirable recreation, and a moral and physical discipline of value to every able-bodied boy. Nay, more, athletics, physical sport, and emulation are necessary to spiritual health. Even excess in them is better, it has often been said, than that moral evil should abound. But is the alternative necessary? Must we have either gladiators or degenerates? Need athletics be professionalized, be specialized? Do specialized athletics benefit the morals of the ninety and nine who don't play? Do they not rather spoil sport, detract from time and tendency to exercise for oneself? Do they not substitute hysteria for muscular development? Football is a noble game; but it is with disgust that one views its degeneration from an exhilarating pastime for all into a profession of the few, a source of newspaper notoriety, a cause of extravagance, orgiastic self-abandonment, and educational shipwreck. This comes of bowing to the idol of Parade.

The university should not adopt the idols of the community. It should set the ideals. The American university is, and ever must be, democratic. It offers education to all who can profit by it. But education itself is aristocratic—of the best and for the best. The educated are those who, having striven, are the chosen few.

Idols of the Academic Market-Place

Bewildered by the advance of democracy, educators not only have accepted fallacies of the Tribe, but have attempted to justify their acceptance by further fallacies of their own—based some upon a juggling with words, others upon the authority of some Pundit (living or dead), others upon individual ignorance and conceit. These are, respectively, what Bacon has called the idols of the Market-place, the idols of the Lecture-room or Theater, the idols of the Cave.

Idols of the Market-place are fallacies proceeding from the misconception of words. Since we educators are an imitative race, many of these misconceptions have been fostered or confirmed by the influence of some great name, Rousseau, or Froebel, or Jacotot, or another; that is to say, by authority. Consequently, the idols of the Market-place are sometimes also idols of the Theater, which is to say, of the Lecture-room, or master by whose words we swear.

"He that will write well in any tongue must follow this counsel of Aristotle, to speak as the common people speak, but think as wise men think." From disregard of such counsel, many of our academic fallacies concerning education have arisen. We are involved in questions and differences because we have followed the false appearances of words, instead of setting down in the beginning the definitions in which as wise men we may concur. In what definition of education is it possible that wise men may concur? All will agree that education is a process: not that of play, nor yet of work, but of artistic activity. Play meanders pleasantly toward an external end of no significance. Work drives straight for an end beyond, that is pleasant because of its worth. The process of Art has an end but not beyond. Its end is in itself; and it is pleasurable in its activity because its true activity is a result. From play the artistic process differs because its end is significant; from work it differs because its end is in its activity, and because its activity possesses the pleasure of worth. It is like religion: a process continually begun, and in its incompleteness complete. Its ideal is incapable of temporal fulfilment, but still, in each moment of development, it is spiritually perfect.

Education, then, is an art—the art of the individual realizing himself as a member of a society whose tabernacle is here, but whose home is a house not built with hands. Education is the process of knowing the best, enjoying the best, producing the best in knowledge, conduct, and the arts. Realization, expression of self, physical, intellectual, social, emotional, is its means and end. It implies faith in a moral order and continuing process, of which it is itself an integral and active part.

It is remarkable with what persistency the race of educators has indulged extremes. There has been accorded from time to time an apostle of the golden mean. But his disciples have ever proceeded to the ulterior limit: among the ancients to the pole of self-culture or to the pole of uncultured service; in the Dark Ages to the ideal of the cloister or the ideal of the castle, to joyless learning or to feudal, and feminine, approval; in the Middle Ages to the bigotry of the obscurantist or the allurement of the material; in the Renaissance to contempt of the ancients or to neo-paganism—to theological quibbles or to Castiglione, to the bonfire of vanities or the carnal songs of Lorenzo; in the Reformation, to compulsory discipline or the apotheosis of natural freedom; in the succeeding age to pedantry or deportment. Still later appear Rousseau and the philanthropists with the "return to nature," the worship of individuality, the methods of coddling and play; and then Jacotot—and the equal fitness of all for higher education, the exaggeration of inductive methods, the chimerical equivalence of studies. And now has arrived the subordination of the art to pure profit, or vaudeville, or seminars for sucklings.

Always the fallacy of the extreme!—If education is not for the fit it must be for imbeciles; if not for culture, for Mammon; if not for knowledge, for power; if not of incunabula, of turbines and limericks; if not by the cat-o'-nine-tails, by gum-drops. Why the mean of a Plato or a Quintilian could not obtain—the sanity of Melanchthon or Erasmus, of Sturm or Comenius, of Milton or the Port Royal, of Pestalozzi, Friedrich Wolf, or Thomas Arnold,—Heaven only knows, which in its inscrutable purpose has permitted the race of educators, following the devices of their own heart, to go astray after idols.

To know, to feel, to do aright and best, each and all in all and each of the fields of human activity, that is the art of education.

If we exaggerate one of these functions to the neglect of the rest, our education is no longer an ideal but an idol. If, forgetting that education is an art, we try to make of it a pleasant meandering, we set up the idol of Play. If, forgetting that the activity of Art is of intrinsic value and delight, we glorify the empty means and merit of drudgery, then we have erected the idol of Pedantry: we beat the air for discipline, shuffle in and out of corners the straw of arid learning, and choke ourselves with the dust of our own sweeping. If we fix our eyes on the cash, we bow to the tribal idol of Quick Returns. If we forget that, as an art, there is for education a progressive ideal and a law of progress, too, we bow to the idol of Caprice. We fall not only into the fallacies already enumerated but into the fallacy of the equivalence of studies, the fallacy of shifting, the fallacy of dissipation. In Art each factor is in relation to the rest, and all to the whole: we proceed fatuously upon the assumption that the part *is* the whole; and therefore each part equal to each; and therefore one study as good as any other. In Art the means, which is the end, is relative, progressive: we assume comfortably that studies are independent of each other, that we can take any in any order, pass an examination and have done. In Art the end, which is the means, is absolute and self-referred and ideal: we figure that, by dissipating our energies, we shall happen to hit, here and now, the ideal. Disregarding the progressive unity of education we bow to Caprice.

The idols of the academic market-place to-day are Caprice and Quick Returns and Play, and, in unexpected corners, Pedantry, against which in reaction these three were set up. Of these, Quick Returns was borrowed from the tribe; and not alone, for of this subvention are other tribal gods too numerous to rehearse—specially

Numbers and Inevitable Grace and Incidental Issues and Parade. To one or other of these false worships are due the wane of scholarship, the utilitarian tendency, the excrescence of non-academic activities, the neglected discipline in our education at the present time.

THE COLLEGE AND AMERICAN LIFE[1]

JAY WILLIAM HUDSON

[Jay William Hudson was born in Cleveland, Ohio, in 1874. After studying at Hiram College and at Oberlin, he received his A.B. degree at the University of California and his PH.D. at Harvard. He is now professor of philosophy at the University of Missouri. Among his publications are the volumes *America's International Ideals* and *The Truths We Live By*.]

OUT of the American vision of what men are and what they may become, evolve all the fundamental expressions of American life; instinctively, for the most part; and so, subject to the deviousness of an experience forever correcting itself; but which, correcting itself in quite definite ways, reveals that the vision which is the soul of its meaning is ever present.

What are some of these expressions of American life? And how shall the American college adjust itself to them?

First, there is the American state. The state is one of many expressions of the American order and exists to guarantee its sure success. All the significant things that belong to political America as an ideal are already implied in America's interpretation of the nature of men and their rights. Thus, the freedom and equality that we have found belonging to the American theory of the

[1] From *The College and New America*. Copyright, 1920, by D. Appleton and Company. Reprinted by permission of and by special arrangement with the publishers.

person translate themselves, politically, into self-government, with its freedom and equality of thought, speech, and ballot; and of civil and political rights. This self-government becomes a government through elected representatives for only one reason,—it is impracticable for each one of the great democracy to govern directly.

In such a government, the functions of the representative are two: To express the people's will; and to lead it in the light of his unusual opportunities for information and wisdom in matters of public concern. On the other hand, the functions of the citizen are to acquaint himself with the issues that constantly arise for his decision; to express and to discuss his convictions freely with his fellows; and freely and fearlessly to register his convictions through the franchise,—in other words, to realize his rational freedom through a thoroughly conscious political responsibility.

If we scan American politics as it actually is, we find that the citizen has failed and that his representative has failed quite notoriously; and in ways in which the American college ought to be conspicuously equipped to remedy. The failure of both the citizen and his representative is, first of all, in the lack of expert intelligence in matters political; both tending to substitute for political wisdom an optimistic fatalism which is convinced that no possible error could ever render American democracy anything but triumphant. Add to this our characteristically American belief, noted the world over, that anybody can do anything, particularly the deeds involved in all phases of governing.

Such faith is fatal. The college can correct it. Precisely here is where the limited but important ideal of "education for citizenship" finds an indispensable place. A course in the American State, including intelligent discussion of vital political problems—yes, and comparative government—should be required of every American college man. And in all this, the institution of American government should not be left unrelated to the larger aspects of the American social order, whose security and progress is its only justification.

The American college can help America to redeem a second noteworthy failure of both its citizens and politicians; namely, the failure to realize government as a social responsibility, before which every whit of selfishness must give away. The indifference of the citizen to the franchise; his submission to the intrenched power of the Bosses; his regarding his government as a far-away thing, somehow abstracted from his private and local concerns—these all are facts; and they are symptoms of an apathy which plays directly into the hands of the politician, who, selfish in his own way, makes of the citizen's indifference his own opportunity; abuses his function as a representative and ignores his responsibilities as a leader; or, deliberately takes advantage of his inside knowledge to mislead. The college can remedy this, too, and in only one way. It can remedy it by making its entire curriculum and its administration a training for the feeling and the conviction of responsibility to the social order, including its political institution—a moral responsibility, conceived as the supreme business of the educated man; not as a mere incident among the things worth while. With the American social order as the aim of education, the American state at once becomes an integral part of that living purpose, in terms of which college education shall exist. One of the most encouraging signs for the future of the American state is the increasing emergence of college men into expert leadership in political life. Education in America may yet be, in fact as well as in theory, what our forefathers wanted it to be, the bulwark of democratic government.

Second, the American order is an economic and industrial order. If, in the American conception, all things must serve the person as the ultimate end and criterion of values, so must all economic institutions. Verily, there is such a thing as economic and industrial democracy—as an ideal. What such economic democracy in detail would be is one of the grave questions for the educated man to solve, and to solve speedily. The question is, certainly, imminent and imperative enough. It is going to be answered in one way or another; quite possibly, in the wrong way. The risk is that the more pressing economic and industrial questions may be decided in one of two equally disastrous ways; either by the one-sided prejudices of the wage-earner, through a growing self-conscious solidarity, which means dictatorship, with or without violence; or, by the equally one-sided prejudices of the wage-payer, through the adroit manipulation of the established order, for which he has some genius. Or, a third way is possible—continuous compromises, out of which shall emerge again and yet again the everlasting conflict, to be compromised once more.

The solution of the economic problems of the American order cannot rightly come through the triumph of the interest of one class, or through the compromise of classes. Such solutions are contradictions to the very being of the American order. Virtually, they make large bodies of men things to be used, not ends in themselves. Such solutions mean the exploitation of the employer by the employee; or the reverse; or both. No, the economic problem must be solved, painfully and slowly as you please, not by prejudice or by special interests on the one side or the other; but by an impartial and expert reason, whose supreme qualification is the possession of a standard of values higher than the merely economic; and expressive of the many-sided good of the social order as a whole. Never and nowhere was rational and judicious leadership through courageous convictions needed more than now and here. It is the business of the college to furnish much of the material for such leadership, if the college be granted to exist for the social order at all. And the American college must afford not only leaders, but a large body of men who can intelligently support intelligent leadership, once it appears. Certainly, every American college man should have a training in economic and industrial fundamentals. But it must not be an economics academically taught. It must mean a learning to think in economic terms, based upon a conviction of the gravity of the economic situation, and stimulated by a sympathetic knowledge of comparative points of view and of contemporary movements of economic import. America and the world seethe with such movements now; the college graduate must meet them not indifferently or ignorantly, but responsibly and intelligently—which means a fundamental recognition of the relation of economic values to the other human values for which his college exists. Once there was a danger that some colleges might find themselves indirectly subsidized, to the exclusion of open-mindedness in economic teaching. But this danger has been minimized as the academic freedom and tenure of the college professor have become more and more secure. Nor may it be forgotten that, added to the direct influence of the college, is the indirect influence of the technical schools of our universities, which yearly send into the world of economic and industrial life trained experts, many of whom have taken part of the college course; including, it is to be hoped, some such training in economic thinking as I have urged. The indirect influence of such men, trained broadly, even if superficially, in economic questions would be invaluable.

Third, the American order means a new conception of social groupings. Most obviously, the social theory of our democracy makes a system of castes or of semi-castes impossible. That is, there can be no group whose existence means the possession of valuable and exclusive privileges for personal advantage over their fellows, and which is not founded upon principles of inclusion for which any person as a person may qualify, in time. Thus, there can be no aristocracy in the European sense, based upon such a forbidding barrier as that of birth. And this has sometimes been urged against American democratic society as a defect. Indeed, the innate monotony, the social dead level, the spiritless and uninteresting uniformity of democratic society (as a theory) often has been enlarged upon. We are told that the doctrine of social equality inevitably carries with it social sameness.

But the criticism of democracy's society as monotonously uniform assumes that the equality of democracy prohibits the institution of social groups of different grades, mutually exclusive in any sense. Yet not all social groups are castes. And there may be, indeed, a highest social group, without its constituting itself an aristocracy.

For, remember that the doctrine of equality means that persons are equals as ends—as possibilities—and that they have freedom—the freedom to seek their self realization in the social goal, through the reason of each. This social goal, this ideal democracy, is theoretically and really the same for all. But while all have the same ideal; and while, thus, and only thus, is the solidarity of democracy secured, not every person is in the same stage of progress toward it. Nor have those in the same stage the same individual problems to meet—the same interests. Men are, indeed, the same in so far as their ideal is the same, and in so far as they have equal opportunities for attaining it. But men are different in so far as they represent different cultural stages toward the ideal, and express their individuality by realizing it in their own ways.

Now, men will naturally and reasonably group themselves according to their fundamental "interest," as we say. And the fundamental interest of democracy's man, apart from the universally shared interest in the common democratic ideal, is his interest in those things which appertain to his own stage of self-realization toward the social goal. The true principle of fundamental groups in a democracy, then, is community in a stage of culture, or of progress toward the common social ideal. This has reference to democracy's fundamental groups. They are formed on an ethical principle; for democracy is an essentially ethical conception. Other social groups may be formed upon more superficial bases; but they are not integral parts of the organization of democracy's society, as such. And they must disappear if, in principle, they are opposed to it.

These social groups of ideal democracy are exclusive in the sense that no one is acceptable to a group unless he fulfills in himself the qualifications that belong to the sort of culture which it represents. These social groups are open to all in the sense that any person has within himself the capacity for attaining any given stage of culture, and so any social group whatever. Thus, no group of democracy can become a fixed aristocracy. One may add that no sane man would want to belong to an association of persons whose cultural attainments and interests were widely different from his own.

Further, the spirit of democracy permits no snobbishness on the part of any of its social groups. A social set might well be formed in strict accord with democracy's principles, and yet not truly represent democracy, if its members looked upon persons of less cultural attainment with the Pharisee's thanksgiving. For, in democracy, the social ideal of the member of a restricted group is the good not only of his kind, but of the whole of society. Should he restrict his aim to those of his own sort, he thereby would turn his back upon democracy and join his fortunes with an abortive aristocracy. If the masses are not as high as he in cultural progress, he will not look down upon them with contempt, or pity, or indifference; his aim, even in his restricted associations, is to put the masses in the way of progress, not as charity, but as social justice. Thus, the members of a truly democratic social set are not exclusive, in the sense that they limit all their social recognitions to their kind alone.

They esteem themselves part of the larger society, whose obligations are forever prior; and for whose obligations, indeed, they are formed into a group the better to discharge.

What can the college do to mold American social sets into an approximation to America's meaning of a social order?

Well, first of all, it can attempt to correct the obvious shortcomings of American social sets as they exist. Best of all, it can do this by correcting these same shortcomings within the society of the college itself. What are these defects that must be minimized within the student's world, for the sake of that later world he is to enter? To put it boldly, how do American social sets, as they are, sin against democracy?

They sin against democracy in so far as they do not try to discover their real relation to the social order as a whole, and are not fully loyal to what they do know.

They sin against democracy in so far as they emphasize exclusiveness for its own sake; an emphasis that is aided and abetted by the inherent and imitative snobbishness of the masses.

They sin against democracy in so far as they emphasize principles of inclusion which are impossible for a person as a person; such as great wealth beyond its cultural worth, and in terms of the unjust deprivation of others.

They sin against democracy in so far as their ideal is the welfare of the restricted group, rather than that of the total society of which they are parts; and in so far as they do not make the obligations of this larger society strictly prior, and are not grouped for the sake of service to it, rather than for selfish glorification.

They sin against democracy in so far as they regard themselves, isolated and apart, as the real Society, over against the masses, who are conceived as socially alien. In a democracy, there should be no Society, in the insidious meaning of Society versus the masses. Any person belongs to some social group; each group, however large or small, however little it may mingle with others, being rightly considered an integral part of that larger society which, alone, is democracy.

And, finally, our hedonistic social sets sin especially against democracy in so far as they tend to become egoistic and unscrupulously, narrowly, self-indulgent; and, therefore, deeply unsocial, and so undemocratic.

Thus, through these sins against democracy, the conditions of genuine social progress are yet far from being fulfilled in America. For, again, the democratic ideal of society came into being and is justified only because, as far as human reason and experience can judge, this conception is the only one that secures an indefinite and complete social progress—a progress which is ethically real. America has adopted democracy; but society, at least in the restricted sense, is not quite loyal to America's cherished hope.

This hope may be realized partially within college walls. The defects of the American social sets must here be corrected as much as is practicable, whether expressed in snobbishness of family, or wealth, or display, or intellect; whether through hedonism, or aimlessness; whether incorporated in social cliques, or in such forms of fraternities and sororities and clubs as defy the American idea. Here in the college, if anywhere, should be found at least a remote suggestion of the true social ranking. But it can exist only if the consciousness of the American social order, and the meaning of its persons, are introduced to the students' minds not only as a theory, but as an atmosphere. It is Utopian to expect too much from the colleges in this respect. But it is not Utopian to hope and demand something. Above all, no college should lend itself, as some few "aristocratic" colleges certainly have, to the perpetuation of those very social distinctions which the American college should exist emphatically to discourage.

Fourth, the American social order has its unmistakable implications in the realm of literature and the other arts. A famous musician said, during the World War: "It is my conviction that art has as much at stake in this war as democracy." His reason was that true art depends upon true democracy for its future. Since literature is the art most familiar to us, and since it ranks high among the arts, we may allow it to be representative of the arts for the purposes of this discussion.

Now, that there is possible an art distinctively American has been challenged for a number of reasons; reasons which, I think, are answerable. In the first place, it is alleged that we are guilty of the fallacy of False Cause if we suppose that a particular form of government has any direct influence upon art. But the question is not whether democracy, in the restricted sense of democratic government, has any influence upon art; but whether democracy as a theory of man and society, exemplified in a total national life, has such influence.

Second, it is argued that America has not yet attained a national unity. To this one may reply that America is rapidly attaining a unified self-consciousness, so far as many of the fundamental meanings of its democracy are concerned; that the war has helped to render this unity still more real; and that even if a national unity were not yet attained, it is a possibility; and that art should do its unique share to realize it.

Third, it is contended that the modern close intercourse of nations tends towards the obliteration of purely national arts. But the intimate interrelations of peoples cannot obliterate the distinctiveness of America, until all peoples adopt the principles of its social order. And, even then, the distinctiveness of America will richly remain in the uniqueness of the content of that order; a content to which I shall presently refer.

Finally, it is urged that true art is universal in its nature; it transcends national boundaries, just as true logic is the same logic, regardless of places and times. The answer is that the formal elements of art are, indeed, universal; but that the contentual elements, while distinguishable from form, cannot be sundered from form; that democracy is most favorable to a sound art, through its insistence upon truth to life and the moral values, in terms of persons, which any genuine esthetic creation involves. Attention should also be called to the fact that, besides furnishing the distinctive content of democracy's life as such, America affords the dramatic content peculiar to America's own specific conditions for democracy's realization. This includes such elements as our concrete historical background and movement; the determinations of our national life by the vastness of the country, sectional differences, opportunities for dramatic tendencies counter to democracy in the chances of fortune, and in our inherited and borrowed tendencies; and, above all, and permeating all, the inevitable conflicts, spiritual and material, tragic and comic, belonging to a democracy as yet only in the earlier stages of being realized.

The American social order has hardly begun to express itself through the arts. Some American literature has come nearest to such an expression, especially such as presents to us an apotheosis of the common man and the common life, interpretative of their real meanings. Of course, the first thing is for the American people to value the arts as worth while; and distinctively American art as a desirable possibility. And one of the best ways to achieve this is for educational institutions to lay some stress upon the appreciation and creation of the beautiful. I much fear that this is contrary to the main American tradition; certainly, it is contrary to the established tradition of the college. And yet, is the assumption of a genuine relation between truth and beauty mere sentiment? Is there not a real relation, too, between moral and esthetic ideals? We remember how thoroughly Plato thought that there was.

This is not to argue that the college of arts shall be turned into a school of art; to have visions of canvases and easels and long hair and Byronic collars and a sublimated Latin Quarter. But one may well have a vision of the time when, in America, the beautiful shall no longer be regarded as merely incidental to life, instead of as an important and integral part of life itself. We have the motive of truth in education; in a small measure, too, the motive of morals under various guises. There is place for the motive of beauty as well. It need not and should not be expressed chiefly in special courses in esthetics. It can best be expressed through the education of the imagination; not only through courses in literature, where, however, the possibilities are obvious; but through the sciences as well. There is richly possible such a thing as the use of the imagination in scientific matters; does the student ever find it? Does the average instructor himself? Whether or no the future of American art, including literature, depends greatly upon the American college, from it might well be expected great things. The college will have missed one very great phase of its responsibility to the social order, if it continues to ignore what is a fundamental note in any completely rounded civilization.

Fifth, the American order implies distinct ideals of the meaning of religion. Casually, this assertion seems radical, even dangerous. It is, if not characterized with some care. But, a fundamental doctrine of what men are, such as the American order indubitably affords, cannot but have its implications within the realm of religion. The pricelessness of the person is not only a democratic doctrine, but a religious doctrine. So, the social nature of the self implies that democracy's person cannot accept any religion but one with social responsibilities; that it cannot be "saved" in terms of any selfish hedonism. Again, if democracy's person is fundamentally rational, religion may not be considered as remote from other intellectual interests, including science, which often seems unwarrantably opposed to it. Further, if persons are free, then religion must spring from within, however validly it may be stimulated from without. And, again, if persons are measureless in capacities, then religion must not be thought of as merely a negative constraint, but as a positive and expanding self-realization.

Such are a few of the religious implications of the American social order. Already, the churches tend to recognize them. Only such religion, whether Christian or Jewish, Catholic or Protestant, can furnish an adequate sanction for democracy's ethical ideals. And such a sanction is needed. Closely allied to a healthy moral consciousness, is the religious consciousness—consciousness of those verities that strongly support and are logically implied by a living moral faith. To fight for the right, effectively and hopefully, is to have some sort of belief in the triumph of the right, which, at any definite moment in human history, is never fully victorious; indeed, often apparently defeated. It means a living faith in some power that makes for righteousness.

While it is not the business of the non-sectarian college, with manifest obligations to the democracy of thought, to insist upon any too particular interpretation of religious verities (beyond their general spirit, as just outlined) no college should prejudice its youths against them, directly or indirectly. Yet, indirectly, and wholly unintentionally, this has certainly been done. It has been done because the concepts of physical science, confident through their successes over all other methods and contents of truth, have been taught in such a context as to insure the corollary of scepticism concerning the unseen verities. The so-called "rationalism" of some of our larger colleges is mostly the pretension of the natural science method to decide all questions; a pretension of concepts to which I have referred, and which a new education must controvert. Almost any expert in the logic of method knows better; but his is a still, small voice, unheeded among the more strident achievements which present themselves for acclaim in the world of the obvious.

Such "rationalism" is irrational. A new emphasis upon the intangible, yet supremely real values which all facts must subserve, if they are to have the least glimmer of educational meaning, will involve the resurrection of the age-old rights of the realities we are accustomed to call "religious" to a consideration at least impartial. True education may yet mean the reasonable transfiguration of life, morally and religiously. After the tyranny of an age of "facts," some of earth's older glories may return to show how indispensable these facts of science indeed are; yet, how insufficient they ever must be, when left to their own barren services to themselves.

Education may yet give us not only life's reason, but something of its inspiration, too!

EDUCATION AS A POSSIBLE CURE FOR CROWD-THINKING[1]

EVERETT DEAN MARTIN

[Everett Dean Martin was born at Jacksonville, Illinois, in 1880. After graduating from the McCormick Theological Seminary and serving as the minister of various churches he became the director of the Cooper Union Forum in New York, "the largest center of discussion" in America.]

WE have seen that Democracy in and of itself is no more sure a guarantee of liberty than other forms of government. This does not necessarily mean that we have been forced by our psychological study into an argument against the idea of democracy as such. In fact, it cannot be denied that this form of human association may have decided advantages, both practical and spiritual, if we set about in the right way to realize them. It does not follow that, because the franchise is exercised by all, democracy must necessarily be an orgy of mob rule. If, under our modern political arrangements, it has been shown that the crowd presumes to regulate acts and thought processes hitherto considered purely personal matters, it is also true that the dominance of any particular crowd has, in the long run, been rendered less absolute and secure by the more openly expressed hostility of rival crowds. But crowd-

[1] From *The Behavior of Crowds,* 1920, Chapter X. Used by permission of the publishers, Harper & Brothers.

behavior has been known in all historic periods. Democracy cannot be said to have caused it. It may be a mere accident of history that the present development of crowd-mindedness has come along with that of democratic institutions. Democracy has indeed given new kinds of crowds their hope of dominance. It has therefore been made into a cult for the self-justification of various modern crowds.

The formula for realizing a more free and humane common life will not be found in any of the proffered cure-alls and propagandas which to-day deafen our ears with their din. Neither are we now in such possession of the best obtainable social order that one would wish to preserve the *status quo* against all change, which would mean, in other words, the survival of the present ruling crowds. Many existing facts belie the platitudes which these crowds speak in their defense, just as they lay bare the hidden meaning of the magic remedies which are proposed by counter-crowds. There is no single formula for social redemption, and the man who has come to himself will refuse to invest his faith in any such thing—which does not mean, however, that he will refuse to consider favorably the practical possibilities of any proposed plan for improving social conditions.

The first and greatest effort must be to *free democracy from crowd-mindedness, by liberating our own thinking.* The way out of this complex of crowd compulsions is the solitary part of self-analysis and intellectual courage. It is the way of Socrates, and Protagoras, of Peter Abelard, and Erasmus, and Montaigne, of Cervantes and Samuel Butler, of Goethe and Emerson, of Whitman and William James.

Just here I know that certain conservatives will heartily agree with me. "That is it," they will say; "begin with the individual." Yes, but which individual shall we begin with? Most of those who speak thus mean, begin with some other individual. Evangelize the heathen, uplift the poor, Americanize the Bolshevists, do something to some one which will make him like ourselves; in other words, bring him into our crowd. The individual with whom I would begin is myself. Somehow or other if I am to have individuality at all it will be by virtue of being an individual, a single, "separate person." And that is a dangerous and at present a more or less lonely thing to do. But the problem is really one of practical psychology. We must come out of the crowd-self, just as, before the neurotic may be normal, he must get over his neurosis. To do that he must trace his malady back to its source in the unconscious, and learn the meaning of his conscious behavior as it is related to his unconscious desires. Then he must do a difficult thing—he must *accept the fact of himself at its real worth.*

It is much the same with our crowd-mindedness. If psychoanalysis has therapeutic value by the mere fact of revealing to the neurotic the hidden meaning of his neurosis, then it would seem that an analysis of crowd-behavior such as we have tried to make should be of some help in breaking the hold of the crowd upon our spirits, and thus freeing democracy to some extent from quackery.

To see behind the shibboleths and dogmas of crowd-thinking the "cussedness"—that is, the primitive side—of human nature at work, is a great moral gain. At least the "cussedness" cannot deceive us any more. We have won our greatest victory over it when we drag it out into the light. We can at least wrestle with it consciously, and maybe, by directing it to desirable ends, it will cease to be so "cussed," and become a useful servant. No such good can come to us so long as this side of our nature is allowed its way only on condition that it paint its face and we encourage it to talk piously of things which it really does not mean. Disillusionment may be painful both to the neurotic and to the crowd-man, but the gain is worth the shock to our pride. The ego, when better understood, becomes at once more highly personalized because more conscious of itself, and more truly social because better adjusted to the demands of others. It is this socialized and conscious selfhood which is both the aim and the hope of true democracy.

Such analysis may possibly give us the gift to see ourselves as others do not see us, as we have not wished them to see us, and finally enable us to see ourselves and others and to be seen by them as we really are.

We shall be free when we cease pampering ourselves, stop lying to ourselves and to one another, and give up the crowd-mummery in which we indulge because it happens to flatter our hidden weaknesses! In the end we shall only begin to solve the social problem when we can cease together taking refuge from reality in systems made up of general ideas that we should be using as tools in meeting the tasks from which as crowd-men and neurotics people run away; when we discontinue making use of commonly accepted principles and ideals as defense formations for shameful things in which we can indulge ourselves with a clear conscience only by all doing them together.

There must be an increase in the number of unambitious men, men who can rise above vulgar dilemmas and are deaf to crowd propaganda, men capable of philosophical tolerance, critical doubt and inquiry, genuine companionship, and voluntary coöperation in the achievement of common ends, free spirits who can smile in the face of the mob, who know the mob and are not to be taken in by it.

All this sounds much like the old gospel of conviction of sin and repentance; perhaps it is just that. We must think differently, change our minds. Again and again people have tried the wide way and the broad gate, the crowd-road to human happiness, only to find that it led to destruction in a *cul-de-sac*. Now let us try the other road, "the strait and narrow path." The crowd-path leads neither to self-mastery nor social blessedness. People in crowds are not thinking together; they are not thinking at all, save as a paranoiac thinks. They are not working together; they are *only sticking together*. We have leaned on one another till we have all run and fused into a common mass. The democratic crowd to-day, with its sweet optimism, its warm "brotherly love," is a sticky, gooey mass which one can hardly touch and come back to himself clean. By dissolving everything in "one great union" people who cannot climb alone expect to ooze into the coöperative commonwealth or kingdom of heaven. I am sick of this oozing democracy. There must be something crystalline and insoluble left in democratic America. Somewhere there must be people with sharp edges that cut when they are pressed too hard, people who are still solid, who have impenetrable depths in them and hard facets which reflect the sunlight. They are the hope of democracy, these infusible ones.

To change the figure, may their tribe increase. And this is the business of every educator who is not content to be a faker. What we need is not only more education, but a different kind of education. There is more hope in an illiterate community where people hate lying than in a high-school educated nation which reads nothing but trash and is fed up on advertising, newspapers, popular fiction, and propaganda.

In the foregoing chapter, reference was made to our traditional educational systems. The subject is so closely related to the mental habits of democracy that it would be difficult to over-emphasize its importance for our study. Traditional educational methods have more often given encouragement to crowd-thinking than to independence of judgment. Thinking has been divorced from doing. Knowledge, instead of being regarded as the foresight of ends to be reached and the conscious direction of activity toward such ends, has been more commonly regarded as the copying of isolated things to be learned. The act of learning has been treated as if it were the passive reception of information imposed from without. The subject to be learned has been sequestered and set apart from experience as a whole, with the result that ideas easily come to be regarded as things in themselves. Systems of thought are built up with little or no sense of their connection with everyday problems. Thus our present-day education prepares in advance both the ready-made logical systems in which the crowd-mind takes refuge from the concretely real and the disposition to accept truth second-hand upon the authority of another, which in the crowd-man becomes the spirit of conformity.

Even science, taught in this spirit, may be destructive of intellectual freedom. Professor Dewey says [1] that while science has done much to modify men's thought, still

> It must be admitted that to a considerable extent the progress thus procured has been only technical; it has provided more efficient means for satisfying pre-existent desires rather than modified the quality of human purposes. There is, for example, no modern civilization which is the equal of Greek culture in all respects. Science is still too recent to have been absorbed into imaginative and emotional disposition. Men move more swiftly and surely to the realization of their ends, but their ends too largely remain what they were prior to scientific enlightenment. This fact places upon education the responsibility of using science in a way to modify the habitual attitude of imagination and feeling, not leave it just an extension of our physical arms and legs. . . .
>
> The problem of an educational use of science is, then, to create an intelligence pregnant with belief in the possibility of the direction of human affairs by itself. The method of science ingrained through education in habit means emancipation from rule of thumb and from the routine generated by rule of thumb procedure. . . .
>
> That science may be taught as a set of formal and technical exercises is only too true. This happens whenever information about the world is made an end in itself. The failure of such instruction to procure culture is not, however, evidence of the antithesis of natural knowledge to humanistic concern, but evidence of a wrong educational attitude.

The new kind of education, the education which is to liberate the mind, will make much of scientific methods. But let us notice what it is to set a mind free. Mind does not exist in a vacuum, nor in a world of "pure ideas." The free mind is the functioning mind, the mind which is not inhibited in its work by any conflict within itself.

[1] *Democracy and Education* (1916).

Thought is not made free by the mere substitution of naturalistic for theological dogma. It is possible to make a cult of science itself. Crowd-propaganda is often full of pseudo-scientific jargon of this sort. Specialization in technical training may produce merely a high-class trained-animal man, of the purely reflex type, who simply performs a prescribed trick which he has learned, whenever an expected motor-cue appears. In the presence of the unexpected such a person may be as helpless as any other animal. It is possible to train circus dogs, horses, and even horned toads, to behave in this same way. Much so-called scientific training in our schools to-day is of this sort. It results not in freedom, but in what Bergson would call the triumph of mechanism over freedom.

Science, to be a means of freedom—that is, science as culture—may not be pursued as pure theorizing apart from practical application. Neither may a calculating utilitarianism gain freedom to us by ignoring, in the application of scientific knowledge to given ends, a consideration of the ends themselves and their value for enriching human experience. It is human interest which gives scientific knowledge any meaning. Science must be taught in the humanist spirit. It may not ignore this quality of human interest which exists in all knowledge. To do so is to cut off our relations with reality. And the result may become a negation of personality similar to that with which the crowd compensates itself for its unconscious ego-mania.

The reference just made to Humanism leads us next to a consideration of the humanities. It has long been the habit of traditional education to oppose to the teaching of science the teaching of the classic languages and the arts, as if there were two irreconcilable principles involved here. Dewey says that

> Humanistic studies when set in opposition to study of nature are hampered. They tend to reduce themselves to exclusively literary and linguistic studies, which in turn tend to shrink to "the classics," to languages no longer spoken. . . . It would be hard to find anything in history more ironical than the educational practices which have identified the "humanities" exclusively with a knowledge of Greek and Latin. Greek and Roman art and institutions made such important contributions to our civilization that there should always be the amplest opportunities for making their acquaintance. But to regard them as *par excellence* the humane studies involves a deliberate neglect of the possibilities of the subject-matter which is accessible in education to the masses, and tends to cultivate a narrow snobbery—that of a learned class whose insignia are the accidents of exclusive opportunity. Knowledge is humanistic in quality not because it is *about* human products in the past, but because of what it *does* in liberating human intelligence and human sympathy. Any subject-matter which accomplishes this result is humane and any subject-matter which does not accomplish it is not even educational.

The point is that it is precisely what a correct knowledge of ancient civilization through a study of the classics *does* that our traditional educators most dread. William James once said that the good which came from such study was the ability to "know a good man when we see him." The student would thus become more capable of discriminating appreciation. He would grow to be a judge of values. He would acquire sharp likes and dislikes and thus set up his own standards of judgment. He would become an independent thinker and therefore an enemy of crowds. Scholars of the Renaissance knew this well, and that is why in their revolt against the crowd-mindedness of their day they made use of the *literæ humaniores* to smash to pieces the whole dogmatic system of the Middle Ages.

With the picture of ancient life before him the student could not help becoming more cosmopolitan in spirit. Here he got a glimpse of a manner of living in which the controlling ideas and fixations of his contemporary crowds were frankly challenged. Here were witnesses to values contrary to those in which his crowd had sought to bring him up in a docile spirit. Inevitably his thinking would wander into what his crowd considered forbidden paths. One cannot begin to know the ancients as they really were without receiving a tremendous intellectual stimulus. After becoming acquainted with the intellectual freedom and courage and love of life which are almost everywhere manifest in the literature of the ancients, something happens to a man. He becomes acquainted with himself as a valuing animal. Few things are better calculated to make free spirits than these very classics, once the student "catches on."

But that is just the trouble; from the Renaissance till now, the crowd-mind, whether interested politically, morally, or religiously; whether Catholic, or Protestant, or merely Rationalist, has done its level best to keep the student from "catching on." Educational tradition, which is for the most part only systematized crowd-thinking, has perverted the classics into instruments for producing spiritual results of the very opposite nature from the message which these literatures contain. Latin and Greek are taught for *purposes of discipline.* The task of learning them has been made as difficult and as uninteresting as possible, with the idea of forcing the student to do something he dislikes, of whipping his spirit into line and rendering him subservient to intellectual authority. Thus, while keeping up the external appearance of culture, the effect is to make the whole thing so meaningless and unpleasant that the student will never have the interest to try to find out what it is all about.

I have said that the sciences and classics should be approached in the "humanistic" spirit. The humanist method must be extended to the whole subject-matter of education, even to a revaluation of knowing itself. I should not say *even*, but *primarily*. It is impossible here to enter into an extended discussion of the humanist theories of knowledge as contrasted with the traditional or "intellectualist" theories. But since we have seen that the conscious thinking of the crowd-mind consists in the main of abstract and dogmatic logical systems, similar to the "rationalizations" of the paranoiac, it is important to note the bearing of humanism upon these logical systems wherever they are found.

A number of years ago, while discussing certain phases of this subject with one of the physicians in charge of a large hospital for the insane, the significance of education for healthy mental life was brought out with great emphasis. It was at the time when psychiatrists were just beginning to make use of analytical psychology in the treatment of mental and nervous disorders.

"The trouble with a great many of our patients," said my friend, "is the fact that they have been wrongly educated."

"Do you mean," I said, "that they have not received proper moral instruction?"

"Yes, but by the proper moral instruction I do not

mean quite the same thing that most people mean by that. It all depends on the way in which the instruction is given. Many of these patients are the mental slaves of convention. They have been terrified by it; its weight crushes them; when they discover that their own impulses or behavior are in conflict with what they regard as absolute standards, they cannot bear the shock. They do not know how to use morality; they simply condemn themselves, they seek reconciliation by all sorts of crazy ideas which develop into psychoneurosis. And the only hope there is of cure for them is re-education. The physician, when it is not too late, often to do any good has to become an educator."

The practice of psychoanalysis as a therapeutic method is really hardly anything more than re-education. The patient must first be led to face the fact of himself as he really is; then he must be taught to revalue conventional ideas in such a way that he can use these ideas as instruments with which he may adjust himself in the various relations of life. This process of education, in a word, is humanistic. It is pragmatic; the patient is taught that his thinking is a way of functioning; that ideas are instruments, ways of acting. He learns to value these tendencies to act and to find himself through the mastery of his own thinking.

Now we have seen that the neurosis is but one path of escape from this conflict of self with the imperative and abstract ideas through which social control is exercised. The second way is to deny, unconsciously, the true meaning of these ideas, and this, as we have seen, is crowd-thinking. Here, as in the other case, the education which is needed is that which acquaints the subject with the functional nature of his own thinking, which directs his attention to results, which dissolves the fictions into which the unconscious takes refuge, by showing that systems of ideas have no other reality than what they do and no other meaning than the difference which their being true makes in actual experience somewhere.

We have previously noted the connection between the intellectualist philosophies with their closed systems of ideas, their absolutists, and the conscious thinking of crowds. The crowd finds these systems ready-made and merely backs into them and hides itself like a hermit crab in a deserted seashell. It follows that the humanist, however social he may be, cannot be a crowd-man. He, too, will have his ideals, but they are not made-in-advance goods which all must accept; they are good only as they may be made good in real experience, true only when verified in fact. To such a mind there is no unctuousness, by which ideas may be fastened upon others without their assent. Nothing is regarded as so final and settled that the spirit of inquiry should be discouraged from efforts to modify and improve it.

Generalizations, such as justice, truth, liberty, and all other intellectualist- and crowd-abstractions, become to the humanist not transcendental things in themselves, but descriptions of certain qualities of behavior, actual or possible, existing only where they are experienced and in definite situations. He will not be swept into a howling mob by these big words; he will stop to see what particular things are they which in a given instance are to be called just, what particular hypothesis is it which it is sought to verify and thus add to the established body of truth, whose liberty is demanded and what, to be definite, is it proposed that he shall do with the greater opportunity for action. Let the crowd yell itself hoarse, chanting its abstract nouns made out of adjectives, the humanist will know that these are but words and that the realities which they point to, if they have any meaning at all, are what "they are known as."

This humanist doctrine of the concreteness of the real is important. It is a reaffirmation of the reality of human experience. William James, who called himself a "radical empiricist," made much of this point. Experience may not be ruled out for the sake of an *a priori* notion of what this world ought to be. As James used to say, we shall never know what this world really is or is to become until the last man's vote is in and counted. Here, of course, is an emphasis upon the significance of unique personality which no crowd will grant. Crowds will admit personality as an abstract principle, but not as an active will having something of its own to say about the ultimate outcome of things.

Another important point in which humanism corrects crowd-thinking is the fact that it regards intellect as an instrument of acting, and not as a mere copyist of realities earthly or super-mundane. Dewey says:[1]

> If it be true that the self or subject of experience is part and parcel of the course of events, it follows that the self becomes a knower. It becomes a mind in virtue of a distinctive way of partaking in the course of events. The significant distinction is no longer between a knower *and* the world, it is between different ways of being in and of the movement of things; between a physical way and a purposive way. . . .
>
> As a matter of fact the pragmatic theory of intelligence means that the function of mind is to project new and more complex ends to free experience from routine and caprice. Not the use of

[1] *Creative Intelligence* (1917).

thought to accomplish purposes already given either in the mechanism of the body or in that of the existent state of society, but the use of intelligence to liberate and liberalize action, is the pragmatic lesson. . . . Intelligence as intelligence is inherently forward looking; only by ignoring its primary function does it become a means for an end already given. The latter is servile, even when the end is labeled moral, religious, esthetic. But action directed to ends to which the agent has not previously been attached inevitably carries with it a quickened and enlarged spirit. A pragmatic intelligence is a creative intelligence, not a routine mechanic.

Hence humanism breaks down the conformist spirit of crowds. From the simplest to the most complex, ideas are regarded as primarily motor, or, rather, as guides to our bodily movements among other things in our environment. James says that the stream of life which runs in at our eyes and ears is meant to run out at our lips, our feet, and our fingertips. Bergson says that ideas are like snapshots of a man running. However closely they are taken together, the movement always occurs between them. They cannot, therefore, give us reality, or the movement of life as such, but only cross-sections of it, which serve as guides in directing the conscious activity of life upon matter. According to James again, there are no permanently existing ideas, or impersonal ones; each idea is an individual activity, known only in the thinking, and is always thought *for a purpose*. As all thinking is purposive, and therefore partial, emphasizing just those aspects of things which are useful for our present problem, it follows that the sum total of partial views cannot give us the whole of it. Existence as a whole cannot be reduced to any logical system. The One and the Absolute are therefore meaningless and are only logical fictions, useful, says James, by way of allowing us a sort of temporary irresponsibility, or "moral holiday."

From all this follows the humanist view of Truth. Truth is nothing complete and existing in itself independent of human purpose. The word is a noun made out of an adjective, as I have said. An idea becomes true, says James, when it fits into the totality of our experience; truth is what we say about an idea when it works. It must be made true, by ourselves—that is, verified. Truth is therefore of human origin, frankly, man-made. To Schiller [1] it is the same as the good; it is the attainment of satisfactory relations within experience. Or, to quote the famous humanist creed of Protagoras, as Schiller is so fond of doing, "Man is the measure of all things." The meaning of the word is precisely, for all purposes, its meaning for us. Its worth, both logical and moral, is not something given, but just what we through our activity are able to assign to it.

The humanist is thus thrown upon his own responsibility in the midst of concrete realities of which he as a knowing, willing being is one. His task is to make such modifications within his environment, physical and social, as will make his own activity and that of others with him richer and more satisfactory in the future.

The question arises—it is a question commonly put by crowd-minded people and by intellectual philosophers; Plato asks it of the Protagoreans—how, if the individual man is the measure of all things, is there to be any common measure? How any agreement? May not a thing

[1] F. C. S. Schiller, professor of philosophy in Corpus Christi College, Oxford, author of *Studies in Humanism,* etc.

be good and true for one and not for another? How, then, shall there be any getting together without an outside authority and an absolute standard? The answer, as Schiller and James showed, is obvious; life is a matter of adjustment. We each constitute a part of the other's environment. At certain points our desires conflict, our valuations are different, and yet our experience at these points overlaps, as it were. It is to our common advantage to have agreement at these points. Out of our habitual adjustments to one another, a body of mutual understanding and agreement grows up which constitutes the intellectual and moral order of life. But this order, necessary as it is, is still in the making. It is not something given; it is not a copy of something transcendent, impersonal, and final which crowds may write upon their banners and use to gain uniform submission for anything which they may be able to express in terms which are general and abstract. This order of life is purely practical; it exists for us, not we for it, and because we have agreed that certain things shall be right and true, it does not follow that righteousness and truth are fixed and final and must be worshiped as pure ideas in such a way that the mere repetition of these words paralyzes our cerebral hemispheres.

Doubtless one of the greatest aids of the humanist way of thinking in bringing the individual to self-consciousness is the way in which it orients us in the world of present-day events. It inspires one to achieve a working harmony, not a fictitious haven of rest for the mind interested only in its relations to its own ideas. The unity which life demands of us is not that of a perfect rational system. It is rather the unity of a healthy organism all the parts of which can work together.

Cut up as we are into what Emerson called "fragments of men," I think we are particularly susceptible to crowd-thinking because we are so disintegrated. Thought and behavior must always be more or less automatic and compulsory where there is no conscious coördination of the several parts of it. It is partly because we are the heirs of such a patchwork of civilization that few people today are able to think their lives through. There can be little organic unity in the heterogeneous and unrelated aggregation of half-baked information, warring interests, and irreconcilable systems of valuation which are piled together in the modern man's thinking.

Life may not be reduced to a logical unity, but it is an organic whole for each of us, and we do not reach that organic unity by adding mutually exclusive partial views of it together.

Something happens to one who grasps the meaning of humanism; he becomes self-conscious in a new way. His psychic life becomes a fascinating adventure in a real world. He finds that his choices are real events. He is "set intellectually on fire," as one of our educators has correctly defined education. As Jung would doubtless say, he has "extroverted" himself; his libido, which in the crowd seeks to enhance the ego feeling by means of the mechanism which we have described, now is drawn out and attached to the outer world through the intellectual channel. Selfhood is realized in the satisfactoriness of the results which one is able to achieve in the very fulness of his activity and the richness of his interests.

Such a free spirit needs no crowds to keep up his faith, and he is truly social, for he approaches his social relationships with intelligent discrimination and judgments of worth which are his own. He contributes to the social, not a copy or an imitation, not a childish wish-fancy furtively disguised, but a psychic reality and a new creative energy. It is only in the fellowship of such spirits, whatever political or economic forms their association may take, that we may expect to see the Republic of the Free.

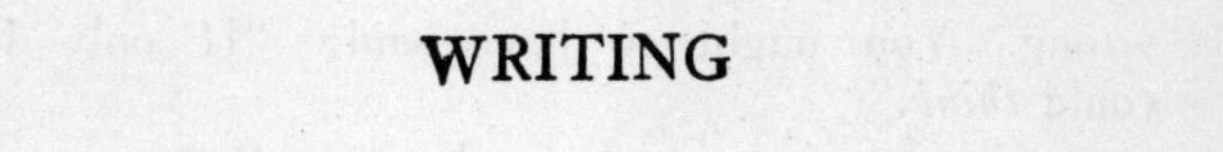

WRITING

You have said to yourself in moments of emotion: "If only I could write—," etc. You were wrong. You ought to have said: "If only I could *think*."

—Arnold Bennett

HOW I LEARNED TO WRITE[1]

Robert Louis Stevenson

[Robert Louis Stevenson (1850–1894) son and grandson of lighthouse builders, was born in Edinburgh. Compelled by physical frailty to give up the inherited profession of civil engineering, he studied law and was admitted to the bar. But his lifelong passion was to express his experiences and his thoughts in words of beauty and power. How he taught himself to write such human reflections as you may read in a later essay in this volume, "Pulvis et Umbra," he relates in the following revelation of his simple, but suggestive method.]

ALL through my boyhood and youth I was known and pointed out for the pattern of an idler; and yet I was always busy on my own private end, which was to learn to write. I kept always two books in my pocket, one to read, one to write in. As I walked, my mind was busy fitting what I saw with appropriate words; when I sat by the roadside, I would either read, or a pencil and a penny version-book would be in my hand, to note down the features of the scene, or commemorate some halting stanzas. Thus I lived with words. And what I thus wrote was for no ulterior use; it was written consciously for practice. It was not so much that I wished to be an author (though I wished that too), as that I vowed I would learn to write. That was a proficiency that tempted me; and I practised to acquire

[1] From *A College Magazine.* Reprinted by permission of Charles Scribner's Sons.

it, as men learn to whittle, in a wager with myself. Description was the principal field of my exercise; for to any one with senses there is always something worth describing, and town and country are but one continuous subject. But I worked in other ways also. . . .

Whenever I read a book or a passage that particularly pleased me, in which a thing was said or an effect rendered with propriety, in which there was either some conspicuous force or some happy distinction in the style, I must sit down at once and set myself to ape that quality. I was unsuccessful, and I knew it, and tried again, and was again unsuccessful, and always unsuccessful; but at least, in these vain bouts, I got some practice in rhythm, in harmony, in construction and the coordination of parts. I have thus played the sedulous ape to Hazlitt, to Lamb, to Wordsworth, to Sir Thomas Browne, to Defoe, to Hawthorne, to Montaigne, to Baudelaire, and to Obermann.

That, like it or not, is the way to learn to write; whether I have profited or not, that is the way. It was so Keats learned, and there was never a finer temperament for literature than Keats's; it was so, if we could trace it out, that all men have learned; and that is why a revival of letters is always accompanied or heralded by a cast back to earlier and fresher models. Perhaps I hear some one cry out: But this is not the way to be original! It is not; nor is there any way but to be born so. Nor yet, if you are born original, is there anything in this training that shall clip the wings of your originality. . . . Nor is there anything here that should astonish the considerate. Before he can tell what cadences he truly prefers, the student should have tried all that are possible; before he can choose and preserve a fitting key of words, he should long have practised the literary scales; and it is only after years of such gymnastic that he can sit down at last, legions of words swarming to his call, dozens of turns of phrase simultaneously bidding for his choice, and he himself knowing what he wants to do and (within the narrow limit of a man's ability) able to do it.

"STYLE IS THE MAN HIMSELF"

M. de Buffon

[George Louis Le Clerc (1707–1788) known by his name indicating noble rank, Comte de Buffon, is famous as the compiler of the *Natural History,* the first encyclopedia of science to present facts in a generally intelligible form. The following address he delivered on the occasion of his reception into the French Academy in 1753.]

IN all times there have been men with the ability to rule their fellows by the power of speech. Yet only in enlightened times have men written and spoken well. True eloquence supposes the exercise of genius, and a cultivated mind. It is far different from that natural facility in speaking which is simply a talent, a gift accorded those whose passions are strong, whose voices are flexible, whose imaginations are naturally quick. Such men perceive vividly, are affected vividly, and display their emotions with force; and by an impression purely mechanical they transmit their own enthusiasm and feelings to others. It is body speaking to body; all movements and all gestures combine equally for service. What, indeed, is requisite in order to arouse and draw on the crowd? What do we need if we would agitate and persuade even the more intelligent? A vehement and affecting tone, expressive and frequent gestures, rapid and ringing words. But for the limited number of those whose heads are steady, whose taste is delicate, whose sense is refined, and who, like you, Gentlemen, set little value on cadence, gestures, and the empty sound of words, one must have substance, thoughts, arguments; and one must know how to present them and shade them and arrange them. It is not enough to strike the ear and hold the eye; one must work on the soul, and touch the sensibilities by addressing the mind.

Style is simply the order and movement one gives to one's thoughts. If these are connected closely, and rigorously compressed, the style will be firm, nervous, and concise. If they are allowed to follow one another loosely and merely at the lead of the diction, however choice this be, the style will be diffuse, nerveless, and languid.

However, before seeking the particular order in which actually to present his thoughts, the writer must first form another more general and more absolute order, where only primary aspects and fundamental ideas shall enter. It is in fixing their places in this prior plan that he sees his subject growing circumscribed, and comes to realize its true extent; and it is by keeping these first outlines continually before him that he is able to determine the proper intervals between the main ideas, and develops the accessory and intermediary ideas that shall serve to fill in. By sheer force of genius he will grasp the sum of these general and particular ideas in their true perspective; by a great delicacy of discernment he will distinguish thoughts that are fertile from such as are sterile; by a sagacity born of long experience in writing he will perceive in advance the ultimate result of all these mental operations. If a subject be at all vast or complex, very seldom can it be taken in at a glance, or penetrated in its entirety by a single and initial effort of genius; and seldom even after much reflection will all its relations be comprehended. Accordingly, one cannot give this matter too much attention; it is, indeed, the sole way to consolidate, develop, and elevate one's thoughts. The more substance and force they receive through meditation, the more easily will they afterward pass into concrete expression.

This plan, though not the resultant style, is nevertheless its basis, supporting it, directing it, regulating its movement, subjecting it to law. Without that basis the best of writers will wander; his pen running on unguided will form haphazard, irregular strokes and incongruous figures. However brilliant the colors he employs, whatever the beauties of detail he introduces, since the ensemble jars or else makes no adequate impression, the work will not really be a construction; hence, though admiring the brilliancy of the author, we may suspect him of lacking true genius. Here is the reason why those who write as they speak, though they may speak excellently, write badly; that those who abandon themselves to the first flashes of their imagination assume a tone which they cannot sustain; that those who are in fear of losing their isolated and fugitive thoughts and who at separate times write in detached fragments, cannot unite these save by forced transitions; that, in a word, there are so many works made up by assemblage of pieces, and so few cast in a single mold.

Every subject, however, is a unit and, no matter how vast it be, can be comprised in a single treatise; hence, interruptions, pauses, sections, and the like, should be employed only when different subjects are under consideration, or when, having to discuss great, thorny, and disparate questions, genius finds its march broken by a multiplicity of obstacles and is constrained by the force of circumstances. Otherwise a great number of divisions, far from rendering a work more solid, destroys its coherence. To the eye the book seems clearer; but the author's design remains obscure. You cannot make an impression on your reader's mind, or even on his feelings, but by continuity of the thread, by harmonious interdependence of the ideas, by a successive development, a sustained gradation, a uniform movement, which every interruption enfeebles or destroys.

Why is it that the works of nature are so perfect? Because each work is a whole, and because nature follows an eternal plan from which she never departs. She prepares in silence the germs of her productions. She sketches the original form of each living being in a single effort. This form she develops and perfects by a continuous movement and in a time prescribed. The result is wonderful; yet what should strike us is the divine imprint that it bears. The human spirit can *create* nothing, nor can it bring forth at all until fertilized by experience and meditation; in its acquired knowledge lie the germs of its productions. But if it imitates nature in its procedure and labor; if it exalts itself by contemplation to the sublimest truths; if it unites these; if it forms of them an entirety systematized by reflection: it will build upon unshakable foundations monuments that cannot pass away.

It is for want of plan, for want of sufficient preliminary reflection on his subject, that a man of intelligence finds himself embarrassed with uncertainty at what point to begin writing. Ideas come to him from many directions at a time; and since he has neither compared nor subordinated them, nothing determines him to prefer one set to another; hence he remains perplexed. When, however, he has made a plan, when he has collected and put in order all the essential thoughts on his subject, he recognizes without difficulty the instant when he ought to take up his pen; he is aware of the critical point when his mind is ready to bring forth; it is urgent with him to come to the birth; nay, he has now only pleasure in writing: his ideas follow one another easily, and the style is natural and smooth. A certain warmth born of that pleasure diffuses itself throughout, giving life to every phrase; there is a gradual increase of animation; the tone grows elevated; individual objects take on color; and a glow of feeling joins with the light of intellect to increase it and carry it on, making it spread from what one is saying to what one is about to say; and the style becomes interesting and luminous.

Nothing is more inimical to this warmth than the desire to be everywhere striking; nothing is more contrary to the light which should be at the center of a work, and which should be diffused uniformly in any composition, than those sparks which are struck only at the cost of a violent collision between words, and which dazzle us for a moment or two, only to leave us in subsequent darkness. These are thoughts that shine only by contrast, when but one aspect of an object is presented, while the remaining sides are put in shadow; and ordinarily the aspect chosen is a point or angle whereon the writer exercises his wit with the greater ease in proportion as he departs farther from the important sides on which good common sense is accustomed to view things.

Again, nothing is more opposed to true eloquence than the employment of superfine thoughts and the anxious search for such ideas as are slender, delicate, and without substance; ideas that, like leaves of beaten metal, acquire brilliancy only as they lose solidity. The more of this attenuated and shining wit there is in a composition, the less will there be of muscle, real illumination, warmth, and style; unless perchance this wit is the mainspring of the subject, and the writer has no other purpose than mere pleasantry. In that case the art of saying trifles will be found more difficult, perhaps, than that of saying things substantial.

Nothing is more opposed to the beauty of naturalness than the pains people take to express ordinary, every-day matters with an air of singularity or pretence; nor is there anything more degrading to the writer. Far from admiring him for this, we may pity him for having spent so much time in making new combinations of syllables, merely to say what everybody else has said already. This is the fault of minds that are cultivated but sterile; they have words in abundance but no ideas. Accordingly they juggle with diction, and fancy that they have put together ideas, because they have been arranging phrases, and that they have refined the language, when they have really corrupted it by warping the accepted forms. Such writers have no style; or, if you wish, they have only its shadow. A style ought to mean the engraving of thoughts; whereas they only know how to trace out words.

To write well, then, an author must be in full possession of his subject; he must reflect on it enough to see clearly the order of his thoughts, and to put them in proper sequence—in a continuous chain, each of whose links represents a unified idea; and when he has taken up his pen, he must direct it successively from one main point to the next, not letting it stray therefrom, nor yet allowing it to dwell immoderately on any, nor, in fact, giving it other movement than that determined by the space to be traversed. Herein consists the rigor of style; and herein lies that which gives it unity and regulates its speed. It is this, too, and this alone, which suffices to render a style precise and simple, even and clear, lively and coherent. If to obedience to this principle—a principle dictated by genius—an author joins delicacy and taste, caution in the choice of phraseology, care in the matter of expressing things only in the most general terms, his style will have positive nobility. If he has, further, a certain distrust of his first impulses, a contempt for what is superficially brilliant, and a steady aversion for what is equivocal and trifling, his style will be not simply grave, but even majestic. In fine, if he writes as he thinks, if he is himself convinced of what he wishes to prove, this good faith with himself, which is the foundation of propriety toward others and of sincerity in style, will make him accomplish his whole purpose; provided always that his inner conviction is not expressed with too violent enthusiasm, and that he shows throughout more candor than confidence and more light than heat.

Gentlemen, it is thus—as it seems to me when I read you—that you would speak to me for my instruction: my soul eagerly receiving such oracles of wisdom would fain take flight and mount on a level with you. How vain the effort! Rules, I hear you add, can never take the place of genius. If that be lacking, they are useless.

To write well—it is at once to think deeply, to feel vividly, and to express clearly; it is to have at once intelligence, sensibility, and taste. Style supposes the united exercise of all the intellectual faculties. Ideas and they alone are its foundation. Well-sounding words are a mere accessory, dependent simply upon the possession of an external sense. One needs only to possess something of an ear for avoiding awkwardness in sound, and to have trained and bettered it by reading the poets and orators, and one is mechanically led to imitate poetical cadence and the turns of oratory. Now imitation never created anything; hence this euphony of words forms neither the basis nor the tone of style. It is, in fact, often found in writings devoid of ideas.

The tone, which is simply an agreement of the style with the nature of the subject, should never be forced, but should arise naturally from the very essence of the material, depending to a large extent upon the generalization one has in mind. If the author rises to the most inclusive ideas, and if his subject itself is lofty, his tone will apparently rise to the same height; and if while sustaining the tone at that altitude his genius proves copious enough to surround each particular object with a brilliant light, if the author can unite beauty of color with vigor of design, if he can, in a word, represent each idea by a lively and well-defined image, and make of each sequence of ideas a picture that is harmonious and energetic, the tone will be not simply elevated but sublime. Here, Gentlemen, the application would avail more than the rule, and illustration be more instructive than precept; but since I am not permitted to cite the sublime passages that have so often transported me in reading your works, I am forced to limit myself simply to reflections. The well-written works are the only ones that will go down to posterity: the amount of knowledge in a book, the peculiarity of the facts, the novelty even of the discoveries, are not sure warrants of immortality. If the works that contain these are concerned with only minor objects; if they are written without taste, without nobility, without inspiration, they will perish; since the knowledge, facts, and discoveries, being easily detached, are passed on to others, and even gain intrinsically when appropriated by more gifted hands. These things are external to the man; the style is the man himself. Style, then, can be neither detached, nor transferred, nor altered by time: if it is elevated, noble, sublime, the author will be admired equally in all ages. For it is truth alone that is permanent, that is even eternal. Now a beautiful style is such in fact only by the infinite number of truths that it presents. All the intellectual graces residing in it, all the interdependences of which it is composed, are truths not less useful, and for the human spirit possibly more precious, than those, whatsoever they be, that form the core of the subject.

The sublime is to be found only in lofty subjects. Poetry, history, and philosophy all deal with the same material, and a most lofty material, namely, man and nature. Philosophy describes and portrays nature; poetry paints and embellishes it; poetry paints men also, enlarges them, intensifies them, creates heroes and divinities. History represents man only, and represents him as he is. Accordingly, the tone of the historian will become sublime only when he draws a picture of the greatest men, when he exhibits the greatest actions, the greatest movements, and the greatest revolutions; under other circumstances it will suffice if he be always majestic and grave. The tone of the philosopher might become sublime whenever he is to speak of the laws of nature, of creatures in general, of space, of matter, of time and motion, of the soul, of the human intellect, of the sentiments, and of the passions; elsewhere it will suffice if he be noble and elevated. But the tone of the orator and the poet, so soon as the subject is lofty, should be ever sublime, because they have the right to bring to the grandeur of their subject just as much color, as much movement, and as much illusion as they please; and because, having at all times to paint and enlarge the objects of their representation, they must at every point employ all the force and display all the extent of their genius.

WORDS THAT LAUGH AND CRY[1]

Editorial in the New York *Sun,* March 16, 1890

DID it ever strike you that there was anything queer about the capacity of written words to absorb and convey feelings? Taken separately they are mere symbols with no more feeling to them than so many bricks, but string them along in a row under certain mysterious conditions and you find yourself laughing or crying as your eye runs over them. That words should convey mere ideas is not so remarkable. "The boy is fat," "the cat has nine tails," are statements that seem obviously enough within the power of written language. But it is different with feelings. They are no more visible in the symbols that hold them than electricity is visible on the wire; and yet there they are, always ready to respond when the right test is applied by the right person. That spoken words, charged with human tones and lighted by human eyes, should carry feelings, is not so astonishing. The magnetic sympathy of the orator one understands; he might affect his audience, possibly, if he spoke in a language they did not know. But written words: How can they do it! Suppose, for example, that you possess remarkable facility in grouping language, and that you have strong feelings upon some subject, which finally you determine to commit to paper. Your pen runs along, the words present themselves, or

[1] Reprinted with the kind permission of the New York *Sun.*

are dragged out, and fall into their places. You are a good deal moved; here you chuckle to yourself, and half a dozen lines further down a lump comes into your throat, and perhaps you have to wipe your eyes. You finish, and the copy goes to the printer. When it gets into print the reader sees it. His eye runs along the lines and down the page until it comes to the place where you chuckled as you wrote; then he smiles, and six lines below he has to swallow several times and snuffle and wink to restrain an exhibition of weakness. And then some one else comes along who has no feelings, and swaps the words about a little, and twists the sentences; and behold the spell is gone, and you have left a parcel of written language duly charged with facts, but without a single feeling.

No one can juggle with words with any degree of success without getting a vast respect for their independent ability. They will catch the best idea a man ever had as it flashes through his brain, and hold on to it, to surprise him with it long after, and make him wonder that he was ever man enough to have such an idea. And often they will catch an idea on its way from the brain to the pen point, turn, twist, and improve on it as the eye winks, and in an instant there they are, strung hand in hand across the page, and grinning back at the writer: "This is our idea, old man; not yours!"

As for poetry, every word that expects to earn its salt in poetry should have a head and a pair of legs of its own, to go and find its place, carrying another word, if necessary, on its back. The most that should be expected of any competent poet in regular practice is to serve a general summons and notice of action on the language. If the words won't do the rest for him it indicates that he is out of sympathy with his tools.

But you don't find feelings in written words unless there were feelings in the man who used them. With all their apparent independence they seem to be little vessels that hold in some puzzling fashion exactly what is put into them. You can put tears into them, as though they were so many little buckets; and you can hang smiles along them, like Monday's clothes on the line, or you can starch them with facts and stand them up like a picket fence; but you won't get the tears out unless you first put them in. Art won't put them there. It is like the faculty of getting the quality of interest into pictures. If the quality exists in the artist's mind he is likely to find means to get it into his pictures, but if it isn't in the man no technical skill will supply it. So, if the feelings are in the writer and he knows his business, they will get into the words; but they must be in him first. It isn't the way the words are strung together that makes Lincoln's Gettysburg speech immortal, but the feelings that were in the man. But how do such little, plain words manage to keep their grip on such feelings? That is the miracle.

ON FAMILIAR STYLE

William Hazlitt

[William Hazlitt (1778–1830) born at Maidstone, Kent, England, had meager schooling and little formal literary training. But he became one of the most brilliant of English critics. He has been called a "glorified journalist" because most of his writings appeared first in magazines and newspapers. Whether he describes a prize fight or characterizes a great poet, the word that best describes him is "gusto," a term which he made popular in our language.]

IT is not easy to write a familiar style. Many people mistake a familiar for a vulgar style, and suppose that to write without affectation is to write at random. On the contrary, there is nothing that requires more precision, and, if I may so say, purity of expression, than the style I am speaking of. It utterly rejects not only all unmeaning pomp, but all low, cant phrases, and loose, unconnected, *slipshod* allusions. It is not to take the first word that offers, but the best word in the common use; it is not to throw words together in any combinations we please, but to follow and avail ourselves of the true idiom of the language. To write a genuine familiar or truly English style is to write as anyone would speak in common conversation, who had a thorough command and choice of words, or who could discourse with ease, force, and perspicuity, setting aside all pedantic and oratorical flourishes. Or to give another illustration, to write naturally is the same thing in regard to common conversation, as to read naturally is in regard to common speech. It does not follow that it is an easy thing to give the true accent and inflection to the words you utter, because you do not attempt to rise above the level of ordinary life and colloquial speaking. You do not assume indeed the solemnity of the pulpit, or the tone of stage-declamation: neither are you at liberty to gabble on at a venture, without emphasis or discretion, or to resort to vulgar dialect or clownish pronunciation. You must steer a middle course. You are tied down to a given and appropriate articulation, which is determined by the habitual associations between sense and sound, and which you can only hit by entering into the author's meaning, as you must find the proper words and style to express yourself by fixing your thoughts on the subject you have to write about. Anyone may mouth out a passage with a theatrical cadence, or get upon stilts to tell his thoughts: but to write or speak with propriety and simplicity is a more difficult task. Thus it is easy to affect a pompous style, to use a word twice as big as the thing you want to express: it is not so easy to pitch upon the very word that exactly fits it. Out of eight or ten words equally common, equally intelligible, with nearly equal pretensions, it is a matter of some nicety and discrimination to pick out the very one, the preferableness of which is scarcely perceptible, but decisive. The reason why I object to Dr. Johnson's style is, that there is no discrimination, no selection, no variety in it. He uses none but "tall, opaque words," taken from the "first row of the rubric":—words with the greatest number of syllables, or Latin phrases with merely English terminations. If a fine style depended on this sort of arbitrary pretension, it would be fair to judge of an author's elegance by the measurement of his words, and the substitution of foreign circumlocutions (with no precise associations) for the mother-tongue.[1] How simple is it to be dignified without ease, to be pompous without meaning! Surely, it is but a mechanical rule for avoiding what is low to be always pedantic and affected. It is clear you cannot use a vulgar English word, if you never use a common English word at all. A fine tact is shown in adhering to those which are perfectly common, and yet never falling into any expressions which are debased by disgusting circumstances, or which owe their signification and point to technical or professional allusions. A truly natural or familiar style can never be quaint or vulgar, for this reason, that it is of universal force and applicability, and that quaintness and vulgarity arise out of the immediate connection of certain words with coarse and disagreeable, or with confined ideas. The last form what we understand by *cant* or *slang* phrases. To give an example of what is not very clear in the general statement. I should say that the phrase *To cut with a knife,* or *To cut a piece of wood,* is perfectly free from vulgarity, because it is perfectly common; but to *cut an acquaintance* is not quite unexceptionable, because it is not perfectly common or intelligible, and has hardly yet escaped out of the limits of slang phraseology. I should hardly therefore use the word in this sense without putting it in italics as a license of expression, to be received *cum grano salis.* All provincial or bye-phrases come under the same mark of reprobation

[1] I have heard of such a thing as an author who makes it a rule never to admit a monosyllable into his vapid verse. Yet the charm and sweetness of Marlowe's lines depended often on their being made up almost entirely of monosyllables. [Hazlitt's Note.]

—all such as the writer transfers to the page from his fireside or a particular *coterie*, or that he invents for his own sole use and convenience. I conceive that words are like money, not the worse for being common, but that it is the stamp of custom alone that gives them circulation or value. I am fastidious in this respect, and would almost as soon coin the currency of the realm as counterfeit the King's English. I never invented or gave a new and unauthorized meaning to any word but one single one (the term *impersonal* applied to feelings) and that was in an abstruse metaphysical discussion to express a very difficult distinction. I have been (I know) loudly accused of reveling in vulgarisms and broken English. I cannot speak to that point: but so far I plead guilty to the determined use of acknowledged idioms and common elliptical expressions. I am not sure that the critics in question know the one from the other, that is, can distinguish any medium between formal pedantry and the most barbarous solecism. As an author, I endeavor to employ plain words and popular modes of construction, as were I a chapman and dealer, I should common weights and measures.

The proper force of words lies not in the words themselves, but in their application. A word may be a fine-sounding word, of an unusual length, and very imposing from its learning and novelty, and yet in the connection in which it is introduced, may be quite pointless and irrelevant. It is not pomp or pretension, but the adaptation of the expression to the idea that clenches a writer's meaning:—as it is not the size or glossiness of the materials, but their being fitted each to its place, that gives strength to the arch; or as the pegs and nails are as necessary to the support of the building as the larger timbers, and more so than the mere showy, unsubstantial ornaments. I hate anything that occupies more space than it is worth. I hate to see a load of band-boxes go along the street, and I hate to see a parcel of big words without anything in them. A person who does not deliberately dispose of all his thoughts alike in cumbrous draperies and flimsy disguises, may strike out twenty varieties of familiar every-day language, each coming somewhat nearer to the feeling he wants to convey, and at last not hit upon that particular and only one, which may be said to be identical with the exact impression in his mind. This would seem to show that Mr. Cobbett is hardly right in saying that the first word that occurs is always the best. It may be a very good one; and yet a better may present itself on reflection or from time to time. It should be suggested naturally, however, and spontaneously, from a fresh and lively conception of the subject. We seldom succeed by trying at improvement, or by merely substituting one word for another that we are not satisfied with, as we cannot recollect the name of a place or person by merely plaguing ourselves about it. We wander farther from the point by persisting in a wrong scent; but it starts up accidentally in the memory when we least expected it, by touching some link in the chain of previous association.

There are those who hoard up and make a cautious display of nothing but rich and rare phraseology;—ancient medals, obscure coins, and Spanish pieces of eight. They are very curious to inspect; but I myself would neither offer nor take them in the course of exchange. A sprinkling of archaisms is not amiss; but a tissue of obsolete expressions is more fit *for keep than wear.* I do not say I would not use any phrase that had been brought into fashion before the middle or the end of the last century; but I should be shy of using any that had not been employed by any approved author during the whole of that time. Words, like clothes, get old-fashioned, or mean and ridiculous, when they have been for some time laid aside. Mr. Lamb is the only imitator of old English style I can read with pleasure; and he is so thoroughly imbued with the spirit of his authors, that the idea of imitation is almost done away. There is an inward unction, a marrowy vein both in the thought and feeling, an intuition, deep and lively, of his subject, that carries off any quaintness or awkwardness arising from an antiquated style and dress. The matter is completely his own, though the manner is assumed. Perhaps his ideas are altogether so marked and individual, as to require their point and pungency to be neutralized by the affectation of a singular but traditional form of conveyance. Tricked out in the prevailing costume, they would probably seem more startling and out of the way. The old English authors, Burton, Fuller, Coryate, Sir Thomas Browne, are a kind of mediators between us and the more eccentric and whimsical modern, reconciling us to his peculiarities. I do not however know how far this is the case or not, till he condescends to write like one of us. I must confess that what I like best of his papers under the signature of Elia (still I do not presume, amidst such excellence, to decide what is most excellent) is the account of *Mrs. Battle's Opinions on Whist,* which is also the most free from obsolete allusions and turns of expression—

A well of native English undefiled.

To those acquainted with his admired prototypes, these *Essays* of the ingenious and highly gifted author have the same sort of charm and relish, that Erasmus's *Colloquies* or a fine piece of modern Latin have to the classical scholar. Certainly, I do not know any borrowed pencil that has more power or felicity of execution than the one of which I have here been speaking.

It is as easy to write a gaudy style without ideas, as it is to spread a pallet of showy colors, or to smear in a flaunting transparency. "What do you read?"—"Words, words, words."—"What is the matter?"—"*Nothing,*" it might be answered. The florid style is the reverse of the familiar. The last is employed as an unvarnished medium to convey ideas; the first is resorted to as a spangled veil to conceal the want of them. When there is nothing to be set down but words, it costs little to have them fine. Look through the dictionary, and cull out a *florilegium,* rival the tulipomania. *Rouge* high enough, and never mind the natural complexion. The vulgar, who are not in the secret, will admire the look of preternatural health and vigor; and the fashionable, who regard only appearances, will be delighted with the imposition. Keep to your sounding generalities, your tinkling phrases, and all will be well. Swell out an unmeaning truism to a perfect tympany of style. A thought, a distinction is the rock on which all this brittle cargo of verbiage splits at once. Such writers have merely *verbal* imaginations, that retain nothing but words. Or their puny thoughts have dragon-wings, all green and gold. They soar far above the vulgar feeling of the *sermo humi obrepens*—their most ordinary speech is never short of an hyperbole, splendid, imposing, vague, incomprehensible, magniloquent, a cento of sounding commonplaces. If some of us, whose "ambition is more lowly," pry a little too narrowly into nooks and corners to pick up a number of "unconsidered trifles," they never once direct their eyes or lift their hands to seize on any but the most gorgeous, tarnished, threadbare patchwork set of phrases, the left-off finery of poetic extravagance, transmitted down through successive generations of barren pretenders. If they criticize actors and actresses, a huddled phantasmagoria of feathers, spangles, floods of light, and oceans of sound float before their morbid sense, which they paint in the style of Ancient Pistol. Not a glimpse can you get of the merits or defects of the performers: they are hidden in a profusion of barbarous epithets and wilful rhodomontade. Our hypercritics are not thinking of these little *fantoccini* beings—

> That strut and fret their hour upon the stage—

but of tall phantoms of words, abstractions, *genera* and *species*, sweeping clauses, periods that unite the Poles, forced alliterations, astounding antitheses—

> And on their pens *Fustian* sits plumed.

If they describe kings and queens, it is an Eastern pageant. The Coronation at either House is nothing to it. We get at four repeated images—a curtain, a throne, a scepter, and a foot-stool. These are with them the wardrobe of a lofty imagination; and they turn their servile strains to servile uses. Do we read a description of pictures? It is not a reflection of tones and hues which "nature's own sweet and cunning hand laid on," but piles of precious stones, rubies, pearls, emeralds, Golconda's mines, and all the blazonry of art. Such persons are in fact besotted with words, and their brains are turned with the glittering, but empty and sterile phantoms of things. Personifications, capital letters, seas of sunbeams, visions of glory, shining inscriptions, the figures of a transparency. Britannia with her shield, or Hope leaning on an anchor, make up their stock in trade. They may be considered as *hieroglyphical* writers. Images stand out in their minds isolated and important merely in themselves, without any ground-work of feeling—there is no context in their imaginations. Words affect them in the same way, by the mere sound, that is, by their possible, not by their actual application to the subject in hand. They are fascinated by first appearances, and have no sense of consequences. Nothing more is meant by them than meets the ear: they understand or feel nothing more than meets their eye. The web and texture of the universe, and of the heart of man, is a mystery to them: they have no faculty that strikes a chord in unison with it. They cannot get beyond the daubings of fancy, the varnish of sentiment. Objects are not linked to feelings, words to things, but images revolve in splendid mockery, words represent themselves in their strange rhapsodies. The categories of such a mind are pride and ignorance—pride in outside show, to which they sacrifice everything, and ignorance of the true worth and hidden structure both of words and things. With a sovereign contempt for what is familiar and natural, they are the slaves of vulgar affectation—of a routine of high-flown phrases. Scorning to imitate realities, they are unable to invent anything, to strike out one original idea.

They are not copyists of nature, it is true: but they are the poorest of all plagiarists, the plagiarists of words. All is far-fetched, dear-bought, artificial, oriental in subject and allusion: all is mechanical, conventional, vapid, formal, pedantic in style and execution. They startle and confound the understanding of the reader, by the remoteness and obscurity of their illustrations: they soothe the ear by the monotony of the same everlasting round of circuitous metaphors. They are the *mock-school* in poetry and prose. They flounder about between fustian in expression, and bathos in sentiment. They tantalize the fancy, but never reach the head nor touch the heart. Their Temple of Fame is like a shadowy structure raised by Dullness to Vanity, or like Cowper's description of the Empress of Russia's palace of ice, "as worthless as in show 'twas glittering"—

It smiled, and it was cold!

A PREFACE TO THE PROFESSION OF JOURNALISM[1]

(BEING AN ANSWER TO A LETTER FROM A COLLEGE STUDENT, ASKING ADVICE AS TO TAKING UP WRITING AS A CAREER)

CHRISTOPHER MORLEY

[Christopher Morley was born at Haverford, Pennsylvania, in 1890 and graduated from Haverford College in 1910. He has been on the staffs of various periodicals and is now contributing editor of the *Saturday Review* for which he writes the weekly column called "The Bowling Green." He is the author of a large number of volumes, including verse, essays, and fiction.]

YOUR inquiry is congenial, and I feel guilty of selfishness in answering it in this way. But he must be a poor workman, whether artisan or artist, who does not welcome an excuse now and then for shutting out the fascinating and maddening complexity of this shining world to concentrate his random wits on some honest and self-stimulating expression of his purpose.

There are exceptions to every rule; but writing, if undertaken as a trade, is subject to the conditions of all other trades. The apprentice must begin with taskwork; he must please his employers before he can earn

[1] From *Plum Pudding,* 1921, with the permission of the author and of the publishers, Doubleday, Page and Company.

the right to please himself. Not only that, he must have ingenuity and patience enough to learn *how* editors are pleased; but he will be startled, I think, if he studies their needs, to see how eager they are to meet him half way. This necessary docility is in the long run a wholesome physic, because, if our apprentice has any gallantry of spirit, it will arouse in him an exhilarating irritation, that indignation which is said to be the forerunner of creation. It will mean, probably, a period—perhaps short, perhaps long, perhaps permanent—of rather meagre and stinted acquaintance with the genial luxuries and amenities of life; but (such is the optimism of memory) a period that he will always look back upon as the happiest of all. It is well for our apprentice if, in this season, he has a taste for cheap tobacco and a tactful technique in borrowing money.

The deliberate embrace of literature as a career involves very real dangers. I mean dangers to the spirit over and above those of the right-hand trouser pocket. For, let it be honestly stated, the business of writing is solidly founded on a monstrous and perilous egotism. Himself, his temperament, his powers of observation and comment, his emotions and sensibilities and ambitions and idiocies—these are the only monopoly the writer has. This is his only capital, and with glorious and shameless confidence he proposes to market it. Let him make the best of it. Continually stooping over the muddy flux of his racing mind, searching a momentary flash of clearness in which he can find mirrored some delicate beauty or truth, he tosses between the alternatives of self-grandeur and self-disgust. It is a painful matter, this endless self-scrutiny. We are all familiar with the addled ego of literature—the writer whom constant self-communion has made vulgar, acid, querulous, and vain. And yet it is remarkable that of so many who meddle with the combustible passions of their own minds so few are blown up. The discipline of living is a fine cooling-jacket for the engine.

It is essential for our apprentice to remember that, though he begin with the vilest hack-work—writing scoffing paragraphs, or advertising pamphlets, or free-lance snippets for the papers—that even in hack-work quality shows itself to those competent to judge; and he need not always subdue his gold to the lead in which he works. Moreover, conscience and instinct are surprisingly true and sane. If he follows the suggestions of his own inward, he will generally be right. Moreover again, no one can help him as much as he can help himself. There is no job in the writing world that he cannot have if he really wants it. Writing about something he intimately knows is a sound principle. Hugh Walpole, that greatly gifted novelist, taught school after leaving Cambridge, and very sensibly began by writing about school-teaching. If you care to see how well he did it, read *The Gods and Mr. Perrin.* I would propose this test to the would-be writer: Does he feel, honestly, that he could write as convincingly about his own tract of life (whatever it may be) as Walpole wrote about that boys' school? If so, he has a true vocation for literature.

The first and most necessary equipment of any writer, be he reporter, advertising copy-man, poet, or historian, is swift, lively, accurate observation. And since consciousness is a rapid, shallow river which we can only rarely dam up deep enough to go swimming and take our ease, it is his positive need (unless he is a genius who can afford to let drift away much of his only source of gold) to keep a note-book handy for the sieving and skimming of this running stream. Samuel Butler has good advice on this topic. Of ideas, he says, you must throw salt on their tails or they fly away and you never see their bright plumage again. Poems, stories, epigrams, all the happiest freaks of the mind, flit by on wings and at haphazard instants. They must be caught in air. In this respect one thinks American writers ought to have an advantage over English, for American trousers are made with hip-pockets, in which a small note-book may so comfortably caress the natural curvature of man.

Fancy is engendered in the eyes, said Shakespeare, and is with gazing fed. By fancy he meant (I suppose) love; but imagination is also so engendered. Close, constant, vivid, and compassionate gazing at the ways of mankind is the laboratory manual of literature. But for most of us we may gaze until our eyeballs twitch with weariness; unless we seize and hold the flying picture in some steadfast memorandum, the greater part of our experience dissolves away with time. If a man has thought sufficiently about the arduous and variously rewarded profession of literature to propose seriously to follow it for a living, he will already have said these things to himself, with more force and pungency. He may have satisfied himself that he has a necessary desire for "self-expression," which is a parlous state indeed, and the cause of much literary villainy. The truly great writer is more likely to write in the hope of expressing the hearts of others than his own. And there are other desires, too, most legitimate, that he may feel. An English humorist said recently in the preface to his book: "I wrote these stories to satisfy an inward craving—not for artistic expression, but for food and drink." But I cannot conscientiously advise any man to turn to writing merely as a means of earning his victual unless he should, by some cheerful casualty, stumble upon a trick of the You-know-me-Alfred sort, what one might call the Attabuoyant style. If all you want is a suggestion as to some honest way of growing rich, the doughnut industry is not yet overcrowded; and people will stand in line to pay twenty-two cents for a dab of ice-cream smeared with a trickle of syrup.

To the man who approaches writing with some decent tincture of idealism it is well to say that he proposes to use as a trade what is, at its best and happiest, an art and a recreation. He proposes to sell his mental reactions to the helpless public, and he proposes not only to enjoy himself by so doing, but to be handsomely recompensed withal. He cannot complain that in days when both honesty and delicacy of mind are none too common we ask him to bring to his task the humility of the tradesman, the joy of the sportsman, the conscience of the artist.

And if he does so, he will be in a condition to profit by these fine words of George Santayana, said of the poet, but applicable to workers in every branch of literature:

> He labors with his nameless burden of perception, and wastes himself in aimless impulses of emotion and reverie, until finally the method of some art offers a vent to his inspiration, or to such part of it as can survive the test of time and the discipline of expression. . . . Wealth of sensation and freedom of fancy, which make an extraordinary ferment in his ignorant heart, presently bubble over into some kind of utterance.

LITERATURE

A Greek got his civilization by talking and looking, and in some measure a Parisian may still do it. But we, who live remote from history and monuments, we must read or we must barbarize.

—William Dean Howells

BOOKS

THOMAS CARLYLE

[Thomas Carlyle (1795–1881) was born at Ecclefechan, Dumfriesshire, Scotland. After completing the undergraduate course at the University of Edinburgh, he studied divinity and then law, and for a time he taught school. During these years he struggled against insomnia, dyspepsia, and deep mental depression, but finally won a victory over his doubts, as described in *Sartor Resartus*. The selection which follows, like the other one in this volume ("The Nature of Human Faiths"), is taken from one of his most original, powerful, and widely read works, *Heroes and Hero-Worship*. Like his disciple Ruskin, he was and is one of the prophets of modern times.]

COMPLAINT is often made, in these times, of what we call the disorganized condition of society: how ill many arranged forces of society fulfil their work; how many powerful forces are seen working in a wasteful, chaotic, altogether unarranged manner. It is too just a complaint, as we all know. But perhaps if we look at this of Books and the Writers of Books, we shall find here, as it were, the summary of all other disorganization;—a sort of *heart,* from which, and to which, all other confusion circulates in the world! Considering what Book-writers do in the world, and what the world does with Book-writers, I should say, It is the most anomalous thing the world at present has to show.—We should get into a sea far beyond sounding, did we attempt to give account of this: but we must glance at it for the sake of our subject. The worst element in the life of these three Literary Heroes was, that they found their business and position such a chaos. On the beaten road there is tolerable traveling; but it is sore work, and many have to perish, fashioning a path through the impassable!

Our pious Fathers, feeling well what importance lay in the speaking of man to men, founded churches, made endowments, regulations; everywhere in the civilized world there is a Pulpit, environed with all manner of complex dignified appurtenances and furtherances, that therefrom a man with the tongue may, to best advantage, address his fellow-men. They felt that this was the most important thing; that without this there was no good thing. It is a right pious work, that of theirs; beautiful to behold! But now with the art of Writing, with the art of Printing, a total change has come over that business. The Writer of a Book, is not he a Preacher preaching not to this parish or that, on this day or that, but to all men in all times and places? Surely it is of the last importance that *he* do his work right, whoever do it wrong;—that the *eye* report not falsely, for then all the other members are astray! Well; how he may do his work, whether he do it right or wrong, or do it at all, is a point which no man in the world has taken the pains to think of. To a certain shopkeeper, trying to get some money for his books, if lucky, he is of some importance; to no other man of any. Whence he came, whither he is bound, by what ways he arrived, by what he might be furthered on his course, no one asks. He is an accident in society. He wanders like a wild Ishmaelite, in a world of which he is as the spiritual light, either the guidance or the misguidance!

Certainly the Art of Writing is the most miraculous of all things man has devised. Odin's *Runes* were the first form of the work of a Hero; *Books,* written words, are still miraculous *Runes,* the latest form! In Books lies the *soul* of the whole Past Time; the articulate audible voice of the Past, when the body and material substance of it has altogether vanished like a dream. Mighty fleets and armies, harbors and arsenals, vast cities, high-domed, many-engined,—they are precious, great: but what do they become? Agamemnon, the many Agamemnons, Pericleses, and their Greece; all is gone now to some ruined fragments, dumb mournful wrecks and blocks: but the Books of Greece! There Greece, to every thinker, still very literally lives; can be called-up again into life. No magic *Rune* is stranger than a Book. All that Mankind has done, thought, gained or been: it is lying as in magic preservation in the pages of Books. They are the chosen possession of men.

Do not Books still accomplish *miracles,* as *Runes* were fabled to do? They persuade men. Not the wretchedest circulating-library novel, which foolish girls thumb and con in remote villages, but will help to regulate the actual practical weddings and households of those foolish girls. So "Celia" felt, so "Clifford" acted: the foolish Theorem of Life, stamped into those young brains, comes out as a solid Practice one day. Consider whether any *Rune* in the wildest imagination of Mythologist ever did such wonders as, on the actual firm Earth, some Books have done! What built St. Paul's Cathedral? Look at the heart of the matter, it was that divine Hebrew BOOK,—the word partly of the man Moses, an outlaw tending his Midianitish herds, four-thousand years ago, in the wilderness of Sinai! It is the strangest of things, yet nothing is truer. With the art of Writing, of which Printing is a simple, an inevitable and comparatively insignificant corollary, the true reign of miracles for mankind commenced. It related, with a wondrous new contiguity and perpetual closeness, the Past and Distant with the Present in time and place; all times and all places with this our actual Here and Now. All things were altered for men; all modes of important work of men: teaching, preaching, governing, and all else.

To look at Teaching, for instance. Universities are a notable, respectable product of the modern ages. Their existence too is modified, to the very basis of it, by the existence of Books. Universities arose while there were yet no Books procurable; while a man, for a single Book, had to give an estate of land. That, in those circumstances, when a man had some knowledge to communicate, he should do it by gathering the learners round him, face to face, was a necessity for him. If you wanted to know what Abelard knew, you must go and listen to Abelard. Thousands, as many as thirty-thousand, went to hear Abelard and that metaphysical theology of his. And now for any other teacher who had also something of his own to teach, there was a great convenience opened: so many thousands eager to learn were already assembled yonder; of all places the best place for him was that. For any third teacher it was better still; and grew ever the better, the more teachers there came. It only needed now that the King took notice of this new phenomenon; combined or agglomerated the various schools into one school; gave it edifices, privileges, encouragements, and named it *Universitas*, or

School of all Sciences: the University of Paris, in its essential characters, was there. The model of all subsequent Universities; which down even to these days, for six centuries now, have gone on to found themselves. Such, I conceive, was the origin of Universities.

It is clear, however, that with this simple circumstance, facility of getting Books, the whole conditions of the business from top to bottom were changed. Once invent Printing, you metamorphosed all Universities, or superseded them! The Teacher needed not now to gather men personally round him, that he might *speak* to them what he knew: print it in a Book, and all learners far and wide, for a trifle, had it each at his own fireside, much more effectually to learn it!—Doubtless there is still peculiar virtue in Speech; even writers of Books may still, in some circumstances, find it convenient to speak also,—witness our present meeting here! There is, one would say, and must ever remain while man has a tongue, a distinct province for Speech as well as for Writing and Printing. In regard to all things this must remain; to Universities among others. But the limits of the two have nowhere yet been pointed out, ascertained; much less put in practice: the University which would completely take-in that great new fact, of the existence of Printed Books, and stand on a clear footing for the Nineteenth Century as the Paris one did for the Thirteenth, has not yet come into existence. If we think of it, all that a University or final highest School can do for us, is still but what the first School began doing,—teach us to *read*. We learn to *read*, in various languages, in various sciences; we learn the alphabet and letters of all manners of Books. But the place where we are to get knowledge, even theoretic knowledge, is the Books themselves! It depends on what we read, after all manner of Professors have done their best for us. The true University of these days is a Collection of Books.

But to the Church itself, as I hinted already, all is changed, in its preaching, in its working, by the introduction of Books. The Church is the working recognized Union of our Priests or Prophets, of those who by wise teaching guide the souls of men. While there was no Writing, even while there was no Easy-writing or *Printing,* the preaching of the voice was the natural sole method of performing this. But now with Books!—He that can write a true Book, to persuade England, is not he the Bishop and Archbishop, the Primate of England and of all England? I many a time say, the writers of Newspapers, Pamphlets, Poems, Books, these *are* the real working effective Church of a modern country. Nay not only our preaching, but even our worship, is not it too accomplished by means of Printed Books? The noble sentiment which a gifted soul has clothed for us in melodious words, which brings melody into our hearts,—is not this essential, if we will understand it, of the nature of worship? There are many, in all countries, who, in this confused time, have no other method of worship. He who, in any way, shows us better than we knew before that a lily of the fields is beautiful, does he not show it us as an effluence of the Fountain of all Beauty; as the *handwriting,* made visible there, of the great Maker of the Universe? He has sung for us, made us sing with him, a little verse of a sacred Psalm. Essentially so. How much more he who sings, who says, or in any way brings home to our heart the noble doings, feelings, darings and endurances of a brother man! He has verily touched our hearts as with a live coal *from the altar*. Perhaps there is no worship more authentic.

Literature, so far as it is Literature, is an "apocalypse of Nature," a revealing of the "open secret." It may well enough be named, in Fichte's style, a "continuous revelation" of the Godlike in the Terrestrial and Common. The Godlike does ever, in very truth, endure there; is brought out, now in this dialect, now in that, with various degrees of clearness: all true gifted Singers and Speakers are, consciously or unconsciously, doing so. The dark stormful indignation of a Byron, so wayward and perverse, may have touches of it; nay the withered mockery of a French sceptic,—his mockery of the False, a love and worship of the True. How much more the sphere-harmony of a Shakespeare, of a Goethe; the cathedral-music of a Milton! They are something too, those humble genuine lark-notes of a Burns,—skylark, starting from the humble furrow, far overhead into the blue depths, and singing to us so genuinely there! For all true singing is of the nature of worship; as indeed all true *working* may be said to be,—whereof such *singing* is but the record, and fit melodious representation, to us. Fragments of a real "Church Liturgy" and "Body of Homilies," strangely disguised from the common eye, are to be found weltering in that huge froth-ocean of Printed Speech we loosely call Literature! Books are our Church too.

Or turning now to the Government of men. Witenagemote, old Parliament, was a great thing. The affairs of the nation were there deliberated and decided; what we were to *do* as a nation. But does not, though the name Parliament subsists, the parliamentary debate go on now, everywhere and at all times, in a far more comprehensive way, *out* of Parliament altogether? Burke said there were Three Estates in Parliament; but, in the Reporters' Gallery yonder, there sat a *Fourth Estate* more important far than they all. It is not a figure of speech, or a witty saying: it is a literal fact,—very momentous to us in these times. Literature is our Parliament too. Printing, which comes necessarily out of Writing, I say often, is equivalent to Democracy: invent Writing, Democracy is inevitable. Writing brings Printing; brings universal every-day extempore Printing, as we see at present. Whoever can speak, speaking now to the whole nation, becomes a power, a branch of government, with inalienable weight in law-making, in all acts of authority. It matters not what rank he has, what revenues or garnitures: the requisite thing is, that he have a tongue which others will listen to; this and nothing more is requisite. The nation is governed by all that has tongue in the nation: Democracy is virtually *there*. Add only, that whatsoever power exists will have itself, by and by, organized; working secretly under bandages, obscurations, obstructions, it will never rest till it get to work free, unencumbered, visible to all. Democracy virtually extant will insist on becoming palpably extant.—

On all sides, are we not driven to the conclusion that, of the things which man can do or make here below, by far the most momentous, wonderful and worthy are the things we call Books! Those poor bits of rag-paper with black ink on them;—from the Daily Newspaper to thc sacred Hebrew Book, what have they not done, what are they not doing!—For indeed, whatever be the outward form of the thing (bits of paper, as we say, and black ink), is it not verily, at bottom, the highest act of man's faculty that produces a Book? It is the *Thought* of man; the true thaumaturgic virtue; by which man works all things whatsoever. All that he does, and brings to pass, is the vesture of a Thought. This London City, with all its houses, palaces, steamengines, cathedrals, and huge immeasurable traffic and tumult, what is it but a Thought, but millions of Thoughts made into One;—a huge immeasurable Spirit of a Thought, embodied in brick, in iron, smoke, dust, Palaces, Parliaments, Hackney Coaches, Katherine Docks, and the rest of it! Not a brick was made but some man had to *think* of the making of that brick.—The thing we called "bits of paper with traces of black ink," is the *purest* embodiment a Thought of man can have. No wonder it is, in all ways, the activest and noblest.

THE LANGUAGE OF ALL THE WORLD[1]

GEORGE EDWARD WOODBERRY

[George Edward Woodberry, born at Beverly, Massachusetts, in 1855, educated at Harvard, and for some years professor of comparative literature at Columbia, has for nearly half a century been one of America's most productive men of letters. His writing is marked by breadth of view and charm of style.]

THE language of literature is the language of all the world. It is necessary to divest ourselves at once of the notion of diversified vocal and grammatical speech which constitutes the various tongues of the earth, and conceals the identity of image and logic in the minds of all men. Words are intermediary between thought and things. We express ourselves really not through words, which are only signs, but through what they signify—through things. Literature is the expression of life. The question, then, is—what things has literature found most effectual to express life, and has therefore habitually preferred? and what tradition in consequence of this habit of preference has been built up in all literatures, and obtained currency and authority in this province of the wider realm of all art? It is an interesting question, and fundamental for any one who desires to appreciate literature understandingly. Perhaps you will permit me to approach it somewhat indirectly.

[1] Reprinted from *The Torch* by permission of Harcourt, Brace and Co.

You are all familiar with something that is called poetic diction—that is, a selected language specially fitted for the uses of poetry; and you are, perhaps, not quite so familiar with the analogous feature in prose, which is now usually termed preciosity, or preciousness of language, that is, a highly refined and æsthetic diction, such as Walter Pater employs. The two are constant products of language that receives any literary cultivation, and they are sometimes called diseases of language. Thus, in both early and late Greek there sprang up literary styles of expression, involving the preference of certain words, constructions, and even cadences, and the teaching of art in these matters was the business of the Greek rhetorician; so in Italy, Spain, and France, in the Renaissance, similar styles, each departing from the common and habitual speech of the time, grew up, and in England you identify this mood of language in Elizabeth's day as Euphuism. The phenomenon is common, and belongs to the nature of language. Poetic diction, however, you perhaps associate most clearly with the mannerism in language of the eighteenth century in England, when common and so-called vulgar words were exiled from poetry, and Gray, for example, could not speak of the Eton schoolboys as playing hoop, but only as "chasing the rolling circles' speed," and when, to use the stock example, all green things were "verdant." This is fixed in our memory because Wordsworth has the credit of leading an attack on the poetic diction of that period, both critically in his prefaces and practically in his verse; he went to the other extreme, and introduced into his poetry such homely words as "tub," for example; he held that the proper language of poetry is the language of common life. So Emerson in his addresses, you remember, had recourse to the humblest objects for illustration, and shocked the formalism of his time by speaking of "the meal in the firkin, the milk in the pan." He was applying in prose the rule of Wordsworth in poetry. Walt Whitman represents the extreme of this use of the actual language of men. But if you consider the matter, you will see that this choice of the homely word only sets up at last a fashion of homeliness in the place of a fashion of refinement, and breeds, for instance, dialect poets in shoals; and often the choice is really not of the word, but of the homely thing itself as the object of thought and expressive image of it; and in men so great as Emerson and Wordsworth the practice is a proof of that sympathy with common life which made them both great democrats. But in addition to the diction that characterizes an age, you must have observed that in every original writer there grows up a particular vocabulary, structure, and rhythm that he affects and that in the end becomes his mannerism, or distinctive style, so marked that you recognize his work by its stamp alone, as in Keats, Browning, and Swinburne in poetry, and in Arnold in prose. In other words there is at work in the language of a man, or of an age even, a constant principle of selection which tends to prefer certain ways and forms of speech to others, and in the end develops a language characteristic of the age, or of the man.

This principle of selection, whether it works toward refinement or homeliness, operates in the same way. It must be remembered—and it is too often forgotten—that the problem of any artistic work is a problem of economy. How to get into the two hours' traffic of the stage the significance of a whole life, of a group of lives; how to pack into a sixteen-line lyric a dramatic situation and there sphere it in its own emotion; how to rouse passion and pour it in a three-minute poem, like Shelley's *Indian Air*—all these are problems in economy, by which speed, condensation, intensity are gained. Now words in themselves are colorless, except so far as their musical quality is concerned; but the thing that a word stands for has a meaning of its own and usually a meaning charged with associations, and often this associative meaning is the primary and important one in its use. A rose, for example, is but the most beautiful of flowers in itself, but it is so charged with association in men's lives, and still more heavily charged with long use of emotion in literature, that the very word and mere name of it awakes the heart and sets a thousand memories unconsciously vibrating. This added meaning is what I am accustomed to term an overtone in words; and it is manifest that, in view of the necessity for economy in poetic art, those words which are the richest and deepest in overtone will be preferred, because of the speed, certainty, and fullness they contain. The question will be what overtones in life appeal most to this or that poet; he will reproduce them in his verse; Pope will use the overtones of a polished society, Wordsworth and Emerson those of humble life. Now our larger question is what overtones are characteristically preferred in great literature, in what objects do they most inhere, and in what way is the authoritative tradition of literature, as respects its means of expression, thus built up?

It goes without saying that all overtones are either of thought or feeling. What modes of expression, then, what material objects, what forms of imagination, what abstract principles of thought, are most deeply charged with ideas and emotions? It will be agreed that, as a mere medium, music expresses pure emotion most directly and richly; music seems to enter the physical frame of the body itself, and move there with the warmth and instancy of blood. The sound of words, therefore, cannot be neglected, and in the melody and echo of poetry sound is a cardinal element; yet, it is here only the veining of the marble, it is not the material itself. In the objects which words summon up, there is sometimes an emotional power as direct and immediate as that of music itself, as for example, in the great features of nature, the mountains, the plains, the ocean, which awe even the savage mind. But, in general, the emotional power of material objects is lent to them by association, that is, by the human use that has been made of them, as on the plain of Marathon, to use Dr. Johnson's old illustration, it is the thought of what happened there that makes the spectator's patriotism "gain force" as he surveys the scene. This human use of the world is the fountain of significance in all imaginative and poetic speech; and in the broad sense history is the story of this human use of the world.

History is so much of past experience as abides in race-memory; and underlies race-literature in the same way that a poet's own experience underlies his expression of life. I do not mean that when a poet unlocks his heart, as Shakspere did in his sonnets, he necessarily writes his own biography; in the poems he writes there may be much of actual event as in Burns's love-songs, or little as in Dante's *New Life*. Much of a poet's experience takes place in imagination only; the life he tells is oftenest the life that he strongly desires to live, and the power, the purity and height of his utterance may not seldom be the greater because experience here uses the voices of desire. "All I could never be," in Browning's plangent line, has been the mounting strain of the sublimest and the tenderest songs of men. All Ireland could never be, thrills and sorrows on her harp's most resonant string, and is the master-note to which her sweetest music ever returns. All man could never be makes the sad majesty of Virgil's verse. As with a man, what a nation strongly desires is no small part of its life, and is the mark of destiny upon it, whether for failure or success; so the note of world-empire is heard in the latest English verse, and the note of humanity—the service of all men—has always been dominant in our own. History, then, must be thought of, in its relation to literature, as including the desire as well as the performance of the race.

History, however, in the narrowest sense, lies close to the roots of imaginative literature. The great place of history and its inspirational power in the literature of the last century I have already referred to; it is one of the most important elements in the extraordinary reach and range of that splendid outburst of imagination throughout Europe. Aristotle recognized the value of history as an aid to the imagination, at the very moment that he elevated poetry above history. In that necessary economy of art, of which I spoke, it is a great gain to have well-known characters and familiar events, such as Agamemnon and the "Trojan War," in which much is already done for the spectator before the play begins. So our present historical novelists have their stories half-written for them in the minds of their readers, and especially avail themselves of an emotional element there, a patriotism, which they do not have to create. The use of history to the imagination, however, goes farther than merely to spare it the pains of creating character and incident and evoking emotion. It assists a literary movement to begin with race-power much as a poet's or—as in Dickens's case—a novelist's own experience aids him to develop his work, however much that experience may be finally transformed in the work. Thus the novel of the last age really started its great career from Scott's historic sense working out into imaginative expression, and in a lesser degree from so minor a writer as Miss Edgeworth in whose Irish stories—which were contemporary history—Scott courteously professed to find his own starting point. It is worth noting, also, that the Elizabethan drama had the same course. Shakspere following Marlowe's example developed from the historical English plays, in which he worked in Scott's manner, into his full control of imagination in the purely ideal sphere. History has thus often been the hand-maid of imagination, and the foster-mother of great literary ages. Yet to vary Aristotle's phrase—poetry is all history could never be.

It appears to me, nevertheless, that history underlies race-literature in a far more profound and universal way. History is mortal: it dies. Yet it does not altogether die. Elements, features, fragments of it survive, and enter into the eternal memory of the race, and are there transformed, and—as we say—spiritualized. Literature is the abiding-place of this transforming power, and most profits by it. And to come to the heart of the matter, there have been at least three such cardinal transformations in the past.

The first transformation of history is mythology. I do not mean to enter on the vexed question of the origin of mythologies; and, of course, in referring to history as its ground, I include much more than that hero-worship such as you will find elaborated or invented in Carlyle's essay on Odin, and especially I include all that experience of nature and her association with human toil and moods that you will find delineated with such marvelous subtleness and fullness in Walter Pater's essay on Dionysus. In mythology, mankind preserved from his primitive experience of nature, and his own heroic past therein, all that had any lasting significance; and, although all mythologies have specific features and a particular value of their own, yet the race, coming to its best, as I have said, bore here its perfect blossom in Greek mythology. I know not by what grace of heaven, by what felicity of blend in climate, blood, and the fortune of mortal life, but so it was that the human soul put forth the bud of beauty in the Greek race; and there, at the dawn of our own intellectual civilization and in the first sunrise of our poetry in Homer, was found a world filled with divine—with majestic and lovely figures, which had absorbed into their celestial being and forms the power of nature, the splendor and charm of the material sphere, the fructifying and beneficent operations of the external universe, the providence of the state and the inspiration of all arts and crafts, of games and wars and song; each of these deities was a flashing center of human energy, aspiration, reliance—with a realm and servants of its own; and mingling with them in fair companionshp was a company of demi-gods and heroes, of kings and princes, and of golden youths, significant of the fate of all young life—Adonis, Hippolytus, Orestes. This mythologic world was near to earth, and it mixed with legendary history, such history as the *Iliad* contained, and also with the private and public life of the citizens, being the ceremonial religion of the state. It was all, nevertheless, the transformation that man had accomplished of his own past, his joys and sorrows, his labors, his insights and desires, the deeds of his ancestors,—the human use that he had made of the world. This was the body of idea and emotion to which the poet appealed in that age, precisely as our historical novelists now appeal to our own knowledge of history and pre-established emotion with regard to it, our patriotism. Here they found a language already full charged with emotion and intelligence, of which they could avail themselves, and speaking which they spoke with the voices of a thousand years. Nevertheless, it was at best a language like others, and subject to change and decay in expressive power. The time came when, the creative impulse in mythology having ceased and its forms being fixed, the mythic world lay behind the mind of the advancing race which had now attained conceptions of the physical universe, and especially ideas of the moral life, which were no longer capable of being held in and expressed by the mythic world, but exceeded the bounds of earlier thought and feeling and broke the ancient molds. Then it was that Plato desired to exile the poets and their mythology from the state. He could not be content, either, with a certain change that had occurred; for the creative power in mythology having long ceased, as I have said, the imagination put forth a new function—a meditative power—and brooding over the old fables of the world of the gods discovered in them, not a record of fact, but an allegorical meaning, a higher truth which the fable contained. Mythology passed thus into an emblematic stage, in which it was again long used by mankind, as a language of universal power. Plato, however, could not free himself from the mythologic habit of imagination so planted in his race, and found the most effective expression for his ideas in the myths of his own invention which he made up by a dexterous and poetic adaptation of the old elements; and others later than Plato have found it hard to disuse the mythologic language; for, although the old religion as a thing of faith and practice died away, it survived as a thing of form and feature in art, as a phase of natural symbolism and of inward loveliness of action and passion in poetry, as a chapter of romance in the history of the race; and the modern literatures of Europe are, in large measure, unintelligible without this key.

The second great transformation of history is chivalry. Here the phenomenon is nearer in time and lies more within the field of observation and knowledge; it is possible to trace the stages of the growth of the story of Roland with some detail and precision; but, on the other hand, the Arthur myth reaches far back into the beginnings of Celtic imagination, and all such race-myths tend to appropriate and embody in themselves the characteristic features both of one another and of whatever is held to be precious and significant in history or even in classical and Eastern legend. The true growth, however, is that feudal culture, which we know as knighthood, working out its own ideal of action and character and sentiment on a basis of bravery, courtesy, and piety, and thereby generating patterns of knighthood, typical careers, and in the end an imaginative interpretation of the purest spiritual life itself in the various legends of the Holy Grail. As in the pagan world the forms and fables of mythology and their interaction downward with the human world furnished the imaginative interpretation of life as it then was, so for the mediæval age, the figures and tales of chivalry and their interaction upward with the spiritual world of Christianity, and also with the magic of diabolism round about, furnished the imaginative interpretation of that later life. It was this new body of ideas and emotion in the minds of men that the mediæval poets appealed to, availed themselves of, and so spoke a language of imagery and passion that was a world-language, charged as I have said with the thought and feeling, the tradition, of a long age. What happened to the language of mythology, happened also to this language; it lost the power of reality, and men arose who, being in advance of its conceptions of life, desired to exile it, denounce it or laugh it out of existence, like Ascham in England, and Cervantes in Spain. It also suffered that late change into an allegorical or emblematic meaning, and had a second life in that form, as in the notable instance of Spenser's *Færie Queene*. It also could not die, but—just as mythology revived in the Alexandrian poets for a season, and fed Theocritus and Virgil—chivalry was reborn in the last century, and in Tennyson's Arthur, and in Wagner's *Parsifal* lived again in two great expressions of ideal life.

The third great transformation of history is contained

in the Scriptures. The Bible is, in itself, a singularly complete expression of the whole life of a race in one volume—its faith and history blending in one body of poetry, thought, and imaginative chronicle. It contains a celestial world in association with human events; its patriarchs are like demi-gods, and it has heroes, legends, tales in good numbers, and much romantic and passionate life, on the human side, besides its great stores of spirituality. In literary power it achieves the highest in the kinds of composition that it uses. It is as a whole, regarded purely from the human point of view, not unfairly to be compared in mass, variety, and scope of expression, with mythology and chivalry as constituting a third great form of imaginative language; nor has its history been dissimilar in the Christian world to which it came with something of that same remoteness in time and reality that belonged equally to mythology and chivalry. It was first used in a positive manner, as a thing of fact and solid belief; but there soon grew up, you remember, in the Christian world that habit of finding a hidden meaning in its historical record, of turning it to a parable, of extracting from it an allegorical signification. It became, not only in parts but as a whole, emblematic, and its interpretation as such was the labor of centuries. This is commonly stated as the source of that universal mood of allegorizing which characterized the mediæval world, and was as strongly felt in secular as in religious writers. Its historical tales, its theories of the universe, its cruder morals in the Jewish ages, have been scoffed at, just as was the case with the Greek myth, from the Apostate to Voltaire and later; but how great are its powers as a language is seen in the completeness with which it tyrannized over the Puritan life in England and made its history, its ideas, its emotions the habitual and almost exclusive speech of that strong Cromwellian age. In our country here in New England it gave the mold of imagination to our ancestors for two whole centuries. A book, which contains such power that it can make itself the language of life through so many centuries and in such various peoples, is to be reckoned as one of the greatest instruments of race-expression that man possesses.

Mythology, chivalry, the Scriptures are the tongues of the imagination. It is far more important to know them than to learn French or German or Italian, or Latin or Greek; they are three branches of that universal language which though vainly sought on the lips of men is found in their minds and hearts. To omit these in education is to defraud youth of its inheritance; it is like destroying a long-developed organ of the body, like putting out the eye or silencing the nerves of hearing. Nor is it enough to look them up in the encyclopædias and notes, and so obtain a piecemeal information; one must grow familiar with these forms of beauty, forms of honor, forms of righteousness, have something of the same sense of their reality as that felt by Homer and Virgil, by the singer of *Roland* and the chronicler of the *Mort d'Arthur,* by St. Augustine, and St. Thomas. He must form his imagination upon these idealities, and load his heart with them; else many a masterpiece of the human spirit will be lost to him, and most of the rest will be impaired. If one must know vocabulary and grammar before he can understand the speech of the mouth, much more must he know well mythology, chivalry, and Bible-lore before he can take possession of the wisdom that the race-mind has spoken, the beauty it has molded life into, as a thing of passion and action, the economy of lucid power it has achieved for perfect human utterance, in these three fundamental forms of a true world-language. The literature of the last century is permeated with mythology, chivalry, and to a less degree with Scripture, and no one can hope to assimilate it, to receive its message, unless his mind is drenched with these same things; and the further back his tastes and desires lead him into the literature of earlier times, the greater will be his need of this education in the material, the modes, and the forms of past imagination.

It may be that a fourth great tongue of the imagination is now being shaped upon the living lips of men in the present and succeeding ages. If it be so, this will be the work of the democratic idea, which is now still at the beginning of its career; but since mythology and chivalry had their development in living men, it is natural to suppose that the human force is still operative in our own generation as it once was in those of Hellenic and mediæval years. The characteristic literature of democracy is that of its ideas, spiritualized in Shelley, and that of the common lot as represented in the sphere of the novel, spiritualized most notably in Victor Hugo. In our own country it is singular to observe that the democratic idea, though efficient in politics, does not yet establish itself in imaginative literature with any great power of brilliancy, does not create great democratic types, or in any way express itself adequately. This democratic idea, in Dickens for example, uses the experience of daily life, that is, contemporary history, or at least it uses an artistic arrangement of such experience: but the novel as a whole has given us in regard to the common lot, rather a description of life in its variety than that concentrated and essential significance of life which we call typical. If democracy in its future course should evolve such a typical and spiritualized embodiment of itself as chivalry found in Arthur and the Round Table, or as the heroic age of Greece found in Achilles and the Trojan War, or as the genius of Rome found in Æneas and his fortunes, then imagination—race-imagination—will be enriched by this fourth great instrument; but this is to cast the horoscope of too distant an hour. I introduce the thought only for the sake of including in this broad survey of race-imagination that experience of the present day, that history in the contemporary process of being transformed, out of which the mass of the books of the day are now made.

Let me recur now to that principle of selection which through the cumulative action of repeated preferences of phrase and image fixes a habit of choice which at last stamps the diction of a man, a school, or an age. It is plain that in what I have called the transformation of history, of which literature is the express image, there is the same principle of selection which, working through long periods of race-life, results at last in those idealities of persons and events in which inhere most powerfully those overtones of beauty, honor, and righteousness that the race has found most precious both for idea and emotion; and to these are to be added what I have had no time to include and discuss, the idealities of persons and events found outside mythology, chivalry, and Scripture, in the work of individual genius like Shakspere, which nevertheless have the same ground in history, in experience, that in them is similarly transformed. Life-experience spiritualized is the formula of all great literature; it may range from the experience of a single life, like Sidney's in his sonnets, to that of an empire in Virgil's *Æneid,* or of a religion in Dante's *Comedy.* In either case the formula which makes it literature is the same. I have illustrated the point by the obvious spiritualizations of history. Race-life, from the point of view of literature, results at last in these molds of imagination, and all else though slowly, yet surely, drops away into oblivion. In truth, it is only by being thus spiritualized that anything human survives from the past. The rose, I said, has been so dipped in human experience that it is less a thing of nature than a thing of passion. In the same way Adonis, Jason and Achilles, Roland and Arthur, Lancelot, Percival and Galahad, Romeo and Hamlet have drawn into themselves such myriads of human lives by admiration and love that from them everything material, contemporary, and mortal has been refined away, and they seem to all of us like figures moving in an immortal air. They have achieved the eternal world. To do this is the work of art. It may seem a fantastic idea, but I will venture the saying of it, since to me it is the truth. Art, I suppose, you think of as the realm and privilege of selected men, of sculptors, painters, musicians, poets, men of genius and having something that has always been called divine in their faculty; but it appears to me that art, like genius, is something that all men share, that it is the stamp of the soul in every one, and constitutes their true and immaterial life. The soul of the race, as it is seen in history and disclosed by history, is an artist soul; its career is an artistic career; its unerring selective power expels from its memory every mortal element and preserves only the essential spirit, and thereof builds its ideal imaginative world through which it finds its true expression; its more perfect comprehension of the world is science, its more perfect comprehension of its own nature is love, its more perfect expression of its remembered life is art. Mankind is the grandest and surest artist of all, and history as it clarifies is, in pure fact, an artistic process, a creation in its fullness of the beautiful soul.

It appears, then, that the language of literature in the race is a perfected nature and a perfected manhood and a perfected divinity, so far as the race at the moment can see toward perfection. The life which literature builds up ideally out of the material of experience is not wholly a past life, but there mingles with it and at last controls it the life that man desires to live. Fullness of life—that fullness of action which is poured in the epic, that fullness of passion which is poured in the drama, that fullness of desire that is poured in the lyric—the life of which man knows himself capable and realizes as the opportunity and hope of life—this is the life that literature enthrones in its dream. You have heard much of the will to believe and of the desire to live: literature is made of these two, warp and woof. Race after race believes in the gods it has come to know and in the heroes it has borne, and in what it wishes to believe of divine and human experience; and the life it thus ascribes to its gods to its own past is the life it most ardently desires to live. Literature, which records this, is thus the chief witness to the nobility, the constancy and instancy of man's effort for perfection. What wonder, then, if in his sublimest and tenderest song there steals that note of melancholy so often struck by the greatest masters in the crisis and climax of their works, and which, when so struck, has more of the infinite in it, more of the human in it, than any other in the slowly triumphant theme!

To sum up—the language of literature is experience; the language of race-literature is race-experience, or history, the human use that the race has made of the world. The law appears to be that history in this sense is slowly transformed by a refining and spiritualizing process into an imaginative world, such as the world of mythology, chivalry, or the Scriptures, and that this world in turn becomes emblematic and fades away into an expression of abstract truth. The crude beginning of the process is seen in our historical fiction; the height of it in Arthur or in Odin; the end of it in the symbolic or allegoric interpretation of even so human a book as Virgil's *Æneid*. Human desire for the best enters into this process with such force that the record of the past slowly changes into the prophecy of the future, and out of the passing away of what was is built the dream of what shall be; so arises in race-life the creed of what man wishes to believe and the dream of the life he desires to live; this human desire for belief and for life is, in the final analysis, the principle of selection whose operation has been sketched, and on its validity rests the validity and truth of all literature.

ON READING FIERCELY[1]

HENRY SEIDEL CANBY

[Henry Seidel Canby, born at Wilmington, Delaware, 1878; Yale A.B. and PH.D; member of the English department at Yale since 1900; editor of the *Literary Review* of the New York *Evening Post,* 1920–4, is now editor of *The Saturday Review.*]

TOO much is said about writing, and not enough of reading. It would seem that whereas only a few can write well and those only when they are prodded until their brains turn over at the proper speed, any one who can spell can read. Not at all. There are 10,000 bad readers for every bad author, and if the number of good readers in proportion to good writers proves to be as much as 500 to one, the Authors' League should give public thanks. For the right kind of reader enters sympathetically into the very purpose of the book he possesses, shares its emotion, and plucks out its thought. He is rare.

Skipping and skimming may be virtues. Not all good books need to be eaten like scallops, a word at a time, as Bacon somewhat differently remarked. But if your brain refuses to follow your author, if your imagination is phlegmatic, if you will not take the trouble to stretch your mind until it can take in a vigorous conception, why, then,

[1] From *Definitions, Second Series.* Copyright, 1924, and published by Harcourt, Brace and Co. Inc. Reprinted with permission of and by special arrangement with the publishers.

who *can* write a book for you that has any width, length, or thickness to it? You are a little wire that will not take a powerful current.

An English critic said recently that the English could not like American novels because the subject matter was unfamiliar and the colloquialisms difficult. How would Walter Scott have fared at his hands; and what welcome would Hardy, Meredith, Kipling, have received from us if we had been as provincial as this cockney critic? The good reader will always make the effort required to climb up to the edge of a good author's mind and peer into the heart of a book. If a little dialect stops him, if a little thinking stops him, if a society unlike any he has ever known stops him, he is a bad reader.

Some of the literary paragraphers have been getting into trouble with the "period" story. They were puzzled by Mrs. Norris' *Certain People of Importance* and by other books that threw upon the screen vivid pictures of the end of the last century. Why all this description of San Francisco in the '80's and '90's? they say. Who cares what they wore and ate, who knows families now where no one breathes without consent of mother?—get on with the story if there is one, we think nothing of your scene. What an attitude! If the Englishman was provincial, these Americans are barbarous, living in a present with no future or past. There is something impotent and unrealized in the life of such readers; they do not feel living with enough vigor to carry it backward or forward; they cannot carry their own egos into scenes where hundreds like them made a different reality for themselves out of a different environment. Take the story out of their street and they will not follow it. Their minds will not travel and therefore they do not properly read.

We cannot afford such meagerness of the imagination here in the United States. Not only the past but the present challenges sympathetic reading. All the racial minds have come to America and are beginning to write. Most American stories used to be about New England or the Far West. Now there are a hundred way stations. And when a poet from the prairies, a Jew from the East Side, a Southern ironist, a New England professor, a naturalized Dutchman, and an Old New Yorker publish books in one week, the reader must cultivate elasticity.

This is no exhortation to read everything and like everything. On the contrary, it is a plea which, if heeded, will lead to a good deal of much needed damning of over-advertised novelties tolerated because, except by their friends, they are only half read. But how can you either love or hate a book unless you grasp somehow the heart of it, tear out its significance, and make it your own? In the controversial days of the seventeenth century, when lives hung on a text, men are described as reading fiercely. That is the way to read, if the book deserves it. Or if not fiercely, then with some lighter emotion, awake and keen. Do not inflict a languid brain upon books that cost time and labor in the breeding. Put such a mind to sleep, or take it to the movies.

POETRY IN A COMMERCIAL AGE[1]

FRED N. SCOTT

[Fred Newton Scott, born at Terre Haute, Indiana, in 1860, was educated at the University of Michigan and has spent his life there as professor of English. He has edited a large number of books valuable to students in American colleges.]

WE can perhaps appreciate the value of poetry in a commercial age by turning the question about and asking what is the value of commerce in an age of poetry. Imagine if you can a country in which poetry is the major interest. The greater part of the population, we may suppose, is engaged for ten hours a day in the composition of verse. There are whole villages, towns, and even cities where very little else is done. There are famous or notorious captains of poetry who organize this activity and control the output. There are great poetic unions, embracing millions of verse-makers, which endeavor to curb the rapacity of the captains, to reduce the number of hours of mental labor, and to restrict the right to make poetry to the members of the union. There are periodic strikes when thousands of poets and versifiers refuse to make verses and try by reason or by force to prevent others from doing so.

In these literary centers there are many grades of

[1] In *The English Journal,* Chicago, December, 1921. Reprinted from *The Standard of American Speech and Other Papers* (Boston, 1926, Allyn and Bacon) by permission.

verse-makers, from the unskilled day-laborer who supplies the patent-medicine almanacs and the monthly magazines, to the skilled artificer who turns out only one polished line in a day or a week. But in the large verse-factories the labor is highly specialized. Of thousands of men sitting at long rows of desks, one set of several hundreds will do nothing all day long except find rhymes in a rhyming dictionary. Another set will turn out metaphors, so many to the minute. Still another will gauge the lines when they are written, count the feet, and throw out superfluous words or insert words when they are necessary to the scansion.

And up and down among them will go specialists in poetic organization, who will measure the output of each man, and reducing his production to a curve, will cut out all lost motions, wastes, and inefficiencies.

And now into this great poetic republic comes a mild-voiced student of commerce and begins to put questions. "Why," he asks of a foreman, "don't you pay some attention to material industries and to commerce?" The foreman blinks at him a moment in surprise, and then says, "Why, we do." "I don't see any evidence of it," replies the visitor. "These men are all engaged in making poetry and apparently the rest of the people are engaged in reading it." "That is true," replies the foreman, "but you are in the wrong department. If you want material productions you must go to the little shanty around the corner, where they keep all that any man can possibly desire." "I have just been there," says the visitor, "and it was closed." "Ah, to be sure," repiles the foreman. "It's open only on Fridays, from two to six." "And this being Friday—" insinuates the visitor. "Yes,

yes," interrupts the foreman, "but this is a holiday for those people, and on holidays all the workmen come over here and help us out on our rush orders." "Well," pursues the visitor, "you can't go on like this. You're starving yourselves. Look at that row of epic poets yonder. See how gaunt and hungry they look. I'll wager they haven't had a square meal in six months. Half of them are on the verge of collapse. Then see what rags they are wearing and how they shiver with cold in this ruinous old building. Man, they are dying by inches. "It may be so," replies the foreman, "but what's the odds if they turn out first-class poetry?" "That's just the point," rejoins the investigator. "How can they produce first-class poetry if they are underfed, badly clothed, exposed to the elements, and depressed by these wretched material surroundings? And whence are they to draw their inspiration? Poetry should deal with life; and the poetic impulse should spring from the vitality of the poet. But if society and the individual are both half-dead, where are the material and the impulse for poetry to come from? Set your poets to living, to working, to doing business with their fellowmen. Then they will have something vital to fill their verses with." "Well, I'll think about it," says the foreman. "Perhaps we can work in a few minutes of vocational study in the night school for apprentices. But it mustn't be allowed to interfere with the preparation of their life-work. It's poetry that keeps this nation going and if you distract the minds of the laboring men from their main business with talk about trade and bookkeeping and machinery and the food-supply, you will overthrow the foundations of organized society."

I might carry this imaginary conversation farther, but perhaps I have gone far enough to suggest by implication some of the important relations of poetry to a commercial age. I have tried, at any rate, to suggest that there are two kinds of nourishment or sustenance which are necessary to human life and progress. One of these is material, the other is spiritual. The first includes all things that are necessary to the life of the body. It embraces food and shelter and fire and clothing and means of transportation and protection. It embraces the manufacture, distribution, buying, and selling of goods, and all of the machinery of exchange. Its importance and value to civilization are immense. Without it, in its simplest form, man could not exist, and without its more elaborate organization, corporate life would be impossible.

The second or spiritual kind of nourishment is supplied by religion, art, philosophy, and literature, but more particularly by that division of literature which we term poetry. Its importance for the well-being and progress of mankind is not less great than that of food and shelter. When it is absent, man rapidly goes back to the dirt from which he has sprung. Poetry lifts him above his sordid wants, humanizes him, opens his heart to all the skyey influences. Like philosophy it bakes no bread, but it can give God, freedom, and immortality.

Although these two great feeders of human life are seemingly at opposite poles of experience, yet, as I have tried to suggest in the dialogue, we must not think of them as isolated one from the other or as hostile. They are coördinate in different spheres, and any system of education which seeks to establish the complete ascendancy of one over the other or to dispense with either, is dangerous and should be put under surveillance.

The gravest charge that has been brought against the present drift toward vocational study is that, by over-emphasis of the material phase of life, it tends to cut the pupil off from his proper share in things of the spirit. It gives him power of one kind at the expense of power of another and of a higher kind. It enables him to live, but it withholds from him that which makes life worth living. It provides his daily bread, but it makes the bread bitter in his mouth.

That this charge is true in some measure, or at least that there is danger of going too fast and too far in this direction will be conceded, I believe, by even the most ardent vocationists. A young and impressionable pupil cannot give his soul and body exclusively to the pursuit of purely practical ends without dulling his senses to the inward vision. It has been proved by experiences that the enjoyment of the finer things of life is an acquired skill. It comes by long practice and it disappears when we cease to practice it. A young man who throughout the whole course of his mental development should hold consistently to the vocational point of view and the vocational program and should occupy himself solely with vocational pursuits would at maturity be a lamentable spectacle. He would be like that "coarse-meated" person discovered by Professor Starbuck in his investigation of the psychology of religion and embalmed in Professor James's *Varieties of Religious Experience:*

> Q.: What does religion mean to you?
>
> A.: It means nothing; and it seems, so far as I can observe, useless to others.

Q.: What comes before your mind corresponding to the words God, Heaven, Angels, etc.?

A.: Nothing whatsoever. I am a man without a religion. These words mean so much mythic bosh.

We need not hope for sensitiveness to poetry in this type of man. In Professor James's words: "His contentment with the finite encases him like a lobster-shell and shields him from all morbid repining at his distance from the Infinite."

But it is not necessary to disparage the practical or business training demanded by a commercial age in order to justify the claims of that training of the imagination and the emotions which comes from the study of poetry. Let us concede at once that both kinds of training, in due measure, are imperative in education and mutually helpful. On the one hand we can then consistently maintain that the ends which the study of poetry seeks are indispensable to industrial success. Thus, an industrial activity which is not the outgrowth of a sensitive intelligence, which lacks imaginative insight, which is not stimulated and sustained by right feeling, which is not guided by an intimate knowledge of human nature and by a broad sympathy with mankind, is a dismal failure, no matter how many million tons of steel or gallons of oil it may turn out in the course of a year.

But it is just as true on the other hand that material activities are essential to the production of the highest type of poetry. A poetry which does not spring out of the preoccupation of the age, that is, out of its prevailing interests and pursuits, and which does not under one guise or another body forth the comedy and tragedy of daily life, which is not in some sense the cry of the people for bread and work and play, is not genuine poetry at all. It is nothing but a chimera bellowing rhythmically in a social vacuum.

If the relation of poetry and the commercial spirit is such as I have indicated, and if this is indeed a commercial age, let us ask next what are the spiritual needs which poetry is adapted to supply. Of these the first and perhaps the most important is the need of regulated emotion. I take this idea from a book by the late Mr. H. R. Haweis, entitled *My Musical Memories,* where the thought is applied most ingeniously to music:

> What is the ruin of art? Ill-regulated emotion.
> What is the ruin of life? Again, ill-regulated emotion.
> What mars happiness? What destroys manliness? What sullies womanhood? What checks enterprise? What spoils success? Constantly the same—ill-regulated emotion. The tongue is a fire; an uncontrolled and passionate outburst swallows up many virtues and blots out weeks of kindness. . . .
> . . . . Music disciplines and controls emotion.
> That is the explanation of the art of music, as distinguished from the mere power of the musical sound. You can rouse with a stroke; but to guide, to moderate, to control, to raise and depress, to combine, to work out a definite scheme involving appropriate relations and proportions of force, and various mobility—for this you require the subtle machinery of an art; and the direct machinery for stirring up and regulating emotion is the wonderful vibratory mechanism created by the art of music.

What the author says of unregulated emotion is especially true of a commercial age. Industry at its lower levels, while it trains the muscles and tends to settled habits of the body, usually leaves the emotions undisciplined and uncontrolled. For this neglect a penalty must be paid. When the barriers of steady employment and routine break down, as in strikes or hard times, the emotions of millions of workingmen are set at liberty to run wild, or worse, to run in the channels prepared for them by designing men. It is of the utmost importance, then, that these emotions should be disciplined, and for this purpose poetry, if it could in some way be brought home to the common people, seems to be even more effective than music, great as the effect of music in this regard undoubtedly is. Poetry has the advantage, first, that more persons can appreciate it, and, second, that the emotional appeal is bound up with a definite thought-content that tends to make its effects more steadfast and enduring.

A second need which poetry can supply is that of a true estimate and evaluation of the world in which we live. In a commercial age this is especially desirable, for the thrust and vibration characteristic of such an age tends to blur the picture of one's fellow-beings in the mass, which is the basis of the social sense, and to throw things out of their due proportions. In such an age men mistake the small for the great, the evil for the good, the temporary for the abiding.

For these distortions poetry is the great corrective. The virtue of good poetry, as Sir Philip Sidney affirmed, is that it cannot lie. It knows not how to deceive, to falsify, to play tricks. "In poetry," says Matthew Arnold, "which is thought and art in one, it is the glory, the eternal hour, that charlatanism shall find no entrance; that this noble sphere be kept inviolate and inviolable."

It may sound absurd to say we can gain a truer picture of the relations of capital and labor from Shakespeare than from Karl Marx exclusively. But it ought to be so and it is so. For my part if I had to make the choice I would rather intrust the solution of this problem to one who had been brought up on the great poets than to one who had been trained only in the fields of business and economics. I think he might do better. He couldn't do much worse.

Passing to another phase of the subject, let us ask: Is there a kind of poetry that is especially suited to a commercial age? Some of the modern poets seem to think so. At any rate they have striven to poetize in one way or another the characteristic features and agencies of industrial life. In these attempts two different methods may be distinguished. One method is by the aid of imagery and poetic diction to throw a romantic glamour over the dull gray facts of machinery and trade: the other is to present with intense vividness and uncompromising realism the harsh, unlovely aspects of toil and of the domestic life of the masses. The first method is illustrated by two recent poems, one a sonnet by Percy MacKaye entitled *The Automobile,* the other a poem by Chester Firkins published under the title *On a Subway Express.* I quote the first entire, and four stanzas from the second:

THE AUTOMOBILE

Fluid the world flowed under us: the hills
  Billow on billow of umbrageous green
  Heaved us, aghast, to fresh horizons, seen
One rapturous instant, blind with flash of rills
And silver-rising storms and dewy stills
  Of dripping boulders, till the dim ravine
  Drowned us again in leafage, whose serene
Coverts grew loud with our tumultuous wills.

Then all of Nature's old amazement seemed
  Sudden to ask us: "Is this also Man?

This plunging, volant, land-amphibian
What Plato mused and Paracelsus dreamed?
Reply!" And piercing us with ancient scan,
The shrill, primeval hawk gazed down—and screamed.

ON A SUBWAY EXPRESS

I, who have lost the stars, the sod,
For chilling pave and cheerless light,
Have made my meeting-place with God
A new and nether Night—

Have found a fane where thunder fills
Loud caverns, tremulous;—and these
Atone me for my reverend hills
And moonlit silences.

. . . .

Speed! Speed! until the quivering rails
Flash silver where the headlight gleams,
As when on lakes the Moon impales
The waves upon its beams.

. . . .

You that 'neath country skies can pray,
Scoff not at me—the city clod;—
My only respite of the Day
Is this wild ride—with God.

Of the second type, I will give a single instance:

HALSTED STREET CAR

Come, you cartoonists,
Hang on a strap with me here
At seven o'clock in the morning
On a Halsted Street car.
Take your pencils

And draw these faces.
Try with your pencils for these crooked faces,
That pig-sticker in one corner—his mouth.
That overall factory girl—her loose cheeks.
Find for your pencils
A way to mark your memory
Of tired empty faces.
After their night's sleep,
In the moist dawn
And cool daybreak,
Faces
Tired of wishes,
Empty of dreams.

In these very commendable pieces of verse the all too obvious purpose is to coat a new subject with old poetic varnish or an old subject with new varnish. Not in such a way, I venture to affirm, can the age of automobiles or of subways be adequately pictured in poetry. The new subject must mold its own form, devise its own diction. What these will be no one can tell until they come.

My own view is that although modern themes must be adequately treated by contemporary poets if poetry is to thrive, nevertheless the effectiveness of the poetry read, its impact upon the reader when it once gets to him, depends very little on its age or its subject. Genuine poetry is like fine gold. It passes current in all markets. Every nation, to be sure, and every time must have its own coinage; but the coin which outlived Tiberius will still buy food—if somewhat less than in the time of that emperor. The poetry which is of most worth in a commercial age is that which, drawn from any source, ancient or modern, brings home to men the truth and beauty of the life which now is. I am not sure that anybody has ever done it better than Homer.

But in any case we must not fall into the common fallacy that poetry can be taught as a thing apart from life. No doubt it is pleasant to retire into the study, draw the curtains, and, burying one's self in another world, forget for a time the existence of this one. Such a withdrawal has its charms and its uses. But that is not the chief function of poetry. I am reminded in this connection of a poem which appeared in a Berlin paper at the beginning of the war, under the title *Und draussen ist Krieg*. Each stanza dwelt upon the preoccupations which please when amid the comforts of home life and peace, but closed with the line *Und draussen ist Krieg:* "And outside is the war." So with our reading of poetry. We may for a time be lulled into unconsciousness of our surroundings, but after all, *Draussen ist Krieg*. The old, bitter, endless warfare of humanity, the tragedy of life and death, goes on. There is no escape. Sooner or later we must confront it. Any reading or study of poetry which does not prepare us to face the truth, which does not give us stay and comfort and courage amid the realities of our daily lives is a delusion and a waste of time.

However far afield the reading and study of poetry may carry us, however far it may lead us into the past or into the future, ultimately it should return us to ourselves. It should say to us in its still small voice: "You thought you were in an alien country, amid unfamiliar scenes, hearkening to a foreign tongue. But it is not so. Lo! this is your own native land, these are your fellows, this is your language. Yours, too, is this joy, this sorrow, this pathos, this terror. I do but reveal yourself to yourself, for in all ages and in all climes man is one and the same."

ART

All passes; Art alone
  Enduring stays to us:
The Bust outlasts the throne,
  The Coin, Tiberius.

—AUSTIN DOBSON

THE FIRST ARTIST AND HIS CRITICS[1]

ROBERT MORSS LOVETT

[Robert Morss Lovett was born at Boston in 1870 and was educated at Harvard. Since 1893 he has been a member of the English department of the University of Chicago and since 1903 he has been dean of the Junior College. He is a member of the editorial board of *The New Republic*.]

THE history of criticism begins with the history of art. When the first artist drew his first horse in red chalk on the walls of his cave, the first critic was at his elbow. And as the other cave dwellers gathered to see and wonder, he doubtless diverted their attention from the artist and his work to himself by raising the pregnant question, "What is criticism, and what is its function at the present time?"

I do not know how he answered that question, but I know that it must have been in one of four ways. There are involved in creative or representative art three factors: there is the artist or creator; there is the material or conception to which he gives form; and there is the public to which he addresses his product. Of course I recognize that in certain cases the first factor and the last are the same—the artist creates for himself alone. Now

[1] This article, reprinted by courtesy of the author and of *The New Republic*, was one of a symposium appearing in the Literary Supplement of *The New Republic* of October 26, 1921.

the resulting work of art will vary according to which of these three factors the artist emphasizes. If he is thinking chiefly of himself he will work in one way; if his loyalty is to his form or material, in quite a different way; and if his leading aim is to capture his public, in a third. So with the critic. He recognizes the three factors in production, and adds to them a fourth, namely himself: and he will answer his question as to the function of criticism according to which of the four he has most insistently in mind.

It may be, though it is unlikely, that the first critic was inspired chiefly by devotion to the artist, whom we may call Ab. Standing by Ab's side in the dim cave he first tried to see what Ab had been about and then explain it to the multitude. He envisaged the function of criticism as that of understanding what the artist had attempted, and of appraising his performance in the light of this understanding. His task was that of interpretation of the masterpiece through the personality of the artist. After the death of Ab, the function of his interpretative critic would be still more important. To scoffers who denied that the object was a horse at all, he would explain that the artist grew up on the plains, where he thought, talked and ate horse, that he loved horsemanship and had remarkable success in picking winners, in short that given the artist's personality and environment —the man and the moment—he could have meant by his marks on the wall nothing but a horse. Thus the critic a few generations after the event became a productive scholar, like Professor Kittredge. Or to other denying spirits who declared that, horse though it might be, it was not the work of Ab but of a follower and pupil, the critic would defend his attribution by pointing out the peculiar trick which Ab had in pointing his horses' ears, and which his pupils forgot to copy. Thus the critic became a connoisseur and professional art critic like Signor Morelli or Mr. Berenson. The chief virtues of this type of criticism are honesty, intelligence, sympathy—and its highest function is interpretation. Its reductio ad absurdum occurs when the critic becomes the judge, and uses his knowledge of Ab's character unfairly against him, declaring, like Ruskin, "Ab was a bad man and therefore he couldn't draw a good horse."

But let us suppose that the first critic had his mind focussed upon the result of Ab's striving, that he forgot the artist in the work of art. Then his problem was to appraise Ab's technique, to point out wherein and why it failed to do justice to the conception. If he insisted on comparing Ab's drawing to a real horse he was a naturalistic critic; if to the eternal and universal concept of horse he was an idealist. He was naturally a superior person and therefore unpleasant, and he gave an unpleasant connotation to the term criticism. When he looked at Ab it was as a pedagogue regards a pupil, training him to produce better results. When he considered the public it was as a lecturer, explaining why the work in question did or did not appeal to the best minds. This line of reasoning might lead him into an examination of the principles of beauty and taste according to laws of psychology, when he would become a philosopher in æsthetics. But he also was under the constant temptation to assume judicial functions. He became the judge before whom Ab was brought to be tried on technical or æsthetic grounds, and who, like Francis Jeffrey, always remembered that the judge is condemned when the guilty are acquitted. But Ab might have had the satisfaction of knowing that to future generation of æsthetic judges he would become a law in himself. To them his first horse would be a standard of achievement, a classic, for the first rule of classical criticism is "To copy nature is to copy Ab."

But let us make the further supposition that the first critic had his mind fixed chiefly on the spectators who crowded the cave to see Ab's masterpiece. What should he say to them? Tell them of Ab's early life, and his fondness for horses and horsey associations? Most unedifying. Point out how truly and sympathetically Ab had seen and reproduced the object of his affection? But what would that do for their business prosperity or their eternal salvation? No, an ethical lesson or judgment was to be extracted from Ab's masterpiece. And thus the critic became the preacher. He reminded his audience that "the horse is a vain thing for safety." He became a moralist, anxiously inquiring of the work of art "What will it do to the beholder? Will it leave him better or worse fitted for life here or hereafter?" He became the social philosopher, seeing in Ab's horse an attack on human standards of living; or the patriot finding in the patient docility of the beast a seditious reference to a virtue on the part of the enemy. He also became the judge. Finding that the public reacted perversely to his warnings he questioned whether it could be trusted to see the drawing at all; and if the temperamental Ab got himself enmeshed in a scandal the critic became the censor and barred Ab's work from the walls of the cave.

I do not mean to suggest that the four types of criticism which I have noted, historical, æsthetic, ethical and impressionistic, afford a complete classification; still less that they exist in classes separate and distinct each from the other, The same critic may partake of more than one type; as he may show more than one critical attitude. He may be by turns interpreter, judge, moralist, and artist. Nearly every critic, however, is predominantly of one type, and shows a tendency to persist in one attitude. Moreover, these different types of criticism predominate in different periods according to the intellectual character of the time. Thus in the eighteenth century and the early nineteenth century criticism was largely æsthetic, divided into schools, classical and romantic, of which Dr. Johnson, Jeffrey, and Coleridge are the expositors. The romantic critic tended toward impressionism, in William Hazlitt. In the middle nineteenth century the interest in humanity finds reflection in ethical criticism, in the shadow of which America remains. Matthew Arnold lamented in an early preface to his poems the lack of a critic as æsthetic school-master for young poets; but when he propounded his famous query as to the function of criticism he answered it, in terms befitting a missionary, "to make known the best that is thought and known in the world," and the bulk of his critical performance rests on the foundation of his dictum that conduct is three-fourths of life. The scientific movement in thought, and the accompanying realistic movement in literature and art, naturally led to a criticism of interpretation, biographical, historical, scientific, scholarly. The famous environment theory of Taine is an illustration. At the close of the century, the period known as the decadence is characterized by impressionistic criticism and the emergence of the critic as an artist in his own right.

Finally, the first critic may have been chiefly absorbed in himself, in his own sensations, impressions, reactions. He was perhaps used to finding "every moment some form or color growing perfect in hand or face, some tone on the hills choicer than the rest," and he may have found something on the walls of the cave which stirred his senses to the same excitement. He may have seen in Ab's crude drawing something that touched him more nearly than the object in life had done, something more real than actuality, and have felt in consequence a certain enhancement of his personality, a sense of more abundant life. He would try to express his emotion in language, to translate Ab's effort into another medium, and he would therefore become an artist himself, using Ab's work as a source of material as freely as he would have used nature. To the people who objected that he talked of an Ab unrecognized by them or even by Ab himself, he would defend his procedure. "What do I know of Ab? A few facts of his life, probably contradicted by others that I don't know, and which are at best misleading. What do I care about principles of beauty and laws of æsthetics? Who am I to say what is good for my fellow men? All I know are my own sensations. Ab's horse like other phenomena exists for me only in them, and only from them can I honestly bear witness to his art."

THE PROVINCES OF THE SEVERAL ARTS[1]

John Addington Symonds

[John Addington Symonds (1840–1895) was born at Bristol, England, and educated at Balliol College, Oxford. Although suffering constantly from ill health he produced a work, *The Renaissance in Italy* in seven volumes, which is described as "monumental." Stevenson speaks of him as the character Opalstein in *Talks and Talkers* in these words: "He was the best of talkers, singing the praises of the earth and the arts." He died at Rome and is buried near Shelley in the Protestant Cemetery there.]

I

"ART," said Goethe, "is but form-giving." We might vary this definition, and say, "Art is a method of expression or presentation." Then comes the question: If art gives form, if it is a method of expression or presentation, to what does it give form, what does it express or present? The answer certainly must be: Art gives form to human consciousness; expresses or presents the feeling or the thought of man. Whatever else art may do by the way, in the communication of innocent pleasures, in the adornment of life and the softening of manners, in the creation of beautiful shapes and sounds, this, at all events, is its prime function.

While investing thought and sentiment, the spiritual

[1] From *Essays Speculative and Suggestive*, 2 vols. Chapman and Hall, London, 1890.

subject-matter of all art, with form, or finding for it proper modes of presentation, each of the arts employs a special medium obeying the laws of beauty proper to that medium. The vehicles of the arts, roughly speaking, are solid substances (like ivory, stone, wood, metal), pigments, sounds, and words. The masterly handling of these vehicles and the realization of their characteristic types of beauty have come to be regarded as the craftsman's paramount concern. And in a certain sense this is a right conclusion; for dexterity in the manipulation of the chosen vehicle, and power to create a beautiful object, distinguish the successful artist from the man who may have had like thoughts and feelings. This dexterity, this power, are the properties of the artist *qua* artist. Yet we must not forget that the form created by the artist for the expression of a thought or feeling is not the final end of art itself. That form, after all, is but the mode of presentation through which the spiritual content must be made. It is the business of art to create an ideal world, in which perception, emotion, understanding, action, and all elements of human life sublimed by thought, shall reappear in concrete forms as beauty. This being so, the logical criticism of art demands that we should not only estimate the technical skill of an artist and his faculty for presenting beauty to the æsthetic sense, but that we should also ask ourselves what portion of the human spirit he has chosen to invest with form, and how he has conceived his subject. It is not necessary that the ideas embodied in a work of art should be the artist's own. They may be common to the race and age; as, for instance, the conception of sovereign deity expressed in the "Olympian Zeus" of Pheidias, or the expression of divine maternity expressed in Raphael's "Madonna di San Sisto." Still the personality of the artist, his own intellectual and moral nature, his peculiar way of thinking and feeling, his individual attitude toward the material given to him in ideas of human consciousness, will modify his choice of subject and of form, and will determine his specific type of beauty. To take an example: supposing that an idea, common to his race and age, is given to the artist for treatment; this will be the final end of the work of art which he produces. But his personal qualities and technical performance determine the degree of success or failure to which he attains in seizing that idea and in presenting it with beauty. Signorelli fails where Perugino excels, in giving adequate and lovely form to the religious sentiment. Michel Angelo is sure of the sublime, and Raphael of the beautiful.

Art is thus the expression of the human spirit by the artist to his fellow-men. The subject-matter of the arts is commensurate with what man thinks and feels and does. It is as deep as religion, as wide as life. But what distinguishes art from religion or from life is, that this subject-matter must assume beautiful form, and must be presented directly or indirectly to the senses. Art is not the school or the cathedral, but the playground, the paradise of humanity. It does not teach, it does not preach. Nothing abstract enters into art's domain. Truth and goodness are transmuted into beauty there, just as in science beauty and goodness assume the shape of truth, and in religion truth and beauty become goodness. The rigid definitions, the unmistakable laws of science, are not to be found in art. Whatever art has touched acquires a concrete sensuous embodiment, and thus ideas presented to the mind in art have lost a portion of their pure thought-essence. It is on this account that the religious conceptions of the Greeks were so admirably fitted for the art of sculpture, and certain portions of the mediæval Christian mythology lent themselves so well to painting. For the same reason the metaphysics of ecclesiastical dogma defy the artist's plastic faculty. Art, in a word, is a middle term between reason and the senses. Its secondary aim, after the prime end of manifesting the human spirit in beautiful form has been accomplished, is to give tranquil and innocent enjoyment.

II

From what has gone before, it will be seen that no human being can make or mold a beautiful form without incorporating in that form some portion of the human mind, however crude, however elementary. In other words, there is no work of art without a theme, without a motive, without a subject. The presentation of that theme, that motive, that subject, is the final end of art. The art is good or bad according as the subject has been well or ill presented, consistently with the laws of beauty special to the art itself. Thus we obtain two standards for æsthetic criticism. We judge a statue, for example, both by the sculptor's intellectual grasp upon his subject, and also by his technical skill and sense of beauty. In a picture of the "Last Judgment" by Fra Angelico we say that the bliss of the righteous has been more successfully treated than the torments of the wicked, because the former has been better understood, although the painter's skill in each is equal. In the Perseus of Cellini we admire the sculptor's spirit, finish of execution, and originality of design, while we deplore that want of sympathy with the heroic character which makes his type of physical beauty slightly vulgar and his facial expression vacuous.

If the phrase "Art for art's sake" has any meaning, this meaning is simply that the artist, having chosen a theme, thinks exclusively in working at it of technical dexterity or the quality of beauty. There are many inducements for the artist thus to narrow his function, and for the critic to assist him by applying the canons of a soulless connoisseurship to his work; for the conception of the subject is but the starting-point in art-production, and the artist's difficulties and triumphs as a craftsman lie in the region of technicalities. He knows, moreover, that however deep or noble his idea may be, his work of art will be worthless if it fail in skill or be devoid of beauty. What converts a thought into a statue or picture, is the form found for it; and so the form itself seems all-important. The artist, therefore, too easily imagines that he may neglect his theme; that a fine piece of coloring, a well-balanced composition, or, as Cellini put it, "*un bel corpo ignudo,*" is enough. And this is especially easy in an age which reflects much upon the arts, and pursues them with enthusiasm, while its deeper thoughts and sentiments are not of the kind which translate themselves readily into artistic form. But, after all, a fine piece of coloring, a well-balanced composition, a sonorous stanza, a learned essay in counterpoint, are not enough. They are all excellent good things, yielding delight to the artistic sense and instruction to the student. Yet when we think of the really great statues, pictures, poems, music of the world, we find that these are really great because of something more—and that more is their theme, their presentation of a noble portion of the human soul. Artists and art students may be satisfied with perfect specimens of a craftsman's skill, independent of his theme; but the mass of men will not be satisfied; and it is as wrong to suppose that art exists for artists and art students, as to talk of art for art's sake. Art exists for humanity. Art transmutes thought and feeling into terms of beautiful form. Art is great and lasting in proportion as it appeals to the human consciousness at large, presenting to it portions of itself in adequate and lovely form.

III

It was necessary in the first place firmly to apprehend the truth that the final end of all art is the presentation of a spiritual content; it is necessary in the next place to remove confusions by considering the special circumstances of the several arts.

Each art has its own vehicle of expression. What it can present and how it can present it, depends upon the nature of this vehicle. Thus, though architecture, sculpture, painting, music, poetry, meet upon the common ground of spiritualized experience—though the works of art produced by the architect, sculptor, painter, musician, poet, emanate from the spiritual nature of the race, are colored by the spiritual nature of the men who make them, and express what is spiritual in humanity under concrete form invented for them by the artist—yet it is certain that all of these arts do not deal exactly with the same portions of this common material in the same way or with the same results. Each has its own department. Each exhibits qualities of strength and weakness special to itself. To define these several departments, to explain the relation of these several vehicles of presentation to the common subject-matter, is the next step in criticism.

IV

Of the fine arts, architecture alone subserves utility. We build for use. But the geometrical proportions which the architect observes, contain the element of beauty and powerfully influence the soul. Into the language of arch and aisle and colonnade, of cupola and façade and pediment, of spire and vault, the architect translates emotion, vague perhaps but deep, mute but unmistakable. When we say that a building is sublime or graceful, frivolous or stern, we mean that sublimity or grace, frivolity or sternness, is inherent in it. The emotions connected with these qualities are inspired in us when we contemplate it, and are presented to us by its form. Whether the architect deliberately aimed at the sublime or graceful—whether the dignified serenity of the Athenian genius sought to express itself in the Parthenon, and the mysticism of mediæval Christianity in the gloom of Chartres Cathedral—whether it was Renaissance paganism which gave its mundane pomp and glory to St. Peter's, and the refined selfishness of royalty its specious splendor to the palace of Versailles—need not be curiously questioned. The fact that we are impelled to raise these points, that architecture more almost than any other art connects itself indissolubly with the life, the character, the moral being of a nation and an epoch, proves that we are justified in bringing it beneath our general definition of the arts. In a great measure because it subserves utility, and is therefore dependent upon the necessities of life, does architecture present to us through form the human spirit. Comparing the palace built by Giulio Romano for the Dukes of Mantua with the contemporary castle of a German prince, we cannot fail at once to comprehend the difference of spiritual conditions, as these displayed themselves in daily life, which then separated Italy from the Teutonic nations. But this is not all. Spiritual quality in the architect himself finds clear expression in his work. Coldness combined with violence marks Brunelleschi's churches; a certain suavity and well-bred taste the work of Bramante; while Michel Angelo exhibits wayward energy in his Library of S. Lorenzo, and Amadeo self-abandonment to fancy in his Lombard chapels. I have chosen examples from one nation and one epoch in order that the point I seek to make, the demonstration of a spiritual quality in buildings, may be fairly stated.

V

Sculpture and painting distinguish themselves from the other fine arts by the imitation of concrete existences in nature. They copy the bodies of men and animals, the aspects of the world around us, and the handiwork of mankind. Yet, in so far as they are rightly arts, they do not make imitation an object in itself. The grapes of

Zeuxis at which birds pecked, the painted dog at which a cat's hair bristles—if such grapes or such a dog were ever put upon canvas—are but evidences of the artist's skill, not of his faculty as artist. These two plastic, or, as I prefer to call them, figurative arts, use their imitation of the external world for the expression, the presentation of internal, spiritual things. The human form is for them the outward symbol of the inner human spirit, and their power of presenting spirit is limited by the means at their disposal.

Sculpture employs stone, wood, clay, the precious metals to model forms, detached and independent, or raised upon a flat surface in relief. Its domain is the whole range of human character and consciousness, in so far as these can be indicated by fixed facial expression, by physical type, and by attitude. If we dwell for an instant on the greatest historical epoch of sculpture, we shall understand the domain of this art in its range and limitation. At a certain point of Greek development the Hellenic Pantheon began to be translated by the sculptors into statutes; and when the genius of the Greeks expired in Rome, the cycle of their psychological conceptions had been exhaustively presented through this medium. During that long period of time, the most delicate gradations of human personality, divinized, idealized, were submitted to the contemplation of the consciousness which gave them being, in appropriate types. Strength and swiftness, massive force and airy lightness, contemplative repose and active energy, voluptuous softness and refined grace, intellectual sublimity and lascivious seductiveness—the whole rhythm of qualities which can be typified by bodily form—were analyzed, selected, combined in various degrees, to incarnate the religious conceptions of Zeus, Aphrodite, Herakles, Dionysus, Pallas, Fauns and Satyrs, Nymphs of woods and waves, Tritons, the genius of Death, heroes and hunters, lawgivers and poets, presiding deities of minor functions, man's lustful appetites and sensual needs. All that men think, or do, or are, or wish for, or imagine in this world, had found exact corporeal equivalents. Not physiognomy alone, but all the portions of the body upon which the habits of the animating soul are wont to stamp themselves, were studied and employed as symbolism. Uranian Aphrodite was distinguished from her Pandemic sister by chastened, lust-repelling loveliness. The muscles of Herakles were more ponderous than the tense sinews of Achilles. The Hermes of the palæstra bore a torso of majestic depth; the Hermes who carried messages from heaven had limbs alert for movement. The brows of Zeus inspired awe; the breasts of Dionysus breathed delight.

A race accustomed, as the Greeks were, to read this symbolism, accustomed, as the Greeks were, to note the individuality of naked form, had no difficulty in interpreting the language of sculpture. Nor is there even now much difficulty in the task. Our surest guide to the subject of a bas-relief or statue is study of the physical type considered as symbolical of spiritual quality. From the fragment of a torso the true critic can say whether it belongs to the athletic or the erotic species. A limb of Bacchus differs from a limb of Poseidon. The whole psychological conception of Aphrodite Pandemos enters into every muscle, every point, no less than into her physiognomy, her hair, her attitude.

There is, however, a limit to the domain of sculpture.

This art deals most successfully with personified generalities. It is also strong in the presentation of incarnate character. But when it attempts to tell a story, we often seek in vain its meaning. Battles of Amazons or Centaurs upon bas-reliefs, indeed, are unmistakable. The subject is indicated here by some external sign. The group Laocoön appeals at once to a reader of Virgil, and the divine vengeance of Leto's children upon Niobe is manifest in the Uffizzi marbles. But who are the several heroes of the Æginetan pediment, and what was the subject of the Pheidian statues on the Parthenon? Do the three graceful figures of a bas-relief which exists at Naples and in the Villa Albani, represent Orpheus, Hermes, and Eurydice, or Antiope and her two sons? Was the winged and sworded genius upon the Ephesus column meant for a genius of Death or a genius of Love?

This dimness of significance indicates the limitations of sculpture, and inclines some of those who feel its charm to assert that the sculptor seeks to convey no intellectual meaning, that he is satisfied with the creation of beautiful form. There is an element of good sense in this revolt against the faith which holds that art is nothing but a mode of spiritual presentation. Truly the artist aims at producing beauty, is satisfied if he conveys delight. But it is impossible to escape from the certainty that, while he is creating forms of beauty, he means something, feels something; and that something, that theme for which he finds the form, is part of the world's spiritual heritage. Only the crudest works of figurative art, capricci and arabesques, have no intellectual content; and even these are good in so far as they convey the playfulness of fancy.

VI

Painting employs colors upon surfaces—walls, panels, canvas. What has been said about sculpture will apply in a great measure to this art. The human form, the world around us, the works of man's hands, are represented in paintings, not for their own sake merely, but with the view of bringing thought, feeling, action, home to the consciousness of the spectator from the artist's consciousness on which they have been impressed. Painting can tell a story better than sculpture, can represent more complicated feelings, can suggest thoughts of a subtler intricacy. Through color, it can play, like music, directly on powerful but vague emotion. It is deficient in the fullness and roundness of concrete reality. A statue stands before us, the soul incarnate in palpable form, fixed and frozen for eternity. The picture is a reflection cast upon a magic glass; not less permanent, but reduced to shadow of palpable reality. To follow these distinctions farther would be alien from the present purpose. It is enough to repeat that, within their several spheres, according to their several strengths and weaknesses, both sculpture and painting present the spirit to us only as the spirit shows itself immersed in things of sense. The light of a lamp enclosed within an alabaster vase is still lamplight, though shorn of luster and toned to colored softness. Even thus the spirit, immersed in things of sense presented to us by the figurative arts, is still spirit, though diminished in its intellectual clearness and invested with hues not its own. To fashion that alabaster form of art with utmost skill, to make it beautiful, to render it transparent, is the artist's function. But he will have failed of the highest if the light within burns dim, or if he gives the world a lamp in which no spiritual flame is lighted.

VII

Music transports us to a different region. Like architecture, it imitates nothing. It uses pure sound, and sound of the most wholly artificial kind—so artificial that the musical sounds of one race are unmusical, and therefore unintelligible, to another. Like architecture, music relies upon mathematical proportions. Unlike architecture, music serves no utility. It is the purest art of pleasure—the truest paradise and playground of the spirit. It has less power than painting, even less power than sculpture, to tell a story or to communicate an idea. For we must remember that when music is married to words, the words, and not the music, reach our thinking faculty. And yet, in spite of all this, music presents man's spirit to itself through form. The domain of the spirit over which music reigns, is emotion—not defined emotion, not feeling even so generally defined as jealousy or anger —but those broad bases of man's being out of which emotions spring, defining themselves through action into this or that set type of feeling. Architecture, we have noticed, is so connected with specific modes of human existence, that from its main examples we can reconstruct the life of men who used it. Sculpture and painting, by limiting their presentation to the imitation of external things, have all the help which experience and association render. The mere artificiality of music's vehicle separates it from life and makes its message untranslatable. Nevertheless, this very disability under which it labors is the secret of its extraordinary potency.

To expect clear definition from music—the definition which belongs to poetry—would be absurd. The sphere of music is in sensuous perception; the sphere of poetry is in intelligence. Music, dealing with pure sound, must always be vaguer in significance than poetry, which deals with words. Nevertheless its effect upon the sentient subject may be more intense and penetrating for this very reason. We cannot fail to understand what words are intended to convey; we may very easily interpret in a hundred different ways the message of sound. But this is not because words are wider in their reach and more alive; rather because they are more limited, more stereotyped, more dead. They symbolized something precise and unmistakable; but this precision is itself attenuation of the something symbolized. The exact value of the counter is better understood when it is a word than when it is a chord, because all that a word conveys has already become a thought, while all that musical sounds convey remains within the region of emotion which has not been intellectualized. Poetry touches emotion through the thinking faculty. If music reaches the thinking faculty at all, it is through fibers of emotion. But emotion, when it has become thought, has already lost a portion of its force, and has taken to itself a something alien to its nature. Therefore the message of music can never rightly be translated into words. It is the very largeness and vividness of the sphere of simple feeling which makes its symbolical counterpart in sound so seeming vague. But in spite of this incontestable defect of seeming vagueness, an emotion expressed by music is nearer to our sentient self, if we have ears to take it in, than the same emotion limited by language. It is intenser, it is more immediate, as compensation for being less intelligible, less unmistakable in meaning. It is an infinite, an indistinct, where each consciousness defines and sets a limitary form.

Nothing intervenes between the musical work of art and the fibers of the sentient being it immediately thrills. We do not seek to say what music means. We feel the music. And if a man should pretend that the music has not passed beyond his ears, has communicated nothing but a musical delight, he simply tells us that he has not felt music. The ancients on this point were wiser than some moderns when, without pretending to assign an intellectual significance to music, they held it for an axiom that one type of music bred one type of character, another type another. A change in the music of a state, wrote Plato, will be followed by changes in its constitution. It is of the utmost importance, said Aristotle, to provide in education for the use of the ennobling and the fortifying moods. These philosophers knew that music creates a spiritual world, in which the spirit cannot live and move without contracting habits of emotion. In this vagueness of significance but intensity of feeling lies the magic of music. A melody occurs to the composer, which he certainly connects with no act of the reason, which he is probably unconscious of connecting with any movement of his feeling, but which nevertheless is the form in sound of an emotional mood. When he reflects upon the melody secreted thus impromptu, he is aware, as we learn from his own lips, that this work has correspondence with emotion. Beethoven calls one symphony Heroic, another Pastoral; of the opening of another he says, "Fate knocks at the door." Mozart sets comic words to the mass-music of a friend, in order to make his sense of its inaptitude for religious sentiment. All composers use phrases like Maestoso, Pomposo, Allegro, Lagrimoso, Con Fuoco, to express the general complexion of the mood their music ought to represent.

VIII

Before passing to poetry, it may be well to turn aside and consider two subordinate arts, which deserve a place in any system of æsthetics. These are dancing and acting. Dancing uses the living human form, and presents feeling or action; the passions and the deeds of men, in artificially educated movements of the body. The element of beauty it possesses, independently of the beauty of the dancer, is rhythm. Acting or the art of mimicry presents the same subject-matter, no longer under the conditions of fixed rhythm, but as an ideal reproduction of reality. The actor is what he represents, and the element of beauty in his art is perfection of realization. It is his duty as an artist to show us Orestes or Othello, not perhaps exactly as Othello and Orestes were, but as the essence of their tragedies, ideally incorporate in action, ought to be. The actor can do this in dumb show. Some of the greatest actors of the ancient world were mimes. But he usually interprets a poet's thought, and attempts to present an artistic conception in a secondary form of art, which has for its advantage his own personality in play.

IX

The last of the fine arts is literature; or, in the narrower sphere of which it will be well to speak here only, is poetry. Poetry employs words in fixed rhythms, which we call metres. Only a small portion of its effect is derived from the beauty of its sound. It appeals to the sense of hearing far less immediately than music does. It makes no appeal to the eyesight, and takes no help from the beauty of color. It produces no palpable, tangible object. But language being the storehouse of all human experience, language being the medium whereby spirit communicates with spirit in affairs of life, the vehicle which transmits to us the thoughts and feelings of the past, and on which we rely for continuing our present to the future, it follows that, of all the arts, poetry soars highest, flies widest, and is most at home in the region of the spirit. What poetry lacks of sensuous fullness, it more than balances by intellectual intensity. Its significance is unmistakable, because it employs the very material men use in their exchange of thoughts and correspondence of emotions. To the bounds of its empire there is no end. It embraces in its own more abstract being all the arts. By words it does the work in turn of architecture, sculpture, painting, music. It is the metaphysic of the fine arts. Philosophy finds place in poetry; and life itself, refined to its last utterance, hangs trembling on this thread which joins our earth to heaven, this bridge between experience and the realms where unattainable and imperceptible will have no meaning.

If we are right in defining art as the manifestation of

the human spirit to man by man in beautiful form, poetry, more incontestably than any other art, fulfills this definition and enables us to gauge its accuracy. For words are the spirit, manifested to itself in symbols with no sensual alloy. Poetry is therefore the presentation, through words, of life and all that life implies. Perception, emotion, thought, action, find in descriptive, lyrical, reflective, dramatic, and epical poetry their immediate apocalypse. In poetry we are no longer puzzled with problems as to whether art has or has not of necessity a spiritual content. There cannot be any poetry whatsoever without a spiritual meaning of some sort: good or bad, moral, immoral, or non-moral, obscure or lucid, noble or ignoble, slight or weighty—such distinctions do not signify. In poetry we are not met by questions whether the poet intended to convey a meaning when he made it. Quite meaningless poetry (as some critics would fain find melody quite meaningless, or a statue meaningless, or a Venetian picture meaningless) is a contradiction in terms. In poetry, life, or a portion of life, lives again, resuscitated and presented to our mental faculty through art. The best poetry is that which reproduces the most of life, or its intensest moments. Therefore the extensive species of the drama and the epic the intensive species of the lyric, have been ever held in highest esteem. Only a paradoxical critic maintains the thesis that poetry is excellent in so far as it assimilates the vagueness of music, or estimates a poet by his power of translating sense upon the border-land of nonsense into melodious words. Where poetry falls short in the comparison with other arts, is in the quality of form giving, in the quality of sensuous concreteness. Poetry can only present forms to the mental eye and to the intellectual sense, stimulate the physical senses by indirect suggestion. Therefore dramatic poetry, the most complicated kind of poetry, relies upon the actor; and lyrical poetry, the intensest kind of poetry, seeks the aid of music. But these comparative deficiencies are overbalanced, for all the highest purposes of art, by the width and depth, the intelligibility and power, the flexibility and multitudinous associations of language. The other arts are limited in what they utter. There is nothing which has entered into the life of man which poetry cannot express. Poetry says everything in man's own language to the mind. The other arts appeal imperatively, each in its own region, to man's senses; and the mind receives art's message by the help of symbols from the world of sense. Poetry lacks this immediate appeal to sense. But the elixir which it offers to the mind, its quintessence extracted from all things of sense, reacts through intellectual perception upon all the faculties that make men what they are.

X

I used a metaphor in one of the foregoing paragraphs to indicate the presence of the vital spirit, the essential element of thought or feeling, in the work of art. I said it radiated through the form, as lamplight through an alabaster vase. Now the skill of the artist is displayed in modelling that vase, in giving it shape, rich and rare, and fashioning its curves with subtlest workmanship. In so far as he is a craftsman, the artist's pains must be bestowed upon this precious vessel of the animating theme. In so far as he has power over beauty, he must exert it in this plastic act. It is here that he displays dexterity; here that he creates; here that he separates himself from other men who think and feel. The poet, more perhaps than any other artist, needs to keep this steadily in view; for words being our daily vehicle of utterance, it may well chance that the alabaster vase of language should be hastily or trivially modelled. This is the true reason why "neither gods nor men nor the columns either suffer mediocrity in singers." Upon the poet it is specially incumbent to see that he has something rare to say and some rich mode of saying it. The figurative arts need hardly be so cautioned. They run their risk in quite a different direction. For sculptor and for painter, the danger is lest he should think that alabaster vase his final task. He may too easily be satisfied with molding a beautiful but empty form.

HOW ARCHITECTURE EXPRESSES A PEOPLE'S SOUL

JOHN RUSKIN

[John Ruskin (1819–1900) son of a prosperous wine merchant, was born in London, was educated principally by private tutors, and took his B.A. degree at Christ Church College, Oxford, in 1842. In the next year appeared the first volume of his first great work, *Modern Painters,* which opened a new epoch in revealing the intimate relations between art and all that world which art reflects. The present address (which he called "Traffic") shows the universality of his interests, the brilliance of his generalizations, and the eloquent earnestness of his plea for all human values.]

MY good Yorkshire friends, you asked me down here among your hills that I might talk to you about this Exchange you are going to build: but, earnestly and seriously asking you to pardon me, I am going to do nothing of the kind. I cannot talk, or at least can say very little, about this same Exchange. I must talk of quite other things, though not willingly; —I could not deserve your pardon, if, when you invited me to speak on one subject, I *wilfully* spoke on another. But I cannot speak, to purpose, of anything about which I do not care; and most simply and sorrowfully I have to tell you, in the outset, that I do *not* care about this Exchange of yours.

If, however, when you sent me your invitation, I had

answered, "I won't come, I don't care about the Exchange of Bradford," you would have been justly offended with me, not knowing the reasons of so blunt a carelessness. So I have come down, hoping that you will patiently let me tell you why, on this, and many other such occasions, I now remain silent, when formerly I should have caught at the opportunity of speaking to a gracious audience.

In a word, then, I do not care about this Exchange—because *you* don't; and because you know perfectly well I cannot make you. Look at the essential conditions of the case, which you, as business men, know perfectly well, though perhaps you think I forget them. You are going to spend £30,000, which to you, collectively, is nothing; the buying a new coat is, as to the cost of it, a much more important matter of consideration to me, than building a new Exchange is to you. But you think you may as well have the right thing for your money, you know there are a great many odd styles of architecture about; you don't want to do anything ridiculous; you hear of me, among others, as *a respectable architectural man-milliner;* and you send for me, that I may tell you the leading fashion; and what is, in our shops, for the moment, *the newest and sweetest thing in pinnacles.*

Now, pardon me for telling you frankly, you cannot have good architecture merely by asking people's advice on occasion. All good architecture is the expression of national life and character, and it is produced by a prevalent and eager national taste, or desire for beauty. And I want you to think a little of the deep significance of this word "taste"; for no statement of mine has been more earnestly or oftener controverted than that *good taste is essentially a moral quality.* "No," say many of my antagonists, "taste is one thing, morality is another. Tell us what is pretty: we shall be glad to know that; but we need no sermons—even were you able to preach them, which may be doubted."

Permit me, therefore, to fortify this old dogma of mine somewhat. *Taste is not only a part and an index of morality;—it is the* ONLY *morality.* The first, and last, and closest trial question to any living creature is, *"What do you like?"* Tell me what you like and I'll tell you what you are. Go out into the street, and ask the first man or woman you meet, what their "taste" is; and if they answer candidly, you know them, body and soul. "You, my friend in the rags, with the unsteady gait, what do *you* like?" "A pipe and a quartern of gin." I know you. "You, good woman, with the quick step and tidy bonnet, what do you like?" "A swept hearth, and a clean tea-table; and my husband opposite me, and a baby at my breast." Good, I know you also. "You, little girl with the golden hair and the soft eyes, what do you like?" "My canary, and a run among the wood hyacinths." "You, little boy with the dirty hands, and the low forehead, what do you like?" "A shy at the sparrows, and a game at pitch farthing." Good; we know them all now. What more need we ask?

"Nay," perhaps you answer; "we need rather to ask what these people and children do, than what they like. If they *do* right, it is no matter that they like what is wrong; and if they *do* wrong, it is no matter that they like what is right. Doing is the great thing; and it does not matter that the man likes drinking, so that he does not drink; nor that the little girl likes to be kind to her canary, if she will not learn her lessons; nor that the little boy likes throwing stones at the sparrows, if he goes to the Sunday school." Indeed, for a short time, and in a provisional sense, this is true. For if, resolutely, people do what is right, in time they come to like doing it. But they only are in a right moral state when they *have* come to like doing it; and as long as they don't like it, they are still in a vicious state. The man is not in health of body who is always thinking of the bottle in the cupboard, though he bravely bears his thirst; but the man who heartily enjoys water in the morning, and wine in the evening, each in its proper quantity and time. And the entire object of true education is to make people not merely *do* the right things, but *enjoy* the right things:—not merely industrious, but to love industry—not merely learned, but to love knowledge—not merely pure, but to love purity—not merely just, but to hunger and thirst after justice.

But you may answer or think, "Is the liking for outside ornaments,—for pictures, or statues, or furniture, or architecture,—a moral quality?" Yes, most surely, if a rightly set liking. Taste for *any* pictures or statues is not a moral quality, but taste for good ones is. Only here again we have to define the word "good." I don't mean by "good," clever—or learned—or difficult in the doing. Take a picture by Teniers, of sots quarrelling over their dice; it is an entirely clever picture; so clever that nothing in its kind has ever been done equal to it; but it is also an entirely base and evil picture. It is an expression of delight in the prolonged contemplation of a vile thing, and delight in that is an "unmannered," or "immoral" quality. It is "bad taste" in the profoundest sense—it is the taste of the devils. On the other hand, a picture of Titian's, or a Greek statue, or a Greek coin, or a Turner landscape, expresses delight in the perpetual contemplation of a good and perfect thing. That is an entirely moral quality—it is the taste of the angels. And all delight in art, and all love of it, resolve themselves into simple love of that which deserves love. That deserving is the quality which we call "loveliness"—(we ought to have an opposite word, hateliness, to be said of the things which deserve to be hated) ; and it is not an indifferent nor optional thing whether we love this or that; but it is just the vital function of all our being. *What we like determines what we are, and is the sign of what we are;* and *to teach taste is inevitably to form character.*

As I was thinking over this, in walking up Fleet Street the other day, my eye caught the title of a book standing open in a bookseller's window. It was—"On the necessity of the diffusion of taste among all classes." "Ah," I thought to myself, "my classifying friend, when you have diffused your taste, where will your classes be? The man who likes what you like, belongs to the same class with you, I think. Inevitably so. You may put him to other work if you choose; but, by the condition you have brought him into, he will dislike the other work as much as you would yourself. You get hold of a scavenger or a costermonger, who enjoyed the Newgate Calendar for literature, and 'Pop goes the Weasel' for music. You think you can make him like Dante and Beethoven? I wish you joy of your lessons; but if you do, you have made a gentleman of him:—he won't like to go back to his costermongering."

And so completely and unexceptionally is this so, that, if I had time to-night, I could show you that a nation cannot be affected by any vice, or weakness, without expressing it, legibly, and for ever, either in bad art, or by want of art; and that there is no national virtue, small or great, which is not manifestly expressed in all the art which circumstances enable the people possessing that virtue to produce. Take, for instance, your great English virtue of enduring and patient courage. You have at present in England only one art of any consequence—that is, iron-working. You know thoroughly well how to cast and hammer iron. Now, do you think, in those masses of lava which you build volcanic cones to melt, and which you forge at the mouths of the Infernos you have created; do you think, on the iron plates, your courage and endurance are not written for ever,—not merely with an iron pen, but on iron parchment? And take also your great English vice—European vice—vice of all the world—vice of all other worlds that roll or shine in heaven, bearing with them yet the atmosphere of hell—the vice of jealousy, which brings competition into your commerce, treachery into your councils, and dishonor into your wars—that vice which has rendered for you, and for your next neighboring nation, the daily occupations of existence no longer possible, but with the mail upon your breasts and the sword loose in its sheath; so that at last, you have realized for all the multitudes of the two great peoples who lead the so-called civilization of the earth,—you have realized for them all, I say, in person and in policy, what was once true only of the rough Border riders of your Cheviot hills—

> They carved at the meal
> With gloves of steel,
> And they drank the red wine through the helmet barr'd;[1]—

do you think that this national shame and dastardliness of heart are not written as legibly on every rivet of your iron armor as the strength of the right hands that forged it?

Friends, I know not whether this thing be the more ludicrous or the more melancholy. It is quite unspeakably both. Suppose, instead of being now sent for by you, I had been sent for by some private gentleman, living in a suburban house, with his garden separated only by a fruit wall from his next door neighbor's; and he had called me to consult with him on the furnishing of his drawing-room. I begin looking about me, and find the walls rather bare; I think such and such a paper might be desirable—perhaps a little fresco here and there on the ceiling—a damask curtain or so at the windows. "Ah," says my employer, "damask curtains, indeed! That's all very fine, but you know I can't afford that kind of thing just now!" "Yet the world credits you with a splendid income!" "Ah, yes," says my friend, "but do you know, at present I am obliged to spend it nearly all in steel-traps?" "Steel-traps! for whom?" "Why, for that fellow on the other side the wall, you know: we're very good friends, capital friends; but we are obliged to keep our traps set on both sides of the wall; we could not

[1] Scott's *Lay of the Last Minstrel,* canto 1, stanza 4.

possibly keep on friendly terms without them, and our spring guns. The worst of it is, we are both clever fellows enough; and there's never a day passes that we don't find out a new trap, or a new gun-barrel, or something; we spend about fifteen millions a year each in our traps, take it altogether; and I don't see how we're to do with less." A highly comic state of life for two private gentlemen! but for two nations, it seems to me, not wholly comic. Bedlam would be comic, perhaps, if there were only one madman in it; and your Christmas pantomime is comic, when there is only one clown in it; but when the whole world turns clown, and paints itself red with its own heart's blood instead of vermilion, it is something else than comic, I think.

Mind, I know a great deal of this is play, and willingly allow for that. You don't know what to do with yourselves for a sensation: fox-hunting and cricketing will not carry you through the whole of this unendurably long mortal life: you liked pop-guns when you were schoolboys, and rifles and Armstrongs are only the same things better made: but then the worst of it is, that what was play to you when boys, was not play to the sparrows; and what is play to you now, is not play to the small birds of State neither; and for the black eagles, you are somewhat shy of taking shots at them, if I mistake not.

I must get back to the matter in hand, however. Believe me, without further instance, I could show you, in all time, that every nation's vice, or virtue, was written in its art: the soldiership of early Greece; the sensuality of late Italy; the visionary religion of Tuscany; the splendid human energy and beauty of Venice. I have no time to do this to-night (I have done it elsewhere before now) ; but I proceed to apply the principle to ourselves in a more searching manner.

I notice that among all the new buildings that cover your once wild hills, churches and schools are mixed in due, that is to say, in large proportion, with your mills and mansions; and I notice also that the churches and schools are almost always Gothic, and the mansions and mills are never Gothic. Will you allow me to ask precisely the meaning of this? For, remember, it is peculiarly a modern phenomenon. When Gothic was invented, houses were Gothic as well as churches; and when the Italian style superceded the Gothic, churches were Italian as well as houses. If there is a Gothic spire to the cathedral of Antwerp, there is a Gothic belfry to the Hôtel de Ville at Brussels; if Inigo Jones builds an Italian Whitehall, Sir Christopher Wren builds an Italian St. Paul's. But now you live under one school of architecture, and worship under another. What do you mean by doing this? Am I to understand that you are thinking of changing your architecture back to Gothic; and that you treat your churches experimentally, because it does not matter what mistakes you make in a church? Or am I to understand that you consider Gothic a pre-eminently sacred and beautiful mode of building, which you think, like the fine frankincense, should be mixed for the tabernacle only, and reserved for your religious services? For if this be the feeling, though it may seem at first as if it were graceful and reverent, you will find that, at the root of the matter, it signifies neither more nor less than that *you have separated your religion from your life.*

For consider what a wide significance this fact has:

and remember that it is not you only, but all the people of England, who are behaving thus, just now.

You have all got into the habit of calling the church "the house of God." I have seen, over the doors of many churches, the legend actually carved, *"This* is the house of God and this is the gate of heaven." Now, note where that legend comes from, and of what place it was first spoken. A boy leaves his father's house to go on a long journey on foot, to visit his uncle: he has to cross a wild hill-desert; just as if one of your own boys had to cross the wolds to visit an uncle at Carlisle. The second or third day your boy finds himself somewhere between Hawes and Brough, in the midst of the moors, at sunset. It is stony ground, and boggy; he cannot go one foot further that night. Down he lies, to sleep, on Wharnside, where best he may, gathering a few of the stones together to put under his head;—so wild the place is, he cannot get anything but stones. And there, lying under the broad night, he has a dream; and he sees a ladder set up on the earth, and the top of it reaches to heaven, and the angels of God are ascending and descending upon it. And when he wakes out of his sleep, he says, "How dreadful is this place; surely this is none other than the house of God, and this is the gate of heaven." This PLACE, observe; not this church; not this city; not this stone, even, which he puts up for a memorial—the piece of flint on which his head has lain.

But this *place;* this windy slope of Wharnside; this moorland hollow, torrent-bitten, snow-blighted! this *any* place where God lets down the ladder. And how are you to know where that will be? or how are you to determine where it may be, but by being ready for it always? Do you know where the lightning is to fall next? You *do* know that, partly; you can guide the lightning; but you cannot guide the going forth of the Spirit, which is that lightning when it shines from the east to the west.

But the perpetual and insolent warping of that strong verse to serve a merely ecclesiastical purpose is only one of the thousand instances in which we sink back into gross Judaism. We call our churches "temples." Now, you know perfectly well they are *not* temples. They have never had, never can have, anything whatever to do with temples. They are "synagogues"—"gathering places"—where you gather yourselves together as an assembly; and by not calling them so, you again miss the force of another mighty text—"Thou, when thou prayest, shalt not be as the hypocrites are; for they love to pray standing in the *churches*" [we should translate it], "that they may be seen of men. But thou, when thou prayest, enter into thy closet, and when thou hast shut thy door, pray to thy Father"—which is, not in chancel nor in aisle, but "in secret."

Now, you feel, as I say this to you—I know you feel—as if I were trying to take away the honor of your churches. Not so; I am trying to prove to you the honor of your houses and your hills; *not that the Church is not sacred—but that the whole Earth is.* I would have you feel, what careless, what constant, what infectious sin there is in all modes of thought, whereby, in calling your churches only "holy," you call your hearths and homes "profane"; and have separated yourselves from the heathen by casting all your household gods to the ground, instead of recognizing, in the place of their many and feeble Lares, the presence of your One and Mighty Lord and Lar.

"But what has all this to do with our Exchange?" you ask me, impatiently. My dear friends, it has just everything to do with it; on these inner and great questions depend all the outer and little ones; and if you have asked me down here to speak to you, because you had before been interested in anything I have written, you must know that all I have yet said about architecture was to show this. The book I called *The Seven Lamps* was to show that certain right states of temper and moral feeling were the magic powers by which all good architecture, without exception, had been produced. *The Stones of Venice* had, from beginning to end, no other aim than to show that the Gothic architecture of Venice had arisen out of, and indicated in all its features, a state of pure national faith, and of domestic virtue; and that its Renaissance architecture had arisen out of, and in all its features indicated, a state of concealed national infidelity, and of domestic corruption. And now, you ask me what style is best to build in, and how can I answer, knowing the meaning of the two styles, but by another question—do you mean to build as Christians or as Infidels? And still more—do you mean to build as honest Christians or as honest Infidels? as thoroughly and confessedly either one or the other? You don't like to be asked such rude questions. I cannot help it; they are of much more importance than this Exchange business; and if they can be at once answered, the Exchange business settles itself in a moment. But before I press them farther, I must ask leave to explain one point clearly.

In all my past work, my endeavor has been to show

that good architecture is essentially religious—the production of a faithful and virtuous, not of an infidel and corrupted people. But in the course of doing this, I have had also to show that good architecture is not *ecclesiastical.* People are so apt to look upon religion as the business of the clergy, not their own, that the moment they hear of anything depending on "religion," they think it must also have depended on the priesthood; and I have had to take what place was to be occupied between these two errors, and fight both, often with seeming contradiction. Good architecture is the work of good and believing men; therefore, you say, at least some people say, "Good architecture must essentially have been the work of the clergy, not of the laity." No—a thousand times no; good architecture [1] has always been the work of the commonalty, *not* of the clergy. "What," you say, "those glorious cathedrals—the pride of Europe—did their builders not form Gothic architecture?" No; they corrupted Gothic architecture. Gothic was formed in the baron's castle, and the burgher's street. It was formed by the thoughts, and hands, and powers of laboring citizens and warrior kings. By the monk it was used as an instrument for the aid of his superstition; when that superstition became a beautiful madness, and the best hearts of Europe vainly dreamed and pined in the cloister, and vainly raged and perished in the crusade,—through that fury of perverted faith and wasted war, the Gothic rose also to its loveliest, most fantastic, and finally, most foolish dreams; and in those dreams, was lost.

I hope, now, that there is no risk of your misunder-

[1] And all other arts, for the most part; even of incredulous and secularly-minded commonalties. [Ruskin's Note.]

standing me when I come to the gist of what I want to say to-night;—when I repeat, that every great national architecture has been the result and exponent of a great national religion. You can't have bits of it here, bits there—you must have it everywhere or nowhere. It is not the monopoly of a clerical company—it is not the exponent of a theological dogma—it is not the hieroglyphic writing of an initiated priesthood; it is the manly language of a people inspired by resolute and common purpose, and rendering resolute and common fidelity to the legible laws of an undoubted God.

Now, there have as yet been three distinct schools of European architecture. I say, European, because Asiatic and African architectures belong so entirely to other races and climates, that there is no question of them here; only, in passing, I will simply assure you that whatever is good or great in Egypt, and Syria, and India, is just good or great for the same reasons as the buildings on our side of the Bosphorus. We Europeans, then, have had three great religions: the Greek, which was the worship of the God of Wisdom and Power; the Mediæval, which was the worship of the God of Judgment and Consolation; the Renaissance, which was the worship of the God of Pride and Beauty: these three we have had—they are past,—and now, at last, we English have got a fourth religion, and a God of our own, about which I want to ask you. But I must explain these three old ones first.

I repeat, first, the Greeks essentially worshipped the God of Wisdom; so that whatever contended against their religion,—to the Jews a stumbling-block,—was, to the Greeks—*Foolishness.*

The first Greek idea of deity was that expressed in the word, of which we keep the remnant in our words "*Di*-urnal" and "*Di*-vine"—the god of *Day,* Jupiter the revealer. Athena is his daughter, but especially daughter of the Intellect, springing armed from the head. We are only with the help of recent investigation beginning to penetrate the depth of meaning couched under the Athenaic symbols: but I may note rapidly, that her ægis, the mantle with the serpent fringes, in which she often, in the best statues, is represented as folding up her left hand, for better guard; and the Gorgon, on her shield, are both representative mainly of the chilling horror and sadness (turning men to stone, as it were), of the utmost and superficial spheres of knowledge—that knowledge which separates, in bitterness, hardness, and sorrow, the heart of the full-grown man from the heart of the child. For out of imperfect knowledge spring terror, dissension, danger, and disdain; but from perfect knowledge, given by the full-revealed Athena, strength and peace, in sign of which she is crowned with the olive spray, and bears the resistless spear.

This, then, was the Greek conception of purest Deity; and every habit of life, and every form of his art developed themselves from the seeking this bright, serene, resistless wisdom; and setting himself, as a man, to do things evermore rightly and strongly;[1] not with any ardent affection or ultimate hope; but with a resolute and continent energy of will, as knowing that for failure there

[1] It is an error to suppose that the Greek worship, or seeking, was chiefly of Beauty. It was essentially of Rightness and Strength, founded on Forethought: the principal character of Greek art is not beauty, but design: and the Dorian Apollo-worship and Athenian Virgin-worship are both expressions of adoration of divine wisdom and purity. Next to these great deities, rank, in power over the national mind, Dionysus and

was no consolation, and for sin there was no remission. And the Greek architecture rose *unerring, bright, clearly defined, and self-contained.*

Next followed in Europe the great Christian faith, which was essentially the religion of Comfort. Its great doctrine is the remission of sins; for which cause, it happens, too often, in certain phases of Christianity, that sin and sickness themselves are partly glorified, as if, the more you had to be healed of, the more divine was the healing. The practical result of this doctrine, in art, is a continual contemplation of sin and disease, and of imaginary states of purification from them; thus we have an architecture conceived in a mingled sentiment of melancholy and aspiration, partly severe, partly luxuriant, which will bend itself to every one of our needs, and every one of our fancies, and be strong or weak with us, as we are strong or weak ourselves. It is, of all architecture, the basest, when base people build it—of all, the noblest, when built by the noble.

And now note that both these religions—Greek and Mediæval—perished by falsehood in their own main purpose. The Greek religion of Wisdom perished in a false philosophy—"Oppositions of science, falsely so called." The Mediæval religion of Consolation perished in false comfort; in remission of sins given lyingly. It was the selling of absolution that ended the Mediæval faith; and I can tell you more, it is the selling of absolution which, to the end of time, will mark false Christian-

Ceres, the givers of human strength and life; then, for heroic example, Hercules. There is no Venus-worship among the Greeks in the great times: and the Muses are essentially teachers of Truth, and of its harmonies. [Ruskin's Note.]

ity. Pure Christianity gives her remission of sins only by *ending* them; but false Christianity gets her remission of sins by *compounding* for them. And there are many ways of compounding for them. We English have beautiful little quiet ways of buying absolution, whether in low Church or high, far more cunning than any of Tetzel's trading.[1]

Then, thirdly, there followed the religion of Pleasure, in which all Europe gave itself to luxury, ending in death. First, *bals masqués* in every saloon, and then guillotines in every square. And all these three worships issue in vast temple building. Your Greek worshipped Wisdom, and built you the Parthenon—the Virgin's temple. The Mediæval worshipped Consolation, and built you Virgin temples also—but to our Lady of Salvation. Then the Revivalist worshipped beauty, of a sort, and built you Versailles and the Vatican. Now, lastly, will you tell me what *we* worship, and what *we* build?

You know we are speaking always of the real, active, continual, national worship; that by which men act, while they live; not that which they talk of, when they die. Now, we have, indeed, a nominal religion, to which we pay tithes of property and sevenths of time; but we have also a practical and earnest religion, to which we devote nine-tenths of our property and sixth-sevenths of our time. And we dispute a great deal about the nominal religion: but we are all unanimous about this practical one; of which I think you will admit that the ruling goddess may be best generally described as the "*Goddess*

[1] **Tetzel's trading in Papal indulgences inspired Luther's protest which ended in the Reformation.**

of Getting-on," or "Britannia of the Market." The Athenians had an "Athena Agoraia," or Athena of the Market; but she was a subordinate type of their goddess, while our Britannia Agoraia is the principal type of ours. And all your great architectural works are, of course, built to her. It is long since you built a great cathedral; and how you would laugh at me if I proposed building a cathedral on the top of one of these hills of yours, taking it for an Acropolis! But your railroad mounds, vaster than the walls of Babylon; your railroad stations, vaster than the temple of Ephesus, and innumerable; your chimneys, how much more mighty and costly than cathedral spires! your harbor-piers; your warehouses; your exchanges!—all these are built to your great Goddess of "Getting-on"; and she has formed, and will continue to form, your architecture, as long as you worship her; and it is quite vain to ask me to tell you how to build to *her;* you know far better than I.

There might, indeed, on some theories, be a conceivably good architecture for Exchanges—that is to say, if there were any heroism in the fact or deed of exchange which might be typically carved on the outside of your building. For, you know, all beautiful architecture must be adorned with sculpture or painting; and for sculpture or painting, you must have a subject. And hitherto it has been a received opinion among the nations of the world that the only right subjects for either, were *heroisms* of some sort. Even on his pots and his flagons, the Greek put a Hercules slaying lions, or an Apollo slaying serpents, or Bacchus slaying melancholy giants, and earthborn despondencies. On his temples, the Greek put contests of great warriors in founding states, or of gods with evil spirits. On his houses and temples alike, the Christian put carvings of angels conquering devils; or of hero-martyrs exchanging this world for another: subject inappropriate, I think, to our manner of exchange here. And the Master of Christians not only left His followers without any orders as to the sculpture of affairs of exchange on the outside of buildings, but gave some strong evidence of His dislike of affairs of exchange within them. And yet there might surely be a heroism in such affairs; and all commerce become a kind of selling of doves, not impious. The wonder has always been great to me, that heroism has never been supposed to be in any wise consistent with the practice of supplying people with food, or clothes; but rather with that of quartering one's self upon them for food, and stripping them of their clothes. Spoiling of armor is an heroic deed in all ages; but the selling of clothes, old, or new, has never taken any color of magnanimity. Yet one does not see why feeding the hungry and clothing the naked should ever become base business, even when engaged in on a large scale. If one could contrive to attach the notion of conquest to them anyhow! so that, supposing there were anywhere an obstinate race, who refused to be comforted, one might take some pride in giving them compulsory comfort! and, as it were, *"occupying* a country" with one's gifts, instead of one's armies? If one could only consider it as much a victory to get a barren field sown, as to get an eared field stripped; and contend who should build villages, instead of who should "carry" them! Are not all forms of heroism conceivable in doing these serviceable deeds? You doubt who is strongest? It might be ascertained by push of spade, as well as push of sword. Who is wisest? There are witty things to be thought of in planning other business than campaigns. Who is bravest? There are always the elements to fight with, stronger than men; and nearly as merciless.

The only absolutely and unapproachably heroic element in the soldier's work seems to be—that he is paid little for it—and regularly: while you traffickers, and exchangers, and others occupied in presumably benevolent business, like to be paid much for it—and by chance. I never can make out how it is that a *knight*-errant does not expect to be paid for his trouble, but a *pedlar*-errant always does;—that people are willing to take hard knocks for nothing, but never to sell ribands cheap; that they are ready to go on fervent crusades, to recover the tomb of a buried God, but never on any travels to fulfill the orders of a living one;—that they will go anywhere barefoot to preach their faith, but must be well bribed to practise it, and are perfectly ready to give the Gospel gratis, but never the loaves and fishes.

If you chose to take the matter up on any such soldierly principle; to do your commerce, and your feeding of nations, for fixed salaries; and to be as particular about giving people the best food, and the best cloth, as soldiers are about giving them the best gunpowder, I could carve something for you on your exchange worth looking at. But I can only at present suggest decorating its frieze with pendant purses; and making its pillars broad at the base, for the sticking of bills. And in the innermost chambers of it there might be a statue of Britannia of the Market, who may have, perhaps advisably, a partridge for her crest, typical at once of her courage in fighting for noble ideas, and of her interest in game; and round its neck, the inscription in golden letters, "Perdix fovit quæ non peperit." [1] Then, for her spear, she might have a weaver's beam; and on her shield, instead of St. George's Cross, the Milanese boar, semi-fleeced, with the town of Gennesaret proper in the field; and the legend, "In the best market," [2] and her corslet, of leather, folded over her heart in the shape of a purse, with thirty slits in it, for a piece of money to go in at, on each day of the month. And I doubt not but that people would come to see your exchange, and its goddess, with applause.

Nevertheless, I want to point out to you certain strange characters in this goddess of yours. She differs from the great Greek and Mediæval deities essentially in two things—first, as to the continuance of her presumed power; secondly, as to the extent of it.

1st, as to the Continuance.

The Greek Goddess of Wisdom gave continual increase of wisdom, as the Christian Spirit of Comfort (or Comforter) continual increase of comfort. There was no question, with these, of any limit or cessation of function. But with your Agora Goddess, that is just the most important question. Getting on—but where to? Gathering together—but how much? Do you mean to gather always—never to spend? If so, I wish you joy of your goddess, for I am just as well off as you, without the trouble of worshipping her at all. But if you do

[1] *Jeremiah* xvii, 11 (best in Septuagint and Vulgate). "As the partridge, fostering what she brought not forth, so he that getteth riches not by right shall leave them in the midst of his days, and at his end shall be a fool." [Ruskin's note.]

[2] Meaning fully, "We have brought our pigs to it." [Ruskin's note.]

not spend, somebody else will—somebody else must. And it is because of this (among many other such errors) that I have fearlessly declared your so-called science of Political Economy to be no science; because, namely, it has omitted the study of exactly the most important branch of the business—the study of *spending.* For spend you must, and as much as you make, ultimately. You gather corn:—will you bury England under a heap of grain; or will you, when you have gathered, finally eat? You gather gold:—will you make your house-roofs of it, or pave your streets with it? That is still one way of spending it. But if you keep it, that you may get more, I'll give you more; I'll give you all the gold you want—all you can imagine—if you can tell me what you'll do with it. You shall have thousands of gold pieces;—thousands of thousands—millions—mountains, of gold: where will you keep them? Will you put an Olympus of silver upon a golden Pelion—make Ossa like a wart? Do you think the rain and dew would then come down to you, in the stream from such mountains, more blessedly than they will down the mountains which God has made for you, of moss and whinstone? But it is not gold that you want to gather! What is it? greenbacks? No; not those neither! What is it then —is it ciphers after a capital I? Cannot you practise writing ciphers, and write as many as you want? Write ciphers for an hour every morning, in a big book, and say every evening, I am worth all those noughts more than I was yesterday. Won't that do? Well, what in the name of Plutus is it you want? Not gold, not greenbacks, not ciphers after a capital I? You will have to answer, after all, "No; we want, somehow or other, money's *worth.*" Well, what is that? Let your Goddess of Getting-on discover it, and let her learn to stay therein.

2d. But there is yet another question to be asked respecting this Goddess of Getting-on. The first was of the continuance of her power; the second is of its extent.

Pallas and the Madonna were supposed to be all the world's Pallas, and all the world's Madonna. They could teach all men, and they could comfort all men. But, look strictly into the nature of the power of your Goddess of Getting-on; and you will find she is the Goddess—not of everybody's getting on—but only of somebody's getting on. This is a vital, or rather deathful, distinction. Examine it in your own ideal of the state of national life which this Goddess is to evoke and maintain. I asked you what it was, when I was last here;—you have never told me.[1] Now, shall I try to tell you?

Your ideal of human life then is, I think, that it should be passed in a pleasant undulating world, with iron and coal everywhere underneath it. On each pleasant bank of this world is to be a beautiful mansion, with two wings; and stables and coach-houses; a moderately-sized park; a large garden and hot-houses; and pleasant carriage drives through the shrubberies. In this mansion are to live the favored votaries of the Goddess; the English gentleman, with his gracious wife, and his beautiful family; always able to have the boudoir and the jewels for the wife, and the beautiful ball dresses for

[1] Refers to a lecture on *Modern Manufacture and Design,* delivered at Bradford, March 1, 1859, published later as Lecture III in *The Two Paths.*

the daughters, and hunters for the sons, and a shooting in the Highlands for himself. At the bottom of the bank, is to be the mill; not less than a quarter of a mile long, with a steam engine at each end, and two in the middle, and a chimney three hundred feet high. In this mill are to be in constant employment from eight hundred to a thousand workers, who never drink, never strike, always go to church on Sunday, and always express themselves in respectful language.

Is not that, broadly, and in the main features, the kind of thing you propose to yourselves? It is very pretty indeed seen from above; not at all so pretty, seen from below. For, observe, while to one family this deity is indeed the Goddess of Getting-on, to a thousand families she is the Goddess of *not* Getting-on. "Nay," you say, "they have all their chance." Yes, so has every one in a lottery, but there must always be the same number of blanks. "Ah! but in a lottery it is not skill and intelligence which take the lead, but blind chance." What then! do you think the old practice, that "they should take who have the power, and they should keep who can," is less iniquitous, when the power has become power of brains instead of fist? and that, though we may not take advantage of a child's or a woman's weakness, we may of a man's foolishness? "Nay, but finally, work must be done, and some one must be at the top, some one at the bottom." Granted, my friends. Work must always be, and captains of work must always be; and if you in the least remember the tone of any of my writings, you must know that they are thought unfit for this age, because they are always insisting on need of government, and speaking with scorn of liberty. But I beg you to observe that there is a wide difference between being captains or governors of work, and taking the profits of it. It does not follow, because you are general of an army, that you are to take all the treasure, or land, it wins; (if it fight for treasure or land;) neither, because you are king of a nation, that you are to consume all the profits of the nation's work. Real kings, on the contrary, are known invariably by their doing quite the reverse of this,—by their taking the least possible quantity of the nation's work for themselves. There is no test of real kinghood so infallible as that. Does the crowned creature live simply, bravely, unostentatiously? probably he *is* a King. Does he cover his body with jewels, and his table with delicates? in all probability he is *not* a King. It is possible he may be, as Solomon was; but that is when the nation shares his splendor with him. Solomon made gold, not only to be in his own palace as stones, but to be in Jerusalem as stones. But, even so, for the most part, these splendid kinghoods expire in ruin, and only the true kinghoods live, which are of royal laborers governing loyal laborers; who, both leading rough lives, establish the true dynasties. Conclusively you will find that because you are king of a nation, it does not follow that you are to gather for yourself all the wealth of that nation; neither, because you are king of a small part of the nation, and lord over the means of its maintenance—over field, or mill, or mine,—are you to take all the produce of that piece of the foundation of national existence for yourself.

You will tell me I need not preach against these things, for I cannot mend them. No, good friends, I cannot; but you can, and you will; or something else can and will. Even good things have no abiding power—and shall these evil things persist in victorious evil? All history shows, on the contrary, that to be the exact thing they never can do. Change *must* come; but it is ours to determine whether change of growth, or change of death. Shall the Parthenon be in ruins on its rock, and Bolton priory in its meadow, but these mills of yours be the consummation of the buildings of the earth, and their wheels be as the wheels of eternity? Think you that "men may come, and men may go," but—mills—go on for ever? Not so; out of these, better or worse shall come; and it is for you to choose which.

I know that none of this wrong is done with deliberate purpose. I know, on the contrary, that you wish your workmen well; that you do much for them, and that you desire to do more for them, if you saw your way to such benevolence safely. I know that even all this wrong and misery are brought about by a warped sense of duty, each of you striving to do his best; but, unhappily, not knowing for whom this best should be done. And all our hearts have been betrayed by the plausible impiety of the modern economist, telling us that, "To do the best for ourselves, is finally to do the best for others." Friends, our great Master said not so; and most absolutely we shall find this world is not made so. Indeed, to do the best for others, is finally to do the best of ourselves; but it will not do to have our eyes fixed on that issue. The Pagans had got beyond that. Hear what a Pagan says of this matter; hear what were, perhaps, the last written words of Plato,—if not the last actually written (for this we cannot know), yet assuredly in fact and power his parting words—in which, endeavoring to give full crowning and harmonious close to all his thoughts, and to speak the sum of them by the imagined sentence of the Great Spirit, his strength and his heart fail him, and the words cease, broken off for ever. They are at the close of the dialogue called *Critias,* in which he describes, partly from real tradition, partly in ideal dream, the early state of Athens; and the genesis, and order, and religion, of the fabled isle of Atlantis; in which genesis he conceives the same first perfection and final degeneracy of man, which in our own Scriptural tradition is expressed by saying that the Sons of God inter-married with the daughters of men, for he supposes the earliest race to have been indeed the children of God; and to have corrupted themselves, until "their spot was not the spot of his children." And this, he says, was the end; that indeed "through many generations, so long as the God's nature in them yet was full, they were submissive to the sacred laws, and carried themselves lovingly to all that had kindred with them in divineness; for their uttermost spirit was faithful and true, and in every wise great; so that, in *all meekness of wisdom, they dealt with each other,* and took all the chances of life; and despising all things except virtue, they cared little what happened day by day, and *bore lightly the burden* of gold and of possessions; for they saw that, if *only their common love and virtue increased, all these things would be increased together with them;* but to set their esteem and ardent pursuit upon material possession would be to lose that first, and their virtue and affection together with it. And by such reasoning, and what of the divine nature remained in them, they gained all this greatness of which we have already told;

but when the God's part of them faded and became extinct, being mixed again and again, and effaced by the prevalent mortality; and the human nature at last exceeded, they then became unable to endure the courses of fortune; and fell into shapelessness of life, and baseness in the sight of him who could see, having lost everything that was fairest of their honor; while to the blind hearts which could not discern the true life, tending to happiness, it seemed that they were then chiefly noble and happy, being filled with an iniquity of inordinate possession and power. Whereupon, the God of Gods, whose Kinghood is in laws, beholding a once just nation thus cast into misery, and desiring to lay such punishment upon them as might make them repent into restraining, gathered together all the gods into his dwelling-place, which from heaven's center overlooks whatever has part in creation; and having assembled them, he said"——

The rest is silence. Last words of the chief wisdom of the heathen, spoken of this idol of riches; this idol of yours; this golden image, high by measureless cubits, set up where your green fields of England are furnace-burnt into the likeness of the plain of Dura: this idol, forbidden to us, first of all idols, by our own Master and faith; forbidden to us also by every human lip that has ever, in any age or people, been accounted of as able to speak according to the purposes of God. Continue to make that forbidden deity your principal one, and soon no more art, no more science, no more pleasure will be possible. Catastrophe will come; or, worse than catastrophe, slow moldering and withering into Hades. But if you can fix some conception of a true human state of life to be striven for—life, good for all men, as for yourselves; if you can determine some honest and simple order of existence; following those trodden ways of wisdom, which are pleasantness, and seeking her quiet and withdrawn paths, which are peace;—then, and so sanctifying wealth into "commonwealth," all your art, your literature, your daily labors, your domestic affection, and citizen's duty, will join and increase into one magnificent harmony. You will know then how to build, well enough; you will build with stone well, but with flesh better; temples not made with hands, but riveted of hearts; and that kind of marble, crimson-veined, is indeed eternal.

SCIENCE

Science refuses to imagine, refuses to believe or to be content. It is inspired with only one motive: a curiosity to discover what the facts are.

—C. H. Ward

HOW AGASSIZ TAUGHT ME TO SEE[1]

NATHANIEL SOUTHGATE SHALER

[Nathaniel Southgate Shaler (1841–1906) was born at Newport, Kentucky. He graduated from Harvard in 1862, served in the army during the Civil War, was professor of geology at Harvard from 1868 to 1906, and after 1891 was dean of the Scientific School. Dean Shaler was one of America's greatest teachers.]

[Louis Agassiz (1807–1873) was born in Switzerland, received his advanced education in German universities, and had achieved an international reputation for his discoveries in ichthyology and in the nature of glaciers before he came to America in 1846. As professor of zoölogy and geology at Harvard he became one of the great founders of American science. Like his pupil, Dean Shaler, he was a remarkable teacher. His method is related in the following incident, one of the most famous in the annals of American education.]

AGASSIZ'S laboratory was then in a rather small two-storied building looking much like a square dwelling house, which stood where the College Gymnasium now stands. . . . Agassiz had recently moved into it from a shed on the marsh near Brighton Bridge, the original tenants, the engineers, having come to riches in the shape of the brick structure now known as the Lawrence Building. In this primitive establishment Agassiz's laboratory, as distinguished from the

[1] From *The Autobiography of Nathaniel Southgate Shaler.* Reprinted with the permission of and by special arrangement with the publishers, Houghton Mifflin Co.

storerooms where the collections were crammed, occupied one room about thirty feet long and fifteen feet wide—what is now the west room on the lower floor of the edifice. In this place, already packed, I had assigned to me a small pine table with a rusty tin pan upon it. . . .

When I sat me down before my tin pan, Agassiz brought me a small fish, placing it before me with the rather stern requirement that I should study it, but should on no account talk to any one concerning it, nor read anything relating to fishes, until I had his permission to do so. To my inquiry, "What shall I do?" he said in effect: "Find out what you can without damaging the specimen: when I think that you have done the work, I will question you." In the course of an hour I thought I had compassed that fish; it was rather an unsavory object, giving forth the stench of old alcohol, then loathsome to me, though in time I came to like it. Many of the scales were loosened so that they fell off. It appeared to me to be a case for a summary report, which I was anxious to make and get on to the next stage of the business. But Agassiz, though always within call, concerned himself no further with me that day, nor the next, nor for a week. At first, this neglect was distressing; but I saw that it was a game, for he was, as I discerned rather than saw, covertly watching me. So I set my wits to work upon the thing, and in the course of a hundred hours or so thought I had done much—a hundred times as much as seemed possible at the start. I got interested in finding out how the scales went in series, their shape, the form and placement of the teeth, etc. Finally, I felt full of the subject, and probably expressed it in my bearing; as for words about it, then, there were none from my master except his cheery "Good morning." At length, on the seventh day, came the question, "Well?" and my disgorge of learning to him as he sat on the edge of my table, puffing his cigar. At the end of the hour's telling, he swung off and away, saying: "That is not right." Here I began to think that, after all, perhaps the rules for scanning Latin verse were not the worst infliction in the world. Moreover, it was clear that he was playing a game with me to find if I were capable of doing hard, continuous work without the support of a teacher, and this stimulated me to labor. I went at the task anew, discarded my first notes, and in another week of ten hours a day labor I had results which astonished myself, and satisfied him. Still there was no trace of praise in word or manner. He signified that it would do by placing before me about a half a peck of bones, telling me to see what I could make of them, with no further directions to guide me. I soon found that they were the skeletons of half a dozen fishes of different species—the jaws told me so much at a first inspection. The task evidently was to fit the separate bones together in their proper order. Two months or more went to this task, with no other help than an occasional looking over my grouping, with the stereotyped remark: "That is not right." Finally, the task was done, and I was again set upon alcoholic specimens—this time a remarkable lot of specimens, representing perhaps twenty species of the side-swimmers or *Pleuronectidæ*.

I shall never forget the sense of power in dealing with things which I felt in beginning the more extended work on a group of animals. I had learned the art of comparing objects, which is the basis of the naturalist's work. At this stage I was allowed to read and to discuss my work with others about me. I did both eagerly, and acquired a considerable knowledge of the literature of ichthyology, becoming especially interested in the system of classification, then most imperfect. I tried to follow Agassiz's scheme of division into the order of ctenoids and ganoids, with the result that I found one of my species of side-swimmers had cycloid scales on one side and ctenoid on the other. This not only shocked my sense of the value of classification in a way that permitted of no full recovery of my original respect for the process, but for a time shook my confidence in my master's knowledge. At the same time I had a malicious pleasure in exhibiting my *find* to him, expecting to repay in part the humiliation which he had evidently tried to inflict on my conceit. To my question as to how the nondescript should be classified, he said: "My boy, there are now two of us who know that."

This incident of the fish made an end of my novitiate. After that, with a suddenness of transition which puzzled me, Agassiz became very communicative; we passed, indeed, into the relation of friends of like age and purpose, and he actually consulted me as to what I should like to take up as a field of study. Finding that I wished to devote myself to geology he set me to work on the *Brachiopoda* as the best group of fossils to serve as data in determining the Palæozoic horizons. So far as his rather limited knowledge of the matter went, he guided me in the field about Cambridge, in my reading, and to acquaintances of his who were concerned with earth structures.

THE METHOD OF SCIENTIFIC INVESTIGATION[1]

Thomas Henry Huxley

[Thomas Henry Huxley (1825–1895) was born at Ealing, a suburb of London. After serving as surgeon in the British Navy, he was for thirty-two years professor of natural history at the Royal School of Mines. He was the greatest popularizer of science in the 19th century.]

THE method of scientific investigation is nothing but the expression of the necessary mode of working of the human mind. It is simply the mode at which all phenomena are reasoned about, rendered precise and exact. There is no more difference, but there is just the same kind of difference, between the mental operations of a man of science and those of an ordinary person, as there is between the operations and methods of a baker or of a butcher weighing out his goods in common scales, and the operations of a chemist in performing a difficult and complex analysis by means of his balance and finely-graduated weights. It is not that the action of the scales in the one case, and the balance in the other, differ in the principles of their construction or manner of working; but the beam of one is set on an infinitely finer axis than the other, and of course turns by the addition of a much smaller weight.

[1] From *Collected Essays.* Reprinted by permission of and arangement with D. Appleton & Company the authorized publishers.

You will understand this better, perhaps, if I give you some familiar example. You have all heard it repeated, I dare say, that men of science work by means of Induction and Deduction, and that by the help of these operations, they, in a sort of sense, wring from Nature certain other things, which are called Natural Laws, and Causes, and that out of these, by some cunning skill of their own, they build up Hypotheses and Theories. And it is imagined by many, that the operations of the common mind can be by no means compared with these processes, and that they have to be acquired by a sort of special apprenticeship to the craft. To hear all these large words, you would think that the mind of a man of science must be constituted differently from that of his fellow-men; but if you will not be frightened by terms, you will discover that you are quite wrong, and that all these terrible apparatus are being used by yourselves every day and every hour of your lives.

There is a well-known incident in one of Molière's plays, where the author makes the hero express unbounded delight on being told that he had been talking prose during the whole of his life. In the same way, I trust that you will take comfort, and be delighted with yourselves, on the discovery that you have been acting on the principles of inductive and deductive philosophy during the same period. Probably there is not one here who has not in the course of the day had occasion to set in motion a complex train of reasoning, of the very same kind, though differing of course in degree, as that which a scientific man goes through in tracing the causes of natural phenomena.

A very trivial circumstance will serve to exemplify

this. Suppose you go into a fruiterer's shop, wanting an apple,—you take up one, and, on biting it, you find it sour; you look at it, and see that it is hard and green. You take up another one, and that too is hard, green, and sour. The shopman offers you a third; but, before biting it you examine it, and find that it is hard and green, and you immediately say that you will not have it, as it must be sour, like those that you have already tried.

Nothing can be more simple than that, you think; but if you will take the trouble to analyze and trace out into its logical elements what has been done by the mind, you will be greatly surprised. In the first place, you have performed the operation of Induction. You found that, in two experiences, hardness and greenness in apples went together with sourness. It was so in the first case, and it was confirmed by the second. True, it is a very small basis, but still it is enough to make an induction from; you generalize the facts, and you expect to find sourness in apples where you get hardness and greenness. You found upon that a general law, that all hard and green apples are sour; and that, so far as it goes, is a perfect induction. Well, having got your natural law in this way, when you are offered another apple which you find is hard and green, you say, "All hard and green apples are sour; this apple is hard and green, therefore this apple is sour." That train of reasoning is what logicians call a syllogism, and has all its various parts and terms,—its major premise, its minor premise, and its conclusion. And, by the help of further reasoning, which, if drawn out, would have to be exhibited in two or three other syllogisms, you arrive at your final determination, "I will not have that apple." So that, you see, you have in the first place, established a law by Induction, and upon that you have founded a Deduction, and reasoned out the special conclusion of the particular case. Well now, suppose, having got your law, that at some time afterward, you are discussing the qualities of apples with a friend: you will say to him, "It is a very curious thing,—but I find that all hard and green apples are sour!" Your friend says to you, "But how do you know that?" You at once reply, "Oh, because I have tried them over and over again, and have always found them to be so." Well, if we were talking science instead of common sense, we should call that an Experimental Verification. And, if still opposed, you go further, and say, "I have heard from the people in Somersetshire and Devonshire, where a large number of apples are grown, that they have observed the same thing. It is also found to be the case in Normandy, and in North America. In short, I find it to be the universal experience of mankind wherever attention has been directed to the subject." Whereupon, your friend, unless he is a very unreasonable man, agrees with you, and is convinced that you are quite right in the conclusion you have drawn. He believes, although perhaps he does not know he believes it, that the more extensive verifications are,—that the more frequently experiments have been made, and results of the same kind arrived at,—that the more varied the conditions under which the same results are attained, the more certain is the ultimate conclusion, and he disputes the question no further. He sees that the experiment has been tried under all sorts of conditions, as to time, place, and people, with the same result; and he says with you, therefore, that the law you have laid down must be a good one, and he must believe it.

In science we do the same thing,—the philosopher exercises precisely the same faculties, though in a much more delicate manner. In scientific inquiry it becomes a matter of duty to expose a supposed law to every possible kind of verification, and to take care, moreover, that this is done intentionally, and not left to a mere accident, as in the case of the apples. And in science, as in common life, our confidence in a law is in exact proportion to the absence of variation in the result of our experimental verifications. For instance, if you let go your grasp of an article you may have in your hand, it will immediately fall to the ground. That is a very common verification of one of the best established laws of nature —that of gravitation. The method by which men of science establish the existence of that law is exactly the same as that by which we have established the trivial proposition about the sourness of hard and green apples. But we believe it in such an extensive, thorough, and unhesitating manner because the universal experience of mankind verifies it, and we can verify it ourselves at any time; and that is the strongest possible foundation on which any natural law can rest.

So much, then, by way of proof that the method of establishing laws in science is exactly the same as that pursued in common life. Let us now turn to another matter (though really it is but another phase of the same question), and that is, the method by which, from the relations of certain phenomena, we prove that some stand in the position of causes toward the others.

I want to put the case clearly before you, and I will

therefore show you what I mean by another familiar example. I will suppose that one of you, on coming down in the morning to the parlor of your house, finds that a tea-pot and some spoons which had been left in the room on the previous evening are gone,—the window is open, and you observe the mark of a dirty hand on the window-frame, and perhaps, in addition to that, you notice the impress of a hob-nailed shoe on the gravel outside. All these phenomena have struck your attention instantly, and before two seconds have passed you say, "Oh, somebody has broken open the window, entered the room, and run off with the spoons and the tea-pot!" That speech is out of your mouth in a moment. And you will probably add, "I know there has; I am quite sure of it!" You mean to say exactly what you know; but in reality you are giving expression to what is, in all essential particulars, an Hypothesis. You do not *know* it at all; it is nothing but an hypothesis rapidly framed in your own mind! And, it is an hypothesis founded on a long train of inductions and deductions.

What are those inductions and deductions, and how have you got at this hypothesis? You have observed, in the first place, that the window is open; but by a train of reasoning involving many Inductions and Deductions, you have probably arrived long before at the General Law—and a very good one it is—that windows do not open of themselves; and you therefore conclude that something has opened the window. A second general law that you have arrived at in the same way is, that tea-pots and spoons do not go out of a window spontaneously, and you are satisfied that, as they are not now where you left them, they have been removed. In the third place, you look at the marks on the window-sill, and the shoe-marks outside, and you say that in all previous experience the former kind of mark has never been produced by anything else but the hand of a human being; and the same experience shows that no other animal but man at present wears shoes with hob-nails in them such as would produce the marks in the gravel. I do not know, even if we could discover any of those "missing links" that are talked about, that they would help us to any other conclusion! At any rate the law which states our present experience is strong enough for my present purpose. You next reach the conclusion, that as these kinds of marks have not been left by any other animals than men, or are liable to be formed in any other way than by a man's hand and shoe, the marks in question have been formed by a man in that way. You have, further, a general law, founded on observation and experience, and that, too, is, I am sorry to say, a very universal and unimpeachable one,—that some men are thieves; and you assume at once from all these premises—and that is what constitutes your hypothesis—that the man who made the marks outside and on the window-sill, opened the window, got in the room, and stole your tea-pot and spoons. You have now arrived at a *Vera Causa;*—you have assumed a Cause which it is plain is competent to produce all the phenomena you have observed. You can explain all these phenomena only by the hypothesis of a thief. But that is a hypothetical conclusion, of the justice of which you have no absolute proof at all; it is only rendered highly probable by a series of inductive and deductive reasonings.

I suppose your first action, assuming that you are a man of ordinary common sense, and that you have established this hypothesis to your own satisfaction, will very likely be to go off for the police, and set them on the track of the burglar, with the view to the recovery of your property. But just as you are starting with this object, some person comes in, and on learning what you are about, says, "My good friend, you are going on a great deal too fast. How do you know that the man who really made the marks took the spoons? It might have been a monkey that took them, and the man may have merely looked in afterward." You would probably reply, "Well, that is all very well, but you see it is contrary to all experience of the way tea-pots and spoons are abstracted; so that, at any rate, your hypothesis is less probable than mine." While you are talking the thing over in this way, another friend arrives, one of that good kind of people that I was talking of a little while ago. And he might say, "Oh, my dear sir, you are certainly going on a great deal too fast. You are most presumptuous. You admit that all these occurrences took place when you were fast asleep, at a time when you could not possibly have known anything about what was taking place. How do you know that the laws of Nature were not suspended during the night? It may be that there has been some kind of supernatural interference in this case." In point of fact, he declares that your hypothesis is one of which you cannot at all demonstrate the truth, and that you are by no means sure that the laws of Nature are the same when you are asleep as when you are awake.

Well, now, you cannot at the moment answer that

kind of reasoning. You feel that your worthy friend has you somewhat at a disadvantage. You will feel perfectly convinced in your own mind, however, that you are quite right, and you say to him, "My good friend, I can only be guided by the natural probabilities of the case, and if you will be kind enough to stand aside and permit me to pass, I will go and fetch the police." Well, we will suppose that your journey is successful, and that by good luck you meet with a policeman; that eventually the burglar is found with your property on his person, and the marks correspond to his hand and of the shoes. Probably any jury would consider those facts a very good experimental verification of your hypothesis, touching the cause of the abnormal phenomena observed in your parlor, and would act accordingly.

Now, in this supposititious case, I have taken phenomena of a very common kind, in order that you might see what are the different steps in an ordinary process of reasoning, if you will only take the trouble to analyze it carefully. All the operations I have described, you will see, are involved in the mind of any man of sense in leading him to a conclusion as to the course he should take in order to make good a robbery and punish the offender. I say that you are led, in that case, to your conclusion by exactly the same train of reasoning as that which a man of science pursues when he is endeavoring to discover the origin and laws of the most occult phenomena. The process is, and always must be, the same; and precisely the same mode of reasoning was employed by Newton and Laplace in their endeavors to discover and define the causes of the movements of the heavenly bodies, as you, with your own common sense, would employ to detect a burglar. The only difference is, that the nature of the inquiry being more abstruse, every step has to be most carefully watched, so that there may not be a single crack or flaw in your hypothesis. A flaw or crack in many of the hypotheses of daily life may be of little or no moment as affecting the general correctness of the conclusions at which we may arrive; but in a scientific inquiry a fallacy, great or small, is always of importance, and is sure to be in the long run constantly productive of mischievous, if not fatal results.

Do not allow yourselves to be misled by the common notion that an hypothesis is untrustworthy simply because it is an hypothesis. It is often urged, in respect to some scientific conclusion, that, after all, it is only an hypothesis. But what more have we to guide us in nine-tenths of the most important affairs of daily life than hypothesis, and often very ill-based ones? So that in science, where the evidence of an hypothesis is subjected to the most rigid examination, we may rightly pursue the same course. You may have hypotheses and hypotheses. A man may say, if he likes, that the moon is made of green cheese: that is an hypothesis. But another man, who has devoted a great deal of time and attention to the subject, and availed himself of the most powerful telescopes and the results of the observations of others, declares that in his opinion it is probably composed of materials very similar to those of which our own earth is made up: and that is also only an hypothesis. But I need not tell you that there is an enormous difference in the value of the two hypotheses. That one which is based on sound scientific knowledge is sure to have a corresponding value; and that which is a mere hasty, random guess, is likely to have but little value. Every great step in our progress in discovering causes has been made in exactly the same way as that which I have detailed to you. A person observing the occurrence of certain facts and phenomena asks, naturally enough, what process, what kind of operation known to occur in nature applied to the particular case, will unravel and explain the mystery? Hence you have the scientific hypothesis; and its value will be proportionate to the care and completeness with which its basis had been tested and verified. It is in these matters as in the commonest affairs of practical life: the guess of the fool will be folly, while the guess of the wise man will contain wisdom. In all cases, you see that the value of the result depends on the patience and faithfulness with which the investigator applies to his hypothesis every possible kind of verification.

THE STRUGGLE FOR EXISTENCE

CHARLES DARWIN

[Charles Darwin (1809–1882) was born at Shrewsbury, Shropshire, England, and studied at Edinburgh and Cambridge Universities. In 1831, on his celebrated voyage in *The Beagle* to South America and the Pacific, he made many observations of plants and animals which after arduous investigations he used to support the theories of his epoch-making book, *The Origin of Species,* published in 1859. In this work and in *The Descent of Man* (1871) he gave the world the doctrine of evolution which has been associated with his name and which has been the most influential scientific doctrine of the past century.]

NOTHING is easier than to admit in words the truth of the universal struggle for life, or more difficult—at least I have found it so—than constantly to bear this conclusion in mind. Yet unless it be thoroughly engrained in the mind, the whole economy of nature, with every fact on extinction and variation, will be dimly seen or quite misunderstood. We behold the face of nature bright with gladness; we often see superabundance of food; we do not see, or we forget, that the birds which are idly singing round us mostly live on insects or seeds, and are thus constantly destroying life; or we forget how largely these songsters, or their eggs or nestlings, are destroyed by birds and beasts of prey; we do not always bear in mind that food is not abundant at all seasons of each recurring year.

A struggle for existence inevitably follows from the

high rate at which all organic beings tend to increase. Every being which during its natural lifetime produces several eggs or seeds must suffer destruction during some period of its life; and during some season or otherwise, on the principle of geometrical increase, its numbers would quickly become so inordinately great that no country could support the product. Hence, as more individuals are produced than can possibly survive, there must in every case be a struggle for existence—either one individual with another or with the physical conditions of life.

There is no exception to the rule that every organic being naturally increases at so high a rate that, if not destroyed, the earth would soon be covered by the progeny of a single pair. We have better evidence on this subject than mere theoretical calculation,—namely, the numerous recorded cases of the astonishingly rapid increase of various animals in a state of nature when circumstances have been favorable to them during two or three seasons. If the statement of the rate of increase of slow-breeding cattle and horses in South America, and latterly in Australia, had not been well authenticated, they would have been incredible. So it is with plants. Cases could be given of introduced plants which have become common throughout whole islands in a period of less than ten years. Several of the plants which are now the commonest over the whole plains of La Plata have been introduced from Europe. In such cases—and endless others could be given—no one supposes that the fertility of the animals or plants has been suddenly increased. The obvious explanation is that the conditions of life have been highly favorable, and that there has consequently been less destruction of the old and young, and that nearly all the young have been enabled to breed. Their geometrical ratio of increase, the result of which never fails to be surprising, simply explains their extraordinary rapid increase and wide diffusion in their new homes.

In a state of nature almost every full-grown plant annually produces seed, and among animals there are very few which do not annually pair. Hence we may confidently assert that all plants and animals are tending to increase at a geometrical ratio—that all would rapidly stock every station in which they could anyhow exist—and that this geometrical tendency to increase must be checked by destruction at some period of life. In looking at nature it is most necessary to keep the foregoing considerations always in mind—never to forget that every single organic being may be said to be striving to the utmost to increase in numbers, that each lives by a struggle at some period of its life, that heavy destruction inevitably falls either on the young or old during each generation or at recurrent intervals. Lighten any check, mitigate the destruction ever so little, and the number of the species will increase to any amount.

The causes which check the natural tendency of each species to increase are most obscure. I will make only a few remarks, just to recall to the reader's mind some of the chief points. Eggs or very young animals seem generally to suffer most. With plants there is a vast destruction of seeds. Seedlings, also, are destroyed in vast numbers by various enemies; for instance, climate plays an important part in determining the average number of a species, and periodical seasons of extreme cold or drought seem to be the most effective of all checks. I estimated that the winter of 1854–5 destroyed four-fifths of the birds in my own grounds; and this is a tremendous destruction. Climate acts chiefly in reducing food, thus bringing on the most severe struggle between the individuals. Even when extreme cold acts directly, it will be the least vigorous individuals which will suffer most. Each species is constantly suffering enormous destruction at some period of its life from enemies or from competitors for the same place and food; and if these enemies or competitors be in the least degree favored by any slight change of climate they will increase in numbers; and as each area is already fully stocked with inhabitants, the other species must decrease.

What a struggle must have gone on during long centuries between the several kinds of trees, each annually scattering its seeds by the thousand; what war between insect and insect, all striving to increase, all feeding on each other, or on the trees or their seeds and seedlings, or on the other plants which first clothed the ground and thus checked the growth of the trees! Throw up a handful of feathers, and all fall to the ground according to definite laws; but how simple is the problem of where each shall fall, compared to that of the action and reaction of the innumerable plants and animals which have determined, in the course of centuries, the proportional numbers and kinds of trees now growing.

The struggle will almost invariably be most severe between the individuals of the same species, for they frequent the same districts, require the same food, and are exposed to the same dangers. For instance, if several varieties of wheat be sown together, and the mixed seed be resown, some of the varieties which best suit the soil or climate, or are naturally the most fertile, will beat the others and so yield more seed, and will consequently in a few years supplant the other varieties. To keep up a mixed stock of sweet peas they must be each year harvested separately; otherwise the weaker kinds will steadily decrease in number and disappear. It may be doubted whether the varieties of any of our domestic plants or animals could be kept up for half a dozen generations if they were allowed to struggle together in the same manner as beings in a state of nature.

The recent extension over parts of the United States of one species of swallow has caused the decrease of another species. The recent increase of the missel thrush in parts of Scotland has caused the decrease of the song thrush. How frequently we hear of one species of rat taking the place of another species under the most different climates. In Russia the small Asiatic cockroach has everywhere driven before it its great relative. In Australia the imported hive bee is rapidly exterminating the small, stingless native bee. One species of wild mustard has been known to supplant another species.

A corollary of the highest importance may be deduced from the foregoing remarks—namely, that the structure of every organic being is related, in the most essential yet often hidden manner, to that of all the other organic beings with which it comes into competition for food or residence, or from which it has to escape, or on which it preys. This is obvious in the structure of the teeth and talons of the tiger, and in that of the legs and claws of the parasite which clings to the hair on the tiger's body; in the beautifully plumed seed of the dandelion and in the flattened and fringed legs of the water beetle. The advantage of plumed seeds no doubt stands in the closest relation to the land being already clothed with other plants; so that the seeds may be widely distributed and fall on unoccupied ground. In the water beetle the structure of its legs, so well adapted for diving, allows it to compete with other aquatic insects, to hunt for its own prey, and to escape serving as prey to other animals.

The store of nutriment laid up within the seeds of many plants seems at first sight to have no sort of relation to other plants. But from the strong growth of young plants produced from such seeds when sown in the midst of long grass it may be suspected that the chief use of the nutriment in the seed is to favor the growth of the seedlings while struggling with other plants growing vigorously all around.

Look at a plant in the midst of its range. Why does it not double or quadruple its numbers? We know that it can perfectly well withstand a little more heat or cold, dampness or dryness; for elsewhere it ranges into slightly hotter or colder, damper or drier districts. In this case we can clearly see that if we wish, in imagination, to give the plant the power of increasing in number, we should have to give it some advantage over its competitors, or over the animals which prey on it. Not until we reach the extreme confines of life, in the Arctic regions or on the borders of an utter desert, will competition cease. The land may be extremely cold or dry, yet there will be competition between some few species for the warmest or dampest spots.

Hence we can see that when a plant or animal is placed in a new country among new competitors, the conditions of its life will generally be changed in an essential manner, although the climate may be exactly the same as in its former home. If its average numbers are to increase in its new home, we should have to modify it in a different way from what we should have had to do in its native country; for we should have to give it some advantage over a different set of competitors or enemies.

Each organic being is striving to increase in a geometrical ratio; each at some period of its life, during some season of the year, during each generation or at intervals, has to struggle for life and to suffer great destruction. When we reflect on this struggle, we may console ourselves with the full belief that the war of nature is not incessant, that no fear is felt, that death is generally prompt, and that the vigorous, the healthy, and the happy survive and multiply.

SCIENCE FROM THE SIDE-LINES[1]

EDWIN E. SLOSSON

[Edwin Emery Slosson was born at Albany, Kansas, in 1865. He was educated at the state university. From 1903 to 1920 he was literary editor of *The Independent* and he is now director of Science Service, Washington, D. C., an organization formed to popularize scientific knowledge. He has written a number of widely read books which carry out the same purpose. Among these are *Creative Chemistry, Chats on Science,* and *Keeping up with Science.*]

I

SCIENCE is advancing more rapidly than ever and is more quickly applied to the needs of life. But the scientific habit of mind is not common or commonly respected. The material contributions of science to our comfort and luxury are accepted as a matter of course with little thought about the prolonged process of research that precedes the practical application.

Science is more than the father of invention. We can get from the reading of science not only new things to think about, but, what is more important, new ways of thinking about things.

Any one who desires to keep in touch with the progress of the world naturally wants to know in a general way what is being done in the various fields of science. But,

[1] From *Chats on Science.* Reprinted by permission of and arrangement with the Century Co.

unfortunately, he does not find it so easy to follow current movements in science as he does in literature, art, music, politics, and other forms of human activity. Science is mostly printed in a foreign language not only when it appears in French, German, Russian, or Japanese, but also when it seems at first sight to be in ordinary English. Translators of foreign tongues are common and competent, but there are comparatively few writers engaged in the interpretation of technical literature for the layman.

II

Science is more than a wonder-worker. Wonders never cease, but we soon cease to wonder at them. Wonder is a fugitive emotion. A "nine-days' wonder" is the normal longevity, and there is no reason why it should live longer, for there are more profitable attitudes. Even when science surprises us by depriving a familiar thing of some attribute deemed essential we do not miss it long. We are quite accustomed to the idea of wireless telephones, smokeless powder, horseless trucks, voiceless drama, fatherless frogs, leatherless soles, strawless straws, tonsilless children, caffeinless coffee, kickless drinks, seedless oranges, and typeless printing.

When a baby sees a strange object,—and to a baby all objects are strange,—he first opens his mouth and stares at it; next, he sticks out his finger and tries to touch it; third, he grabs it and tries to do something with it. These are the three stages through which persons and races pass in their attitude toward the unknown in nature: wonder, curiosity, utilization. The first sentence of each new chapter of the *History of Human Progress* (by various authors, Published in Parts) ends with! Later sentences may be punctuated with? and finally perhaps with $.

Some persons and peoples remain always in the earliest infantile attitude of empty awe, and take pride in it. They do not even attempt to pass to the stage of idle curiosity, as does the normal child. From the open mouth to the open mind is often a long and toilsome progress in the history of the race. The ancient Athenians had passed from the "Oh!" stage, to the "Why?" stage, but never reached the "What for?" stage. That is why they were overwhelmed by the barbarians, who did not know so much, but knew how to kill people quite as well.

In the earlier culture stages people are curious only about "curiosities." They are not interested in the ordinary. It is the "Wonders of Science" period of literature. The museums are jackdaw nests of pretty stones, queer shells, and outlandish trinkets. Crowds flock to the side-show tents to see the two-headed calf and the bearded lady. They may even go as far as to wonder why the calf is bicephalous and the lady pogoniastic, but they do not even raise the more important question why most calves have only one head and most ladies no beard. They listen with eagerness to the tales of travelers, like Herodotus and Mandeville, who have been, or profess to have been, in remote regions. They are curious of all customs except their own, which, being customary, require no explanation. "Why do they act so?" they ask about foreigners, but never, "Why do we act so?" though that is a question that they might more easily answer.

Man began his study of the world with the more distant things. He gazed long at the stars before it occurred to him to look at the ground on which he stood, and longer yet before he tried to turn his attention inward to find out what was going on inside of his own head. Astronomy was well grown before geology was born, and psychology has only recently been admitted to the family of the sciences.

III

Ignorance is commonly referred to as "darkness," but it is not so easy as that would imply. The darkness of space offers no impediment to the penetration of light, but the human mind often opposes a specific resistance to the entrance of a new idea. Especially, if it is a big idea that requires some rearrangement of the mental furniture before room can be found for it.

There are those who love darkness rather than light, not because their deeds are evil, but just because they like to sit around in the dark and tell ghost-stories to one another. They prefer mystery, where they can imagine whatever they wish, and they fear that science will

> Conquer all mysteries by rule and line,
> Empty the haunted air, and gnomed mine,
> Unweave a rainbow, as it erewhile made
> The tender-personed Lamia melt into a shade.

They even seem to regard God, quite blasphemously, as a great conjuror whose tricks may be exposed by some impertinent scientist who turns too much light upon the phenomena of nature. They do not know the simple geometrical principle that as the area of enlightenment enlarges, it lengthens the circle of the surrounding darkness.

The method of science is economy of thought. The aim of science is control of the future. A science arises from some human need, and returns to earth to satisfy some, often some other, human need. It may soar so high into the empyrean as to be out of our sight, but it always comes back in the course of time, bringing food, like Elijah's ravens.

So do not believe a mathematician when he boasts that his newly discovered theorem is of no possible use to anybody. Before he knows it some mechanic will snatch it out of his hand and set it to work in the shops. No occupation seemed idler than the study of geometry of four dimensions when anybody could see that there were only three; yet now all of a sudden the symbols of the fourth dimension appear in astronomical and physical calculations, and are likely to get into chemistry and biology soon.

IV

One cannot, of course, become a scientist by merely reading science, however diligently and long. For a scientist is one who makes science, not one who learns science. A novelist is one who writes novels, not one who reads them. A contortionist is one who makes contortions, not one who watches them. Every real scientist is expected to take part in the advancement of science, to go over the top at least once in his life when he takes his PH.D. degree, if never again. But of course the number of those who are in reserve or in training must always outnumber those at the front.

The highest reward of science, the secret satisfaction of standing where no mortal man has ever stood before, is rightly reserved to those who contribute most of its advance. The pure thrill of primal discovery comes only to the explorer who first crosses the crest of the mountain-range that divides the unknown from the known. But if we cannot all feel that thrill to the full, we can at least catch a resonance of it in our own souls by reading about it, as we know something of how Balboa felt when he stared at the Pacific from a peak in Darien, as well as how Keats felt on first opening Chapman's *Homer*. The lives of explorers are always exciting whether they penetrate to the heart of Africa, like Livingstone, or to the heart of the atom, like Bohr.

At a baseball game there may be five thousand spectators and only one man at the bat, but do not imagine he is the only one having any fun. He alone can feel the whack on the wood that tells him that he has made a three-base hit, but the five thousand participate by proxy in his pleasure, their muscles tense, and their pulses quicken.

There is also fun to be found in sitting on the side-lines of science and watching the international game. Those who are not musicians may get delight from music; those who are not architects, from architecture; those who are not cooks, from food. It is not necessary to be a scientist to get pleasure and profit from scientific researches. This is not a faculty confined to a few. It is common to all who have any capacity for intellectual enjoyment, and those who do not avail themselves of it are curtailing their opportunities for happiness. Appreciation of good music was supposed to be over the ears of the masses until the phonograph brought Beethoven and Wagner to every farm house and tenement.

Science, too, needs to be democratized and brought within reach of the many, not as a task forced upon children, but as a lifelong recreation. That is one difficulty with our excellent school system; it is so comprehensive that if you suggest to a person that he might find it interesting to study, say, botany or chemistry, he is apt to reply that he "had it" when he was a boy, implying that, like the mumps or measles, he could never catch it again. He does not realize that the sciences are making such rapid progress that even if it "took" well in the first place, the immunity would not last longer than ten years.

The investigator does not like to be bothered when he is busy any more than other people. If you lean over his shoulder and jog his elbow when he is picking a chomosome out of a cell with a Barber pipette, he is apt to say: "Run away, child! You could not understand what I'm doing if I explained it to you." Doubtless you could not if he explained it to you in his own language. But somebody else who did understand what he was doing and who spoke your language could explain it to you in a way that would be very interesting. This translation of technical terminology into the vulgar tongue is quite another man's job,—no easy job at that,—and the few men of each generation who have the ability and opportunity to do original research of a high order ought not to be expected to take time off for such secondary work.

But the fact that scientists have been compelled to construct a trade language of their own is undoubtedly one reason why they are commonly misunderstood and disesteemed. It is hard not to feel that a foreigner who does not speak our language is a bit stupid or crazy. Then, too, our pride comes into play and constructs a defensive mechanism for us. Our subconscious self suggests to us to say, "Well, if he can't put it into plain English, I guess it does not amount to much, anyway." This is the time to be reminded of an observation by Quiller-Couch: "I hold there is no surer sign of ill breeding than to speak, even to feel, slightingly of any knowledge oneself does not happen to possess."

V

If there were only one language of science, the layman might learn it once for all in order to get access to the whole of its literature. But "science" is one of those abstract collective terms that get us into trouble. It would be safer always to speak of "the sciences" rather than of "science," since there are many of them and they are not all on speaking terms with one another. Corridor conversations at a session of the American Association for the Advancement of Science sound like a Balkan peace conference, for each is speaking in his own tongue. If a chemist gets by mistake into Section F, and hears a paper being read on "Ecdysis in the Teleostean Agriopus," the chances are that he does not understand any more of it than you or I would, and, between you and me, he is just as much bored by it, though he may grin and bear it, hoping that the biologist will happen in at Section C and hear his paper on "The Internal Strains of the Molecule of Cyclohexane-spiro-cyclopentane-dicardoxylic Acid." Just so in polite conversation you may see a person listening with flattering attention to an unintelligible tale in the hope that he may earn like courtesy when his turn comes. The scientific specialist requires the services of an interpreter as much as the layman, and he needs it more, for he has all he can do to keep up with the voluminous literature of his own subject; yet he must keep an eye out for what is going on in all other fields, even the most remote, for something may happen there that will throw light on his own problems.

Then, too, there is danger that the investigator may become so absorbed in his subject that he will lose sight of its wider aspects, its human interest, its practical possibilities, its relation to the world at large. If one keeps his eye too closely fixed to a microscope, or even a telescope, he is apt to become a trifle near-sighted. A botanist, for instance, may concentrate his attention so exclusively upon questions of taxonomy that it might be said of him

> A primrose by the river's brim
> Primula flava was to him,
> And it was nothing more.

VI

The popularization of science does not mean falsification, but its translation from technical terms into ordinary language. Popular science need not be incorrect, but has to be somewhat indefinite. It differs from the exact sciences in being inexact.

The scientific mind is set at too sharp a focus for ordinary use. The would-be popularizer is always confronted by the dilemma of comprehensible inaccuracy or incomprehensible accuracy, and the fun of his work lies mainly in the solution of that problem.

It is amusing to see that scientists are stricter with others than they are with themselves, though this is a common human failing. For instance, the bacteriologist is a very insistent that the layman shall not confound protozoa and bacteria, but in the laboratory he himself calls them all alike "bugs." The electrician is particular that other people shall use volt and ampere properly, but he tells his assistant to "turn on the juice."

The humanist and the scientist may think they are quarreling when they are merely saying the same thing in different words. Take, for instance, the phenomenon known as "the vernal erethic diathesis" or, in other circles, as "spring's awakening":

"In the spring a young man's fancy lightly turns to thoughts of love," is the way it is put by the poet. (Tennyson)

"In the spring the chief activating gland of the kinetic system, the thyroid, shows a distinct enlargement," is the way it is said by the scientist. (Crile)

The so-called "conflict between science and religion" is largely a question of using words in a technical or a general sense. Volumes have been written on the question of whether "the great fish" which the Lord prepared to swallow Jonah might be a whale, and, if so, whether "the whale's belly" could be interpreted to mean his lungs, where the imprisoned prophet would find plenty of air, rather than the whale's stomach, where he would be in danger of digestion.

The ordinary man wants to include whales among fish and potatoes among roots. The zoölogist and the botanist want to confine these words to the stricter meaning that they have imposed upon them. If the question of the use of these words were put up to a court composed of philologists to decide the issue on its historic grounds, the common man would win his case. But it is never good policy to quarrel about words. The writer of popular science will be wise to evade the issue by using, where he can, words to which scientists have not given a restrictive meaning. We may speak of "ocean life" or "the denizens of the deep" to avoid getting entangled with the distinction between mammalian and non-mammalian pelagic forms, and he is still allowed to talk about "the underground parts of plants" without going too deep into radical nomenclature. Since science has appropriated so many common words and has created a language of its own over which it has original proprietary rights, it is becoming increasingly difficult to put it in "a tongue understanded of the people," to use the Prayer-Book expression, but there is still some playground left.

"Studies," said Lord Bacon, "serve for delight, for ornament, and for ability." The kind of studies classed as natural sciences are, as he was the first clearly to point out, the most useful of all, and their pursuit gives to the mind the same delight as any other, but it must be confessed that they do not serve so well for "ornament," which may in part account for their comparative unpopularity. It is not easy to steer the conversation around to the point where one can quote a quadratic equation or a chemical formula with effect and without affectation, and when one does, it is likely to be no more intelligible than a chorus ending from Euripides. It is true that one may for the moment lightly refer to Einstein or Freud in conversation, and thereby give an impression of erudition that one by no means possesses, but that moment will soon pass, if indeed it has not already passed. In any case, one may only mention their names in common conversation, for if he attempted to explain what either man meant, he would for one reason or another be suppressed.

SCIENCE AND RELIGION[1]

ROBERT ANDREWS MILLIKAN

[Robert Andrews Millikan, born at Morrison, Illinois, in 1868, received degrees from Oberlin and Columbia and studied in Germany. From 1896 to 1921 he taught physics at the University of Chicago. In 1923 he received the Nobel prize (the most famous scientific award in the world) for isolating and measuring the ultimate electrical unity, the electron. At present he is director of the Norman Bridge Laboratory of Physics of the California Institute of Technology.]

THERE seems to be at the present time a strange recrudescence of a point of view which is completely out of keeping with the developments of the age in which we live, a point of view which thoughtful leaders of both science and religion have in all ages realized never had any basis for existence. In the time of Galileo it is perhaps understandable, in view of the crudity of the sixteenth century, that certain misguided religious leaders should have imagined that the discovery of the earth's motions might tend to undermine in some way the basis of religion and who, therefore, attempted to suppress Galileo's teachings. Yet it is to me not a little surprising that men even of such opportunities as Galileo's persecutors could have got religion upon such an entirely false basis in their thinking as to make its

[1] From *Science and Life.* Reprinted with the permission of the publishers, the Pilgrim Press.

fundamental verities, its very existence, dependent in any way upon any scientific discovery. It is not a question of whether Galileo was right or wrong, whether the earth actually revolves about the sun or the sun about the earth. That is a scientific matter with which religion as such has nothing whatever to do, and which should not have given it the slightest concern. Science could be counted upon to take care of that. It is its business to doubt, and it always does so as long as there is any room left for uncertainty. That even those inquisitors were far behind their own times in supposing that there could be any real contradiction between religion, properly understood, and the findings of astronomers cannot perhaps be better demonstrated than by the following quotation from St. Augustine, who lived twelve hundred years earlier, about 400 A. D., and is probably recognized as the most influential authority, next to Jesus and St. Paul, of the early Christian church.

"It very often happens," says Augustine, in commenting upon the entire distinctness from his point of view of the two great lines of thought, the natural and spiritual, "that there is some question *as to the earth or the sky, or the other elements of this world* . . . . respecting which one who is not a Christian has knowledge derived from most certain reasoning or observation: and it is very disgraceful and mischievous, and of all things to be carefully avoided, that a Christian, speaking of such matters as being according to the Christian scriptures, should be heard by an unbeliever talking such nonsense that the unbeliever, perceiving him to be as wide from the mark as east from west, can hardly restrain himself from laughing."

That this same controversy that Augustine thus saw nearly sixteen hundred years ago had no basis for existence, because it is outside the proper field of religion, but which nevertheless flared up so violently in Galileo's time, and then died out as men grew in intelligence, should have appeared again in as enlightened a country as America, in the year 1922, is one of the most amazing phenomena of our times. But it is not less amazing than it is deplorable, for the damage which well meaning but small visioned men can do to the cause of organized religion as represented in the Christian church through the introduction inside the organization of such a disintegrating influence is incalculably greater than any which could possibly be done by attacks from outside. Indeed, should the movement succeed the church would inevitably soon lose all its most vital elements and society would be obliged to develop some other agency to do the work which the church was organized to do, which in the main it has always done, and which to a very large extent it now does, namely, the work of serving as the great dynamo for injecting into human society the sense of social responsibility, the spirit of altruism, of service, of brotherly love, of Christlikeness and of eliminating as far as possible the spirit of greed and self-seeking.

But I am not going to place the whole blame for the existence of this situation upon misguided leaders of religion. The responsibility is a divided one, for science is just as often misrepresented as is religion by men of little vision, of no appreciation of its limitations, and of imperfect comprehension of the real rôle which it plays in human life—by men who lose sight of all spiritual values and therefore exert an influence upon youth which is unsettling, irreligious, and sometimes immoral. The two groups, the one in the religious field, the other in the scientific, are in reality very much alike. They represent essentially the same type of mind, or perhaps I should say, the same stage of intellectual development. Each interprets the Bible, for example, essentially literally, instead of historically, the one to support, the other to condemn. Both may be assumed to be sincere, but the one is wholly unacquainted with science, while presuming to judge it; the other is in almost complete ignorance of what religion is, while scoffing at it. I am ready to admit that it is quite as much because of the existence of scientists of this type as of their counterparts in the field of religion that the fundamentalist controversy has flared up to-day, and it is high time for scientists to recognize their share of the responsibility and take such steps as they can to remove their share of the cause.

I do not suppose that anything which I may say will exert much influence upon the groups whose prejudices have already been aroused, and who are therefore not interested in an objective analysis of the situation, but I may perhaps hope that some of the youth whose minds have been confused by the controversy may profit somewhat from a restatement of what seem to me the perfectly obvious and indisputable facts.

The first fact which seems to be altogether obvious and undisputed by thoughtful men is that there is actually no conflict whatever between science and religion when each is correctly understood. The simplest and probably the most convincing proof of the truth of that statement is found in the testimony of the greatest minds who have been leaders in the field of science, upon the one hand,

and in the field of religion, upon the other. Suppose, for example, that we select the greatest names in the last two centuries of the history of British sciences, or, for that matter, of world science. Everyone would agree that the stars that shine brightest in that history, as one's glance sweeps down from 1650 to 1920, are found in the names of Newton, whose life centered about 1680; Faraday, living about 1830; Maxwell, 1870; Kelvin, 1890, and Lord Raleigh, who died in 1921. No more earnest seekers after truth, no intellects of more penetrating vision, can be found anywhere, at any time, than these, and yet every one of them has been a devout and professed follower of religion. It was Kelvin who first estimated the age of the earth at something like a hundred million years without seeing the least incompatibility, in spite of the first chapters of Genesis, between that scientific conclusion and his adherence to the church, of which he was a lifelong member and a constant attendant. Indeed, in 1887, when he was at the very height of his powers, he wrote: "I believe that the more thoroughly science is studied the further does it take us from anything comparable to atheism." Again in 1903, toward the end of his life, he wrote: "If you think strongly enough you will be forced by science to the belief in God, which is the foundation of all religion. You will find it not antagonistic, but helpful, to religion." His biographer, Silvanus P. Thompson, says: "His faith was always of a very simple and childlike nature, undogmatic and untainted by sectarian bitterness. *It pained him to hear crudely atheistic views expressed by young men who had never known the deeper side of existence.*" Just as strong a case of the same sort can be made by turning to the biographies of any of the other men mentioned, and these were chosen, let it be remembered, not because they were religious men, but because they are universally recognized as the foremost of scientists. Indeed, I doubt if the world has ever produced in any field of endeavor men of more commanding intellects than two of them, Sir Isaac Newton and James Clerk-Maxwell.

If someone says that I am calling only on the testimony of physicists and of Englishmen, then listen to the man whom the French nation has repeatedly voted the foremost of all Frenchmen, and who is also easily the peer of any biologist who has ever lived anywhere, Louis Pasteur, of whom his biographer says, "Finally, let it be remembered that Pasteur was a deeply religious man." Over his tomb in the Institute Pasteur are inscribed these words of his: "Happy is he who carries a God within him, an ideal of beauty to which he is obedient—an ideal of art, an ideal of science, an ideal of the fatherland, an ideal of the virtues of the Gospel."

Or, again, if I am accused of calling merely on the testimony of the past, on the thinking which preceded the advent of this new twentieth century in which we live, I can bring the evidence strictly up to date by asking you to name the dozen most outstanding scientists in America to-day and then showing you that the great majority of them will bear emphatic testimony, not only to the complete lack of antagonism between the fields of science and religion, but to their own fundamental religious convictions. One naturally begins with the man who occupies the most conspicuous scientific position in the United States, namely, the President of the National Academy of Sciences, who is at present both the head of the Smithsonian Institute of Washington and the president of the American Association for the Advancement of Science, Dr. Charles D. Walcott, one of the foremost of American students of the evolution of life in the early geologic ages. He is personally known to me to be a man of deep religious conviction and has recently written me asking that he be described for the purposes of this address, which he has seen, as "an active church worker." The same is true of Henry Fairfield Osborn, the director of the American Museum of Natural History of New York, and one of the foremost exponents of evolution in the country. Another rival for eminence in this field is Edwin G. Conklin of Princeton, who in recently published articles has definitely shown himself a proponent of the religious interpretation of life. In the same category I know, also from direct correspondence, that I may place John C. Merriam, president of the Carnegie Institution of Washington and America's foremost paleontologist; Michael Pupin, the very first of our electrical experts who has "approved every word" of this address and recently delivered a better one at Columbia University on this same subject; John Coulter, dean of American botanists; A. A. and W. A. Noyes, foremost among our chemists; James R. Angell, president of Yale University, and eminent psychologist, with whom I have had an exchange of letters on this subject; James A. Breasted, our most eminent archeologist, who served with me for years on the board of trustees of a Chicago church, upon which also T. C. Chamberlin, dean of American geologists, was a constant attendant; Dr. C. G. Abbot, home secretary of the National Academy of Sciences, eminent astronomer and active churchman; and so on through the list of a large number of the scientists of eminence in this country.

Turn now to the other side of the picture and ask what have been the views of the most outstanding and most inspired religious leaders upon the relations of science to religion, and you obtain altogether similar testimony. Was it not Jesus himself, who said, "You shall know the truth and the truth shall make you free?" There is not one syllable in all that he taught nor one idea which he introduced into human life which would justify one in arraying him on the side of those who would see antagonism between any scientific truth and the deepest of spiritual values. There were no creeds in Jesus' teaching, no verbal inspirations of any sort. Religion was to him a life of love and duty, the simple expression of the Golden Rule.

Turning next to great religious personalities since Jesus' day, I have already quoted Augustine to show how he warned against religious leaders of such narrow insight as to make religion a laughing-stock by the presentation of an antagonism which did not exist. John Wesley, the founder of the Methodist church, in the chapter of his Compendium of Natural Philosophy on "A General View of the Gradual Progression of Beings," has a passage which speaks of "the ostrich with the feet of a goat which unites birds to quadrupeds," and then continues, "By what degrees does Nature raise herself to man? . . . How will she rectify this head that is always inclined toward earth? How change these paws into flexible arms? What method will she make use of to transform these crooked feet into skillful and supple hands? Or how will she widen and extend this contracted stomach? In what manner will she place the breasts and give them a roundness suitable to them? The ape is this rough draft of man, this rude sketch, an imperfect representation which nevertheless bears a resemblance to him, and is the last creature that serves to display the admirable progression of the works of God. . . . But mankind have their gradations as well as other productions of our globe. *There is a prodigious number of continued links between the most perfect man and the ape.*" (Italics mine.) I am not here asserting that Wesley's point of view was correct. For our present purposes that is quite immaterial. But he was a supreme religious leader and the quotation shows that he saw too clearly to allow his scientific thinking to be trammeled by any man-made religious dogmas.

Again, in our own time, there has been no more spiritual religious leader than Henry Drummond, whose most inspiring work was in showing the contribution of science to religion, and I think I might name practically all of the outstanding religious leaders now living and say that there is not one in ten of them who would not take his place beside Jesus and Augustine and Drummond and Beecher and Lyman Abbot and Fosdick and Soares and King and Brown and Burton and Mathews and a host of other *men of broad vision and deep experience who have seen science and religion as twin sisters which are effectively coöperating in leading the world on to better things.*

My argument thus far has been merely this, that there can be no conflict between science and religion if the greatest minds in the two fields, the minds to which we look for our definitions of what both science and religion are, have not only not seen such a conflict but have clearly seen and clearly stated that there is none.

But now let me go to my second obvious fact and show why in the nature of things there can be no conflict. This appears at once as soon as one attempts to define for himself what is the place of science and what the place of religion in human life. *The purpose of science is to develop without prejudice or preconception of any kind a knowledge of the facts, the laws, and the processes of nature. The even more important task of religion, on the other hand, is to develop the consciences, the ideals, and the aspirations of mankind.*

The definition of science I think all will agree with. The definition of religion is in essence that embodied in the teachings of Jesus, who, unlike many of his followers of narrower vision, did not concern himself at all with creeds, but centered his whole teaching about a life of service and the spread of the spirit of love. It is of course true that the scientific and the religious sides of life often come into contact and mutually support each other. Science without religion obviously may become a curse, rather than a blessing to mankind, but science dominated by the spirit of religion is the key to progress and the hope of the future. On the other hand, history has shown that religion without science breeds dogmatism, bigotry, persecution, religious wars, and all the other disasters which in the past have been heaped upon mankind in the name of religion, disasters which have been so fatal to organized religion itself that at certain times and in certain countries the finest characters and the most essentially religious men have been found outside the church. In some countries that is the situation to-day, and *wherever this is true it is because the essence of religion has been lost sight of, buried under theologies and other external trappings which correspond exactly to the "mint, the anise, and the cummin" of Jesus' day.* If anyone wishes to see what disaster these excrescences can bring upon the cause of real religion let him read the history of the church in Asia Minor for the first six centuries and see for himself what sects and schisms and senseless quarrels over the nature of the person of Jesus can do in the way of sucking the life-blood out of the spirit of his teachings and out of the effectiveness of the organization which was started for the sole purpose of spreading that spirit.

Yet in America, at least, it is not primarily those inside the church who thus misinterpret and misunderstand it, though we must sorrowfully admit that such a group does exist here. It is, however, for the most part the outsiders, the critics who have never seen the inside of church walls, and many of whom know so little about the church in America as to actually believe that Christianity is to be identified with mediæval theology, when the fact is so obvious that he who runs may read, that all that is vital in Christianity has remained altogether untouched by the most complete revolutions in theology, such as have gone on, for example, during the past hundred years. Many of us were brought up under creeds and theologies which have now completely passed on, as such things will continue to do as the world progresses, and yet, as we look back, we see that the essential thing which the churches of our childhood were doing for us and for our neighbors then is precisely what they are doing now, namely, stimulating us to right conduct, as each of us sees it, inspiring us to *do as we know* we ought to do, developing our ideals and our aspirations. There is a very simple and a very scientific way of finding out for yourself what is the heart and center of the Christian religion, the fundamental and vital thing which it stands for in human society, and that is to get far enough back so that details are lost sight of and then to observe what is the element which is common to all Christian churches in the United States. He who does that will see at once that *it is the life and the teachings of Jesus which constitute all that is essential to Christianity, that the spread of his spirit of unselfishness, of his idealism, and of his belief in the brotherhood of man and the fatherhood of God is the great purpose of the Christian religion.* In other words, that religion exists, as stated above, for the sake of developing the consciences, the ideals, and the aspirations of mankind.

My third obvious fact is that *both science and religion have reached their present status through a process of development from the crudest beginnings.* This will be universally recognized in the case of science, and in the case of religion the most superficial study of history shows that this is true. The religious ideals and practices of the American Indians and of all other primitive tribes, with their totem-poles and incantations, have obviously been of the most primitive type. The ideas of duty, of responsibility, have always been involved in these religions, but the motives of right conduct, as primitive man conceived it, have been, from our present point of view, of the most unenlightened and even unworthy sort.

But is it not altogether obvious that religion cannot

possibly rise higher than the stage of development of the people of whose ideals it is the expression? Nothing could show that process of development better than the Bible itself, for the early books of the Old Testament reveal the conception of God, characteristic indeed of the age, but not at all satisfying to us, for it was a God who was indeed benevolent and just toward his own chosen people, but vindictive and cruel and utterly regardless of the welfare of those outside this chosen group. This imperfect conception is developed and refined through the history of the Jews as portrayed in the Bible until it culminates in the all-embracing love and fatherhood preached by Jesus. He who would deny this developmental process going on in both science and religion and clearly revealed in all the records of the past which we have, must shut his eyes to the indisputable facts as they are presented in all history, including sacred history.

To me it has always been of the utmost interest and profit, especially when I was disposed to judge severally great religious leaders of the past, like Paul or Moses, to try to conceive myself living in their surroundings, with their lack of scientific knowledge, interpreting life from the limited point of view which they had, formulating rules of conduct relating, for example, to matters of hygiene, such as those dealt with in Deuteronomy, trying to interpret mysterious phenomena of nature like eclipses, the possession of evil spirits, etc., and when I do this my wonder always is that these men saw as clearly as they did, and succeeded as well as they did in separating the fundamental from the incidental. Difficult as it is to judge the great leaders of the past by their standards rather than by ours, it is imperative that we do so if we are to form any just appreciation of them and of their contributions to the development of the race. Indeed, this is the essence of the whole problem. Once get this point of view and you will never think of asking whether Genesis is to be taken as a modern text-book of *science.* It was written long before there was any such thing as science. It is of the utmost importance from every point of view to realize that the Bible itself makes no claims whatever of *scientific* correctness or, for that matter, of verbal inspiration. It is rather the record of the *religious* experiences and development of a great race.

My fourth obvious fact is that *every one who reflects at all believes in one way or another in God.* From my point of view, the word atheism is generally used most carelessly, unscientifically, and unintelligently, for it is to me unthinkable that a real atheist should exist at all. I may not, indeed, believe in the conception of deity possessed by the Congo negro who pounds the tom-tom to drive away the god whose presence and influence he fears; and it is certain also that no modern religious leader believes in the god who has the attributes which Moses, Joshua and the Judges ascribe to their deity. But it seems to me as obvious as breathing that every man who is sufficiently in his senses to recognize his own inability to comprehend the problem of existence, to understand whence he himself came and whither he is going, must in the very admission of that ignorance and finiteness recognize the existence of a Something, a Power, a Being in whom and because of whom he himself "lives and moves and has his being." *That Power, that Something, that Existence, we call God.* Primitive man, of course, had anthropomorphic conceptions of that being. He was not able to think of a god who was very different from himself. His god became angered and had to be appeased, he was jealous and vindictive and moody; but man's conceptions have widened with the process of the suns, and as he has grown up he has slowly been putting away childish things.

I am not much concerned as to whether I agree precisely with you in my conception or not, for "can men with thinking find out God?" Both your conception and mine must in the nature of the case be vague and indefinite. Least of all am I disposed to quarrel with the man who spiritualizes nature and says that God is to him the Soul of the universe, for spirit, personality, and all these abstract conceptions which go with it, like love, duty, and beauty, *exist* for you and for me just as much as do iron, wood and water. They are in every way as real for us as are the physical things which we handle. No man, therefore, can picture nature as devoid of these attributes which are a part of your experience and mine, and which you and I *know* are in nature. If you, then, in your conception identify God with nature, you must perforce attribute to him *consciousness* and *personality*, or better, *superconsciousness* and *superpersonality*. You cannot possibly synthesize nature and leave out its most outstanding attributes. Nor can you get these *potentialities* out of nature, no matter how far back you go in time. In other words, materialism, as commonly understood, is an altogether absurd and an utterly irrational philosophy, and is indeed so regarded by most thoughtful men.

Without attempting, then, to go further in defining what in the nature of the case is undefinable, let me reassert my conviction that although you may not believe in some particular conception of God which I may try to give expression to, and although it is unquestionably true that many of our conceptions are sometimes childishly anthropomorphic, every one who is sufficiently in possession of his faculties to recognize his own inability to comprehend the problem of existence bows his head in the presence of the Nature, if you will, the God, I prefer to say, who is behind it all and whose attributes are partially revealed to us in it all, so that it pains me as much as it did Kelvin "to hear crudely atheistic views expressed by men who have never known the deeper side of existence." Let me then henceforth use the word God to describe *that which is behind the mystery of existence and that which gives meaning to it.* I think you will not misunderstand me, then, when I say that I have never known a thinking man who did not believe in God.

My fifth obvious fact is *that there have been two great influences in the history of the world which have made goodness the outstanding characteristic in the conception of God.* The first influence was Jesus of Nazareth; the second influence has been the growth of modern science, and particularly the growth of the theory of evolution. All religions, including Christianity, have impersonated the spirit of evil and the spirit of good, and in many instances the former has been given the controlling influence. All of us see much in life which tends to make us pessimists. The good does not always prevail. Righteousness does not always triumph. What is the meaning of existence? Is it worth while? Are we going anywhere? Jesus and modern science have both answered that question in the affirmative—Jesus took it as his mission in life to preach *the news of the goodness of God.* He came in an age which was profoundly ignorant of modern science. He used the terms, in dealing with disease and evil, which were appropriate to his day, the only terms which his audiences could have understood, but he saw a God who was caring for every sparrow and who was working out through love a world planned for the happiness and well being of all creatures. Similarly science in the formulation of the theory of evolution has seen the world developing through countless ages higher and higher qualities, moving on to better and better things. It pictures God, however you may conceive him, as essentially good, as providing a reason for existence and a motive for making the most of existence, in that we may be a part of the great plan of world progress. No more sublime conception of God has ever been presented to the mind of man than that which is furnished by science when it represents him as revealing himself through countless ages in the development of the earth as an abode for man and in the age-long inbreathing of life into its constituent matter, culminating in man with his spiritual nature and all his godlike powers.

But let me go a step further. Science in bringing to light the now generally admitted, thought not as yet obvious and undisputed fact, that this is not a world in which things happen by caprice, but a world governed throughout by law, has presented the most powerful motive to man for goodness which has ever been urged upon him, more powerful even than any which Jesus found. That "whatsoever a man soweth that shall he also reap" is no longer merely a biblical text; it is a truth which has been burned into the consciousness of mankind by the last hundred years of the study of physics, chemistry and biology. Science, then, not only teaches that God is good, but it furnishes man with the most powerful of motives to fit in with the scheme of goodness which God has provided in nature. It teaches him not only that disease breeds disease, but also, by inference at least, that hate breeds hate, that dishonesty breeds dishonesty, that the wages of sin is death, and on the other hand that love begets love. *It teaches him that the moral laws and the physical laws alike are all laws of nature, and that violations of either of them lead to disaster and to misery.*

In closing this brief statement of the faith of the scientist, let me present a situation and a question. In the spring of 1912 the great ship *Titanic* had collided with an iceberg and was doomed. She was about to sink. The lifeboats were insufficient. The cry went up, "The women first!" The men stepped back. The boats were loaded and the men sank with the ship. You call it an heroic act. Why did they do it? Perhaps you answer, because it was the law of the sea and the men preferred to die rather than to live after having broken that law. Then take a simpler case, for I want a more fundamental answer. Two men were clinging after the wreck to a floating piece of timber. It would not support them both. One of them voluntarily let go and sank. Heroisms of just this sort happened thousands of times during the war. *Men threw away their lives for a cause.* Such events happen every day in times of peace. Why do they happen? Because men and women prefer to die rather than to live in the consciousness of having played the coward, of having failed to play their part worthily *in the great scheme of things*. It is true that not all men are like that, but I am optimist enough to think that most men are. But now come back to the question, Why are most men like that? Simply because *most men believe that there is such a world scheme; that they are a part of it, that their deaths are going to contribute to its development, in short, because most men believe in God.* This is the obvious inference from the fact that men are willing to die for a cause. They may not know whether there is personal immortality for them or not, but they *do knew with absolute certainty that they live on in memory and in influence;* many of them, too, have faith to believe that they live on in consciousness, but in either case they are a part of a plan of development *which gives meaning to life.* In other words, men who have the stuff in them which makes heroes all believe in God, in "a power in the world which makes for righteousness." Without that belief there is no motive for heroism or for self-sacrifices of any sort, nor any such thing as "the development of the consciences, the ideals, and the aspirations of mankind," which I said above, was the task of religion, for there is then no basis for ideals or for aspirations. This is why Kelvin said that "belief in God is the foundation of all religion."

If there be a man who does not believe, either through the promptings of his religious faith or through the objective evidence which the evolutionary history of the world offers, in a progressive revelation of God to man, if there be a man who in neither of these two ways has come to feel that there is a meaning to and a purpose for existence, if there be such thorough-going pessimism in this world, then may I and mine be kept as far as possible from contact with it. If the beauty, the meaning and the purpose of this life as revealed by both science and religion are all a dream, then let me dream on forever!

PHILOSOPHY AND SOCIAL SCIENCE

The political problem of mankind is to combine three things: economic efficiency, social justice, and individual liberty.

—J. M. Keynes

ADVENTURES IN PHILOSOPHY[1]

ELLWOOD HENDRICK

[Ellwood Hendrick was born at Albany, New York, in 1861. After studying with some of the leading chemists in Europe he engaged in a number of business enterprises. He has been prominently identified with organizations for promoting industrial chemistry. Since his retirement in 1915 he has written books and articles on a wide range of subjects.]

I

A LITTLE HOMILY ON THE TRUTH

WE sorely need a clearer conception of the truth. We need it in the business of living; especially as a means of avoiding misunderstandings. If we have an abstract idea of what the truth is we are less likely to err in the belief that we are right before we know the truth. In adventuring upon a theory which for the past few years has seemed to me to hold we shall hardly be charged with applying new meanings to old words if we say that facts and the truth are not the same. Facts are parts of the truth, just as wheels, rods, levers, and the like are parts of a machine. If we say "the whole truth" every time we refer to the truth, it might make the idea more clear, but let us agree to consider it so,

[1] From *Percolator Papers;* copyright, 1919, by Harper & Brothers. Reprinted by permission of the author and the publishers.

without the need of saying two words where one will do.

If you strike me, that becomes a fact as soon as you have done it. Whether you have struck me or not is a question of fact and not a question of truth. The truth may be that you struck me to call my attention to impending danger, or you may have struck me in anger, or the blow may be an unimportant episode in a long fight between us.

The truth, as I conceive it, is all the facts in their right or correct relation, the relation which they must bear to one another when the truth is attained. Thus the truth becomes an abstract thing, because we know *what* it is, although we may not know *it*. Rarely, indeed, are we able to gather all the facts in relation to a subject, on the one hand, or to correlate them, on the other; nevertheless, we must do this if we would know the truth.

If this definition is unfamiliar, if we are not accustomed to consider the truth in this sense, I think it will do us no harm to bear it in mind. In courts of law, according to current practice, it might not hold, but we are, fortunately, under no obligation to order our thinking according to processes of law.

If we exalt the truth and reverence it, the glib and hysterical brothers and sisters who, grasping a single fact, proceed to preach that and that only as the truth, will cause less annoyance. We may acknowledge their facts as facts, which is all they ask of us. If we still remain unconvinced of the truth of their preachments we shall be contradicting no one. The truth is very great, very large, and when Lessing prayed that to him be given the privilege to seek the truth rather than to know it, because to know it he was not worthy, he spoke as one of the wisest of men. To seek it, to get nearer to it, sometimes perhaps to get a glimpse of it, is all that we may hope for; it is the best that we can do.

Suppose you and I look at a tree on a hillside. We see only the leaves, and we observe that the tree is green. The tree *is* green; that is a fact. Let us make a note of it. Then suppose we go a distance away and look at it again. The tree is blue. It is idle for us to say, "It seems blue, but it really is green," because our very organs which gave the reaction of green a while ago now give the reaction of blue. By the same token that the tree was green when we saw it near by it is blue when we see it from afar. So let us make a second note: the tree is blue. Here we have two contradictory statements of fact, neither false, and yet neither the whole truth. The truth about the color of the tree involves a great range of subjects, including the physics of light, the anatomy and physiology of the human eye, photochemistry—in short, a vast store of learning and understanding.

Many facts which seem irreconcilable become harmonious parts of the truth when all the facts are arranged in their right order. So the truth should make us humble and patient with one another. None of us has faculties of universal coördination, and our blind spots, instead of being little delinquencies of perception, are in reality vast areas. The most we can claim is that we have a few sighted spots. To see all the facts in their right relation is what we might call the Olympian Vision.

II

THE GREEN TREE

The first time I visited Charlotte, North Carolina, I had some business to transact with a charming, soft-spoken old gentleman who wore a broad-brimmed felt hat. When our business was completed for the day we walked leisurely about the town. "Charlotte," said the gentleman of the sombrero, "is all to' up over a dispute which is ragin' among our people."

"What is the cause of it?" I asked.

"Free grace and fo'ordination," he answered.

I was delighted, and wrote a long letter home about it that night. Charlotte seemed so very archaic! This was many years ago, and since then Charlotte has grown to be a great manufacturing town with a grand hotel and clubs and all the things that modern industry and wealth bring about. In those days there were the Presbyterians and Baptists on the one side and the Methodists and Lutherans on the other, and the adherents of the little Episcopal Church, who were divided on the question. These included substantially the whole white population. Now, unless I am sorely mistaken, Charlotte has ceased to worry over "free grace and fo'ordination"; she is modern and up-to-date. But if my surmise be correct, she has gone backward intellectually; she only thinks herself modern; she has become commercial and has ceased to participate in the intellectual life of the day. For the old question whereby Charlotte was "all to' up" abides in philosophy. Turn whichever way we will, we meet that same old nagging problem, teasing us, on the one hand, with what seems to be proof that we have no free will at all, and insisting, on the other, that a very good reason why we have free will is because we know we have it.

Many of us have ceased to be Presbyterians or Baptists or Methodists or Episcopalians, but as soon as we venture into biology we find ourselves urged to join either the Mechanist or the Vitalist denomination, and there we find the same old dispute raging again among our biological people.

This is, indeed, the comedy domain of philosophy. The Greeks used to dispute over it. St. Paul appeared to have the problem solved, and so did St. Augustine. Pelagius differed from them, and so did his followers—with some warmth. The harmony between Luther and John Calvin over the matter was not striking; Servetus had an opinion which went up in smoke; the savants of Charlotte, North Carolina, talked themselves out over it—and now behold the biologists in battle array! If it were given to us to live to a prodigious number of years and to observe the earth from afar, we should see the philosophers in dispute over this problem throughout the ages, never agreeing and never persuading one another. It is a very enduring subject.

But is not this dispute over the question whether we have free will or not very like a dispute that we might engage in over the color of a tree—whether it be green or blue? It hardly seems worth while to boast or to grow angry in protesting that we have absolute free will, when a little surgical operation of one sort of another, or a shock, or a blow upon the head, may change our nature entirely. Why not proceed along the mechanistic way seeking the mechanical, physical, and chemical causes of every act, and thus gather as many facts as we can? If every act seems to be a response to a stimulus, why deny it? We shall not have achieved the truth when we have learned the exact process of every act, but we shall be much wiser than we are now. We shall advance toward the truth when we learn the relation to one another of those processes of which we are now so ignorant. And if from the study of the facts at hand we reach the conclusion that we have no free will at all, but are mere automata, with no power of choice or selection throughout our lives, is it not time to pause and admit that we may not have all the facts yet? Also that such as we have may not be in their right order before our vision?

There are some verses by John Godfrey Saxe, called "The Blind Men and the Elephant," which are very instructive. According to Saxe, six wise men of Indostan, all of them very wise, but all of them blind, went to sce the elephant. One examined its side and declared the elephant was very like a wall; another, feeling its trunk, was sure the elephant was very like a snake; another concluded from its leg that it was very like a tree; another, examining one of its tusks, knew that the elephant was very like a spear; the expert who examined its ear found it to resemble a fan, and the authority who grasped its tail was equally certain that the elephant was very like a rope. According to the legend, they are still disputing over it.

Now the truth is bigger than an elephant, and our vision of it is narrower than the observations of each of the blind men. And we should bear in mind that they were right, every one of them. Each had a fact; none knew the truth. None had a theory of the truth; each knew what he knew, and that was enough for him. We can well imagine one of them saying, "If a thing is so, it's so, and you can't get around it; my senses bear me witness; the elephant is very like a snake."

If we have a good working method of dealing with facts it is a good thing to hold to it just as we do well to hold fast to the fact that the tree is green when we look at it near by. It seems to be a part of the truth. And the mechanistic theory, which will have nothing to do with spooks or ghosts or with vital sparks with qualities that are not material, is helpful, wholesome, and illuminating. It makes for clean thinking. It will not countenance the Pickwickian point of view, which is very popular and current in our day. It provides that facts be gathered by observation and the study of cause and effect. It also seems to lead to the conclusion that every act is the only one possible under conditions as they exist. Now if this reasoning appears sound, let us, instead of frothing at the mouth and denouncing the sincere men who have reached these conclusions, admit it—as a part of the truth.

If through another chain of reasoning, or through consciousness, or by any other means, we come to a conclusion opposed to this, there is no occasion to boast that the first conclusion is disproved. If we reach both conclusions, we may know that we have not yet achieved the truth, but, for aught we know, both may be right. That we have free will and that we have not free will may be, both of them, parts of the truth, just as the opposed statements that the tree is green and that it is blue are parts of the truth.

We may say that the whole organization of human conduct is based upon the free will of the individual; but the organization of human conduct, like many another good thing, is based in large part upon fancy. When we consider acts from anear we might as well admit that free will seems to play very little, if any, part in them. Here is the human machine with its equipment, the consciousness including a part of that group of records and nerve centers which are "connected up," the connecting up occurring automatically along the line of least resistance; and then, given the stimulus, the one and only reaction which can occur does occur. There would need to be a difference in the equipment or the stimulus to bring about a different reaction. The conclusion, you observe, is precisely the same as that reached by the late and occasionally lamented John Calvin, except that he maintained that every current through the colloidal content of every nerve was a special, volitional act of the Deity, "for His own glory."

This view, that every act is automatic if considered by itself, has great merit. If we consider it to be a part of the truth, we are likely to have far more abundant charity for one another. By it we enlarge our sympathy. For instance, we may say that everybody always does his best at the time he acts. If he does evil, there is a reason for it, a structural reason. His sympathetic equipment may be atrophied. Or he may be angry. In either case we are dealing with facts close at hand and our business is with his condition. The cause of it may be due to his grandfather, or to a false leading in his early childhood. We should diagnose his case and determine what part of his equipment is atrophied or what part so congested that his way was the path of crime. And if he is angry we should regard him as a nervous invalid until his attack is over and the anger bodies are eliminated from his system or until his injured brain cells are restored.

There is an illuminating book by Doctor Crile, of Cleveland, on *The Origin and Nature of the Emotions,* that is very enlightening about anger. He postulates that by evolution we have developed what he calls "nociceptors," which give the warning of pain in the presence of danger, and that these warnings are given according to the experience of the race. The equipment provides against such external injuries as the goring and tearing by an animal's teeth in far greater measure than against the more modern devices of swift-moving bullets and very sharp instruments, because the experience of the race against teeth is so much greater than with bullets and swords. It is imaginable that if a sword were sharp enough and thin enough and swung with sufficient speed, the old Chinese legend of the master headsman might almost escape fiction. In this, it may be recalled, the executioner graciously gave a pinch of snuff to each of his victims, who remained comfortably unaware that his head had been severed from his body. By the sneezes which followed the perfect swordsmanship was revealed; the heads rolled off, and the surprised offenders proceeded to die with all haste and propriety.

Another interesting warning is found in the fact that we are ticklish in our ears and nostrils and on the soles of our feet, where buzzing insects are likely to sting.

Now in danger these warnings elicit the response either of flight or of turning and facing it, and so we become either afraid or angry. Doctor Crile notes two features in connection with these emotions which are interesting in regard to what we are discussing: he finds that during the processes of anger and fear we suffer inhibitions of all other faculties than those which are of value in fighting or running away. We are useless, inefficient, incompetent, in every other respect. When we are angry we have not our normal equipment because the greater part is blocked off, and we are no more our complete selves than when, if ever, we are very drunk. The second observation is that under anger or fear there occurs a destruction of brain cells that are but slowly repaired, and, under stress of severe and prolonged emotion, the brain is permanently injured. These notes have been vastly illuminating to me in regard to the dreadful war which now rages, and I think we may well pause to consider how difficult the recovery will be after it is over, when so many minds that are crippled by passion must attempt the work that calls for entire men.

The Man of Wrath with a great lust to kill ceases to inspire us. We know that he is of value in hand-to-hand combats, but he is a nuisance, and even worse, in a fight where cool heads and steady hands are needed for machine-guns. He is potential in instigating war, but he is incompetent to end it. He is a drum-major of anarchy.

We also learn that the emotional hurrah of the man in high authority is evidence that he is unfit for his job, because under emotion his qualities of judgment are paralyzed and his sense of coördination is atrophied.

While confining ourselves to the mechanistic point of view we may describe judgment as the operation of selecting the best thing available to do at the time—just as the tree reaches out toward the light—and we may regard it as mechanical. As in a Jacquard loom the woof is run through those openings that are before it, so the judgment, the determining bobbin, as we might call it, passes through those channels of the mind that are open to it, and determines the act which we mechanically perform.

We may regard impulse as something different from reason if we want to, but to me the difference seems to be in name rather than in fact. If judgment is automatic it may operate so rapidly that it skips consciousness, but that is no ground for calling it a thing apart. Under impulse we act rapidly, so that consciousness is often skipped in the process, and usually there is an emotional drive to it. An impulse seems to me to be a quick, emotional leading or drive to an act, and as much of an automatic response to stimulus as to eat when we are hungry or to drink when we are thirsty. In doing many things we skip consciousness after we are used to doing them, although at first, when we are learning how, they involve great effort.

There are also automatic vanities which we have discussed elsewhere, of which a notable example is our disposition to justify ourselves, any time and all the time. We are apt to think that we thought, when we were acting so rapidly that the act skipped consciousness. And in explaining afterward, our sense of veracity is under the greatest strain. We fool ourselves into the belief that we deliberated over every possibility, when in fact we were following blindly the drive within us to do that which was the only possible thing that we could do under existing conditions.

III

THE BLUE TREE

Free will is a long way from our acts, yet we have a constructive faculty. Although often within a very narrow range, we have the ordering of our lives in our hands. This constructive faculty is in use when we are conjuring up our ideals. We can of our own volition say, "I will plan my life to do this thing." We can of our own will select a picture in our minds and hold it in our consciousness as a stimulus. More likely than not we get the idea from some one else; but such ideas, as they are given to us, become our property, to do with as we will, to adopt as ideas or to reject. Many things influence us in this; we are not as free as we think we are; we generate our own energy, and some of us are equipped with very low-power dynamos; but the process of selecting those purposes and ways of life which we project into our consciousness by our own will is the occasion of our greatest freedom.

As we grow older we become either more firm of purpose or more obedient to any stimulus; what we have made of our lives becomes more fixed; but at no time are we complete. We may change our whole nature at fifty as well as at thirty or fifteen—but we are less likely to. This business of combining impressions and setting them up as ideals is the substance of our free will. We may fall short of our ideals, we may be entirely different from what we meant to be, and yet be following them as nearly as we can. The question of responsibility is: With what earnestness do we select our ideals, and with what effort do we project them into our consciousness?

The difference between achieving an ideal and performing an act is rather hazy, I'll admit; but I imagine the one to be the little push we give of our own desire and choice when a picture comes into consciousness that we want to have represent us. "That is mine!" we say, and we proceed to conform to the picture, to drive it into consciousness, to recall it, to urge it upon ourselves until in the end we act that way, and this because we want to. The picture is the stimulus, but the process of selection seems supermechanical. Although I cannot imagine how we can think without our thinking-machines, it seems that somewhere in the process freedom has entered in and we thus become, let us say, the navigating officers of our lives. On the other hand, the direct performance of an act seems an automatic response to the strongest stimulus in the mind at the time.

This may seem like arguing in a circle, because the mechanism that we employ when we are selecting our ideals is substantially the same as that which we use when we perform an act. But the stimulus comes from within. Responsibility is a quality that we recognize, and to consider it a fiction seems premature—as though we had not yet a clear vision of the truth of the matter.

In the late Christian Herter's remarkable and, in many respects, illuminating book called *Biologic Aspects of Human Problems* he develops consciousness as an "awareness of self" that arises in a certain complexity of organism under certain conditions. This awareness of self becomes more abundant as what we might call the harmonious complexity of the organism increases. Now, responsibility, or the capacity to choose of our own accord, like consciousness, is a quality that seems to be present in us. It would be futile to deny consciousness because we do not understand just how and where it begins. And it seems equally idle to deny responsibility. It seems to me to be a late accompaniment of this awareness of self which we know we have, and to my way of thinking it functions when we order our lives.

So we conceive these two statements as being parts of the truth—that whatever any one does, it seems the best that he can do at the time, and also that whatever any one does is qualified by the manner in which he has ordered his life. This idealizing ego, then, is as much a part of ourselves as are our fingers and toes. It is also selective. Now, if it appears that we have no free will when we commit an act, but have free will when we order our lives, we surely have not the whole truth in hand, but the theory may lead us nearer to it.

IV

THE GOD IN THE MACHINE

Here I respectfully ask your pardon. Despite my protestations I have already burdened you with a definition of the truth that is not in the dictionaries, and now I am about to ask you to consider religion from a point of view that does not seem to be current. I admit frankly that it is not only distressing to the reader, but also that it makes for confusion, to frame new definitions for old words as one proceeds; but, *"Gott hilf mir; ich kann nicht anders!"*

It seems to me that, so far as our civilization is concerned, the concept of religion *per se* is modern. There is no Germanic word for it; in English, German, Dutch, and Scandinavian, the Latin word has been imported and substituted for faith, belief, and even for dogma and theology. In the sense in which I want to use the word there is no plural. Christianity, Buddhism, Brahminism, Judaism, Mohammedanism are not so many religions (although I must admit that the Latins, who gave us the word, would have used it in this sense) ; they are, let us say, faiths or beliefs or confessions. At all events, if we agree to call them such, it will leave us free to use the word religion without thinking of the minister, the Sunday-school, or the choir in which we used to sing. Of course, the minister and the Sunday-school and the church choir may have functioned as parts of religion, but to think of them as the substance of it might get them out of their right relation to the idea which I am trying to express.

In the chapter called "The Blue Tree" we considered how we may, of our own free will, select impressions or ideas, and by making ideals of them drive them into consciousness so that they shall serve both as stimuli and inhibitions to our actions. We called this the ordering of life. In the process we are open to impressions, although we determine within ourselves, subject, of course, to our limitations, which of these impressions we shall select. Now, the function of providing ideals and offering them and teaching them, so that we may order our lives aright and thus approach the truth, seems to me to be the great province of religion. We may practise religion either with or without dogma. The man of faith may have great religious value, and again he may have no religious value at all. There are, for example, religious Christians, and, on the other hand, Christians of great piety who are not religious. The anchorite who whips and distresses himself to save his own soul is not practising religion; he is exercising his faith. The Samaritan who picks up the fallen wanderer by the wayside and by his act also enlarges the vision of the man he helps, so that the stimulus of sympathy enters into him, is doing a religious act. Faith may be a stimulus to religious acts, and we know that it often is; but since often it is not, we may as well address ourselves to that aspect of religion which we can understand, regarding it as having to do with the ordering of our lives, and not as related to dogma or faith save as dogma or faith may induce it. Then we find that everybody has the religious equipment, just as he has a sympathetic equipment although both may be greatly atrophied. With his mind, although we cannot fail to recognize a conflict between science and the Bible and science and dogma, there is no conflict between science and religion.

This view of religion takes the subject out of the domain of metaphysics and mysteries and recognizes it as a specific department of human life. By it we reach the conclusion that it is a necessary function, in which we are all interested. The truly religious man is he who helps you and me to be of positive value to the world in which we live and, in one way or another, to approach the truth. Whether he be a Christian or a Jew or anything else is his affair—his faith, his profession. His religion is in his ideals and his use of them.

We must have ideals. We can do nothing without them. And this essay is written in the sincere belief that as we approach the truth with understanding, one human problem after another will be solved. Only, we must order our lives aright or else we cannot approach the truth. We cannot, otherwise, get the facts into focus. So all the world needs religion—to-day, it would seem, more than ever before. Dogmas that we cannot believe will not answer the purpose. Apologetics often offend more than they aid. Religion is bigger than any church or any creed or any faith, and its business is the development of a wiser and a better humanity.

V

INTO THE UNKNOWN

We have discussed the problem of free will and found it not very free, and yet I have tried to develop the idea that we have the ordering of our lives in our own hands. Now let us adventure farther, and this time into the unknown, with analogy as our guide.

We have seen how facts are parts of the truth and that we reap confusion if we consider them as substitutes for it. We might postulate a law of arrangement, a law of order, that holds good in regard to the truth and applies also to animate and inanimate things. We see this ordering of the composite parts into their right relation in the formation of a crystal. We need not question now why the molecules join according to a mathematical scale to form a symmetrical body; suffice it for the present to observe that they do. The molecules are individual, but they group themselves into something that is not a molecule—into a crystal. We may compare a crystal to the truth, and the molecules to the facts which constitute it. Until the molecules are in their right order there is no crystal. Until the facts are in their right order there is no truth.

We, as men and women, are composed of innumerable particles of many different kinds. Their good condition and orderly arrangement are necessary to our being. Let us consider, for example, our white blood corpuscles or leucocytes. They work with what almost appears to be intelligence in overcoming disease. They are not simple little things by any means; they are marvelously complex. They respond to a stimulus and go to work, just as we do. Sometimes they are weak, inefficient, and sick; and then we languish or die because they do not do their work. They are mechanical entities, and are subject to physical and chemical laws.

Now we are mechanical entities and we constitute something greater than ourselves. We group ourselves artificially into nations which a congress has power to change by moving a boundary line from one side of us to the other. We divide humanity into other groups, as into families, because of immediate consanguinity, and into races, based on what appears to be a remoter consanguinity. We divide ourselves again into long-headed and broad-headed classes. The facts upon which these groupings are based do not accord with one another, nor do they tell us much about what humanity means. They are desirable facts and, in a way, it is worth knowing that some of us are of one nation and some of another;

some long-headed and some broad; some onc thing and others something else; but a new and greater meaning might be applied to us by a master mind, the greater anthropologist who could explain the human family as it has not been explained before.

The news of battles does not tell us what is really happening to us all; and there are problems ahead even graver and more important than who shall win. Is not victory itself a curse to the winner who lacks the character to meet his obligations? Some day, let us hope, a wiser generation will follow that will refuse to accept the wrath and hate that we cherish, and will work diligently to repair the havoc of this war. Then perhaps the greater anthropologist will come.

Collective humanity is, indeed, a strange phenomenon. Constantly destroying itself, it is at war with half of nature and cultivates as richly as it can the other half. It has a marvelous faculty for helping itself, and then, when a part of it has achieved a high order of living and gathered in those things of the earth which it desires, there is usually a great fall, and as the years roll on, the dull, stupid toiler guides his plow over the land that once was Carthage and Nineveh. What is it that makes collective humanity sick? What was the disease of Babylon and of the forgotten city that underlies it? After all the analyses, what was the sickness of Rome? Why did Europe go to sleep for a thousand years, and what was it that killed the intellect of the Saracens? Why did Persia die?

Collective humanity is a thing, a being that grows well and is strong and becomes godlike, and then again sickens and becomes foolish, and the spirit of it fades away until slavery under a benign master would be an advantage. Collective humanity as we see it is a great jumble of parts, related, unrelated, and in dire confusion. What is it doing? Not one of us can tell.

Now let us imagine leucocytes to have consciousness and vision, and let us consider a single one of them. Its abode is in the blood of somebody—of you, let us say; and its life is very exciting for it because it never knows what its path will be. Sometimes it is driven into one of your fingers, again into one of your toes; it may be busy on a little scratch well covered up, or it may suddenly have to do battle with a tetanus bacillus. Ask a leucocyte what it knows of life, and it might well answer that it is a continuous problem; it would tell you all sorts of interesting things about your interior—which is its whole world—but it could not tell anything about you. Even so simple a detail as that, for instance, you do not like parsnips, could not occur to this leucocyte, because you do not eat them, and so it has no experience with parsnips. Really, the leucocytes with consciousness, which I am imagining, are very like us; they are in their world and we in ours. And we may be very like them—parts of a Great Intelligence as much beyond us as we are beyond the leucocytes which form parts of us.

Humanity has always been speculating about this Greater Intelligence, and yet speculation has always been discouraged on the ground that the matter is all settled. This conservatism is what gives us such amazing dicta as the Westminster Shorter Catechism and the Thirty-nine Articles. The usual human concept of the Greater Intelligence is as of one apart from us and appearing in all manifestations of power. It has been proposed that we may come into sight and communication with it after death; and the fear of it, described as the beginning of wisdom, has also been used to make us do strange things in accordance with traditions and myths older than history.

Even analogy will only help us occasionally here, and otherwise we have nothing to guide us in these vaster regions but the imagination. And yet, if we can imagine some relation between human beings and a possible Greater Intelligence, a relation which does not seem false or impossible, we may be taking steps in advance. If we imagine this and imagine that and then something else, it may be that some day somebody will imagine a working hypothesis which does not seem to offend against the truth.

Now suppose the working hypothesis should involve the conception of human beings as minute particles of the Greater Intelligence, citing the analogy of the leucocytes or any other swarm of microscopic units. We need not then restrict ourselves to their reactions in the human body. We are different, are differently constructed, and this remarkable quality of consciousness is, at all events, far greater in the human being than it is, for instance, in a leucocyte. Without doubt it reaches farther. Nor need we restrict the Greater Intelligence to our own limitations. We are not conscious of our blood corpuscles, but that is no reason why the Greater Intelligence may not be conscious of us. We know, as we have said, that if our white blood corpuscles are weak, inefficient, or sick, we languish, and that our welfare requires that they be in health. So, if we consider collective humanity and observe that it advances in knowledge, in understanding, in order, and in righteousness, we may then feel that it is well with the Greater Intelligence of which we are a part. But if we live in idleness and waste and hatred and cruelty and malice, and cause misery and degradation, it would seem that we are offending and injuring the Greater Intelligence, the God of all of us. This makes the Great Intelligence in a way dependent upon us, so that it loses health and welfare and power when we undermine the health and welfare of one another.

Sometime when we know more than we do now, there may be available a working hypothesis along these lines and in accord with familiar facts. It is interesting to speculate upon what the results may be. Hebrew poetry has given us a tradition and a conception of a deity apart from ourselves and pregnant with the greatest conceivable measure of power. The Christian, Jewish, and Mohammedan peoples worship an Almighty Divinity that rules the stars and the uttermost heavens, the nebulæ as well as the sun and its planets, including the earth. The thought of any other is condemned. Beginning with a tribal master of its fate inspired by selfishness, lust, and wrath, humanity has magnified its conception of its god until it has exalted him beyond the earth and projected him through the ether into a million other worlds. It may be that we shall be guided back again to a God of all men and women, exercising vast powers of the spirit when in health and when His component particles are doing their work as they should, but losing power to lead or guide if mankind is wayward and corrupt.

THE NATURE OF HUMAN FAITHS

Thomas Carlyle

[For biographical sketch see page 123]

IT is well said, in every sense, that a man's religion is the chief fact with regard to him. A man's, or a nation of men's. By religion I do not mean here the church-creed which he professes, the articles of faith which he will sign and, in words or otherwise, assert; not this wholly, in many cases not this at all. We see men of all kinds of professed creeds attain to almost all degrees of worth or worthlessness under each or any of them. This is not what I call religion, this profession and assertion; which is often only a profession and assertion from the outworks of the man, from the mere argumentative region of him, if even so deep as that. But the thing a man does practically believe (and this is often enough *without* asserting it even to himself, much less to others); the thing a man does practically lay to heart, and know for certain, concerning his vital relations to this mysterious Universe, and his duty and destiny there, that is in all cases the primary thing for him, and creatively determines all the rest. That is his *religion;* or, it may be, his mere scepticism and *non-religion:* the manner it is in which he feels himself to be spiritually related to the Unseen World or No-World;

[1] From "The Hero as Divinity," *Heroes and Hero Worship.*

and I say, if you tell me what that is, you tell me to a very great extent what the man is, what the kind of things he will do is. Of a man or of a nation we inquire, therefore, first of all, What religion they had? Was it Heathenism,—plurality of gods, mere sensuous representation of this Mystery of Life, and for chief recognized element therein Physical Force? Was it Christianism; faith in an Invisible, not as real only, but as the only reality; Time, through every meanest moment of it, resting on Eternity; Pagan empire of Force displaced by a nobler supremacy, that of Holiness? Was it skepticism, uncertainty and inquiry whether there was an Unseen World, any Mystery of Life except a mad one;—doubt as to all this, or perhaps unbelief and flat denial? Answering of this question is giving us the soul of the history of the man or nation. The thoughts they had were the parents of the actions they did; their feelings were parents of their thoughts: it was the unseen and spiritual in them that determined the outward and actual;—their religion, as I say, was the great fact about them. In these Discourses, limited as we are, it will be good to direct our survey chiefly to that religious phasis of the matter. That once known well, all is known. We have chosen as the first Hero in our series, Odin the central figure of Scandinavian Paganism; an emblem to us of a most extensive province of things. Let us look for a little at the Hero as Divinity, the oldest primary form of Heroism.

Surely it seems a very strange-looking thing this Paganism; almost inconceivable to us in these days. A bewildering, inextricable jungle of delusions, confusions, falsehoods, and absurdities, covering the whole field of

Life! A thing that fills us with astonishment, almost, if it were possible, with incredulity,—for truly it is not easy to understand that sane men could ever calmly, with their eyes open, believe and live by such a set of doctrines. That men should have worshiped their poor fellow-man as a God, and not him only, but stocks and stones, and all manner of animate and inanimate objects; and fashioned for themselves such a distracted chaos of hallucinations by way of Theory of the Universe: all this looks like an incredible fable. Nevertheless, it is a clear fact that they did it. Such hideous inextricable jungle of misworships, misbeliefs, men, made as we are, did actually hold by, and live at home in. This is strange. Yes, we may pause in sorrow and silence over the depths of darkness that are in man; if we rejoice in the heights of purer vision he has attained to. Such things were and are in man; in all men; in us too.

Some speculators have a short way of accounting for the Pagan religion: mere quackery, priestcraft, and dupery, say they; no sane man ever did believe it,—merely contrived to persuade other men, not worthy of the name of sane, to believe it! It will be often our duty to protest against this sort of hypothesis about men's doings and history; and I here, on the very threshold, protest against it in reference to Paganism, and to all other *isms* by which man has ever for a length of time striven to walk in this world. They have all had a truth in them, or men would not have taken them up. Quackery and dupery do abound; in religions, above all in the more advanced decaying stages of religions, they have fearfully abounded; but quackery was never the originating influence in such things; it was not the health and life of such things, but their disease, the sure precursor of their being about to die! Let us never forget this. It seems to me a most mournful hypothesis, that of quackery giving birth to any faith even in savage men. Quackery gives birth to nothing; gives death to all things. We shall not see into the true heart of anything, if we look merely at the quackeries of it; if we do not reject the quackeries altogether; as mere diseases, corruptions, with which our and all men's sole duty is to have done with them, to sweep them out of our thoughts as out of our practice. Man everywhere is the born enemy of lies. I find Grand Lamaism itself to have a kind of truth in it. Read the candid, clear-sighted, rather sceptical Mr. Turner's *Account of his Embassy* to that country, and see. They have their belief, these poor Thibet people, that Providence sends down always an Incarnation of Himself into every generation. At bottom some belief in a kind of Pope! At bottom still better, belief that there is a *Greatest* Man; that *he* is discoverable; that, once discovered, we ought to treat him with an obedience which knows no bounds! This is the truth of Grand Lamaism; the "discoverability" is the only error here. The Thibet priests have methods of their own of discovering what Man is Greatest, fit to be supreme over them. Bad methods: but are they so much worse than our methods,—of understanding him to be always the eldest-born of a certain genealogy? Alas, it is a difficult thing to find good methods for!—We shall begin to have a chance of understanding Paganism, when we first admit that to its followers it was, at one time, earnestly true. Let us consider it very certain that men did believe in Paganism; men with open eyes, sound senses, men made altogether like ourselves; that we, had we been there, should have believed in it. Ask now, What Paganism could have been?

Another theory, somewhat more respectable, attributes such things to Allegory. It was a play of poetic minds, say these theorists; a shadowing-forth, in allegorical fable, in personification and visual form, of what such poetic minds had known and felt of this Universe. Which agrees, add they, with a primary law of human nature, still everywhere observably at work, though in less important things. That what a man feels intensely he struggles to speak-out of him, to see represented before him in visual shape, and as if with a kind of life and historical reality in it. Now doubtless there is such a law, and it is one of the deepest in human nature; neither need we doubt that it did operate fundamentally in this business. The hypothesis which ascribes Paganism wholly or mostly to this agency, I call a little more respectable; but I cannot yet call it the true hypothesis. Think, would *we* believe, and take with us as our life-guidance, an allegory, a poetic sport? Not sport but earnest is what we should require. It is a most earnest thing to be alive in this world; to die is not sport for a man. Man's life never was a sport to him; it was a stern reality, altogether a serious matter to be alive!

I find, therefore, that though these Allegory theorists are on the way towards truth in this matter, they have not reached it either. Pagan Religion is indeed an Allegory, a Symbol of what men felt and knew about the Universe; and all Religions are Symbols of that, altering always as that alters: but it seems to me a radical perversion, and even *in*version, of the business, to put that forward as the origin and moving cause, when it was rather the result and termination. To get beautiful allegories, a perfect poetic symbol, was not the want of men; but to know what they were to believe about this Universe, what course they were to steer in it; what, in this mysterious Life of theirs, they had to hope and to fear, to do and to forbear doing. The *Pilgrim's Progress* is an Allegory, and a beautiful, just and serious one: but consider whether Bunyan's [1] Allegory could have *preceded* the Faith it symbolizes! The Faith had to be already there, standing believed by everybody;—of which the Allegory could *then* become a shadow; and, with all its seriousness, we may say a *sportful* shadow, a mere play of the Fancy, in comparison with that awful Fact and scientific certainty which it poetically strives to emblem. The Allegory is the product of the certainty, not the producer of it; not in Bunyan's nor in any other case. For Paganism, therefore, we have still to inquire, Whence came that scientific certainty, the parent of such a bewildered heap of allegories, errors and confusions? How was it, what was it?

Surely it were a foolish attempt to pretend "explaining," in this place, or in any place, such a phenomenon as that far-distant distracted cloudy imbroglio of Paganism,—more like a cloudfield than a distant continent of firm land and facts! It is no longer a reality, yet it was one. We ought to understand that this seeming cloudfield was once a reality; that not poetic allegory, least of all that dupery and deception was the origin of

[1] John Bunyan: 1628–1688, *Pilgrim's Progress,* First Part, 1678; Second Part, 1684.

it. Men, I say, never did believe idle songs, never risked their soul's life on allegories: men in all times, especially in early earnest times, have had an instinct for detecting quacks, for detesting quacks. Let us try if, leaving out both the quack theory and the allegory one, and listening with affectionate attention to that far-off confused rumor of the Pagan ages, we cannot ascertain so much as this at least, That there was a kind of fact at the heart of them; that they too were not mendacious and distracted, but in their own poor way true and sane!

You remember that fancy [1] of Plato's, of a man who had grown to maturity in some dark distance, and was brought on a sudden into the upper air to see the sun rise. What would his wonder be, his rapt astonishment at the sight we daily witness with indifference! With the free open sense of a child, yet with the ripe faculty of a man, his whole heart would be kindled by that sight, he would discern it well to be Godlike, his soul would fall down in worship before it. Now, just such a childlike greatness was in the primitive nations. The first Pagan Thinker among rude men, the first man that began to think, was precisely this child-man of Plato's. Simple, open as a child, yet with the depth and strength of a man. Nature had as yet no name to him; he had not yet united under a name the infinite variety of sights, sounds, shapes and motions, which we now collectively name Universe, Nature, or the like, —and so with a name dismiss it from us. To the wild deep-hearted man all was yet new, not veiled under

[1] "Behold! human beings living in an underground den." Plato's *Republic,* beginning of Bk. vii. See Jowett's translation (N. Y. 1892), iii, 214–217.

names or formulas; it stood naked, flashing-in on him there, beautiful, awful, unspeakable. Nature was to this man, what to the Thinker and Prophet it for ever is, *preter*natural. This green flowery rock-built earth, the trees, the mountains, rivers, many-sounding seas;—that great deep sea of azure that swims overhead; the winds sweeping through it; the black cloud fashioning itself together, now pouring out fire, now hail and rain; what *is* it? Ay, what? At bottom we do not yet know; we can never know at all. It is not by our superior insight that we escape the difficulty; it is by our superior levity, our inattention, our *want* of insight. It is by *not* thinking that we cease to wonder at it. Hardened round us, encasing wholly every notion we form, is a wrappage of traditions, hearsays, mere *words*. We call that fire of the black thunder-cloud "electricity," and lecture learnedly about it, and grind the like of it out of glass and silk: but *what* is it? What made it? Whence comes it? Whither goes it? Science has done much for us; but it is a poor science that would hide from us the great deep sacred infinitude of Nescience, whither we can never penetrate, on which all science swims as a mere superficial film. This world, after all our science and sciences, is still a miracle; wonderful, inscrutable, *magical* and more, to whosoever will *think* of it.

That great mystery of TIME, were there no other; the illimitable, silent, never-resting thing called Time, rolling, rushing on, swift, silent, like an all-embracing ocean-tide, on which we and all the Universe swim like exhalations, like apparitions which *are*, and then *are not:*

this is for ever very literally a miracle; a thing to strike us dumb,—for we have no word to speak about it. This Universe, ah me—what could the wild man know of it; what can we yet know? That it is a Force, and thousandfold Complexity of Forces; a Force which is *not we.* That is all; it is not we, it is altogether different from *us.* Force, Force, everywhere Force; we ourselves a mysterious Force in the center of that. "There is not a leaf rotting on the highway but has Force in it: how else could it rot?" Nay surely, to the Atheistic Thinker, if such a one were possible, it must be a miracle too, this huge illimitable whirlwind of Force, which envelops us here; never-resting whirlwind, high as Immensity, old as Eternity. What is it? God's creation, the religious people answer; it is the Almighty God's! Atheistic science babbles poorly of it, with scientific nomenclatures, experiments and what-not, as if it were a poor dead thing, to be bottled-up in Leyden jars and sold over counters: but the natural sense of man, in all times, if he will honestly apply his senses, proclaims it to be a living thing,—ah, an unspeakable, godlike thing; towards which the best attitude for us, after never so much science, is awe, devout prostration and humility of soul; worship if not in words, then in silence.

But now I remark further: What in such a time as ours it requires a Prophet or Poet to teach us, namely, the stripping-off of those poor undevout wrappages, nomenclatures and scientific hearsays,—this, the ancient earnest soul, as yet unencumbered with these things, did for itself. The world, which is now divine only to the gifted, was then divine to whosoever would turn his eye upon it. He stood bare before it face to face. "All was Godlike or God:"—Jean Paul [1] still finds it so; the giant Jean Paul, who has power to escape out of hearsays: but there then were no hearsays. Canopus [2] shining-down over the desert, with its blue diamond brightness (that wild blue spirit-like brightness, far brighter than we ever witness here), would pierce into the heart of the wild Ishmaelitish man, whom it was guiding through the solitary waste there. To his wild heart, with all feelings in it, with no *speech* for any feeling, it might seem a little eye, that Canopus, glancing-out on him from the great deep Eternity; revealing the inner Splendor to him. Cannot we understand how these men *worshiped* Canopus; became what we call Sabeans [3] worshiping the stars? Such is to me the secret of all forms of Paganism. Worship is transcendent wonder; wonder for which there is now no limit or measure; that is worship. To these primeval men, all things and everything they saw exist beside them were an emblem of the Godlike, of some God.

And look what perennial fiber of truth was in that. To us also, through every star, through every blade of grass, is not a God made visible, if we will open our minds and eyes? We do not worship in that way now: but is it not reckoned still a merit, proof of what we call a "poetic nature," that we recognize how every

[1] Jean Paul Friedrich Richter (1763–1825), the greatest humorist in modern German literature. His rather barbarous and chaotic style and his idealism powerfully influenced Carlyle, who wrote two essays on him, and quotes him constantly. The quotation here is from Carlyle's translation of Richter's *Quintus Fixlein,* end.

[2] A bright star in Argo, in the Southern Hemisphere, invisible in most of North America.

[3] From *Saba,* the host of heaven. They worshiped the sun, moon, and stars, which they believed to be the bodily appearances of celestial spirits.

object has a divine beauty in it; how every object still verily is "a window through which we may look into Infinitude itself"? He that can discern the loveliness of things, we call him Poet, Painter, Man of Genius, gifted, lovable. These poor Sabeans did even what he does,—in their own fashion. That they did it, in what fashion soever, was a merit: better than what the entirely stupid man did, what the horse and camel did,—namely, nothing!

But now if all things whatsoever that we look upon are emblems to us of the Highest God, I add that more so than any of them is man such an emblem. You have heard of St. Chrysostom's [1] celebrated saying in reference to the Shekinah,[2] or Ark of Testimony, visible Revelation of God, among the Hebrews: "The true Shekinah is Man!" Yes, it is even so: this is no vain phrase; it is veritably so. The essence of our being, the mystery in us that calls itself "I,"—ah, what words have we for such things?—is a breath of Heaven; the Highest Being reveals himself in man. This body, these faculties, this life of ours, is it not all as a vesture for that Unnamed? "There is but one Temple in the Universe," says the devout Novalis, [3] "and that is the Body of Man. Nothing is holier than that high form. Bending before men is a reverence done to this Revelation in

[1] Chysostom, the "Golden-mouthed" (347–407), preacher of the early Greek Church.

[2] The symbol of the Divine Presence in shape of a cloud or light over the Jewish Ark of the Covenant. Exodus xxv, 10 ff.; Numbers vii, 89; ix, 15 ff.

[3] The pseudonym of Friedrich Leopold von Hardenberg (1772–1801), German poet and mystic. Novalis adapts these words from 1 Cor. iii: "Know ye not that ye are the temple of God, and that the Spirit of God dwelleth in you? If any man defile the temple of God, him shall God destroy; for the temple of God is holy, which temple ye are."

the Flesh. We touch Heaven when we lay our hand on a human body!" This sounds much like a mere flourish of rhetoric; but it is not so. If well meditated, it will turn out to be a scientific fact; the expression, in such words as can be had, of the actual truth of the thing. *We* are the miracle of miracles,—the great inscrutable mystery of God. We cannot understand it, we know not how to speak of it; but we may feel and know, if we like, that it is verily so.

WHAT MAKES A SOCIAL SYSTEM GOOD OR BAD?[1]

BERTRAND AND DORA RUSSELL

[Bertrand (Arthur William) Russell, son of Viscount Amberley, was born at Trelleck, England, in 1872. After graduating from Trinity College, Cambridge, he was for many years lecturer there on mathematics and philosophy. He is one of the world's foremost thinkers on social questions at the present time. In 1921 he married Dora Winifred, daughter of Sir Frederick Black.]

I

ANY man who desires, as I do, a fundamental change in the structure of society is forced sooner or later to ask himself the question: what is it that makes one social system seem to him good and another bad? This is undoubtedly very largely a matter of individual caprice. In history, for example, some prefer one epoch, some another. Some admire the polished and civilized ages, while others profess to admire the rude virtues of more barbarous times. One does not wish to think that one's political opinions result from mere fanciful preferences of this sort, yet I believe that an enormous proportion of political opinion comes, in the last analysis, from some untested, unexamined, almost unconscious love for a certain type of society

[1] From *Prospects of Industrial Civilization*, by Bertrand and Dora Russell. Copyright, 1923, by The Century Company. Reprinted by permission of and by special arrangement with the publishers.

actual or imagined. I think it is possible to arrive at something less subjective than such tastes and fancies, and I think the advocate of fundamental change, more obviously than anyone else, needs to find ways of judging a social system which do not embody merely his individual tastes.

Men's proximate political opinions are defended by arguments—arguments as to the effect of this course or that: such a course will lead to war; such another to economic slavery; such another to starvation. But in choosing the danger we most wish to avoid or the advantage we most wish to secure, we are almost all of us dominated by some more or less vague picture of the sort of society we should like to see existing. One man is not afraid of war because he has a picture of Homeric heroes whose fighting he finds it agreeable to contemplate. Another is not afraid of economic slavery because he thinks that he himself and his friends will be the slave-drivers rather than the slaves. Another is not afraid of starvation because he has a secret hoard and therefore believes that privation brings out the latent heroism in men. And so they differ as to the course which is best to be pursued, and the grounds of their differences remain obscure to themselves and others. Being obscure, they are suitable subjects for endless quarrels. The only way to make people's political judgments more conscious, more explicit, and therefore more scientific is to bring to the light of day the conception of an ideal society which underlies each man's opinion, and to discover, if we can, some method of comparing such ideals in respect of the universality, or otherwise, of their appeal.

I propose first of all to examine some ways of judging a social system which are common but which I believe to be erroneous, and then to suggest the ways in which I think such judgments should be formed.

Among most people at most times, the commonest way of judging is simply by inherited prejudices. Any society which is not in a state of rapid transition has customs and beliefs which have been handed down from previous generations. The peculiar merit of the Greeks was due largely to the fact that, being a commercial and seafaring people, they came across the customs and beliefs of innumerable and widely differing nations and were thus led to a skeptical examination of the basis of all such customs, including their own. If my memory serves me, there is somewhere in Herodotus a story of a conversation between some Greeks and a barbarian tribe, in which the Greeks expressed horror of the barbarians for the practice of eating their dead; but the barbarians expressed quite equal horror of the practice of burying the dead, which to them was just as shocking as the other to the Greeks. Such experiences of intercourse with other nations diminish the hold which merely inherited beliefs have upon the man who lives in a fixed environment. In our age, this effect is produced not only by travel and commerce, but also by the changes in social custom inevitably produced by the growth of industrialism. Wherever industry is well developed and not very new, one finds that religion and the family, which are the twin props of every merely traditional social structure, lose their hold over men's minds. Consequently the force of tradition is less in the present age than it has ever been before. Nevertheless, it is even now as great probably as all other forces combined. Take, for example, the belief in the sacredness of private property—a belief bound up originally with the patriarchal family, the right which a man was supposed to have to the produce of his own labor, and the right which he was able to extort to what he had conquered by the sword. In spite of the antiquity and diminishing strength of these ancient grounds of belief in private property, and in spite of the fact that no new grounds are suggested, the enormous majority of mankind have a deep and unquestioning belief in its sacredness, due largely to the taboo effect of the words "Thou shalt not steal." It is clear that private property is an inheritance from the pre-industrial era when an individual man or family could make an individual product. In an industrial system a man never makes the whole of anything, but makes the thousandth part of a million things. Under these circumstances, it is totally absurd to say that a man has a right to the produce of his own labor. Consider a porter on a railway whose business it is to shunt goods-trains: what proportion of the goods carried can be said to represent the produce of his labor? The question is wholly insoluble. Therefore it is impossible to secure social justice by saying that each man shall have what he himself produces. Early socialists in the days before Marx were apt to suggest this as a cure for the injustices of capitalism, but their suggestions were both utopian and retrograde, since they were incompatible with large-scale industry. It is therefore evident that the injustice of capitalism cannot be cured so long as the sacredness of private property is recognized. The Bolsheviks have seen this and have therefore confiscated all private capital for the use of the state. It is because they have challenged men's belief in the sacredness of private property that the outcry against them has been so great. Even among professing socialists there are many who feel a thrill of horror at the thought of turning rich men out of their mansions in order to make room for overcrowded proletarians. Such instinctive feelings are difficult to overcome by mere reason. The few men who do so, like the leading Bolsheviks, have to face the hostility of the world. But by the actual creation of a social order which does not respect merely traditional prejudices, more is done to destroy such prejudices in ordinary minds than can be done by a century of theoretical propaganda. I believe it will appear, when time enables men to see things in due proportion, that the chief service of the Bolsheviks lies in their practical challenge to the belief in private property, a belief existing by no means only among the rich, and forming at the present time an obstacle to fundamental progress—so great an obstacle that only its destruction will make a better world possible.

Another thing which affects people's instinctive judgment of a social system, whether actual or imagined, is whether it would provide a career for the sort of person they think they are. One cannot imagine that Napoleon, even in youth, could have been very enthusiastic about dreams of universal peace, or that captains of industry would be attracted by Samuel Butler's *Erewhon,* where all machines were illegal. Similarly, the artist will not enjoy the thought of a society where no man is allowed to paint unless his pictures are pleasing to the town council. And on this ground many artists are opponents of socialism. Men of science struggled against the system which existed in the seventeenth century and compelled them to teach nothing contradictory to revealed religion; and in like manner intellectuals in Russia object to having to teach their subjects from a Marxian point of view. People who find a pleasure in ordering others about (and this includes most of the energetic people in the world) will not like anarchism, where every man can do as he pleases. They will be in rebellion against existing authority unless they are part of it, but will wish to replace it by their own authority, not to abolish it, because in a world where every man could do as he pleases executive people would find no career. On the other hand, easy-going people will hate strenuous systems. They will oppose the setting up of drill and severe educational methods. During the war, they called such things "Prussianism." If they were better informed about Russia, they would now call them "Bolshevism." I confess to a temperamental sympathy with this point of view, and my sympathy was confirmed by what I saw of China, the most easy-going country left in the world. But this is not an easy-going age, nor one in which such temperamental preferences can be allowed to weigh. It is an age in which we have to think less of the present than of the future, less of the lives of our own generation than of the lives they are preparing for the generations to come.

Another thing which influences people, more or less unconsciously, in their judgment as to a suggested social system, is the question whether the activities involved in the creating of it would be agreeable to them. I fear that revolutionaries are not always exempt from this motive. There are certainly some in whom hatred of the possessing classes is stronger than love for the dispossessed; there are some to whom mere benevolent feeling appears to be repulsive humbug, and who derive the zeal of their revolutionary ardor mainly from the delight which they feel in the thought of punishing the bourgeoisie. Such men will, of course, always be found among the advocates of violent tactics, since without violence there is no satisfaction for their impulses. Patriotism and militarism have, in many men, a similar origin. The thought of fighting, or, more probably, the thought of setting others to fight, is delightful to them, and patriotism recommends itself to them as a creed likely to produce fighting. I do not mean that men are conscious of these impulsive sources of their beliefs, but I do mean that such impulses operate in the kind of way studied by psychoanalysis, and I believe that it is of great importance to drag the operation of these impulses into the light of day, to be aware of their operation in ourselves, and to do what we can to make others similarly aware; for an underground, unconscious force operates against reason, eludes discussion, and makes objectivity impossible while it remains undetected.

Among writers on sociology and political theorists generally, a very common way of judging the social structure is by whether it constitutes a pleasant pattern to contemplate. Many social theorists forget that a community is composed of individuals, and that whatever of good or bad it may contain must be embodied in those individuals. They think of the state as something having a good of its own, quite distinct from the good of the citizens; and what they call the good of the state is usually, unconsciously to themselves, what gives them a certain æsthetic or moral satisfaction. We know that when God created the world he saw that it was good, obviously not from the point of view of the unfortunates who have to live in it, but from a higher point of view, presumably that of æsthetic contemplation. In like manner, social theorists create worlds in their imagination which they also see to be good in spite of the fact that they would be intolerable to live in. Such worlds are neat and tidy; everybody does at each moment something which is in accordance with the central plan; they obey the will of the administrator as the universe obeys the will of God. The theorist, of course, is always in imagination himself the administrator. This kind of social theory was made popular among professors by Hegel; it was used by him to laud the Prussian state, and has been used by his academic followers to support the conservatisms of their several countries. Since the war, the Hegelian theory has been at a discount, having been supposed in some mysterious way to have inspired the invasion of Belgium; but in other forms a similar outlook remains common. Much of the belief in industrialism, particularly as applied to backward countries, is of this sort; it is intolerable to the industrially minded to think of lazy populations sitting under banana-trees, eating the fruit as it drops, and being happy in unproductive idleness. Some forms of socialism are not free from this defect: they aim rather at creating the kind of state which is pleasing to theoretical contemplation than the kind which will suit the temperaments of its citizens. A very great deal of imperialism is also of this sort; it is pleasant to see much of one's national color on the map, and it is unpleasant to see one's dominions jagged and scattered owing to the intrusion of foreign territories. The habit of judging the state as it is to contemplate, not as it is to live in, arises from giving more importance to the faint and transient sentiments of an observer (when that observer happens to be oneself) than to the vivid and continual experiences of those who have to live under the government of the state. It is certainly a very potent source of bad social theory. Whoever wishes to be a social theorist should daily remind himself of the very simple but important maxim that a state is something in which people have to live, and not merely something to be read about in books, or contemplated as we contemplate the view from a mountain-top.

II

So far we have been concerned with ways of judging a society which we believe to be mistaken. It is time to turn to those to which we can assent.

There are two elements in a good society, namely: first, the present well-being of those who compose it, and secondly, its capacity for developing into something better. These two do not, by any means, always go together. Sometimes a society in which there is little present well-being may contain within itself the seeds of something better than any previous system. Sometimes, on the other hand, a society in which there is much diffused well-being may be unprogressive, for a time static, and ultimately decadent. It is, therefore, necessary to take account of both elements as independent ingredients of the sort of society we should wish to see existing. If the science of social dynamics were more developed and the art of prophecy less insecure, progressiveness would be a much more important quality in a society than present well-being. But politics is so far from scientific and the social future so very uncertain that present well-being, which is indubitable, must be allowed as much weight as an uncertain future good, although this future good, if realized, will outweigh anything merely present because of its longer extension in time. "A bird in the hand is worth two in the bush"; and this is particularly true when we are not sure there are any birds in the bush at all. Let us therefore begin with what makes the present well-being of a community.

In judging of the present well-being of a community, there are two opposite fallacies to be avoided. We may call these, respectively, the fallacy of the aristocrat and the fallacy of the outside observer. We considered a moment ago the fallacy of the outside observer. The fallacy of the aristocrat consists in judging a society by the kind of life it affords to a privileged minority. The ancient empires of Egypt and Babylonia afforded a thoroughly agreeable existence for kings and priests and nobles, but the rest of the community were mostly slaves or serfs, and must have had an existence composed of unremitting toil and hardship. Modern capitalism affords a delightful existence for the captains of industry: for them there is adventure and free initiative, luxury and the admiration of contemporaries. But for the great mass of the workers, there is merely a certain place in the great machine. To that place they are confined by the need of a livelihood, and no effective choice is open to them except the collective stopping of the whole machine by strikes or revolutions, which involve imminent risk of starvation. Defenders of the capitalist régime are apt to vaunt the liberty which it grants to men of enterprise, but this is an example of the aristocratic fallacy. In new countries, such as the United States used to be, and such as South America still is, there may be some truth in it, and therefore in such countries one sees capitalism at its best; but in older countries, whose resources are developed and whose population is nearly as great as present methods of industry can support, the supposed freedom of enterprise exists only for a few. The early history of railways in the United States is full of bold piratical adventures; the railroad kings of that period remind one of Elizabethan buccaneers. But a railway in modern England is a very sober affair: its capital is held largely by innumerable maiden ladies and orphans whose funds are administered by trustees; its directors are sleepy peers; its policy is traditional; and it does nothing to encourage new men with bold schemes. This is not due, as superficial observers suppose, to a difference between the British and American temperaments, but to a difference in their geography and industrial antiquity. But even taking the capitalist case at its best, even considering America as it was forty years ago, it was only the men of unusual enterprise and push and unscrupulousness who came to the top. Such men are, by definition, the minority, and a society which suits only them cannot be considered satisfactory except by one who commits the aristocratic fallacy. I am afraid there are many socialists who commit the same fallacy; they imagine industry developed under state control, and they visualize themselves in that future millennium as part of the state control, not as part of the ordinary workaday labor. In a system of centralized bureaucratic state socialism, those who direct the machine will have all the advantages at present enjoyed by the captains of industry, with the exception of enormous wealth, which to a vigorous, executive, and combative person is one of the smallest advantages of business success, being valued mainly as a tangible proof of ability and power and as a means of acquiring the respect of the herd. But it is not only the great captains of industry who will enjoy an exceptionally agreeable life under state socialism; it is also the whole army of officials. It is obvious that the man who sits in a government office, and spends his time interfering with the other people, has a pleasanter life than the man who works in a mine or stokes a liner. Yet there are many forms of socialism which would do nothing to remedy this inequality. The industrial machine as it has been developed by capitalism is full of injustices other than the inequality of wealth. Unless these other injustices are also remedied, a socialistic society may be scarcely pleasanter to the average manual worker than the existing system. This is concealed from labor politicians and from men with bureaucratic minds because they envisage themselves in the new order as leaders or officials, not as ordinary workers. Their judgment of the society they aim at creating is, in fact, vitiated by the aristocratic fallacy. It may be that the evils of the present world must be cured one by one, that inequality of wealth must be tackled first, leaving inequality of power for a later stage, and inequality in the pleasantness of labor for perhaps a still later stage. It may be that a bureaucratic centralized state socialism is the necessary first step. It is not this that I am denying. What I am denying is that such a society is good in itself, and that I do not think that any one who imagines with equal vividness the lives of all the members of the community can remain contented with an ideal which confines initiative, power, and the use of intelligence to a few.

A society which is to bring diffused well-being not only to one class or to one type of character, but as far as possible to every member of the community, must not be too systematic nor too orderly. It must not be the kind of society which a man of administrative temperament plans in his head and enforces by bayonets and the criminal law. Different individuals have different needs, and it is important to suit all needs that can be suited without damage to others. It is, of course, necessary to restrain predatory impulses. The insufficient amount of such restraint is one of the greatest evils of the world as it is. But it is at least equally disastrous to restrain creative impulses. This is the danger of what one may call tight systems. A military machine or an industrial machine treats men as all alike, with the exception of the privileged few who direct it; it has no room for other exceptions, no desire for the kind of work that would not be ordered from above, no toleration for the kind of person to whom it is difficult to become a mere cog in the machinery.

Perhaps the most important of all the qualities that a social system can possess is that it must be such as people can *believe* in. Europe during the last five centuries has advanced with quite extraordinary rapidity in all that makes what we call civilization, but step by step with this advance has gone a progressive disintegration of belief. I do not mean merely belief in religious dogma, though this also has played its part. I mean belief in all the assumptions on which the social order is based; all the sources of authority have become suspect, and all inherited institutions have ceased to command assent. The war and the Russian revolution gave the *coup de grâce* to such beliefs as remained. At the beginning of the war, democracy was still a fighting creed, something for which men were willing to die. At the end, poor President Wilson was left its one remaining votary, proclaiming his gospel in pathetic isolation to a world which shrugged its shoulders and went about its business as if he had not spoken. It may be that some element of injustice is essential to the existence of a social order, at any rate for many ages to come. But in ages of faith men believe in the social order even when it makes them suffer, even when they are victims of what to a later age appears unmerited misfortune. Nowadays this is not the case. The only men nowadays who believe in injustice are those who profit by it, and even they in their hearts feel that their belief is not genuine but merely as embodiment of self-interest. I except from this indictment the big capitalists of America, who are more naïve, more untouched by modern thought, than any other set of men with the exception possibly of a few Central African negroes. American business men still believe in the capitalist system, but business men elsewhere merely hope it will last their lifetime, provided they can obtain sufficient machine-guns and ships to shoot down or starve those who advocate systems which, in their hearts, they know to be better. Such half-hearted belief does not bring happiness. The capitalists tried to persuade themselves that their war against Russia was a holy crusade, but in this attempt they were very unsuccessful throughout Europe. And everybody except the capitalists is unable to create in himself even a semblance of belief in the old order, the order which made the war and blockaded Russia, the order which devastated Ireland, starves Germany and Austria, imprisons or kills socialists, and, amid the tottering ruins of our old civilization, pursues the old absurd diplomatic game of haggling for territories and arming against nominally friendly nations. This old order is no longer capable of bringing happiness. It is not only its nominal victims who suffer; it is not only the defeated nations or the proletarians who find that life has lost its meaning. Even the well-to-do classes of western Europe have no longer the sense of anything to live for. Having no purpose in life, they have plunged into a frantic pursuit of pleasure. But with every added pleasure comes added unhappiness; while the senses are gratified, the soul remains hungry—there is no inward sense of well-being, but only futility and despair.

There is only one cure for this despair, and that is a faith that a man can believe. No man can be happy unless he feels his life in some way important; so long as his life remains a futile round of pleasures or pains leading to no end, realizing no purpose that he can believe to be of value, so long it is impossible to escape despair. In most men at the present time this despair is dumb and unconscious, and, because it is unconscious, it cannot be avoided. It is like a specter always looking over a man's shoulder and whispering acid words into his ear, but never seen, never looked at face to face. Once acknowledged, once faced, this despair can be coped with, but it can be coped with only by a new belief, by something which supersedes the search for pleasure. Although it may sound old-fashioned to say so, I do not believe that a tolerable existence is possible for an individual or a society without some sense of duty.

There is only one kind of duty that the modern man can acknowledge without superstition, and that is a duty to the community. There was a time when such ideals as God, country, family, could move men. That time is past. All such ideals were used by elderly rulers throughout the war to drive the young to slaughter each other in futile carnage. Most of the young at the time believed that the war was about something important, but, now that it is nominally over, they see their mistake. Nothing good has come out of it except revolt against the system which caused it; the vices of the vanquished have been acquired by the victors, and the only new hope has come from Russia, the most defeated of all the nations in the Great War. Socialism is, I believe, the only faith which can restore happiness to the world, which can cure it of the sickness left by the war, which can give men the sense that their lives are capable of something better than pleasure and can end the despair that drives men to frivolous cruelty. The faith of the Russian communists in the new thing they are endeavoring to create is rather crude, rather ruthless, possibly rather premature, but it makes their lives happy as hardly any western life is happy; it enables them to endure privations and dangers, and preserves throughout a kind of joy and freshness in the soul such as one does not find in the weary West. If there were no other argument for socialism, the fact that it is a creative faith which the modern man can believe would be alone enough to make it the hope of the world.

And this brings me to the second of the two characteristics which a good society must have. It must be progressive; it must lead on to something still better. Now fundamental progress seldom comes from those who fit comfortably and easily into the existing system. It is not, for example, from trust magnates that we expect the inauguration of the new era. In like manner, if we imagine socialism established, it will not be from those who administer it or from those who have least difficulty in adapting themselves to it that new growth will come. New growth will come from the creative people, the men of science, the artists, the thinkers, many of whom very probably will be critics of the new order. Under the influence of commercialism, many men have come to think that the important progress is progress in the technical methods of production, better machinery, better means of communication, and so on. This has been true, since in the past labor was not sufficiently productive to provide a good life for all. But it is true no longer, and with our existing technical knowledge, if we had a scientific socialist organization, every man could have enough without long hours of work. When once men have enough of material commodities, there is no great importance in providing them with a superfluity. It is only commercialism, the competitive struggle for markets, as reinforced by the luxury of the very rich, that has made mere quantity of goods seem so important. We have reached the point where we could organize our material resources in a way that would leave sufficiency and leisure for all. Therefore the important progress now is not in industrial production but in ideas. One might hope that under socialism the energy liberated from the production of luxuries and armaments would be employed in the pursuit of knowledge and in the beautifying of life, bringing back for the many that artistic excellence which existed in the pre-industrial era for the few. But if this is to happen, there must be freedom for the creative people, the men of science and the artists. They must not be controlled at every point by state officials, or obliged to do work at every moment which is pleasing to existing prejudices. Without freedom, the man who is ahead of his age is rendered impotent. All innovations are, to begin with, displeasing to the majority, yet without innovations no society can progress. Freedom for exceptional people, provided their work is creative and not predatory, is the most important condition of progress in any society. There is always a tendency for the administrator to think of himself as God Almighty and to imagine himself capable of judging the good or bad in every new idea. This tendency is dangerous, and would be particularly dangerous in the earlier phases of socialism, where the administrator may be expected to have more power than he has ever had before. The danger can only be met by acknowledging the importance of creative work and the fact that the best creative work often does not commend itself to contemporaries. It is not in the least necessary that the artists and men of science should be rewarded for their work, since the best of them are indifferent to rewards and do their work merely because they love it. But it is necessary that they should be free to do it and free to make it known—that, for example, a man of science should be able to print his work without having first to find favor in the eyes of officials. All this will come about of itself if socialism comes as a liberation for the many, not as a punishment for the few, if it is love for the good we are creating that inspires us, and not merely hatred for the evil we are destroying. It would be demanding the impossible to suggest that hatred should be wholly absent as a generator of energy in the time of transition, but it is important that it should not be the fundamental motive. If hatred is the fundamental motive, the régime created will be oppressive and restrictive, not only where it must be, but also in many directions where oppression and restriction must be avoided if progress is not to cease. It is a world full of hope and joy that we must seek to create, not a world mainly designed to restrain men's evil impulses. Evil impulses must be restrained, especially during the time of transition while they are still strong, but this is an incidental part of our task, not its main purpose or inspiration. The main purpose and inspiration of any reconstruction which is to make a better world must be the liberation of creative impulses, so that men may see that out of them a happier life can be built than out of the present frantic struggle to seize and hold what others desire. Socialism, once established, may so regulate the material side of existence as to enable men to take it for granted and to leave their minds free to employ their leisure in those things which make the true glory of man.

THE FORGOTTEN MAN[1]

WILLIAM GRAHAM SUMNER

[William Graham Sumner (1840–1910) born at Paterson, New Jersey, graduated from Yale in 1863. There he served as professor of social science from 1872 to 1909 and in his generation was Yale's most powerful teacher. Among his many stimulating books the one called *The Challenge of Facts and Other Essays* will suggest by its title the uncompromising and fearless nature of his teaching and writing.]

THE type and formula of most schemes of philanthropy or humanitarianism is this: A and B put their heads together to decide what C shall be made to do for D. The radical vice of all these schemes, from a sociological point of view, is that C is not allowed a voice in the matter, and his position, character, and interests, as well as the ultimate effects on society through C's interests, are entirely overlooked. I call C the Forgotten Man. For once let us look him up and consider his case, for the characteristic of all social doctors is, that they fix their minds on some man or group of men whose case appeals to the sympathies and the imagination, and they plan remedies addressed to the particular trouble; they do not understand that all the parts of society hold together, and that forces which are set in action act and react throughout the

[1] Copyrighted by Graham Sumner and Eliot Sumner. Reprinted by their permission and that of the publishers, The Yale University Press.

whole organism, until an equilibrium is produced by a re-adjustment of all interests and rights. They therefore ignore entirely the source from which they must draw all the energy which they employ in their remedies, and they ignore all the effects on other members of society than the ones they have in view. They are always under the dominion of the superstition of government, and, forgetting that a government produces nothing at all, they leave out of sight the first fact to be remembered in all social discussion—that the State cannot get a cent for any man without taking it from some other man, and this latter must be a man who has produced and saved it. This latter is the Forgotten Man.

The friends of humanity start out with certain benevolent feelings toward "the poor," "the weak," "the laborers," and others of whom they make pets. They generalize these classes, and render them impersonal, and so constitute the classes into social pets. They turn to other classes and appeal to sympathy and generosity, and to all the other noble sentiments of the human heart. Action in the line proposed consists in a transfer of capital from the better off to the worse off. Capital, however, as we have seen, is the force by which civilization is maintained and carried on. The same piece of capital cannot be used in two ways. Every bit of capital, therefore, which is given to a shiftless and inefficient member of society, who makes no return for it, is diverted from a reproductive use; but if it was put to reproductive use, it would have to be granted in wages to an efficient and productive laborer. Hence the real sufferer by that kind of benevolence which consists in an expenditure of capital to protect the good-for-nothing is the industrious laborer. The latter, however, is never thought of in this connection. It is assumed that he is provided for and out of the account. Such a notion only shows how little true notions of political economy have as yet become popularized. There is an almost invincible prejudice that a man who gives a dollar to a beggar is generous and kind-hearted, but that a man who refuses the beggar and puts the dollar in a savings-bank is stingy and mean. The former is putting capital where it is very sure to be wasted, and where it will be a kind of seed for a long succession of future dollars, which must be wasted to ward off a greater strain on the sympathies than would have been occasioned by a refusal in the first place. Inasmuch as the dollar might have been turned into capital and given to a laborer who, while earning it, would have reproduced it, it must be regarded as taken from the latter. When a millionnaire gives a dollar to a beggar the gain of utility to the beggar is enormous, and the loss of utility to the millionnaire is insignificant. Generally the discussion is allowed to rest there. But if the millionnaire makes capital of the dollar, it must go upon the labor market, as a demand for productive services. Hence there is another party in interest—the person who supplies productive services. There always are two parties. The second one is always the Forgotten Man, and anyone who wants to truly understand the matter in question must go and search for the Forgotten Man. He will be found to be worthy, industrious, independent, and self-supporting. He is not, technically, "poor" or "weak"; he minds his own business, and makes no complaint. Consequently the philanthropists never think of him, and trample on him.

We hear a great deal of schemes for "improving the condition of the working-man." In the United States the farther down we go in the grade of labor, the greater is the advantage which the laborer has over the higher classes. A hod-carrier or digger here can, by one day's labor, command many times more days' labor of a carpenter, surveyor, book-keeper, or doctor than any unskilled laborer in Europe could command by one day's labor. The same is true, in a less degree, of the carpenter, as compared with the book-keeper, surveyor, and doctor. This is why the United States is the great country for the unskilled laborer. The economic conditions all favor that class. There is a great continent to be subdued, and there is a fertile soil available to labor, with scarcely any need of capital. Hence the people who have strong arms have what is most needed, and, if it were not for social consideration, higher education would not pay. Such being the case, the working-man needs no improvement in his condition except to be freed from the parasites who are living on him. All schemes for patronizing "the working classes" savor of condescension. They are impertinent and out of place in this free democracy. There is not, in fact, any such state of things or any such relation as would make projects of this kind appropriate. Such projects demoralize both parties, flattering the vanity of one and undermining the self-respect of the other.

For our present purpose it is most important to notice that if we lift any man up we must have a fulcrum, or point of reaction. In society that means that to lift one man up we push another down. The schemes for improving the condition of the working classes interfere in the competition of workmen with each other. The beneficiaries are selected by favoritism, and are apt to be those who have recommended themselves to the friends of humanity by language or conduct which does not betoken independence and energy. Those who suffer a corresponding depression by their interference are the independent and self-reliant, who once more are forgotten or passed over; and the friends of humanity once more appear, in their zeal to help somebody, to be trampling on those who are trying to help themselves.

Trades-unions adopt various devices for raising wages, and those who give their time to philanthropy are interested in these devices, and wish them success. They fix their minds entirely on the workmen for the time being *in* the trade, and do not take note of any other *workmen* as interested in the matter. It is supposed that the fight is between the workmen and their employers, and it is believed that one can give sympathy in that contest to the workmen without feeling responsibility for anything farther. It is soon seen, however, that the employer adds the trades-union and strike risk to the other risks of his business, and settles down to it philosophically. If, now, we go farther, we see that he takes it philosophically because he has passed the loss along on the public. It then appears that the public wealth has been diminished, and that the danger of a trade war, like the danger of a revolution, is a constant reduction of the well-being of all. So far, however, we have seen only things which could *lower* wages—nothing which could raise them. The employer is worried, but that does not raise wages. The public loses, but the loss goes to cover extra risk, and that does not raise wages.

A trades-union raises wages (aside from the legitimate and economic means noticed in Chapter VI) by restricting the number of apprentices who may be taken into the trade. This device acts directly on the supply of laborers, and that produces effects on wages. If, however, the number of apprentices is limited, some are kept out who want to get in. Those who are in have, therefore, made a monopoly, and constituted themselves a privileged class on a basis exactly analogous to that of the old privileged aristocracies. But whatever is gained by this arrangement for those who are in is won at a greater loss to those who are kept out. Hence it is not upon the masters nor upon the public that the trades-unions exert the pressure by which they raise wages; it is upon other persons of the labor class who want to get into the trades, but, not being able to do so, are pushed down into the unskilled labor class. These persons, however, are passed by entirely without notice in all the discussions about trades-unions. They are the Forgotten Men. But, since they want to get into the trade and win their living in it, it is fair to suppose that they are fit for it, would succeed at it, would do well for themselves and society in it; that is to say, that, of all persons interested or concerned, they most deserve our sympathy and attention.

The cases already mentioned involve no legislation. Society, however, maintains police, sheriffs, and various institutions, the object of which is to protect people against themselves—that is, against their own vices.

Almost all legislative effort to prevent vice is really protective of vice, because all such legislation saves the vicious man from the penalty of his vice. Nature's remedies against vice are terrible. She removes the victims without pity. A drunkard in the gutter is just where he ought to be, according to the fitness and tendency of things. Nature has set up on him the process of decline and dissolution by which she removes things which have survived their usefulness. Gambling and other less mentionable vices carry their own penalties with them.

Now, we never can annihilate a penalty. We can only divert it from the head of the man who has incurred it to the heads of others who have not incurred it. A vast amount of "social reform" consists in just this operation. The consequence is that those who have gone astray, being relieved from Nature's fierce discipline, go on to worse, and that there is a constantly heavier burden for the others to bear. Who are the others? When we see a drunkard in the gutter we pity him. If a policeman picks him up, we say that society has interfered to save him from perishing. "Society" is a fine word, and it saves us the trouble of thinking. The industrious and sober workman, who is mulcted of a percentage of his day's wages to pay the policeman, is the one who bears the penalty. But he is the Forgotten Man. He passes by and is never noticed, because he has behaved himself, fulfilled his contracts, and asked for nothing.

The fallacy of all prohibitory, sumptuary, and moral legislation is the same. A and B determine to be teetotalers, which is often a wise determination, and sometimes a necessary one. If A and B are moved by considerations which seem to them good, that is enough. But A and B put their heads together to get a law passed which shall force C to be a teetotaler for the sake of D, who is in danger of drinking too much. There is no pressure on A and B. They are having their own way, and they like it. There is rarely any pressure on D. He does not like it, and evades it. The pressure all comes on C. The question then arises, Who is C? He is the man who wants alcoholic liquors for any honest purpose whatsoever, who would use his liberty without abusing it, who would occasion no public question, and trouble nobody at all. He is the Forgotten Man again, and as soon as he is drawn from his obscurity we see that he is just what each one of us ought to be.

AMERICA AND THE CHANGING WORLD

Toiling centuries have struggled upward on a stony
way,
Just to set the torch of freedom where it flames
aloft today.

Shall the children of the ages fail them in this
mighty trust,
Let their beacon pale and dwindle, quench its
beauty in the dust?

Rather, we shall hold it higher, shake its splendor
through the sky,
Searching out each nook of shadow till the things
of darkness die.

—ODELL SHEPARD

HOW THE PROMISE HAS BEEN REALIZED[1]

HERBERT CROLY

[Herbert Croly was born in New York City in 1869 and was educated at Harvard. From 1900 to 1906 he was editor of *The Architectural Record* and since 1914 he has been editor of *The New Republic*. In the *World's Work* for June, 1910, he tells us that this volume is partly a protest against the fact that "American patriotic formulas could be used . . . to discourage specialized individual effort."]

ALL the conditions of American life have tended to encourage an easy, generous, and irresponsible optimism. As compared to Europeans, Americans have been very much favored by circumstances. Had it not been for the Atlantic Ocean and the virgin wilderness, the United States would never have been the Land of Promise. The European Powers have been obliged from the very conditions of their existence to be more circumspect and less confident of the future. They are always by way of fighting for their national security and integrity. With possible or actual enemies on their several frontiers, and with their land fully occupied by their own population, they need above all to be strong, to be cautious, to be united, and to be opportune in their policy and behavior. The case

[1] From *The Promise of American Life* by Herbert Croly. Copyrighted, 1914, by The Macmillan Company. Reprinted by permission.

of France shows the danger of neglecting the sources of internal strength, while at the same time philandering with ideas and projects of human amelioration. Bismarck and Cavour seized the opportunity of making extremely useful for Germany and Italy the irrelevant and vacillating idealism and the timid absolutism of the third Napoleon. Great Britain has occupied in this respect a better situation than have the Continental Powers. Her insular security made her more independent of the menaces and complications of foreign politics, and left her free to be measurably liberal at home and immeasurably imperial abroad. Yet she has made only a circumspect use of her freedom. British liberalism was forged almost exclusively for the British people and the British peace for colonial subjects. Great Britain could have afforded better than France to tie its national life to an overnational idea, but the only idea in which Britons have really believed was that of British security, prosperity, and power. In the case of our own country the advantages possessed by England have been amplified and extended. The United States was divided from the mainland of Europe not by a channel but by an ocean. Its dimensions were continental rather than insular. We were for the most part freed from alien interference, and could, so far as we dared, experiment with political and social ideals. The land was unoccupied, and its settlement offered an unprecedented area and abundance of economic opportunity. After the Revolution the whole political and social organization was renewed, and made both more serviceable and more flexible. Under such happy circumstances the New World was assuredly destined to become to its inhabitants a Land of Promise—a land in which men were offered a fairer chance and a better future than the best which the Old World could afford.

No more explicit expression has ever been given to the way in which the Land of Promise was first conceived by its children than in the *Letters of an American Farmer.* This book was written by a French Immigrant, Hector St. John de Crèvecœur, before the Revolution, and is informed by an intense consciousness of the difference between conditions in the Old and in the New World.

"What, then, is an American, this new man?" asks the Pennsylvania farmer.

> He is either a European or the descendant of a European; hence the strange mixture of blood, which you will find in no other country. . . .
>
> He becomes an American by being received in the broad lap of our great *Alma Mater.* Here individuals of all nations are melted into a new race of men, whose labors and prosperity will one day cause great changes in the world. Here the rewards of his industry follow with equal steps the progress of his labor; this labor is founded on the basis of *self-interest;* can it want a stronger allurement? Wives and children, who before in vain demanded a morsel of bread, now fat and frolicsome, gladly help their father to clear those fields, whence exuberant crops are to arise to feed them all; without any part being claimed either by a despotic prince, a rich abbot, or a mighty lord. . . . The American is a new man, who acts upon new principles; he must therefore entertain new ideas and form new opinions. From involuntary idleness, servile dependence, penury, and useless labor he has passed to toils of a very different nature rewarded by ample subsistence. This is an American.

Although the foregoing is one of the first, it is also one of the most explicit description of the fundamental American; and it deserves to be analyzed with some care. According to this French convert the American is a man, or the descendant of a man, who has emigrated from Europe chiefly because he expects to be better able in the New World to enjoy the fruits of his own labor. The conception implies, consequently, an Old World, in which the ordinary man cannot become independent and prosperous, and, on the other hand, a New World in which economic opportunities are much more abundant and accessible. America has been peopled by Europeans primarily because they expected in that country to make more money more easily. To the European immigrant—that is, to the aliens who have been converted into Americans by the advantage of American life—the Promise of America has consisted largely in the opportunity which it offered of economic independence and prosperity. Whatever else the better future, of which Europeans anticipate the enjoyment in America, may contain, these converts will consider themselves cheated unless they are in a measure relieved of the curse of poverty.

This conception of American life and its prosperity is as much alive to-day as it was in 1780. Its expression has no doubt been modified during four generations of democratic political independence, but the modification has consisted of an expansion and a development rather than of a transposition. The native American, like the alien immigrant, conceives the better future which awaits himself and other men in America as fundamentally a future in which economic prosperity will be still more abundant and still more accessible than it has yet been either here or abroad. No alteration or attenuation of this demand has been permitted. With all their professions of Christianity their national idea remains thoroughly worldly. They do not want either for themselves or for their descendants an indefinite future of poverty and deprivation in this world, redeemed by beatitude in the next. The Promise, which bulks so large in their patriotic outlook, is a promise of comfort and prosperity for an ever increasing majority of good Americans. At a later stage of their social development they may come to believe that they have ordered a larger supply of prosperity than the economic factory is capable of producing. Those who are already rich and comfortable, and who are keenly alive to the difficulty of distributing these benefits over a larger social area, may come to tolerate the idea that poverty and want are an essential part of the social order. But as yet this traditional European opinion has found few echoes in America, even among the comfortable and the rich. The general belief still is that Americans are not destined to renounce, but to enjoy.

Let it be immediately added, however, that this economic independence and prosperity has always been absolutely associated in the American mind with free political institutions. The "American Farmer" traced the good fortune of the European immigrant in America, not merely to the abundance of economic opportunity, but to the fact that a ruling class of abbots and lords had no prior claim to a large share of the products of the soil. He did not attach the name of democracy to the improved political and social institutions of America, and when the political differences between Great Britain and her American colonies culminated in the Revolutionary War, the converted "American Farmer" was filled with anguish at this violent assertion of the "New Americanism." Nevertheless he was fully alive to the benefits which the immigrant enjoyed from a larger dose of political and social freedom; and so, of course, have been all the more intelligent of the European converts to Americanism. A certain number of them, particularly during the early years, came over less for the purpose of making money than for that of escaping from European political and religious persecution. America has always been conventionally conceived, not merely as a land of abundant and accessible economic opportunities, but also as a refuge for the oppressed; and the immigrant ships are crowded both during times of European famine and during times of political revolution and persecution.

Inevitably, however, this aspect of the American Promise has undergone certain important changes since the establishment of our national independence. When the colonists succeeded in emancipating themselves from political allegiance to Great Britain, they were confronted by the task of organizing a stable and efficient government without encroaching on the freedom, which was even at that time traditionally associated with American life. The task was by no means an easy one, and required for its performance the application of other political principles than that of freedom. The men who were responsible for this great work were not, perhaps, entirely candid in recognizing the profound modifications in their traditional ideas which their constructive political work had implied; but they were at all events fully aware of the great importance of their addition to the American idea. That idea, while not ceasing to be at bottom economic, became more than ever political and social in its meaning and contents. The Land of Freedom became in the course of time also the Land of Equality. The special American political system, the construction of which was predicted in the "Farmer's" assertion of the necessary novelty of American modes of thought and action, was made explicitly, if not uncompromisingly, democratic; and the success of this democratic political system was indissolubly associated in the American mind with the persistence of abundant and widely distributed economic prosperity. Our democratic institutions became in a sense the guarantee that prosperity would continue to be abundant and accessible. In case the majority of good Americans were not prosperous, there would be grave reasons for suspecting that our institutions were not doing their duty.

The more consciously democratic Americans became, however, the less they were satisfied with a conception of the Promised Land, which went no farther than a pervasive economic prosperity guaranteed by free institutions. The amelioration promised to aliens and to future Americans was to possess its moral and social aspect. The implication was, and still is, that by virtue of the more comfortable and less trammeled lives which Americans were enabled to lead, they would constitute a better society and would become in general a worthier set of men. The confidence which American institutions placed in the American citizen was considered equivalent to a greater faith in the excellence of human nature. In our favored land political liberty and economic opportunity were by a process of natural education inevitably making for individual and social amelioration. In Europe the people did not have a fair chance. Population increased more quickly than economic opportunities, and the opportunities which did exist were largely monopolized by privileged classes. Power was lodged in the hands of a few men, whose interest depended upon keeping the people in a condition of economic and political servitude; and in this way a divorce was created between individual interest and social stability and welfare. The interests of the privileged rulers demanded the perpetuation of unjust institutions. The interest of the people demanded a revolutionary upheaval. In the absence of such a revolution they had no sufficient inducement to seek their own material and moral improvement. The theory was proclaimed and accepted as a justification for this system of popular oppression that men were not to be trusted to take care of themselves—that they could be kept socially useful only by the severest measures of moral, religious, and political discipline. The theory of the American democracy and its practice was proclaimed to be the antithesis of this European theory and practice. The people were to be trusted rather than suspected and disciplined. They must be tied to their country by the strong bond of self-interest. Give them a fair chance, and the natural goodness of human nature would do the rest. Individual and public interest will, on the whole, coincide, provided no individuals are allowed to have special privileges. Thus the American system will be predestined to success by its own adequacy, and its success will constitute an enormous stride toward human amelioration. Just because our system is at bottom a thorough test of the ability of human nature to respond admirably to a fair chance, the issue of the experiment is bound to be of more than national importance. The American system stands for the highest hope of an excellent worldly life that mankind has yet ventured—the hope that men can be improved without being fettered, that they can be saved without even vicariously being nailed to the cross.

Such are the claims advanced on behalf of the American system; and within certain limits this system has made good. Americans have been more than usually prosperous. They have been more than usually free. They have, on the whole, made their freedom and prosperity contribute to a higher level of individual and social excellence. Most assuredly the average Americanized American is neither a more intelligent, a wiser, nor a better man than the average European; but he is likely to be a more energetic and hopeful one. Out of a million well-established Americans, taken indiscriminately from all occupations and conditions, compared to a corresponding assortment of Europeans, a larger proportion of the former will be leading alert, active, and useful lives. Within a given social area there will be a smaller amount of social wreckage and a larger amount of wholesome and profitable achievement. The mass of the American people is, on the whole, more deeply stirred, more thoroughly awake, more assertive in their personal demands, and more confident of satisfying them. In a word, they are more alive, and they must be credited with the moral and social benefit attaching to a larger amount of vitality.

Furthermore, this greater individual vitality, although

intimately connected with the superior agricultural and industrial opportunities of a new country, has not been due exclusively to such advantages. Undoubtedly the vast areas of cheap and fertile land which have been continuously available for settlement have contributed, not only to the abundance of American prosperity, but also to the formation of American character and institutions; and undoubtedly many of the economic and political evils which are now becoming offensively obtrusive are directly or indirectly derived from the gradual monopolization of certain important economic opportunities. Nevertheless, these opportunities could never have been converted so quickly into substantial benefits had it not been for our more democratic political and social forms. A privileged class does not secure itself in the enjoyment of its advantages merely by legal intrenchments. It depends quite as much upon disqualifying the "lower classes" from utilizing their opportunities by a species of social inhibition. The rail-splitter can be so easily encouraged to believe that rail-splitting is his vocation. The tragedy in the life of Mr. J. M. Barrie's *The Admirable Crichton* was not due to any legal prohibition of his conversion in England, as on the tropic island, into a veritable chief, but that on English soil he did not in his own soul want any such elevation and distinction. His very loyalty to the forms and fabric of English life kept him fatuously content with the mean truckling and meaner domineering of his position of butler. On the other hand, the loyalty of an American to the American idea would tend to make him more aggressive and self-confident. Our democratic prohibition of any but occasional social distinctions and our democratic dislike to any suggestion of authentic social inferiority have contributed as essentially to the fluid and elastic substances of American life as have its abundant and accessible economic opportunities.

The increased momentum of American life, both in its particles and its mass, unquestionably has a considerable moral and social value. It is the beginning, the only possible beginning, of a better life for the people as individuals and for society. So long as the great majority of the poor in any country are inert and are laboring without any hope of substantial rewards in this world, the whole associated life of that community rests on an equivocal foundation. Its moral and social order is tied to an economic system which starves and mutilates the great majority of the population, and under such conditions its religion necessarily becomes a spiritual drug, administered for the purpose of subduing the popular discontent and relieving the popular misery. The only way the associated life of such a community can be radically improved is by the leavening of the inert popular mass. Their wants must be satisfied and increased with the habit of satisfaction. During the past hundred years every European state has made a great stride in the direction of arousing its poorer citizens to be more wholesomely active, discontented, and expectant; but our own country has succeeded in traveling farther in this direction than has any other, and it may well be proud of its achievement. That the American political and economic system has accomplished so much on behalf of the ordinary man does constitute the fairer hope that men have been justified in entertaining of a better worldly order; and any higher social achievement, which America may hereafter reach, must depend upon an improved perpetuation of this process. The mass of mankind must be aroused to still greater activity by a still more abundant satisfaction of their needs, and by a consequent increase of their aggressive discontent.

The most discriminating appreciation, which I have ever read, of the social value of American national achievement has been written by Mr. John B. Crozier; and the importance of the matter is such that it will be well to quote it at length. Says Mr. Crozier in his chapter on "Reconstruction in America," in the third volume of his *History of Intellectual Development:*

There [in America] a natural equality of sentiment, springing out of and resting on a broad equality of material and social conditions, has been the heritage of the people from the earliest time. . . . This broad natural equality of sentiment, rooted in equal material opportunities, equal education, equal laws, equal opportunities, and equal access to all positions of honor and trust, has just sufficient inequality mixed with it—in the shape of greater or less mental endowments, higher or lower degrees of culture, larger or smaller material possessions, and so on—to keep it sweet and human; while at the same time it is all so gently graded, and marked by transitions so easy and natural, that no gap was anywhere to be discovered on which to found an order of privilege or caste. Now an equality like this, with the erectness, independence, energy and initiative it brings with it, in men, sprung from the loins of an imperial race is a possession, not for a nation only, but for civilization itself and for humanity. It is the distinct raising of the entire body of a people to a higher level, and so brings civilization a stage nearer its goal. It is the first successful attempt in recorded history to get a healthy, natural equality which should reach down to the foundations of the state and to the great masses of men; and in its results corresponds to what in other lands (excepting, perhaps, in luxury alone) has been attained only by the few—the successful and the ruling spirits. To lose it, therefore, to barter it or give it away, would be in the language of

Othello "such deep damnation that nothing else could match," and would be an irreparable loss to the world and to civilization.

Surely no nation can ask for a higher and more generous tribute than that which Mr. Crozier renders to America in the foregoing quotation, and its value is increased by the source from which it comes. It is written by a man who, as a Canadian, has had the opportunity of knowing American life well without being biased in its favor, and who, as the historian of the intellectual development of our race, has made an exhaustive study of the civilizations both of the ancient and the modern worlds. Nothing can be soberly added to it on behalf of American national achievement, but neither should it be diminished by any important idea and phrase. The American economic, political, and social organization has given to its citizens the benefits of material prosperity, political liberty, and a wholesome natural equality; and this achievement is a gain, not only to Americans, but to the world and to civilization.

WANDERING BETWEEN TWO ERAS[1]

STUART P. SHERMAN

[Stuart Pratt Sherman, born at Anita, Iowa, and educated at Williams and at Harvard, was for seventeen years a professor of English at the University of Illinois. Since 1924 he has been the literary editor of the New York *Herald-Tribune*. He is one of the most prominent critics of present-day America.]

LITERARY as well as political historians are certain to fix upon 1918 as the end of an old era, the beginning of a new one; and with increasing assurance, as that date recedes into the past, they will distinguish and insist upon the differences between the buzzing blooming confusion that preceded it and the buzzing blooming confusion that followed it. They will give to the ante-bellum era a significant name and to the post-bellum era a significant name; and by their names we shall know them; and from their names the wayfaring man will be able to deduce the characteristics of the authors who lived in those eras, without the annoyance of having to read them. This will be a convenience to those who wish to find time for reading Plato or *Clarissa Harlowe*.

I suggest that we call the span from 1832 to 1867 The Era of Middle Class Society or The Age of Gentlemen,

[1] Reprinted from *The Review* of May 17, 1919, by permission of the author.

that from 1867 to 1918 The Era of Biological Considerations or The Age of Vital Forces, and the half century for the dawn of which the cocks are now crowing, The Proletarian Millennium or The Age of Economic Units. These epithets have at least the merit of indicating a whence and a whither. When I have shown how the three periods are reflected in their respective literatures, and how they are related to one another, and how, finally, they are related to the deep current which bears the affairs of men onward whether they will or no, then the gentle reader may return to his classics, assured that his house or his houseboat has been set in order; or he may propose an arrangement of his own.

As mirrored in literature and seen through the soft blue haze of time, that early Victorian interval which we have called The Age of Gentlemen lies before us enveloped in its own atmosphere, serene, changeless, finished, like a classical landscape, only a little damaged by the slashing of Mr. Wells and the Militant Suffragettes. What first catches the dreaming eye is the towers of the cathedral at Barchester, that Trollope built, embosomed high in lofty trees, neighbored by Bishop Proudie's palace and the comfortable dwellings of Archdeacon Grantly and Dean Arabin. Then at wide intervals in a countryside tufted with woodlands one makes out the seats of great county families like the Luftons and the Crawleys and the Austin Feverels and odd places like Crotchet Castle and Gryll Grange. Piercing the greenery here and there, rise the ivory towers of the poets: in one of them Tennyson is writing with pearl-handled gold pen his *Idylls of the King,* in another Arnold is meditating his *Tristram and Iseult,* in a third Swinburne is murmuring his *Atalanta in Calydon,* and in still another Morris is chanting his *Earthly Paradise.* These towers and castles are but the accents of the scene. For look! What populous towns and villages have emptied all their folk this pious morn to stream up by twos and threes to hear the Archdeacon's sermon? Colonel Newcome heads the line, followed by an endless procession of clergymen, lawyers, doctors, army officers, civil servants, journalists, merchants, tradesmen, farmers, and other representatives of that great class of *bourgeois gentilshommes* which began in 1832 significantly to displace the old aristocracy as the center of English society. Some of these people have a long way to go before they overtake Colonel Newcome; but they all know where they are going, and they approve of the expedition.

The predominance of a respectable middle class was England's slowly matured response to the radical challenge of the French Revolution and to the contention that all men came to the social compact with equal rights in their hands, naked from the arms of nature. To the searching question put afresh in every age, What is man that he should inherit the earth? England replied, still cherishing fondly in her troubled heart the traditions of an ancient Christian chivalry: "Man is a creature of miscellaneous instincts and unpredictable conduct, as I have freely admitted by the mouth of Mr. Thackeray; but, as I have insisted also by the mouth of Mr. Tennyson, he has the aspirations of a Galahad, the ideals of an Arthur. Man is a being of dual personality; one side is as real as the other; if you would see him whole, you must take them both together. In his sentiments, if not always in his creed and conduct, he is a Christian, a patriot, and a gentleman. With that understanding, I admit him to my society; and I think that I can make a fairly human and creditable place of it." While that understanding endured, a considerable number of the inhabitants of England of course remained outside in mine and factory and unregarded corner, mute or clamoring for a revolution.

In the last fifty years the revolution took place. It created The Era of Biological Considerations. What we actually discover there is the destruction—not by the lower orders but by the intellectuals—of the bonds which held that earlier society together. The Era of Biological Considerations, for which Darwin and Huxley prepared the way, is not properly a society at all. Its characteristic business is not to establish man's relations in a human community but to establish his relations in the animal kingdom. This business generates a new type of literary imagination, a new notion of realism, a new criticism. Equipped with a fresh conception of man, the children of The Era of Biological Considerations reëxamine the professed aspirations of The Age of Gentlemen and pronounce them hypocrisy. What the first age revered as ideals, the second denounces as shams. "Talk not to us," cry the Butlers, the Shaws, the Wellses, the Cannans, the Mackenzies of this veracious epoch, "talk not to us of the duality of human nature, of Tennyson's Arthur and the Victorian ideality; the grand Victorian type is Pecksniff. Man is neither a Christian, a patriot, nor a gentleman; he is a 'bad monkey.' And we have had him under the scalpel. We have seen him under the microscope. He is an agitated congeries of chemical and physical forces. He is a bit of passionate protoplasm. He is a vital force."

We are all, except the very young and the very old, acquainted with the resolute and measurably successful efforts made by writers of the last half century to prove that men are not destined to be Christians, patriots, or gentlemen. It was perhaps Samuel Butler who led off by demonstrating this truth in the case of Ernest Pontifex in *The Way of All Flesh,* a novel which I thought rather dull, till I found all my intelligent contemporaries praising it to the skies as a "brilliant attack upon the institution of the family, especially the relations between parents and children." Thomas Hardy, singular in his sense of the tragic nature of his task, developed with somber and genuine poetic power the thesis that man is a bit of passionate protoplasm plastic on the wheel of Chance, the whimsical Potter, blindly worshiped by the Age of Gentlemen as the Divine Providence. George Moore joined in with a series of novels presenting vital forces in full evening dress, yet not for a moment mistakable for ladies and gentlemen; and he has recently added what I am assured is a very brilliant travesty on the life of Jesus. G. B. Shaw contributed to the bright bonfire of shams the garments of clergymen, prize-fighters, duchesses, and chauffeurs whom he had stripped down to the naked reality of vital forces and set speechifying in a parlor; and in recent years he has launched many a brilliant attack upon patriotism. Mr. Wells, eagerly reeking of the laboratory, has also specialized on heroes and heroines who are emancipated vital forces, and he has supplemented these representations by brilliant attacks upon humanistic education and other institutions designed to perpetuate The Age of

Gentlemen. Mr. Galsworthy has scattered some brilliant aspersions on the institution of property; but, since the success of *The Dark Flower* has rather eclipsed his effusions on the Under Dog, he and his satellites tend to specialize on exhibitions of man as exquisitely palpitating protoplasm. I have just read, for example, in a current magazine his brilliant beginning of a new story about a London rector (of The Age of Gentlemen) and his palpitating cousin and daughter (of The Age of Vital Forces). The rector's cousin, having got rid of two husbands, is now the mistress of attractive Captain Fort. The daughter, having given herself to an officer departing for the war, "with the sole thought of making him hers forever," seems on the point of giving herself also to Captain Fort. While the Captain waits, says my author, he is "turning the leaves of an illustrated journal wherein society beauties, starving Serbians, actresses with pretty legs, prize dogs, sinking ships, royalties, shells bursting, and padres reading funeral services testified to the catholicity of the public taste but did not assuage his nerves."

One cannot compose the literature of this period into a picture of society; it doesn't compose. Like Captain Fort's journal, it presents us a bewildering medley of impressions. It is a picture of disorganization, of a human welter without top or bottom, such as one finds in the novels of Goncharóv, Dostoévsky, and Artzybashev. The writers who express the prevailing spirit of the time represent society as breaking up under biological criticism into the social anarchy of a state of nature. The more vigorous poets have left the ivory towers to go a-vagabonding and ballad-singing down the highways of the earth; others palpitate like exquisite jelly-fish responding to physical stimuli in a protoplasmic prose, sometimes called free verse. Only the novelists are lyrical; and they are lyrical perforce in the general decadence of the dramatic imagination and the confusion of the social scene.

The exceptions—Meredith with his picture of a coherent prosperous intellectual aristocracy, Bennett with his picture of a coherent prosperous canny bourgeoisie, Gissing with his picture of a miserable "ignobly decent" one—these exceptions must be regarded as survivors, retaining in a hostile environment the standards, the aspirations of a former age. Mr. Chesterton is obviously Dickensian. . . . De Morgan is not mentioned at all. The "ethicist" Stevenson with his knightly pose is of course still more out of his setting. As for Conrad and Kipling, neither of them is a painter of society. Conrad is the voice of the vast wistfulness of men who remember hearth and home and household gods but are exiles roaming in African wildernesses, sailing desolate seas, outcasts on solitary islands, mixing with human derelicts and savages, defeated, forgotten. Kipling, on the other hand, is the celebrant of vital forces adventurous, successful, disciplined to the level of military and administrative efficiency, better for the barracks than the parlor, many pegs below the fine wits of Meredith's world, several pegs above the palpitating protoplasms of Mr. Galsworthy's, good for imperial adventure, good for deciding in a world-society that is lapsing into barbarism which forces are fittest to survive.

On this scene the Great War breaks—surely not as an interruption but as the completion of the overmastering drift of the age towards a return to nature. It was precipitated by Germany, because she first among the nations worked up the results of her biological considerations into a clearly defined national policy. Checking the naturalistic reversion at Mr. Kipling's level rather than at Mr. Galsworthy's she sent to the battle line not exquisite protoplasms but efficient vital forces. As fast as we could, we all followed suit. And for four years human society in the greater part of the world gave place to a primitive physical conflict in an ingenious and sophisticated branch of the animal kingdom.

The war is over, and every pleasant person one meets talks hopefully of a new age. Those with the faintest idea of how it is to differ from its predecessor usually betray the vacancy of their imaginations by a facile use of the word "reconstruction." But no hopeful person wants to reconstruct The Age of Vital Forces; that has been too thoroughly discredited. What considerations are going to take the place of those biological reveries which so profoundly affected the imagination of the preceding generation? Patriotism is still a little under the cloud of "vitalistic" nationalism. Christianity is not the prime concern of the reuniting churches, but the minimum wage. There is nothing visibly pointing to an immediate restoration of The Age of Gentlemen. In recognition of certain signs of the times—notably those great bodies of men who have discovered a bond strong enough to hold them together and to make them feel alike, think alike, act alike, and make the Government "stand and deliver"—I have ventured to call the coming period The Proletarian Millennium or The Age of Economic Units. In the new age, when the searching question is asked, What is man that he should inherit the earth? the response will be: "Man is a paid laborer. He is a wage-earner. Give the words what breadth and scope you like." I don't think these definitions quite satisfy every aspiration of the heart; but they are an immense improvement over those which were current in The Age of Biological Considerations. They lift man at once out of the animal kingdom; animals are not wage-earners. They place him in a society at least rudimentarily human. They suggest rough elementary forms of individual and social discipline for other ends than battle.

As we have had only six months of the Millennium, its literature is not yet abundant. The front pages of even the current magazines are still filled with the naturalistic work of the old school. But happily the advertising sections, always written by men of great talent who understand the latest condition of the heart of the people, contain many jewels of the new economic imagination. I select one which indicates pretty well the direction which the march of progress may be expected to take in the next fifty years under the new social leaders. It is headed "Free Proof That I Can Raise Your Pay." It recites a truly inspiriting little tale about a young man who, when he consulted the advertiser, had nothing: "To-day this young man is worth $200,000. He is building a $25,000 home—and paying cash for it. *He has three automobiles. His children go to private schools.* He goes hunting, fishing, traveling whenever the mood strikes him. His income is over a thousand dollars a week."

I think that two automobiles might suffice, unless one can also afford a cook. But is there an impecunious

Economic Unit that does not thrill responsively to literature like that? And in that thrill do we not discern "organic filaments" of a new order? Man is a worshiper of clothes—and woman, too, though at present she seems to prize them in inverse ratio to their quantity. Even in the shaggy "Bolshevik" breast there lurks a furtive desire for a silk hat and a fur-trimmed overcoat, and a slumbering but inextinguishable liking for the manners that go with the clothes, the sentiments that go with the manners, and the principles that support the sentiments. In this universal and ineradicable passion for clothes lies, at present, the reformer's chief hope of bringing the whole body of English society "into one harmonious and truly humane life," that far-off goal towards which the current sets beneath all the whirl of conflicting tendencies.

THE CHANGING MIND OF MAN[1]

EDWIN E. SLOSSON

[For biographical sketch, see page 247]

WHEN this weary old World got to the end of Chapter XIX of his history he turned over the page with a yawn and the wish that he would find Chapter XX more exciting than the *fin de siècle* stuff he had been reading. He found it so.

The real dividing line between the two eras is not the century mark, but August 1, 1914. If any book written after that date is the same as though it had been written before we may safely say that it has little relation to actual life. It is not merely in trivial externalities such as the use of Petrograd instead of St. Petersburg but an indefinable though easily detectable alteration of spirit. In more than one post bellum novel it is possible to tell just how far the author had got when he opened the morning paper and saw that war was declared. We of the present generation used to be amused at our parents because they dated every event in their lives as "before the war" or "after." But we are already falling into the habit.

What an effect the Civil War had upon American litterature is more readily realized by an outsider than by

[1] An address at Dartmouth College. Reprinted by permission of the author.

one of us. It is not merely that the struggle against slavery brought out the best of our poetry and prose, but that the great conflict is still furnishing our writers with motives and plots. A few years before the War when I was on a Pacific steamer, I got to talking with a young New Zealander about American literature. "I have stopped reading American novels," he said. "They are all the same and I know the formula. Virginia mansion —southern girl—northern lover—southern rival—Fort Sumter fired upon—war—wounded—she saves him— he saves her—peace and wedding bells."

Of course I denied the slander on American literature, but I could not help thinking of it the other night when I dropped into a motion picture show and found them reeling off this same old plot. Now if sixty years after the Civil War is over its incidents are still the staple of our stories, we may imagine how long literature will be concerned with the Great War.

There was at first manifest as a reaction from the long strain upon our sympathies a disposition to ignore not only the war but whatever else is repugnant in life. This feeling gave rise to an ostrich-literature of astonishing extent and variety. The movement in its best forms may be what William James called it, "the religion of healthy-mindedness"; in its worst forms it is hardly more than a callous hedonism. A single Mark Tapley is a blessing to the community, but when everybody tries to look on the bright side of things all at once, there is apt to be a jam, and toes are likely to get stepped on. Someone has defined a pessimist as "one who has been living in the society of optimists." It was natural that an overdose of the gladiola books should plunge us later into Schopenhauerean gloom. If we do too much whistling to keep our courage up we are likely to get down in the mouth.

Now we are in the midst of a reaction from the war enthusiasm. Pessimism is a dominant note among conquerors and conquered, alike victims of the great catastrophe.

Anatole France says: "Europe is ill, dying. It is Europe that is now the sick man of the world. And peace has not brought its balm."

In France Professor Demangeon of the Sorbonne writes of *Le Déclin de l'Europe,* published in the United States under the title of *America and the Race for World Dominion.* He sees the center of gravity of international politics removed from Europe and the hegemony of the world passing into the hands of Asiatic and American peoples. In England Webb's *Collapse of Capitalism,* in our own country Stoddard's *Revolt Against Civilization* are indicative of this trend.

In Germany Oswald Spengler has produced a book which in scope of scholarship and eloquence of style reminds one of Schopenhauer, Hegel, and Hartmann. British writers already speak of the "Spengler School" of younger historians. It is *Der Untergang des Abendlandes,* "The Downfall of Western Europe"; a comparative morphology of world history, in two large volumes. Spengler claims to have discovered the universal formula for the development and decline of political institutions, art, science, religion, and philosophy. He shows the courage of his convictions in daring to project his curve into the future and lay out a course of events. According to Spengler's theory Europe passed from the stage of Culture to that of Civilization in 1800 and has before it the stage of Cæsarism (2000 to 2200) manifested by increasing naturalism in political forms; decomposition of folk organisms into amorphous masses of men; their reabsorption in an empire gradually assuming the character of primitive despotism. The final state (after 2200) is "Egyptianism, Mandarinism, Byzantinism"; torpidity and dissolution of the imperial mechanism; the booty of younger peoples or foreign robbers; slow relapse into the state of early man.

Whether or not we believe with Spengler that political life and philosophic thought move in cycles, it is evident that there is in history an alternation of periods of integration and disintegration, of synthesis and analysis. The political and intellectual worlds are, like the physical world, balanced between centrifugal and centripetal forces and they sway alternately to either side. The nineteenth century was an epoch of aggregation, of the drawing together of nations into empires and of like-minded groups of different nationalities into world-wide organizations. In the twentieth century the opposite tendency obviously prevails. The great empires are split up into little, isolated, jealous, and antagonistic nationalities. Probably none of us—perhaps no future generation—will live to see as much international intercourse and individual freedom of movement as we saw in 1914. While engineering is reducing the national barriers that have held peoples apart, while railroads and radios are short-circuiting time and space and, as we say, "making the world smaller," the artificial barriers of national boundaries, tariff walls, divergent speech, and hostile attitude are being erected or resurrected. It is an era of secession, of separation, when the desire for self-determination may overcome the instinct for self-preservation and the lure of self-interest. Languages are being resolved into their constituent dialects and obsolescent tongues revived to serve as a basis for further sub-division. The Ukrainian, Irish, Finnish, Latvian, Lithuanian, and Hebrew languages are ardently cultivated, but the advocates of Esperanto and Ido are now rarely heard. Race prejudices are encouraged and systematically cultivated. Sectarian distinctions are being emphasized.

The partition of the common world is naturally followed by the partition of the common mind. The Balkanization of Europe results necessarily in the Balkanization of the mentality. The new map of Europe looks like a patch-work crazy-quilt, and doubtless our brains seen under the proper rays would look the same. We are living in an era of speeding up and splitting up. The general trend of the times is toward particularization in politics, science, art, and philosophy.

In literature we have shorter stories and shorter paragraphs, shorter sentences and shorter words. The jerky journalistic style has taken the place of the long sweeping sentences of classic English. The short story is the popular form. A volume of fiction is usually made up of a chain of short stories. We might call it the catenary type of fiction as distinguished from the reticulate of the last century.

In painting we see the stipple, the pointillist, the separately discernible brush-strokes. In a futuristic portrait arms, legs, ears, and eyes are scattered over the canvas as though it were a battlefield.

In the most popular form of art to-day, the motion picture, each scene lasts but a thirtieth of a second and an act of over thirty-five seconds is considered long and tedious.

In education specialization has been carried to the extreme and the field of scholarship is parceled out in private claims like the map of an oil field in a boom.

Nature study in its modern form is characterized by the recognition of individuality in animals and plants. The old idea of evolution was a long slow accumulation of minute differences, no sudden breaks. The new theory is evolution by jerks. Darwin's favorite was *Natura non fecit saltum,* "Nature never makes a jump." The Mendelist keeps nature on the jump all the time.

In physics we have the jerk theory of energy taking the place of the old continuum. The ether is abrogated by edict of Einstein. He denies the possibility of simultaneity and has given us the conception of local time. Instead of an infinite expansion of space and time Einstein confines us to a cozy universe of only a hundred million light-years around. The ultimate indivisible unit of matter that the Greek named the "atom" proves to be divisible. It should henceforth be deprived of its alpha privative and be called the "tom." The elusive electron, though thousands of times smaller than the atom and moving with almost the speed of light, can be handled as an individual. Professor Millikan catches and counts them as though they were baseballs.

In philosophy we may trace the same trend in the dominance of pluralism over monism and of pragmatism over universalism.

It would be highly improbable that all these converging tendencies should be disconnected. We must assume that they are all characteristic of the man's mental mood in the present time, though what may be their common cause we may be able to discover.

I must not be understood as meaning that I object to all these movements or any of them. That would be as erroneous as it would be futile. Some of them I like and some I do not like, but that makes no difference to anybody but myself. I do not say that they are right or wrong. I merely say they exist. I am not criticizing. I am describing. The same tendency that is an advance in science and philosophy may be a retrogression in art or literature.

What makes our age different from all the preceding and invalidates the deductions from history is the possession of inanimate power. Man is drawing upon the accumulated capital of the millions of years prior to his advent. In his use of coal and oil he is lighting his houses and running his machines with the sunshine of the Carboniferous Era. Science has given each of us, every man, woman, and child in America, if the apportionment were equal, a train of twenty slaves to wait upon him night and day.

What this acquisition of inanimate energy might mean for the advancement of civilization we can hardly conceive, for of late it has been largely used for the destruction of civilization.

We have now come to realize that what is done by an engine depends as much on the character of the engineer as on the power of the machine. Our horse-power per capita has risen to an unprecedented height. But has our mind-power per capita increased with it in proportion? If not this new-found force may prove dangerous to us. The question on which the future depends is whether men can muster up among them enough mentality and morality to manage the stupendous powers which applied science has recently placed in their hands. Once upon a time, long before the oldest of us was born, before any man was born for that matter—I refer to the Jurassic Era—the ruling race was composed of creatures much larger and more powerful than we are. There were giants on the earth in those days, gigantic saurians which when they stood up on their hind legs would tower up four times as tall as a man. But their cranial cavity was smaller than ours. The Jurassic saurians had grown too big for their brains; so they perished.

Now the addition of machine power to the natural strength of man is equivalent to adding more powerful arms and legs, more skillful hands, and sharper senses. It increases his physical capacity but does not directly enlarge his mental ability. It endows him with a giant's strength but does not teach him how to use it.

Among the horrid fancies that haunted the head of Samuel Butler of Erewhon was a nightmare of a coming age when the machines that man has made for his service should rise in Spartacan revolt and enslave man. This skit of Butler's on "The Mechanical Creation" is brought to mind by recent events.

The last few years have made it manifest that in our civilization the mechanical forces have got ahead of the moral forces. Man is mounted on a bigger horse than he can ride. Making war was an efficient process; making peace is—not. The chemist did his bit with amazing, even alarming, proficiency. The diplomat fell down on his job. The physical sciences have evidently been developed so far beyond the political sciences as to constitute a menace to civilization. The modern man, like the Arabian fisherman, has liberated from the bottle genii that he does not know how to control.

The late War revealed to the horror of the world the possibilities for destruction that science has placed in the hands of mortal man. Unless he has undergone a moral reformation, of which there is no apparent sign, he is not likely to be deterred from using them by a paper prohibition. The Prince of Power of the Air will be the ruling spirit in the next war—if there is a next war. It is now possible to send an airplane, with or without a pilot, by day or night, over the enemy's country to sprinkle the ground with a liquid so deadly that a whiff inhaled or a few drops touching the skin will cause death. There is no need for fine sighting and mathematical calculations such as the artillery man requires; no need to know where the enemy is. The airships of self-propelled projectiles will simply move over the land, as a farmer's potato-bug sprinkler goes over a field, and a certain strip of territory, say a mile wide and a hundred miles long, will be instantaneously depopulated and will remain uninhabitable for days to come. In the next war there will be no frontiers, no entrenched line, no exempt cities, no distinction between combatant and non-combatant. Fortifications will be futile, for the wall that will withstand a forty-two centimeter projectile is easily penetrable to a molecule of poison gas. On sea the revolution will be quite as complete. There will be no need to sink ships in the next war, for the reason that it is not worth while shooting a riderless cavalry horse.

Can we say that man has reached a moral and mental maturity so that he can be safely entrusted with such dangerous weapons? We cannot take them from him as we can take a revolver from a child. But it is clear that unless man can learn how to make proper use of his new-found knowledge he is likely to destroy himself. Science has endowed man with the power of a superman, but his mind remains human, all too human. He is like a pauper come into a fortune, a laborer who has been put into the position of boss of the shop, a private promoted to command the regiment, a slave made the master of slaves. Man has had no training for such responsibilities as have now been thrust upon him. This new command of time and space, this mastery of unknown forces, this apparition of new perils, this entrance into untried fields, all these are too much for man of today. He secretly shrinks and openly blusters. He alternately cowers and brags. He lacks confidence in himself and therefore he suspects others. He is afraid of the dark. He is afraid of his shadow, for that is dark. He shudders with ancient fears. The modern man is suffering from shell shock. He has all the various symptoms. Those who stayed at home are often worse than those that went over there. The victorious nations show the same symptoms as the defeated.

The causeless suspicions, the sudden hatreds, the erratic actions, the intolerance of opposing opinion, the unwillingness to face facts, the return to primitive modes of thought, the alternations of despair and dissipation, the substitution of emotionalism for rationality, the revival of superstition—such are the stigmata of hysteria and such are the characteristics of our time.

In mental diseases where the conscious will relaxes and the more recent centers of thought decay, the patient relapses into a sort of second childhood, using baby-talk, drawing the crude pictures that he made when first he took pencil in hand and reverting consciously to the unconscious voices of infancy.

An uprush of infantilism from the unconscious mind of the human race is dragging the modern world back to the superstitions, obscurantism, formalism, gargoylism, and parochialism of the Dark Ages.

Our most advanced artists take as their teachers the most backward savages surviving on the earth. Formerly ambitious young painters went to Greece or Rome to study. Now they journey to Tahiti or the Congo. If a modernist art gallery should be preserved for several thousand years the archæologist of that day studying the style would unhesitatingly assign it to a period prior to, and more primitive than, the Upper Palæolithic when the Cro-Magnon man depicted the mammoth and the reindeer on the walls of the caves of Altamira, 25,000 years ago.

Modern literature, especially poetry, shows marked reversion to infantile types, in the breaking up of the logical sentence into disconnected fragments, in the appearance of nouns without verbs and adjectives without nouns, in the shortened paragraphs, in the ejaculatory style, in the overruling of sense by sound, in the repetitions almost reaching the point of echolalia.

In music the same reversion to the childhood of the race is apparent. The tom-tom sets the pace for modern progress and the primitive piper calls the tune to which we dance.

The movement toward mediævalism in art, religion, industrial organization, and social forms is gaining strength under the leadership of such brilliant writers as Gilbert K. Chesterton. It seems as if man, with his eyes half opened, resents the light. "Pull down the curtain," he shouts to the scientist, "or I'll pitch you out of the window." Then he rolls over and pulls the cover over his head to get another nice long sleep such as he had from A. D. 300 to A. D. 1200.

The world, like a child at Christmas, is willing to receive the material gifts of science but refuses its moral lessons. The world will accept from the hands of science, railroads and radios, soft raiment and foreign foods, airplanes and submarines, but turns a deaf ear when science would talk of peace, efficiency, economy, foresight, and the frank facing of facts.

It was commonly supposed that the fights for evolution and the higher criticism of the Bible which had absorbed so large a part of the intellectual activity of the nineteenth century had been virtually won by the beginning of the twentieth, but we see now a strong movement against both. Our eloquent ex-Secretary of State, Mr. Bryan, carried on a vigorous campaign against evolution and the Fundamentalists are endeavoring to eliminate the teaching of evolution in the schools and colleges. It is even proposed to go further and to prohibit by law the teaching of anything that offends the religious sentiment or undermines the faith of anyone. Under this law it would be impossible to teach that the earth is round or that the Indians are not descendants of the lost Jewish tribes or that there is any such thing as disease in a school containing a Dowieite, Mormon, or Christian Science child.

We became accustomed to the censorship and the mass

suppression of unpopular opinions during the war, and the disposition to use such legal and illegal means for the repression of undesirable views has been growing ever since. The most remarkable feature of the situation is that there is almost universal acquiescence in the restriction of the rights of free speech and propaganda for which our ancestors fought and suffered martyrdom.

One of the curious though natural results of the War is the millennialist movement which is now sweeping over the country and has appeared in Europe. It is not due to the influence of one powerful personality, but has sprung up spontaneously in various churches and localities, an instinctive outbreak of the folk-psychology, of a state of mind such as prevailed in the year 1000 when it was commonly believed that the end of the world was at hand. In the United States the movement is admirably organized and substantially financed and its missionaries enter in all sorts of circles, preaching the literalist interpretation of the Scriptures and its prophecies.

Along with the suspicion of science and scholarship comes a distrust and dislike of modern civilization, which is built on a scientific foundation. People are looking back with longing eyes to a presumed primitive paradisiaical period, to an Edenic or Arcadian life. Some would have us take to the woods; some to the South Seas. "Back to Nature" is the theme of poets, romancers and even preachers. In India Mahatma Ghandi heads a powerful movement for the elimination of machine power and its products.

The revival of the worship of the heathen earth-goddess, Magna Mater, began in an inoffensive fashion in the literature of the latter part of the eighteenth century and has since infected all classes and countries. It is now securely enthroned in the two strongholds that were erected against it, church and school. The neo-pagan poet Swinburne, who wrote

> Thou hast conquered, O pale Galilean;
> The world has grown gray from thy breath.

was premature in his despair. He might better have written

> Thou hast conquered, O rosy Rousseau;
> The world has grown gay from thy breath.

Those who say "God made the country but the devil made the city" are reading history backward. The word "pagan" means literally "countryman" (paganus). "Civilization" is by self-definition a product of the city dweller (civis). Our modern nature-lovers are trying to rob the Creator of credit for the highest products of creative activity. They would make a scapegoat of God and drive him out of the town into the desert. But God is not in the thunder of whirlwind, but in the voice, the artificial creation of man. It is only by overcoming nature that man can rise.

The cult of naturalism is now dominant everywhere. The call of the wild is drowning out the appeal of civilization. "Back to barbarism!" is the slogan of the hour. Sink into savagery. Praise the country and denounce the city. Admire cliffs but make fun of skyscrapers. Extol forests and despise laboratories. Exalt the physical and ignore the intellectual. Spend \$250,000 on a new gymnasium and let the old library go to ruin. Abolish compulsory Latin and establish compulsory swimming.

Patronize football and neglect debating. Up with the soldier and down with the savant. Jazz your music and cube your painting. Roughcast your walls, corrode your bricks, deckle your bookedges, wormhole your furniture, coarsen your fabrics, and deform your pottery. Condemn everything new and worship everything old. Regenerate obsolescent languages, restore antiquated spelling, adopt mediæval costumes, revive ancient rituals, inflame traditional animosities, resurrect forgotten realms, reërect overthrown barriers. Cultivate the primitive virtues of personal bravery and clan loyalty. Reprove and repress the Christian virtues of kindness and universal sympathy.

Some of the signs of the times I have enumerated are good things in themselves, some are trifles of no consequence, but they all hang together and a floating straw shows the current of a river as well as a log. A change in taste is often the precursor of a shift of the trend of human affairs. The dominant tendency of the times is undoubtedly downward and backward, and the advance of science has not yet availed to check it.

It is a reactionary spirit, antagonistic to progress and destructive to civilization. Science and Christianity are at one in abhorring the natural man and calling upon the civilized man to fight and subdue him. The conquest of nature, not the imitation of nature, is the whole duty of man.

We should "move upward, working out the brute, and let the ape and tiger die." Our sins are mostly survivals. Like the vermiform appendix they are vestigial organs, needing excision. It is those who believe in perpetuating the pugnacious propensities of the lower animals and man in his lower stages who are responsible for these years of war and the consequent anarchy. Modern literature is tainted throughout by that most pestilential heresy, zoölatry. From the child's primer to the sociological treatise, animals and insects are held up for our admiration and imitation.

The back-to-Nature movement is more psychological than actual. Hundreds of books appear annually in favor of country life, and the only volume in opposition is the decennial census report. For in spite of the eloquent advocates of rurality the cities continue to grow. Thousands of square miles of forests are ground to pulp in order to proclaim the witchery of forestry. Thousands of men are forced to labor in dark coal mines in order that they may read the praises of God's own sunshine. Thousands of editors, artists, and nature-writers live in the largest city in the world all the year round in order that they may depict its horrors and hardships and urge others to flee to the freedom of the country.

I have often seen and admired the editor of some metropolitan garden magazine, sticking bravely at his desk in the hottest days of summer and pursuing his studies late at night in the roof garden or the winter garden. Others may take his advice and take to the woods but he, like Casabianca, still stands upon the burning deck of the mammoth metropolis. Such heroism inspires like unselfishness. The youths and maidens of our villages and farms, reading in these journals how much more happily situated they are near to nature's heart, are seized with compassion for the unfortunate urbanite and rush into the largest city within reach in order to leave more room in the country for the over-crowded city dwellers.

I have referred to the reversion to primitive modes of thought and expression, the blind worship of Nature, meaning by that the sub-human, or sub-civilized.

Along with the increasing admiration for the natural comes an increasing belief in the supernatural. The modern believer is disposed to repudiate the Saints and prophets and to pin his faith on Sir Oliver Lodge and Eusapia Palladino. Amulets are again in fashion. The ouija board rivals the typewriter in the production of literature. Astrology has more adherents than lived in ancient Egypt and Babylon. Palmistry is more studied than botany. Rosicrucianism has had a renaissance. The old Roman method of divination has been revived and the apparatus consisting of a ball on the end of a thread is being sold for $2.00 to determine the sex of a chicken from the egg. The magic wand, the divining rod, is used now to find water and gold and lost articles. Witchcraft has appeared again in our courts. In a recent French trial evidence was brought forward in court to prove that the accused had killed people by sticking pins into their wax figures. Satan-worship has become a cult and the Black Mass is celebrated in Paris. That Lord Carnarvon was the victim of Tut-Ankh-Amen's curse is commonly believed. Bleeding images appear in Ireland and weeping virgins in France. Necromancy, or communion with the spirits of the dead, is the fashionable faith of the hour. Sir Conan Doyle, doctor and detective, published photographs of fairies. The Great War was most prolific in miracles. Volumes have been written on the visions and legends of this War. St. George and St. Jeanne d'Arc made up their ancient quarrel and fought on the same side, as numerous witnesses attest. The angels of Mons formed the theme of many a sermon and learned article, and the fact that the vision was traced back to a short story in a London daily did not shake faith in it. The 80,000 Russian soldiers who were transported from Archangel to Scotland and down through England to France were seen by many people *en route*. One lady who reported seeing them in a railway station said she knew they were Russians because "they wore their cossacks." It seems this legend originated in the fact that the supply of Russian eggs was cut off when Petrograd was blockaded, and so the exporter telegraphed to the London house, "80,000 Russians shipped via Archangel."

Against witchcraft and necromancy State and Church fought for hundreds of years by all the means in their power. It must not be assumed that the warfare against witches was altogether irrational and unjustified. There was really never any such thing as witchcraft, but there have always been witches. Some of them were harmless; some of them were harmful. A malignant old woman who was believed and believed herself to have the power to inflict injury on her neighbors by her curses and conjurations was undeniably a nuisance to the community. There were two ways the community might have adopted to get rid of the nuisance; one was to punish witches, the other was not to believe in them. The latter course was impracticable in most communities until recent times; so the former was generally adopted. The same penalty was imposed as for catching a hare or cutting down a tree; that is to say, death. But killing off witches did not eliminate the belief in witchcraft. On the contrary it gave it judicial confirmation. So the laws against witchcraft have been abrogated or allowed to fall into innocuous desuetude.

The last prosecution under the witchcraft law in England took place in 1904, when Sir Alfred Harmsworth, editor of the *Daily Mail,* instituted proceedings against Professor and Madame Keiro, palmists and crystal gazers. The jury found them guilty of both fortune telling and of obtaining money under false pretenses, but the judge only took into consideration the latter count and suspended sentence at that. Instead of burning witches we advertise them.

One of the changes that we must frankly face is the rebellion against the code of morals on which our civilization is based. Formerly those who broke with the Church were careful to declare that they acted in the interests of a purer religion and a higher morality. Those who denied the divinity of Christ were loud in their profession of admiration for the teachings of Jesus. Now, however, we must recognize that a large and increasing class of people in every country not only violate the standards of Christian ethics, but explicitly repudiate them. Violence is advocated as a necessity of the class struggle and even as a desirable thing in itself. Murder is taught as a fine art; the opium dream of De Quincey has become a reality. The destruction of property, the smashing of machines, the damaging of products, the ruination of business, are urged as a sacred duty. Handbooks on the theory and practice of sabotage are published. Work is neglected, not merely from natural laziness, but from conscientious causes. The violation of contract, the breaking of promises, is regarded as the highest ethics. Hatred is diligently cultivated. Licentiousness is openly advocated. Altruism is denied as undesirable or impossible. Sympathy is denounced as a symptom of weakness and degeneracy. Charity is considered as a double injury; it curses him that gives and him that takes. Thrift and industry are classed as vices instead of virtues. Cursing is commended; drunkenness is defended; family quarrels are encouraged; and wife-beating is advocated by popular writers of the day.

Such sentiments in one form or another crop up in current literature so frequently and in such varied forms that it is vain to try to suppress them by any sort of censorship. If it were possible to crush out the Bolsheviki in Russia, the syndicalists of France, the anarchists of Italy, the Nietzscheans of Germany and the I. W. W. of America, there would still persist this spirit of denial of the established principles of ethics. It is not merely anti-Christian; it is clearly anti-moral, for it is a challenge to all that has been regarded as the code of morality throughout the recorded history of the human race. The code of Hammurabi of Babylon, the maxims of Ptah-Hotep of Egypt and the laws of Moses show that essentially the same fundamental principles of right and justice were held then as now. In the seven thousand years since, few persons have questioned them though many have disregarded them. The new thing is that now we hear them openly and emphatically denied and denounced. We can only hope that the advocates of the new immorality may be as unsuccessful as the preachers of the old morality in persuading the people to follow their injunctions.

AMERICA AND ACCELERATION[1]

G. LOWES DICKINSON

[(Goldsworthy) Lowes Dickinson, an English scholar, was educated at Cambridge, where he was for a time fellow and lecturer. He has been for many years a profound student of the civilizations of Europe, America, and the Orient, and in numerous books has presented keen appraisals of those civilizations in a style full of charm and vigor.]

IN ATTEMPTING to estimate what progress means, one could not do better, I suppose, than describe the civilization of the United States. For in describing that, one will be describing the whole civilization of the future, seeing that what America is our colonies are, or will become, and what our colonies are we, too, may hope to attain, if we make the proper sacrifices to preserve the unity of the empire. Let us see, then, what, from an objective point of view, really is the future of this progressing world of ours.

Perhaps, however, before proceeding to analyze the spiritual ideals of the American people, I had better give some account of their country. For environment, as we all know now, has an incalculable effect upon character. Consider, then, the American continent! How simple it is! How broad! How large! How grand in design! A strip of coast, a range of mountains, a plain, a second

[1] From *A Modern Symposium.* Reprinted by permission of the author, and of the publishers, Doubleday, Page & Co.

range, a second strip of coast! That is all! Contrast the complexity of Europe, its lack of symmetry, its variety, irregularity, disorder and caprice! *The geography of the two continents already foreshadows the differences in their civilizations.* On the one hand simplicity and size; on the other a hole-and-corner variety: there are immense rivers, endless forests, interminable plains, *indefinite repetition of a few broad ideas;* here distracting transitions, novelties, surprises, shocks, distinctions in a word, already suggesting Distinction. Even in its physical features America is the land of quantity, while Europe is that of quality. And as with the land, so with its products. How large are the American fruits! How tall the trees! How immense the oysters! What has Europe by comparison? Mere flavor and form, mere beauty, delicacy and grace! America, one would say, is the latest work of the great artist—we are told, indeed, by geologists, that it is the youngest of the continents—conceived at an age when he had begun to repeat himself, broad, summary, impressionist, audacious in empty space; whereas Europe would seem to represent his pre-Raphaelite period, in its wealth of detail, its variety of figure, costume, architecture, landscape, its crudely contrasted colors and minute precision of individual form.

And as with the countries, so with their civilizations. Europe is the home of class, America of democracy. By democracy I do not mean a mere form of government—in that respect, of course, America is less democratic than England; I mean the mental attitude that implies and engenders Indistinction. Indistinction, I say, rather than equality, for the word equality is misleading, and might seem to imply, for example, a social and economic parity of conditions, which no more exists in American than it does in Europe. Politically, as well as socially, America is a plutocracy; her democracy is spiritual and intellectual; and its essence is, the denial of all superiorities save that of wealth. Such superiorities, in fact, hardly exist across the Atlantic. All men there are intelligent, all efficient, all energetic; and as these are the only qualities they possess, so they are the only ones they feel called upon to admire. How different is the case with Europe! How innumerable and how confusing the gradations! For diversities of language and race, indeed, we may not be altogether responsible; but we have superadded to these, distinctions of manner, of feeling, of perception, of intellectual grasp and spiritual insight, unknown to the simpler and vaster consciousness of the West. In addition, in short, to the obvious and fundamentally natural standard of wealth, we have invented others impalpable and artificial in their character; and however rapidly these may be destined to disappear as the race progresses, and the influence of the West begins to dominate the East, they do, nevertheless, still persist, and give to our effete civilization the character of Aristocracy, that is of Caste. In all this we see, as I have suggested, the influence of environment. The old-world stock, transplanted across the ocean, imitates the characteristics of its new home. Sloughing off artificial distinctions, it manifests itself in bold simplicity, broad as the plains, turbulent as the rivers, formless as the mountains, crude as the fruits of its adopted country.

Yet while thus forming themselves into the image of the new world, the Americans have not disdained to make use of such acquisitions of the Past as might be useful to them in the task that lay before them. They have rejected our ideals and our standards; but they have borrowed our capital and our inventions. They have thus been able—a thing unknown before in the history of the world—to start the battle against Nature with weapons ready forged. On the material results they have thus been able to achieve it is the less necessary for me to dilate, that they keep us so fully informed of them themselves. But it may be interesting to note an important consequence in their spiritual life, which has commonly escaped the notice of observers. Thanks to Europe, America has never been powerless in the face of Nature; therefore has never felt Fear; therefore never known Reverence; and therefore never experienced Religion. It may seem paradoxical to make such an assertion about the descendants of the Puritan Fathers; nor do I forget the notorious fact that America is the home of the sects, from the followers of Joseph Smith to those of Mrs. Eddy. But these are the phenomena that illustrate my point. A nation which knew what religion was, in the European sense; whose roots were struck in the soil of spiritual conflict, of temptations and visions in haunted forests or desert sands by the Nile, of midnight risings, scourgings of the flesh, dirges in vast cathedrals, and the miracle of the Host solemnly veiled in a glory of painted light—such a nation would never have accepted Christian Science as a religion. No! Religion in America is a parasite without roots. The questions that have occupied Europe from the dawn of her history, for which she has fought more fiercely than for empire or liberty, for which she has fasted in deserts, agonized in cells, suffered on the cross, and at the stake, for which she has sacrificed wealth, health, ease, intelligence, life, these questions of the meaning of the world, the origin and destiny of the soul, the life after death, the existence of God, and his relation to the universe, for the American people simply do not exist. They are as inaccessible, as impossible to them, as the Sphere to the dwellers in Flatland. That whole dimension is unknown to them. Their healthy and robust intelligence confines itself to the things of this world. Their religion, if they have one, is what I believe they call "healthy-mindedness." It consists in ignoring everything that might suggest a doubt as to the worth of existence, and so conceivably paralyze activity. "Let us eat and drink," they say, with a hearty and robust good faith; omitting as irrelevant and morbid the discouraging appendix, "for to-morrow we die." Indeed! What has death to do with buildings twenty-four stories high, with the fastest trains, the noisiest cities, the busiest crowds in the world, and generally the largest, the finest, the most accelerated of everything that exists? America has sloughed off religion; and as, in the history of Europe, religion has underlain every other activity, she has sloughed off, along with it, the whole European system of spiritual life. Literature, for instance, and Art, do not exist across the Atlantic. I am aware, of course, that Americans write books and paint pictures. But their books are not Literature, nor their pictures Art, except in so far as they represent a faint adumbration of the European tradition. The true spirit of America has no use for such activities. And even if, as must occasionally happen in a population of eighty millions, there is born among them a man of artistic instincts, he is immediately and inevitably repelled to Europe, whence he derives his training and his inspiration, and where alone he can live, observe and create. That this must be so from the nature of the case is obvious when we reflect that *the spirit of Art is disinterested contemplation,* while *that of America is cupidinous acquisition.* Americans, I am aware, believe that they will produce Literature and Art, as they produce coal and steel and oil, by the judicious application of intelligence and capital; but here they do themselves injustice. The qualities that are making them masters of the world, unfit them for slighter and less serious pursuits. The Future is for them, the kingdom of elevators, of telephones, of motor-cars, of flying-machines. Let them not idly hark back, misled by effete traditions, to the old European dream of the kingdom of heaven. "*Excudent alii*" let them say, "for Europe, Letters and Art; *tu regere argento populos, Morgane, memento,* let America rule the world by Syndicates and Trusts!" For such is her true destiny; and that she conceives it to be such, is evidenced by the determination with which she has suppressed all irrelevant activities. Every kind of disinterested intellectual operation she has severely repudiated. In Europe we take delight in the operations of the mind as such, we let it play about a subject, merely for the fun of the thing; we approve knowledge for its own sake; we appreciate irony and wit. But all this is unknown in America. The most intelligent people in the world, they severely limit their intelligence to the adaptation of means to ends. About the ends themselves they never permit themselves to speculate; and for this reason, though they calculate, they never think, though they invent, they never discover, and though they talk, they never converse. For thought implies speculation; reflection, discovery; conversation, leisure; and all alike imply a disinterestedness which has no place in the American system. For the same reason they do not play; they have converted games into battles; and battles in which every weapon is legitimate so long as it is victorious. An American foot-ball match exhibits in a type the American spirit, short, sharp, scientific, intense, no loitering by the road, no enjoyment of the process, no favor, no quarter, but a fight to the death with victory as the end, and anything and everything as the means.

A nation so severely practical could hardly be expected to attach the same importance to the emotions as has been attributed to them by Europeans. Feeling, like Intellect, is not regarded, in the West, as an end in itself. And it is not uninteresting to note that the Americans are the only great nation that has not produced a single lyric of love worth recording. Physically, as well as spiritually, they are a people of cold temperament. Their women, so much and, I do not doubt, so legitimately admired, are as hard as they are brilliant; their glitter is the glitter of ice. Thus happily constituted, Americans are able to avoid the immnse waste of time and energy involved in the formation and maintenance of subtle personal relations. They marry, of course, they produce children, they propagate the race; but, I would venture to say, they do not love, as Europeans have loved; they do not exploit the emotion, analyze and enjoy it, still less express it in manners, in gesture, in epigram, in verse. And hence the kind of shudder produced in a cultivated European by the treatment of emotion in American fiction. The authors are trying to express something they have never experienced, and to graft the European tradition on to a civilization which has none of the elements necessary to nourish and support it.

From this brief analysis of the attitude of Americans towards life, the point with which I started will, I hope, have become clear, that it is idle to apply to them any of the tests which we apply to a European civilization. For they have rejected, whether they know it or not, our whole scheme of values. What, then, is their own? What do they recognize as an end? This is an interesting point on which I have reflected much in the course of my travels. Sometimes I have thought it was wealth, sometimes power, sometimes activity. But a poem, or at least a production in meter, which I came across in the States, gave me a new idea upon the subject. On such a point I speak with great diffidence; but I am inclined to think that my author was right; that the real end which Americans set before themselves is *Acceleration*. To be always moving, and always moving faster, that they think is the beatific life; and with their happy detachment from philosophy and speculation, they are not troubled by the question, *Whither?* If they are asked by Europeans, as they sometimes are, what is the point of going so fast? their only feeling is one of genuine astonishment. Why, they reply, you go fast! And what more can be said? Hence, their contempt for the leisure so much valued by Europeans. Leisure they feel, to be a kind of standing still, the unpardonable sin. Hence, also, their aversion to play, to conversation, to everything that is not work. I once asked an American who had been describing to me the scheme of his laborious life, where it was that the fun came in? He replied, without hesitation and without regret, that it came in nowhere. How should it? It could only act as a brake; and *a brake upon Acceleration is the last thing tolerable to the American genius.*

The American genius, I say: but after all, and this is the real point of my remarks, what America is Europe is becoming. We, who sit here, with the exception, of course, of Wilson, represent the Past, not the Future. Politicians, professors, lawyers, doctors, no matter what our calling, our judgments are determined by the old scale of values. Intellect, Beauty, Emotion, these are the things we count precious; to wealth and to progress we are indifferent, save as conducing to these. And thus, like the speakers who preceded me, we venture to criticize and doubt, where the modern man, American or European, simply and wholeheartedly accepts. For this it would be idle for us to blame ourselves, idle even to regret; we should simply and objectively note that we are out of court. All that we say may be true, but it is irrelevant. "True," says the man of the Future, "we have no religion, literature, or art; we don't know whence we come, nor whither we go; but, what is more important, we don't care. What we do know is, that we are moving faster than anyone ever moved before; and that there is every chance of our moving faster and faster. To inquire *Whither?* is the one thing that we rocognize as blasphemous. The principle of the Universe is Acceleration, and we are its exponents; what is not accelerated will be extinguished; and if we cannot answer ultimate questions, that is the less to be regretted in that, a few centuries hence, there will be nobody left to ask them."

Such is the attitude which I believe to be that of the Future, both in the West and in the East. I do not pretend to sympathize with it; but my perception of it gives a peculiar piquancy to my own position. I rejoice that I was born at the end of an epoch; that I stand as it were at the summit, just before the plunge into the valley below; and looking back, survey and summarize in a glance the ages that are past. I rejoice that my friends are Socrates and Plato, Dante, Michelangelo, Goethe, instead of Mr. Carnegie and Mr. Pierpont Morgan. I rejoice that I belong to an effete country; and that I sit at table with almost the last representatives of the culture, the learning and the ideals of centuries of civilization. I prefer the tradition of the Past to that of the Future; I value it the more for its contrast with that which is to come; and I am the more at ease inasmuch as I feel myself divested of all responsibility towards generations whose ideals and standards I am unable to appreciate.

All this shows, of course, merely that I am not one of the people so aptly described by Wilson as the "new generation." But I flatter myself that my intellectual apprehension is not colored by the circumstances of my own case, and that I have given you a clear and objective picture of what it is that really constitutes progress.

MAKING DEMOCRACY SAFE FOR ENLIGHTENMENT[1]

ROBERT ANDREWS MILLIKAN

[For biographical sketch, see page 259]

THE supreme question which the present generation faces is, Can we make democracy work, not merely for America, but for the world? *Can we replace bullets by ballots?* That question is being asked more searchingly and more fearfully to-day than it was in 1891. *If an affirmative answer is found at all it will be because the nations of the earth, including our own, learn to take a more rational, a more objective, a more scientific attitude toward life and all its problems than any of them have as yet learned to take.* Some wag has said that the anti-evolutionist is opposed to evolution because it never did very much for him. I wish to take that witticism altogether seriously. It is literally true that a good many individuals are still *in the jungle* so far as their method of meeting life's problems, so far as the mainsprings of their conduct are concerned.

For in the jungle ignorance and prejudice and impulse and emotion *must* determine conduct, and *so long as that*

---

[1] From *Science and Life*, copyright, 1924, by Sidney A. Weston and published by the Pilgrim Press. Reprinted by permission of the publishers. This selection is a part of the chapter entitled "Science and Society." It was originally delivered as the Commencement Address at Stanford University, June 18, 1923.

is the case none other save the law of the jungle is possible. Man himself is just now emerging from the jungle. It was only a few hundred years ago that he began to try to use the experimental and the objective method, to try to set aside all his prejudices and his preconceptions, to suspend his judgment until he had all the facts before him, to spare no pains to first see all sides of the situation and then to let his reason and his intelligence, instead of his passion and his prejudice, control his decisions. That is called the scientific method. Why? Not because it is applied only in the study of science, but because it has had its most striking development in the sciences, and because it finds its finest application to-day, though not its only one, in the analytical subjects of mathematics, physics, and chemistry. It is because of that method that these sciences have very recently made the astounding strides referred to a moment ago. It is because of it and what it has done already that scientists dare to hope that the law of the jungle can ultimately be displaced by the law of reason, not only in our domestic affairs but in our international ones as well. It is because of it that scientists in general believe that human life may be indefinitely enriched and human happiness enormously multiplied.

But how far are we from the application of that method now, even in our so-called enlightened United States? Let a few illustrations answer. A few weeks ago the daily press reported that the New York Legislature had passed a bill requiring that the history of the revolutionary period be taught in the New York schools so as to develop patriotism. The only possible interpretation of that act was that the legislature desired the facts of the revolution to be distorted to suit the prejudices of dwellers in New York. It is fortunate, indeed, that this was the same legislature that has just passed a bill which, whatever its purely legal and technical status, is yet deliberately *aimed* at the nullification within New York State of the present constitution of the United States, since otherwise there would be two such legislatures instead of only one in this country. And yet New York thinks that it is representative at least of the average state of evolution and of intelligence of the country. Let us hope that it is mistaken!

My second illustration, however, is not taken from New York. I recently asked a prominent school-book publisher if it would be possible to begin a slow process of eliminating the misunderstandings which lead to war between peoples by inducing publishers of school histories in all countries to submit their proposed school books to three or four international historians of world repute, who would endorse them, if they were able to do so, by the statement that these histories pictured essentially correctly the portions of the field of history with which they dealt. His reply was, "No. It is not yet possible to take such a step in the United States, for the reason that school boards do not yet in this country want history to be taught as it happened. They want something to be called history which pleases their pride and appeals to their prejudices, and I know it because we are ourselves just having our histories attacked in the State of Washington on the ground, not that they are incorrect but that they are unpatriotic." And this sort of thing is happening to publishers all over the United States. This means that we are doing in our America to-day precisely what the whole world condemned Germany for doing in all the years preceding 1914, namely, *teaching nationalism in preference to truth.*

The American newspaper which claims to have the largest circulation of any newspaper in the world displays as its motto the words of Stephen Decatur completely inexcusable, at least as they are usually understood, "Our country! May she always be right, but our country right or wrong." It was in very fact the international hates and misunderstandings caused by just that sort of teaching which brought on the Great War. And yet there are a dozen American newspapers which are sedulously spreading not merely anti-British but anti-international propaganda of every description.

A British visitor who has traveled and lived in this country recently told me that if his analysis were correct the United States was more likely to start another war than was any nation of Europe. But if another such war as the last is started, I, for one, fear that the world may bid good-by to civilization. I am far from being a pessimist, but the history of central Asia, once at the center of the earth's civilization, and again, the very recent history of Russia, both show that it is possible to destroy civilization completely in a very few years of time. *Let those who deliberately set to work by distortion and untruth, by misrepresentation and cynical mistrust of motives, to stir up class hates and class prejudices in America, reflect well upon these things.* Some of them do it from base motives, because the mob has votes or pennies; others have good enough intentions but neither the intelligence nor the training to catch the scientific spirit and to be able, or even to try, to distinguish truth from falsehood. Well-meaning men without poise or any sort of scientific discrimination, and highly trained and able men without conscience are about equally grave dangers to the wholesome development of human society.

Another glaring example. Look at the storm of protest raised in the United States Senate when Mr. Harding proposed that we begin to try to establish a machinery for settling judicially our international difficulties by joining the Hague court of international justice, a body organized largely through the genius of our own Mr. Elihu Root and advocated in essence by both political parties for twenty years, and then ask yourself whether that protest was dictated by ignorance and prejudice or by intelligence and the scientific spirit.

But I do not need to go to Washington, to Chicago, or to New York, nor even to the field of politics for illustrations. We have not, indeed, passed anti-evolution laws as yet in California, but we have many people even here who hasten to condemn evolution without having the remotest conception of what it is that they are condemning, nor the slightest interest in an objective study *of the evidence in the case which is all that "the teaching of evolution" means,* men whose decisions have been formed, as are all decisions in the jungle, by instinct, by impulse, by inherited loves and hates, instead of by reason. Such people may be amiable and lovable, just as is any house dog, but they are a menace to democracy and to civilization because ignorance and the designing men who fatten upon it control their votes and their influence. The churches are often charged by their critics with having more than their share of this type of jungle dwellers, but my own observation is that there are almost as many among the leaders of the churches who have caught the scientific spirit as there are among the so-called scientists themselves, and many more who have caught what is even more essential to progress, the altruistic spirit. Medical science certainly is full of the jungle dwellers, as is shown by the existence of such a scientific anomaly as sects in medicine. *For science is an objective study of the facts of nature.* It uses any and all hypotheses which assist in correlating these facts, and its many hypotheses have had varying degrees of success in making such correlations, but science never commits itself as a matter of faith to any of them, not even to evolution. When it does so it ceases to be science.

But what, now, is the remedy? Is there any hope for the improvement of the situation and the elimination of the dangers which threaten the permanence and success of our modern society inside our commonwealth and outside of it? I have no nostrums to propose. The longer one lives the less confidence does he have in any universal formula. The situation itself which I have portrayed suggests the only solution which there can be, namely, the slow growth of a larger degree of *both public intelligence and public conscience than we now have. Intelligence enables one to know better what he ought to do, while conscience keeps him doing as he knows he ought.* In America the school has concerned itself primarily with the first field, the church with the second. Which will play the larger rôle in getting us out of the jungle I will not attempt to say, but it appears to me fairly obvious that without both of them human society is headed for the rocks. But science, imbued with the spirit of service, which is the essence of religion, and religion guided by the intelligence, the intellectual honesty, the objectiveness, and the effectiveness which is characteristic of the spirit of science, can between them, without a shadow of a doubt, in view of the rate at which discoveries are now being made and at which changes are being brought about, transform this world in a generation. If that transformation actually gets very far in your lifetime, members of the class of 1923, it will be because of the following sorts of influences:

First, it will be because you, graduates, and others of your opportunities, act as centers for the growth in the communities in which you live of both the scientific spirit and the altruistic spirit, and a relatively few such centers can accomplish wonders, for most men follow while but few men lead. It will be because you do not sit idly and thoughtlessly by, expecting that leadership to come from New York or Chicago or other great centers of population. Athens, with its hundred thousand Greeks, did more to shape the development of the race than any city of fifty times its population has ever done, and an insignificant village in Galilee did more than Athens. The only way in which public sentiment, the sovereign power in a democracy, can be developed is by having hundreds and thousands of such centers as we may ourselves create in the communities in which we live. There is nothing new nor spectacular about that remedy any more than there is about any of the processes of growth; but these are, after all, the processes by which most of the progress of this world comes about.

Secondly, I think that people of intelligence will soon take steps to so reorganize the teaching of science in the public schools as to give a larger fraction of the pupils who go through our high schools and colleges more training, particularly in the mathematical and physical sciences, for from my point of view there is no training in objective, analytical thinking, nor in honesty and soundness of judgment, which is comparable to the training furnished by these sciences. I know of no training for life which is equal to it, whether one is to be an engineer, lawyer, business man, or preacher. It is an exceedingly wholesome thing to work at some time in one's life in a field in which *the distinction between right and wrong, between loose and correct thinking, cannot be obliterated or escaped;* to learn that there are eternal physical laws and presumably also eternal æsthetic, moral, and social laws in conformity with which one must proceed if he is to arrive at correct results; to learn, too, that four-fifths of all the experiments which we make in our physical laboratories in the hope of developing new relations, establishing new laws, or opening up new avenues of progress, are found to be directed along wrong lines and have to be abandoned. There is no reason to suppose that any larger percentage of the efforts which are made toward social, political, or educational reform are in the actual direction of progress. With a better realization of these facts we should have less worship of the new *merely because it is new,* fewer cubists in art, in literature, in education, in politics, in social reform. A well-known resident of Southern California who had a fine training in physics and mathematics but has spent his later life as a farmer and fruit grower said to me the other day, "I do not use my science much on my ranch. I guess and blindly follow tradition almost as much as my neighbors, but I know *when I don't know* and they do not. That is worth all my education cost me." If such a change in our public school curriculum as I am suggesting is brought about at all, it is going to be done, I think, through a reorganization of the required group of studies rather than by important changes in methods of instruction in the individual sciences. This is primarily a matter for the attention of the superintendents and principals of our public schools.

In the third place, public-spirited men are going to see more and more that the support in a large way of scientific research is an investment which brings the largest returns of satisfaction to themselves and of progress to mankind which can be made at all. It is my own belief that no efforts toward social readjustments or toward the redistribution of wealth, such as so many well-meaning people are urging in a thousand different ways. have one-tenth part as good a chance of contributing to human well-being as have the efforts of the physicists, the chemists, the biologists, and the engineers toward the better understanding and the better control of nature. The distribution of wealth can, of course, be improved, and I welcome every constructive and sane effort toward its improvement, but the results which can be accomplished for the well-being of mankind by efforts in this direction seem to me to be utterly trivial in comparison with those which may be brought about by physical and biological research. An eminent and progressive economist told me lately that no sort of redistribution of the wealth now available could possibly add more than ten per cent to the income of the average man, and probably much less than that. To replace for the toiler a dollar meal by a dollar and ten cent meal is scarcely my idea of the millennium.

In the fourth place—and this is in my opinion most important of all—*the spirit of religion and the spirit of science are going to join hands,* because the leaders of both religion and of science are coming increasingly to see life as a whole instead of from the pathetically narrow and unscientific point of view from which some in both fields have in the past looked upon it. This is one of the places at which you, young graduates, have your greatest opportunity to exert a very large influence upon your generation.

I should like, in closing, to call two recent events to the attention of any man who is wondering whether after all there is any progress, whether mankind gets farther away from the method of the jungle, and develops any more of the spirit of science, or of the spirit of service than he had in the past. Both of these events seem small, but I think they are pregnant with meaning and with encouragement for the man who has begun to wonder whether human society can ever really catch both the *scientific spirit and the altruistic spirit* and realize the immense possibilities which are before it when it does.

My first event is in the field of medical education. I am informed by my medical friends that the medical fraternity has actually educated itself up to the point where allopaths and homœopaths have got together, to abolish, so far as they themselves are concerned, sectarian schools of medicine. The last of these particular sectarian schools, so I am told, has gone, having been simply and rationally combined into schools which teach merely *medical science* as it is known to-day. Truly "the thoughts of men *are* widened with the process of the suns!"

The second ground for encouragement is found in the following fact: A statement upon the relations of science and religion was recently drawn up, which Bishop Johnson of Los Angeles characterized as a "thoroughly pious statement." It asserted that religion and science were not only not antagonistic, but that both were necessary to the progress and the happiness of mankind. Further, this statement definitely recognized God, and it definitely assigned to religion an even more important place in human life than to science. On the other hand, it called for the recognition by all the signers of the scientific method. *Fifteen-sixteenths of all the scientists to whom that statement was submitted signed it at once without a question as the statement of their belief,* and these men were chosen, let it be remembered, solely because of their outstanding character as scientists and without any knowledge of their religious views. Three-fourths of all the men of affairs approached signed and none expressed dissent, a few, however, preferring for political reasons not to join in the statement. Two-thirds of the religious leaders who were interrogated signed, most of whom were of the more conservative groups. The response of the scientists is particularly significant and possibly has some bearing upon the breadth of view developed by scientific training. After this showing who is he who is asserting that science is materialistic and irreligious? There are a few scientists, it is true, but only a few, who forget the scientific method when they touch the field of religion and scoff at it without knowing anything about it, and these men, too, have their exact counterparts, perhaps in slightly larger numbers, in the field of religion where there is, I regret to say, a group of blind leaders of the blind, men who still follow the method of the jungle and are still imbued with its spirit of prejudice, preconception and intolerance. Yet there is here the best of evidence that the leadership in both science and religion is in the main imbued with both the spirit of intellectual honesty and objectiveness which is characteristic of science, and the spirit of altruism and service which is the glory of religion. *This combination is the only nostrum which there is for human ills, the only hope for a paradise on earth, and each of us has the opportunity to do his bit toward bringing it about.*

(*The purpose of the following statement is to assist in correcting two erroneous impressions which seem to be current among certain groups of persons. The first is that religion to-day stands for mediæval theology; the second, that science is materialistic and irreligious.*)

A JOINT STATEMENT UPON THE RELATIONS OF SCIENCE AND RELIGION [1]

By a Group of Scientists, Religious Leaders, and Men of Affairs.

We, the undersigned, deeply regret that in recent controversies there has been a tendency to present science and religion as irreconcilable and antagonistic domains of thought, for in fact they meet distinct human needs, and in the rounding out of human life they supplement rather than displace or oppose each other.

The purpose of science is to develop, without prejudice or preconception of any kind, a knowledge of the facts, the laws, and the processes of nature. The even more important task of reli-

[1] This is the statement referred to in the preceding address and published in the press of the United States in June, 1923.

gion, on the other hand, is to develop the consciences, the ideals, and the aspirations of mankind. Each of these two activities represents a deep and vital function of the soul of man, and both are necessary for the life, the progress, and the happiness of the human race.

It is a sublime conception of God which is furnished by science, and one wholly consonant with the highest ideals of religion, when it represents him as revealing himself through countless ages in the development of the earth as an abode for man and in the age-long inbreathing of life into its constituent matter, culminating in man with his spiritual nature and all his God-like powers.

RELIGIOUS LEADERS

Bishop WILLIAM LAWRENCE, Episcopalian, Bishop of Massachusetts, Boston.

Bishop WILLIAM THOMAS MANNING, Episcopalian, Bishop's House, Cathedral Heights, New York City.

Bishop JOSEPH H. JOHNSON, Episcopalian, Bishop of Los Angeles, California.

Dr. HENRY VAN DYKE, Presbyterian, Preacher and Poet, Princeton, New Jersey.

Dr. JAMES I. VANCE, Presbyterian, First Presbyterian Church, Nashville, Tennessee.

Dr. JOHN D. DAVIS, Presbyterian, Professor of Old Testament Literature, Princeton Theological Seminary, Princeton, New Jersey.

President, JAMES GORE KING MCCLURE, Presbyterian, McCormick Theological Seminary, Chicago, Illinois.

President CLARENCE A. BARBOUR, Baptist, Rochester Theological Seminary, Rochester, New York.

President ERNEST D. BURTON, Baptist, Theologian, President of University of Chicago, Illinois.

President WILLIAM LOUIS POTEAT, Baptist, Wake Forest College, Wake Forest, North Carolina.

President HENRY CHURCHILL KING, Congregationalist, Oberlin Graduate School of Theology, Oberlin, Ohio.

Dr. ROBERT E. BROWN, Congregationalist, Second Congregational Church, Waterbury, Connecticut.

Bishop FRANCIS JOHN MCCONNELL, Methodist, Pittsburgh, Pennsylvania.

Dr. Merle N. Smith, Methodist, First Methodist Church, Pasadena, California.

Dr. Peter Ainslie, Disciple, Christian Temple, Baltimore, Maryland.

Dr. Herbert L. Willett, Disciple, Theologian, Associate Editor, *Christian Century,* Chicago, Illinois.

SCIENTISTS

Charles D. Walcott, Geologist, President of the National Academy of Sciences, President of the American Association for the Advancement of Science, and Head of the Smithsonian Institution of Washington.

Henry Fairfield Osborn, Paleontologist, President of the American Museum of Natural History, New York.

Edwin Grant Conklin, Zoölogist, Head of the Department of Zoology, Princeton University.

James Rowland Angell, Psychologist, President of Yale University.

John Merle Coulter, Botanist, Head of the Department of Botany, University of Chicago.

Michael I. Pupin, Physicist and Engineer, Professor of Electromechanics and Director of Phœnix Research Laboratory, Columbia University.

William James Mayo, Surgeon, Mayo Foundation for Medical Education and Research, Rochester, Minnesota.

George David Birkhoff, Mathematician, Head of the Department of Mathematics, Harvard University, Cambridge, Massachusetts.

Arthur A. Noyes, Chemist, Director of the Gates Chemical Laboratory, California Institute of Technology, Pasadena, California.

William Wallace Campbell, Astronomer, Director of Lick Observatory and President-elect of the University of California.

John J. Carthy, Engineer, Vice-President in Charge of Research, American Telephone and Telegraph Company, New York.

Robert A. Millikan, Physicist, Director of Norman Bridge Laboratory of Physics, Pasadena, California.

William Henry Welch, Pathologist, Director of the School of Hygiene and Public Health, Johns Hopkins University, Baltimore.

JOHN C. MERRIAM, Paleontologist, President of The Carnegie Institute of Washington.

GANO DUNN, Engineer, Chairman of the National Research Council, Washington, D. C.

MEN OF AFFAIRS

HERBERT HOOVER, Secretary of Commerce, Washington, D. C.

JAMES JOHN DAVIS, Secretary of Labor, Washington, D. C.

ELIHU ROOT, ex-Secretary of State, New York City.

DAVID F. HOUSTON, ex-Secretary of the Treasury, 195 Broadway, New York City.

FRANK O. LOWDEN, ex-Governor of Illinois, Oregon, Illinois.

JOHN SHARPE WILLIAMS, ex-United States Senator, Yazoo City, Mississippi.

Rear Admiral WILLIAM S. SIMS, Commander United States Naval Forces in European Waters during the World War, Newport, Rhode Island.

HARRY BATES THAYER, President American Telephone and Telegraph Company, 195 Broadway, New York City.

JULIUS KRUTTSCHNITT, Chairman of the Executive Committee, Southern Pacific Railway, 165 Broadway, New York City.

FRANK VANDERLIP, ex-President National City Bank of New York, Scarborough, N. Y.

HENRY S. PRITCHETT, President Carnegie Corporation of New York.

WILLIAM ALLEN WHITE, Writer and Editor of Emporia *Gazette,* Emporia, Kansas.

VICTOR F. LAWSON, Editor and Publisher of the Chicago *Daily News.*

JOHN G. SHEDD, ex-President of The Marshall Field Company, Chicago.

THE DUTY OF INTERNATIONALISM[1]

ALBERT EDWARD WIGGAM

[Albert Edward Wiggam was born in Austin, Indiana, in 1871, and was educated at Hanover College in his native state. He has had a varied career in business, mining, and lecturing. In 1923 he became nationally known through the striking book from which the following chapter is taken. This chapter is his "Ninth Commandment" and like the rest of the volume is in the form of direct address to the President of the United States.]

THE ninth commandment of science to statesmanship and to all mankind is the duty of internationalism. As Professor Giddings has suggested in his profound analysis entitled, *Studies in the Theory of Society,* there looms before every dream and achievement of man huge, defiant, portentous, the one eternal, inescapable question: *"Is it peace or is it war?"*

If you should write upon the cover of every book, above the entrance to every school and church, above the door of every home and the cradle of every babe this black and terrifying question, "IS IT PEACE OR IS IT WAR?" you would describe the precise situation of the human species on this globe. It always has been so; it always will be. The answer has always come in the sepulchral voice of hell—"War!" Surely, surely, surely

[1] From *The New Decalogue of Science,* copyright, 1922, and published by the Bobbs-Merrill Co. Reprinted by permission of and by special arrangement with the publishers.

the spirit of man is capable of answering it in the angelic voice of heaven—"Peace!"

I think, Your Excellency, we can discuss this question with clasped hands, common desires, united hopes and similar sympathies. The agony of the world is too great, too much of its soil is still wet with tears and blood for men to approach the problem of peace or war to-day in any other spirit. Yet, there is one man who, I think, cannot help us—the pacifist. He might achieve a world of stagnation, but not a world of virile and adventurous peace. He would have you believe that men hate war. Do not let him deceive you with any such fantastic biological buncombe. It will lead you into fantastic and futile undertakings. You must understand and legislate for a human being that exists, not for one that does not. Men love war. They always have; they always will. "All wild animals die a tragic death." And in doing so even the timidest live one moment of superlative ecstasy. And men, in their brief moment of civilization, have not forgotten this most precious teaching of evolution. If nature had not taught every organic thing to rush to its death in one last flame of ecstatic life, the courage which makes us believe that peace is possible would never have bloomed.

I think this is basic to all discussion of this irrepressible issue. I can see no natural peace in nature. I can see only the peace of educated intelligence. Nature is war to the death. It was she who taught men to meet their "rendezvous with death" with the gaiety of wedding bells. But in doing this she had to develop within the organism two characters that are at war—intelligence and sympathy. Intelligently guided sympathy is our only biological hope. Intelligence and sympathy made the group possible, yet the moment the group either attacks or is attacked they are both lost. Hate and selfishness instantly resume their primal sway. We are told by those who still live in the ancient world of 1913, "In time of peace prepare for war." Quite the contrary. In time of peace prepare for eternal peace. Prepare men's intelligence and sympathy, by education, art, ethics, philosophy, religion, by new social, economic and political objectives, so that in the hour of passion, reason and humanity will not lose their majestic sanctions to the mad terror of tooth and claw. The human spirit has bloomed out of blood and only an insistent air of intelligent humanism will preserve and spread its perfume.

There are three main biological causes for war. Deepest and oldest is self-preservation—the first necessity, therefore the first "law" of nature. Second, the preservation of offspring, and third, preservation of the group. But, within the historic period, war in the larger sense, has been mainly motivated, I think by two things: first, "the bitter cry of the children,"—the preservation of the offspring—and second, social, economic and political nationalism—the aggrandizement of the group. This is not group preservation but satisfaction of its egotism. It is the one great extra-biological cause for war, and, therefore, the most susceptible to education.

The bitter cry of the children often causes war, because children cry for but one thing, food. You and I cry for wealth, culture, economic imperialism, national expansion, upholstered furniture and fine homes. But children cry for but one thing, something to eat. And when children have nothing to eat, nations go to war.

There are also many psychological causes of war. But the bio-economic situation of humanity can always be summed up in the very simple formula that when population outruns food supply nature leaps from her lair with her three swords of organic destiny, Famine, Pestilence and War, and reaps her human harvest. Especially does she mow down the children—the children at one end in the cradle and the children at the other end in their dotage, while the prime manhood of the nation dies fighting for food on the battle-field.

"But," exclaims the *laissez faire* selectionist, "this gives natural selection her happy chance to produce strength and genius!" True enough. But what is the use of strength and genius in a world not fit to live in?

Yet, unless through "adaptive fecundity" you do adapt the numbers of your people to the capacity of the soil to feed them, and unless through preferential fecundity you elevate their intelligence and character that they may make the most of the soil nature has allotted them, and, still further, unless by education you train them to a high coöperative life with their neighbor peoples, then this heartless, triple-headed Juggernaut, Famine, Pestilence and War, will grind on its ruthless way. By and by, no matter how beautiful your temples nor how bountiful your culture, your hungry, diseased, bleeding civilization will go down before some other hungry, diseased, bleeding civilization, fighting for food for its children. And the thing we call "Christian" civilization becomes a travesty upon the name.

If you doubt this dénouement to your brilliant social order and colossal mechanical power, let me remind you that at last our scientists have been able, for the first time, to make a truly planetary survey of the food and population problems. In a summary by Prof. E. M. East, of Harvard, which is characterized by the eminent Dr. Raymond Pearl, of Johns Hopkins, as the "most brilliant survey of the population question of this generation," Professor East points out that every civilized land, Europe, America, the Orient, has long ago exceeded the food capacity of its own soil, and is feeding its people from the uncivilized, more sparsely settled quarters of the globe. Within fifteen years, he tells us, the United States will not have a pound of food to export, unless it be in exchange for some other form of food, and that a short crop will mean the universal rationing of food more severe than during the Great War. The bitter cry of your own children for food is not so far away as you so comfortably, even egotistically, think. The scientist can already hear their faint but terrifying wail in the near distance.

Further than this, Havelock Ellis, the British scientist-essayist, calls attention to a fact obvious to common sense but utterly overlooked by statesmanship. This significant fact is that throughout its millions of years on earth up until 1800, the human race had increased from its first pair to only eight hundred and fifty millions. But in 1800 the industrial revolution mechanized civilization. As a result, an enormous increment of wealth, transportation and food began. And, within the mere flash of a century, the human race has leaped from eight hundred fifty millions to nearly two thousand millions!

But, more significant still, East and Pearl have shown, the latter by brilliant experiments upon the fruit fly, *drosophila,* and by ingenious biometrical calculations upon human populations, that the final goal of man on earth, as to mere numbers, is already clearly in sight. You talk glibly of a half billion in the United States alone. You have not reckoned, Sir, with nature. Pearl has shown that they will never reach more than two hundred millions. You think to feed them continuously from the luxuriant under-populated tropics. But, under the world-wide birth release of wealth and science, they, too, are filling up. Knibbs, a statistician quoted by Ellis, believes the world is filling up at the rate of twenty millions a year—a new France every twenty-four months. East estimates it at fifteen millions, two new Belgiums—almost two new Canadas every year! Despite every triumph of science, East believes that the whole earth will never feed more than five billion human beings, and that the day when they will all be here is not more than six to eight generations away. Our great-grandchildren, possibly some of our grandchildren, will be numbered among them.

Three things, as Ellis elaborates, have occurred but yesterday that should give statesmanship pause. First, the industrial revolution, which, as wealth and food always do, speeded up procreation enormously. Second, the growth of hygiene, medicine and sanitation, which prolongs life, as I have shown, particularly among the weaklings. And third, the growth of humanitarian sentiment—especially under the influence of Christianity—which has again saved feeble life at one end of the scale, and prolonged its existence, and period of child-bearing, at the other. The world, then, will soon be full, but what will it be full of? When you can already sail round the earth, and can soon fly round it, and send your voice round it eight times within a second, it has shrunk from the "vast new worlds" of Magellan and Columbus, or even the "limitless prairies" of our own boyhood, to a tiny biological experiment station. And yet it is an experiment so great, so tumbling with gigantic forces, so incalculable in its evolutionary trends, that statesmanship may well stand aghast at the prospect of guiding it to anything but chaos.

What have you done so far to guide it? Wealth, more goods, more wages, power, leisure, amusement, speed—these have been your personal ideals. Nationalism and economic imperialism have been your goals of statesmanship. So-called democratic peoples have called it more tenderly national expansion, national development. These phrases make a more soothing emollient to the national conscience. Here in America you pride yourself that you have finished the physical conquest of the continent. Indeed you have. You gave the Indian the doctrine of the atonement in exchange for his lands. You traded him cheap whisky, measles, typhoid, tuberculosis, syphilis, and a sex-morals worse than his own, for his natural resources, so long ago that you have comfortably forgotten about it. You did little better by Mexico. It merely happened that they could breed too fast to make room for you to occupy their soil. The treatment of every "Christian" nation by every other has been precisely on a par with this. It is merely typical of all internationalism up to date.

As the biologist sees war to-day, there are two great conceptions of the social destiny of man which lie back of it; first, nationalism, and second, nationality. The latter conception of nationhood, natural nationality, is the fruition of the finest things in human nature. Economic and political nationalism is the blackest, ghastliest thing that ever stalked with its blood-spattered seven-league boots across this fair earth. Nationality, as pointed out by that most brilliant of our social philosophers, Everett Dean Martin, is the flower of all that is most distinctive and unique in the cultures of the world's varied peoples. As suggested by Glenn Frank, it makes "cultural nationalism," as opposed to political and economic nationalism, the proper ideal of every state.

A man naturally loves his country. It may be poor but it is his own. He loves the rocks and hillsides, the breezes that blow across them, the trees, the very vegetation amid which he was born. He loves the old home, its folks and folkways; he loves the path he trod to school, the schoolroom, the college, the university. He loves his nation's art and literature. They give him nearly all his world wisdom and criticism of life. He loves his country's history, although so far his school-books have been too much steeped in the records of its nationalism, instead of its cultural development and spiritual conquests. But these things make up nationality. A man will fight for them, and he is a poor thing if he will not. They are the things men live by, love by, die by. They ought to be. This earth offers nothing richer.

There be those who for all this would substitute a "World State." Mr. H. G. Wells has, I think, set out for inspection all there is to this conception. Its romance appeals much more to Mr. Wells' imagination, I think, than its common sense will appeal to the judgment of mankind. I am opposed to it for six distinct reasons, any one of which I believe fatal to such a fantastic project.

First, it is beyond the intellectual power of mankind. Evolution does not throw up leaders fast enough to carry it on. It would require the continuous presence in the world of Genghis Khan, Pericles, Alexander the Great, Cæsar, Napoleon, Lincoln, Roosevelt and Henry Ford, all working together with the spirit of the Twelve Apostles, with the immediacy of a social heaven before them to make a go of it.

Second, there is no existent psychology to-day to build it on. Nobody much wants it. The vast social ardors and political enthusiasm necessary to put it over, even for trial, simply do not exist. I beg Mr. Wells to point to any evidence of them anywhere.

Third, "liberty," as Edmund Burke said, "must inhere in some sensible object." So must all loyalties. Men require something which they can touch, see, feel, something which their imaginations can enclose. Men can be loyal to their homes, their county, state or nation because they are theirs. They are personal possessions. But men cannot possess a World State even in imagination. They can't belong to it. They could nearly as easily be loyal to the planetary system. Men will fight for a red or white rose, but not for the size or color of the planets.

Fourth, it would not only fail to create the new loyalties necessary, but it would destroy the old ones—the great deep loyalties of nationality—all those nourishing things that give uniqueness, distinctiveness, picturesqueness, peculiarity and quaintness to the inhabitants of each separate nation. These are too precious, too interesting, too native. No people would ever give them up. They give fragrance to a people's life—they are its essence and perfume, if you please, its local color. They constitute the personality, the national character of any people.

Fifth, the benefits, even in theory, of a World State are not obvious enough to make it seem a fair exchange for the rich possessions already in hand.

Sixth, I think it biologically and, therefore, politically impossible if man is ever to progress toward richer inborn endowment, or even maintain his present organic level. It would shortly plunge the world back into savagery. This latter is because, as emphasized by Prof. Edward A. Ross, national boundaries prevent the peoples of lower development from wandering and migrating en masse hither and thither over the earth, pouring their mongrel blood into richer racial streams. With indiscriminate mixture of all peoples three things would result; first, a lowering of the blood of the enterprising pioneers who discovered and developed any country; second, a lowering of morality, of social and cultural standards; and third, a lowering of its political efficiency with a resulting chaos in its economic and political machinery. The latter two are certainly beginning to show up in America, owing to its low immigrations of the past two generations.

Nations cannot progress to any high standards of social life, gentility and polish, nor to any ordered working of political institutions, without a homogeneous national mind, a common racial outlook, similar cultural traditions, common language and literature. In short, there must be a national like-mindedness, which is the outcome of biological like-mindedness, inner similarity of physio-psychological organization. The fact, as witnessed by the writer, that during the great Dayton, Ohio, flood, many of the foreigners of lower cultures, and doubtless of inferior racial make-up, had to be forced to clean the mud from their beds and houses at the point of the bayonet, is a poignant national reminder. This has a world political significance. Those who recklessly think the mining of a few more tons of coal, or the manufacture of a few more pounds of steel, is worth this price have reckoned in dollars instead of national character. This lowering of the bars of our American development which was rapidly trending toward unique, picturesque national individuality in art, politics, social life, education, folkways, speech and literature has probably robbed us forever of our manifest destiny. We had clearly before us to become a greater Greece, a grander Rome, a more puissant England with a still nobler influence. We are the children of these cultures and should enrich them. With wise statesmanship, we may do it yet, but you have thus infinitely delayed such a consummation.

The ideal, therefore, of nationality which should be wrought into the fabric of all social thought, is that of a stable population in every nation, whether large or small, of very great racial homogeneity, constantly balanced between numbers and food supply, developing its national personality and slowly elevating the biological quality of its people by every eugenical agency. With nationalism rampant, permanent national eugenics is impossible. With a world state it is equally so. It is only those who do not understand eugenics who advocate such a scheme. A world state would not end war but promote it. It would not speed up evolution but largely end it. You must set up immigration barriers or the development of unique and virile peoples is impossible. And the moment you set up immigration barriers, as Ross has pointed out, you are back into the old nationhood again. And whether that nationhood becomes the rich fruition of character and culture of nationality, or the damnable, blasting, war-breeding thing of nationalism, depends wholly upon the intelligence and idealism that animates the statesmanship of to-morrow. Nationality, coupled with coöperative internationality, is the biological as well as the cultural, economic and political hope of mankind.

Do not imagine, therefore, Sir, that the biologist is looking forward to some new baptism of brotherly love descending upon men; or that the world is suddenly going to become a mutual admiration society. Men in the mass will not keep the peace unless they are forced to. Nations are made up of crowds, and crowds have to be watched and guided. For a long time yet, occasionally somebody will have to be shot and others hanged. The more the national ringleaders in such cases can be haled into court, and this salutary process personally administered, the more rapidly will international peace progress. Had a dozen of the right men, not all of them in Germany, been shot in 1913, when it was obvious they were starting out with intent to kill, the war would not and could not have occurred. The world is to-day allowing a great many of these arch-criminals to be at large with nothing more effective to restrain them than pious resolutions of peace societies and prayer by the churches on Sunday.

But the more the mad license of nationalism can be,

by force, moral suasion, education and the development of practical international agencies, reduced to the liberty of free nationalities under duly enforced law, the fewer the hangings and the farther between. But there is no evidence that either the tongues or spirits of angels are about to possess mankind. Internationality will come only by hard work, virile thinking, immense tolerance and patience, and education. We cannot as yet safely lay the big stick on the shelf, but we can enormously reduce its size and make it an international instead of a national weapon. In the end the chief weapons of internationalism are books, not cannon; exchange professorships, not poison gas; commercial coöperation and rationing of world-resources, not cut-throat competition; business, not bullets. But this ideal will come about neither through a world state, nor a sudden baptism of brotherly love, but through a rational education of man's present psychology and the direction to more intelligent ends of those agencies and institutions of national life which alone will express present human nature and give it its natural satisfactions.

Finally, then, it is evident that even a scientific civilization, if it be only national, will soon be crushed by war. It will never make war, but it must defend itself. Internationalism is no longer a theory but a condition; not a dream but a necessity of national existence. No nation, therefore, can remain civilized until all nations become civilized. As a selective agent for killing the unfit and preserving the fit, it is probable that modern war has scarcely more survival value than an earthquake. And just as earthquakes are going out of fashion, so must war go the same way. Your nationalistic slogans, ambitions and power propagandas are not only not sufficient unto a world order, but they are not even sufficient unto a permanent national order.

Moreover, as I have shown, these vast problems of race migrations, mixtures, hybridizations, and the pressures of populations upon food, no matter how many times you multiply your food, will to-morrow tax all the genius, both of science and statesmanship. Biology has exploded the myth of the melting pot as it has the myth of war. Each race and nation must still continue to create its own culture, its own national or racial psychology, its own specific intellectual discipline. But if one culture is to continue to crush another by war, or if great spiritual disciplines are to be lost by the hybridization of strange and disharmonic peoples, all civilization will periodically go down in the biological holocaust. It is only the abounding development of humanism amid the free air of individualistic, distinctive, undisturbed nationality, free because it is free from the fear of war, free because it has espoused the scientific spirit, free because it has thus developed the power and passion to create for all mankind a true world-wisdom through the friendly fraternity of nations that will ever give this blood-drenched, but still "moonlit and dream-visited planet" a virile, virtuous and adventurous peace. And to attain this freedom, your narrow nationalistic patriotisms, loyalties and ambitions must merge—not disappear, for men must not become stagnant—but merge into the larger loyalties, the wider moralities and the higher processes of the unitary development of man.

HORIZONS

Something hidden. Go and find it. Go and look
behind the Ranges—
Something lost behind the ranges. Lost and waiting for you. Go!

—Kipling

THE AMERICAN SCHOLAR[1]

RALPH WALDO EMERSON

[Ralph Waldo Emerson (1803-1882) was born in Boston. He graduated at Harvard in 1821. He made three visits to England and lectured extensively in America, but during the greater part of his life he lived quietly at Concord. Through his essays and other writings he has exerted probably more influence than any other American author. The following memorable address, while delivered for a specific purpose, gathers up much of the best in his thought. It has been justly called America's spiritual Declaration of Independence and in its importance as an American heritage must be ranked beside our original political Declaration.]

MR. PRESIDENT AND GENTLEMEN, I greet you on the recommencement of our literary year. Our anniversary is one of hope, and, perhaps, not enough of labor. We do not meet for games of strength or skill, for the recitation of histories, tragedies, and odes, like the ancient Greeks; for parliaments of love and poesy, like the Troubadours; nor for the advancement of science, like our contemporaries in the British and European capitals. Thus far, our holiday has been simply a friendly sign of the survival of the love of letters amongst a people too busy to give to letters any more. As such it is precious as the sign of an indestructible in-

[1] An oration delivered before the Phi Beta Kappa Society, at Cambridge, August 31, 1837; now printed in the volume entitled *Nature, Addresses, and Lectures:* Houghton Mifflin Co., authorized publishers.

stinct. Perhaps the time is already come when it ought to be, and will be, something else; when the sluggard intellect of this continent will look from under its iron lids and fill the postponed expectation of the world with something better than the exertions of mechanical skill. Our day of dependence, our long apprenticeship to the learning of other lands, draws to a close. The millions that around us are rushing into life, cannot always be fed on the sere remains of foreign harvests. Events, actions arise, that must be sung, that will sing themselves. Who can doubt, that poetry will revive and lead in a new age, as the star in the constellation Harp, which now flames in our zenith, astronomers announce, shall one day be the pole-star for a thousand years?

In this hope, I accept the topic which not only usage, but the nature of our association, seem to prescribe to this day,—the "American Scholar." Year by year, we come up hither to read one more chapter of his biography. Let us inquire what light new days and events have thrown on his character, and his hopes.

It is one of those fables, which, out of an unknown antiquity, convey an unlooked-for wisdom, that the gods, in the beginning, divided Man into men, that he might be more helpful to himself; just as the hand was divided into fingers, the better to answer its end.

The old fable covers a doctrine ever new and sublime; that there is One Man,—present to all particular men only partially, or through one faculty; and that you must take the whole society to find the whole man. Man is not a farmer, or a professor, or an engineer, but he is all. Man is priest, and scholar, and statesman, and producer, and soldier. In the *divided* or social state these functions are parcelled out to individuals, each of whom aims to do his stint of the joint work, whilst each other performs his. The fable implies that the individual, to possess himself, must sometimes return from his own labor to embrace all the other laborers. But, unfortunately, this original unit, this fountain of power, has been so distributed to multitudes, has been so minutely subdivided and peddled out, that it is spilled into drops, and cannot be gathered. The state of society is one in which the members have suffered amputation from the trunk, and strut about so many walking monsters,—a good finger, a neck, a stomach, an elbow, but never a man.

Man is thus metamorphosed into a thing, into many things. The planter, who is Man sent out into the field to gather food, is seldom cheered by any idea of the true dignity of his ministry. He sees his bushel and his cart, and nothing beyond, and sinks into the farmer, instead of Man on the farm. The tradesman scarcely ever gives an ideal worth to his work, but is ridden by the routine of his craft, and the soul is subject to dollars. The priest becomes a form; the attorney a statute-book; the mechanic a machine; the sailor a rope of the ship.

In this distribution of functions the scholar is the delegated intellect. In the right state he is *Man Thinking*. In the degenerate state, when the victim of society, he tends to become a mere thinker, or still worse, the parrot of other men's thinking.

In this view of him, as Man Thinking, the theory of his office is contained. Him Nature solicits with all her placid, all her monitory pictures; him the past instructs; him the future invites. Is not indeed every man a student, and do not all things exist for the student's behoof? And, finally, is not the true scholar the only true master? But the old oracle said, "All things have two handles: beware of the wrong one." In life, too often, the scholar errs with mankind and forfeits his privilege. Let us see him in his school, and consider him in reference to the main influences he receives.

I. The first in time and the first in importance of the influences upon the mind is that of Nature. Every day, the sun; and, after sunset, Night and her stars. Ever the winds blow; ever the grass grows. Every day, men and women, conversing, beholding and beholden. The scholar is he of all men whom this spectacle most engages. He must settle its value in his mind. What is nature to him? There is never a beginning, there is never an end, to the inexplicable continuity of this web of God, but always circular power returning into itself. Therein it resembles his own spirit, whose beginning, whose ending, he never can find,—so entire, so boundless. Far too as her splendors shine, system on system shooting like rays, upward, downward, without center, without circumference,—in the mass and in the particle, Nature hastens to render account of herself to the mind. Classification begins. To the young mind every thing is individual, stands by itself. By and by, it finds how to join two things and see in them one nature; then three, then three thousand; and so, tyrannized over by its own unifying instinct, it goes on tying things together, diminishing anomalies, discovering roots running under ground whereby contrary and remote things cohere and flower out from one stem. It presently learns that since the dawn of history there has been a constant accumulation and classifying of facts. But what is classification but the perceiving that these objects are not chaotic, and are not foreign, but have a law which is also a law of the human mind? The astronomer discovers that geometry, a pure abstraction of the human mind, is the measure of planetary motion. The chemist finds proportions and intelligible method throughout matter; and science is nothing but the finding of analogy, identity, in the most remote parts. The ambitious soul sits down before each refractory fact; one after another reduces all strange constitutions, all new powers, to their class and their law, and goes on forever to animate the last fiber of organization, the outskirts of nature, by insight.

Thus to him, to this school-boy under the bending dome of day, is suggested that he and it proceed from one root; one is leaf and one is flower; relation, sympathy, stirring in every vein. And what is that root? Is not that the soul of his soul? A thought too bold; a dream too wild. Yet when this spiritual light shall have revealed the law of more earthly natures,—when he has learned to worship the soul, and to see that the natural philosophy that now is, is only the first gropings of its gigantic hand, he shall look forward to an ever expanding knowledge as to a becoming creator. He shall see that nature is the opposite of the soul, answering to it part for part. One is seal and one is print. Its beauty is the beauty of his own mind. Its laws are the laws of his own mind. Nature then becomes to him the measure of his attainments. So much of nature as he is ignorant of, so much of his own mind does he not yet possess. And, in fine, the ancient precept, "Know thyself," and the modern precept, "Study nature," become at last one maxim.

II. The next great influence into the spirit of the scholar is the mind of the Past,—in whatever form, whether of literature, of art, of institutions, that mind is inscribed. Books are the best type of the influence of the past, and perhaps we shall get at the truth,—learn the amount of this influence more conveniently,—by considering their value alone.

The theory of books is noble. The scholar of the first age received into him the world around; brooded thereon; gave it the new arrangement of his own mind, and uttered it again. It came into him life; it went out from him truth. It came to him short-lived actions; it went out from him immortal thoughts. It came to him business; it went from him poetry. It was dead fact; now, it is quick thought. It can stand, and it can go. It now endures, it now flies, it now inspires. Precisely in proportion to the depth of mind from which it issued, so high does it soar, so long does it sing.

Or, I might say, it depends on how far the process had gone, of transmuting life into truth. In proportion to the completeness of the distillation, so will the purity and imperishableness of the product be. But none is quite perfect. As no air-pump can by any means make a perfect vacuum, so neither can any artist entirely exclude the conventional, the local, the perishable from his book, or write a book of pure thought, that shall be as efficient, in all respects, to a remote posterity, as to contemporaries, or rather to the second age. Each age, it is found, must write its own books; or rather, each generation for the next succeeding. The books of an older period will not fit this.

Yet hence arises a grave mischief. The sacredness which attaches to the act of creation, the act of thought, is transferred to the record. The poet chanting was felt to be a divine man: henceforth the chant is divine also. The writer was a just and wise spirit: henceforward it is settled the book is perfect; as love of the hero corrupts into worship of his statue. Instantly the book becomes noxious: the guide is a tyrant. The sluggish and perverted mind of the multitude, slow to open to the incursions of Reason, having once so opened, having once received this book, stands upon it, and makes an outcry if it is disparaged. Colleges are built on it. Books are written on it by thinkers, not by Man Thinking; by men of talent, that is, who start wrong, who set out from accepted dogmas, not from their own sight of principles. Meek young men grow up in libraries, believing it their duty to accept the views which Cicero, which Locke, which Bacon, have given; forgetful that Cicero, Locke, and Bacon were only young men in libraries when they wrote these books.

Hence, instead of Man Thinking, we have the bookworm. Hence the book-learned class, who value books, as such; not as related to nature and the human constitution, but as making a sort of Third Estate with the world and the soul. Hence the restorers of readings, the emendators, the bibliomaniacs of all degrees.

Books are the best of things, well used; abused, among the worst. What is the right use? What is the one end which all means go to effect? They are for nothing but to inspire. I had better never see a book than to be warped by its attraction clean out of my orbit, and made a satellite instead of a system. The one thing in the world, of value, is the active soul. This every man is entitled to; this every man contains within him, although, in almost all men, obstructed, and as yet unborn. The soul active sees absolute truth and utters truth, or creates. In this action it is genius; not the privilege of here and there a favorite, but the second estate of every man. In its essence it is progressive. The book, the college, the school of art, the institution of any kind, stop with some past utterance of genius. This is good, say they,—let us hold by this. They pin me down. They look backward and not forward. But genius looks forward: the eyes of man are set in his forehead, not in his hindhead; man hopes: genius creates. Whatever talents may be, if the man creates not, the pure efflux of the Deity is not his; —cinders and smoke there may be, but not yet flame. There are creative manners, there are creative actions, and creative words; manners, actions, words, that is, indicative of no custom or authority, but springing spontaneous from the mind's own sense of good and fair.

On the other part, instead of being its own seer, let it receive from another mind its truth, though it were in torrents of light, without periods of solitude, inquest, and self-recovery, and a fatal disservice is done. Genius is always sufficiently the enemy of genius by over-influence. The literature of every nation bears me witness. The English dramatic poets have Shakspearized now for two hundred years.

Undoubtedly there is a right way of reading, so it be

sternly subordinated. Man Thinking must not be subdued by his instruments. Books are for the scholar's idle times. When he can read God directly, the hour is too precious to be wasted in other men's transcripts of their readings. But when the intervals of darkness come, as come they must,—when the sun is hid and the stars withdraw their shining,—we repair to the lamps which were kindled by their ray, to guide our steps to the East again, where the dawn is. We hear, that we may speak. The Arabian proverb says, "A fig tree, looking on a fig tree, becometh fruitful."

It is remarkable, the character of the pleasure we derive from the best books. They impress us with the conviction that one nature wrote and the same reads. We read the verses of one of the great English poets, of Chaucer, of Marvell, of Dryden, with the most modern joy,—with a pleasure, I mean, which is in great part caused by the abstraction of all *time* from their verses. There is some awe mixed with the joy of our surprise, when this poet, who lived in some past world, two or three hundred years ago, says that which lies close to my own soul, that which I also had well-nigh thought and said. But for the evidence thence afforded to the philosophical doctrine of the identity of all minds, we should suppose some preëstablished harmony, some foresight of souls that were to be, and some preparation of stores for their future wants, like the fact observed in insects, who lay up food before death for the young grub they shall never see.

I would not be hurried by any love of system, by any exaggeration of instincts, to underrate the Book. We all know, that as the human body can be nourished on any food, though it were boiled grass and the broth of shoes, so the human mind can be fed by any knowledge. And great and heroic men have existed who had almost no other information than by the printed page. I only would say that it needs a strong head to bear that diet. One must be an inventor to read well. As the proverb says, "He that would bring home the wealth of the Indies, must carry out the wealth of the Indies." There is then creative reading as well as creative writing. When the mind is braced by labor and invention, the page of whatever book we read becomes luminous with manifold allusion. Every sentence is doubly significant, and the sense of our author is as broad as the world. We then see, what is always true, that as the seer's hour of vision is short and rare among heavy days and months, so is its record, perchance, the least part of his volume. The discerning will read, in his Plato or Shakspeare, only that least part,—only the authentic utterances of the oracle; —all the rest he rejects, were it never so many times Plato's and Shakspeare's.

Of course there is a portion of reading quite indispensable to a wise man. History and exact science he must learn by laborious reading. Colleges, in like manner, have their indispensable office,—to teach elements. But they can only highly serve us when they aim not to drill, but to create; when they gather from far every ray of various genius to their hospitable halls, and by the concentrated fires, set the hearts of their youth on flame. Thought and knowledge are natures in which apparatus and pretension avail nothing. Gowns and pecuniary foundations, though of towns of gold, can never countervail the least sentence or syllable of wit. Forget this, and our American colleges will recede in their public importance, whilst they grow richer every year.

III. There goes in the world a notion that the scholar should be a recluse, a valetudinarian,—as unfit for any handiwork or public labor as a pen-knife for an ax. The so-called "practical men" sneer at speculative men, as if, because they speculate or *see,* they could do nothing. I have heard it said that the clergy,—who are always, more universally than any other class, the scholars of their day,—are addressed as women; that the rough, spontaneous conversation of men they do not hear, but only a mincing and diluted speech. They are often virtually disfranchised; and indeed there are advocates for their celibacy. As far as this is true of the studious classes, it is not just and wise. Action is with the scholar subordinate, but it is essential. Without it he is not yet man. Without it thought can never ripen into truth. Whilst the word hangs before the eye as a cloud of beauty, we cannot even see its beauty. Inaction is cowardice, but there can be no scholar without the heroic mind. The preamble of thought, the transition through which it passes from the unconscious to the conscious, is action. Only so much do I know, as I have lived. Instantly we know whose words are loaded with life, and whose not.

The world,—this shadow of the soul, or *other me,* lies wide around. Its attractions are the keys which unlock my thoughts and make me acquainted with myself. I run eagerly into this resounding tumult. I grasp the hands of those next me, and take my place in the ring to suffer and to work, taught by an instinct that so shall the dumb abyss be vocal with speech. I pierce its order; I dissipate its fear; I dispose of it within the circuit of my expanding life. So much only of life as I know by experience, so much of the wilderness have I vanquished and planted, or so far have I extended my being, my dominion. I do not see how any man can afford, for the sake of his nerves and his nap, to spare any action in which he can partake. It is pearls and rubies to his discourse. Drudgery, calamity, exasperation, want, are instructors in eloquence and wisdom. The true scholar grudges every opportunity of action past by, as a loss of power.

It is the raw material out of which the intellect molds her splendid products. A strange process, too, this by which experience is converted into thought, as a mulberry leaf is converted into satin. The manufacture goes forward at all hours.

The actions and events of our childhood and youth are now matters of calmest observation. They lie like fair pictures in the air. Not so with our recent actions, —with the business which we now have in hand. On this we are quite unable to speculate. Our affections as yet circulate through it. We no more feel or know it than we feel the feet, or the hand, or the brain of our body. The new deed is yet a part of life,— remains for a time immersed in our unconscious life. In some contemplative hour it detaches itself from the life like a ripe fruit, to become a thought of the mind. Instantly it is raised, transfigured; the corruptible has put on incorruption. Henceforth it is an object of beauty, however base its origin and neighborhood. Observe too the impossibility of antedating this act. In its grub state, it cannot fly, it cannot shine, it is a dull grub. But suddenly, without observation, the selfsame thing unfurls beautiful wings, and is an angel of wisdom. So is there no fact, no event, in our private history, which shall not, sooner or later, lose its adhesive, inert form, and astonish us by soaring from our body into the empyrean. Cradle and infancy, school and playground, the fear of boys, and dogs, and ferules, the love of little maids and berries, and many another fact that once filled the whole sky, are gone already; friend and relative, profession and party, town and country, nation and world, must also soar and sing.

Of course, he who has put forth his total strength in fit actions has the richest return of wisdom. I will not shut myself out of this globe of action, and transplant an oak into a flower-pot, there to hunger and pine; nor trust the revenue of some single faculty, and exhaust one vein of thought, much like those Savoyards, who, getting their livelihood by carving shepherds, shepherdesses, and smoking Dutchmen, for all Europe, went out one day to the mountain to find stock, and discovered that they had whittled up the last of their pine-trees. Authors we have, in numbers, who have written out their vein, and who, moved by a commendable prudence, sail for Greece or Palestine, follow the trapper into the prairie, or ramble round Algiers, to replenish their merchantable stock.

If it were only for a vocabulary, the scholar would be covetous of action. Life is our dictionary. Years are well spent in country labors; in town; in the insight into trades and manufactures; in frank intercourse with many men and women; in science; in art; to the one end of mastering in all their facts a language by which to illustrate and embody our perceptions. I learn immediately from any speaker how much he has already lived, through the poverty or the splendor of his speech. Life lies behind us as the quarry from whence we get tiles and copestones for the masonry of to-day. This is the way to learn grammar. Colleges and books only copy the language which the field and the work-yard made.

But the final value of action, like that of books, and better than books, is that it is a resource. That great principle of Undulation in nature, that shows itself in the inspiring and expiring of the breath; in desire and satiety; in the ebb and flow of the sea; in day and night; in heat and cold; and, as yet more deeply ingrained in every atom and every fluid, is known to us under the name of Polarity, —these "fits of easy transmission and reflection," as Newton called them, are the law of nature because they are the law of spirit.

The mind now thinks, now acts, and each fit reproduces the other. When the artist has exhausted his materials, when the fancy no longer paints, when thoughts are no longer apprehended and books are a weariness,—he has always the resource *to live.* Character is higher than intellect. Thinking is the function. Living is the functionary. The stream retreats to its source. A great soul will be strong to live, as well as strong to think. Does he lack organ or medium to impart his truth? He can still fall back on this elemental force of living them. This is a total act. Thinking is a partial act. Let the grandeur of justice shine in his affairs. Let the beauty of affection cheer his lowly roof. Those "far from fame," who dwell and act with him, will feel the force of his constitution in the doings and passages of the day better than it can be measured by any public and designed display. Time shall teach him that the scholar loses no hour which the man lives. Herein he unfolds the sacred germ of his instinct, screened from influence. What is lost in seemliness is gained in strength. Not out of those on whom systems of education have exhausted their culture, comes the helpful giant to destroy the old or to build the new, but out of unhandselled savage nature; out of terrible Druids and Berserkers come at last Alfred and Shakspeare.

I hear therefore with joy whatever is beginning to be said of the dignity and necessity of labor to every citizen. There is virtue yet in the hoe and the spade, for learned as well as for unlearned hands. And labor is everywhere welcome; always we are invited to work; only be this limitation observed, that a man shall not for the sake of wider activity sacrifice any opinion to the popular judgments and modes of action.

I have now spoken of the education of the scholar by nature, by books, and by action. It remains to say somewhat of his duties.

They are such as become Man Thinking. They may all be comprised in self-trust. The office of the scholar is to cheer, to raise, and to guide men by showing them facts amidst appearances. He plies the slow, unhonored, and unpaid task of observation. Flamsteed and Herschel, in their glazed observatories, may catalogue the stars with the praise of all men, and the results being splendid and useful, honor is sure. But he, in his private observatory, cataloguing obscure and nebulous stars of the human mind, which as yet no man has thought of as such,—watching days and months sometimes for a few facts; correcting still his old records;—must relinquish display and immediate fame. In the long period of his preparation he must betray often an ignorance and shiftlessness in popular arts, incurring the disdain of the able who shoulder him aside. Long he must stammer in his speech; often forego the living for the dead. Worse yet, he must accept—how often!—poverty and solitude. For the ease and pleasure of treading the old road, accepting the fashions, the education, the religion of society, he takes the cross of making his own, and, of course, the self-accusation, the faint heart, the frequent uncertainty and loss of time, which are the nettles and tangling vines in the way of the self-relying and self-directed; and the state of virtual hostility in which he seems to stand to society, and especially to educated society. For all this loss and scorn, what offset? He is to find consolation in exercising the highest functions of human nature. He is one who raises himself from private considerations and breathes and lives on public and illustrious thoughts. He is the world's eye. He is the world's heart. He is to resist the vulgar prosperity that retrogrades ever to barbarism, by preserving and communicating heroic sentiments, noble biographies, melodious verse, and the conclusions of history. Whatsoever oracles the human heart, in all emergencies, in all solemn hours, has uttered as its commentary on the world of actions,—these he shall receive and impart. And whatsoever new verdict Reason from her inviolable seat pronounces on the passing men and events of to-day,—this he shall hear and promulgate.

These being his functions, it becomes him to feel all

confidence in himself, and to defer never to the popular cry. He and he only knows the world. The world of any moment is the merest appearance. Some great decorum, some fetish of a government, some ephemeral trade, or war, or man, is cried up by half mankind and cried down by the other half, as if all depended on this particular up or down. The odds are that the whole question is not worth the poorest thought which the scholar has lost in listening to the controversy. Let him not quit his belief that a popgun is a popgun, though the ancient and honorable of the earth affirm it to be the crack of doom. In silence, in steadiness, in severe abstraction, let him hold by himself; add observation to observation, patient of neglect, patient of reproach, and bide his own time,—happy enough if he can satisfy himself alone that this day he has seen something truly. Success treads on every right step. For the instinct is sure, that prompts him to tell his brother what he thinks. He then learns that in going down into the secrets of his own mind he has descended into the secrets of all minds. He learns that he who has mastered any law in his private thoughts, is master to that extent of all men whose language he speaks, and of all into whose language his own can be translated. The poet, in utter solitude remembering his spontaneous thoughts and recording them, is found to have recorded that which men in crowded cities find true for them also. The orator distrusts at first the fitness of his frank confessions, his want of knowledge of the persons he addresses, until he finds that he is the complement of his hearers;—that they drink his words because he fulfils for them their own nature; the deeper he dives into his privatest, secretest presentiment, to his wonder he finds this is the most acceptable, most public, and universally true. The people delight in it; the better part of every man feels, This is my music; this is myself.

In self-trust all the virtues are comprehended. Free should the scholar be,—free and brave. Free even to the definition of freedom, "without any hindrance that does not arise out of his own constitution." Brave; for fear is a thing which a scholar by his very function puts behind him. Fear always springs from ignorance. It is a shame to him if his tranquillity, amid dangerous times, arise from the presumption that like children and women his is a protected class; or if he seek a temporary peace by the diversion of his thoughts from politics or vexed questions, hiding his head like an ostrich in the flowering bushes, peeping into microscopes, and turning rhymes, as a boy whistles to keep his courage up. So is the danger a danger still; so is the fear worse. Manlike let him turn and face it. Let him look into its eye and search its nature, inspect its origin,—see the whelping of this lion,—which lies no great way back; he will then find in himself a perfect comprehension of its nature and extent; he will have made his hands meet on the other side, and can henceforth defy it and pass on superior. The world is his who can see through its pretension. What deafness, what stone-blind custom, what overgrown error you behold is there only by sufferance,—by your sufferance. See it to be a lie, and you have already dealt it its mortal blow.

Yes, we are the cowed,—we the trustless. It is a mischievous notion that we are come late into nature; that the world was finished a long time ago. As the world was plastic and fluid in the hands of God, so it is ever to so much of his attributes as we bring to it. To ignorance and sin, it is flint. They adapt themselves to it as they may; but in proportion as a man has anything in him divine, *the firmament flows before him and takes his signet and form.* Not he is great who can alter matter, but he who can alter my state of mind. They are the kings of the world who give the color of their present thought to all nature and all art, and persuade men by the cheerful serenity of their carrying the matter, that this thing which they do, is the apple which the ages have desired to pluck, now at last ripe, and inviting nations to the harvest. The great man makes the great thing. Wherever Macdonald sits, there is the head of the table. Linnæus makes botany the most alluring of studies, and wins it from the farmer and the herb-woman; Davy, chemistry; and Cuvier, fossils. The day is always his, who works in it with serenity and great aims. The unstable estimates of men crowd to him whose mind is filled with a truth, as the heaped waves of the Atlantic follow the moon.

For this self-trust, the reason is deeper than can be fathomed,—darker than can be enlightened. I might not carry with me the feeling of my audience in stating my own belief. But I have already shown the ground of my hope, in adverting to the doctrine that man is one. I believe man has been wronged; he has wronged himself. He has almost lost the light that can lead him back to his prerogatives. Men are become of no account. Men in history, men in the world of to-day, are bugs, are spawn, and are called "the mass" and "the herd." In a century, in a millennium, one or two men; that is to say, one or two approximations to the right state of every man. All the rest behold in the hero or the poet their own green and crude being,—ripened; yes, and are content to be less, so *that* may attain to its full stature. What a testimony, full of grandeur, full of pity, is borne to the demands of his own nature, by the poor clansman, the poor partisan, who rejoices in the glory of his chief. The poor and the low find some amends to their immense moral capacity, for their acquiescence in a political and social inferiority. They are content to be brushed like flies from the path of a great person, so that justice shall be done by him to that common nature which it is the dearest desire of all to see enlarged and glorified. They sun themselves in the great man's light, and feel it to be their own element. They cast the dignity of man from their own downtrod selves upon the shoulders of a hero, and will perish to add one drop of blood to make that great heart beat, those giant sinews combat and conquer. He lives for us, and we live in him.

Men such as they are, very naturally seek money or power; and power because it is as good as money,—the "spoils," so called, "of office." And why not? for they aspire to the highest, and this, in their sleep-walking, they dream is highest. Wake them and they shall quit the false good and leap to the true, and leave governments to clerks and desks. This revolution is to be wrought by the gradual domestication of the idea of Culture. The main enterprise of the world for splendor, for extent, is the upbuilding of a man. Here are the materials strewn along the ground. The private life of one man shall be a more illustrious monarchy, more formidable to its enemy, more sweet and serene in its influence to its friend, than any kingdom in history. For a man, rightly viewed, comprehendeth the particular natures of all men. Each philosopher, each bard, each actor has only done for me, as by a delegate, what one day I can do for myself. The books which once we valued more than the apple of the eye, we have quite exhausted. What is that but saying that we have come up with the point of view which the universal mind took through the eyes of one scribe; we have been that man, and have passed on. First, one, then another, we drain all cisterns, and waxing greater by all these supplies, we crave a better and more abundant food. The man has never lived that can feed us ever. The human mind cannot be enshrined in a person who shall set a barrier on any one side to this unbounded, unboundable empire. It is one central fire, which, flaming now out of the lips of Etna, lightens the capes of Sicily, and now out of the throat of Vesuvius, illuminates the towers and vineyards of Naples. It is one light which beams out of a thousand stars. It is one soul which animates all men.

But I have dwelt perhaps tediously upon this abstraction of the Scholar. I ought not to delay longer to add what I have to say of nearer reference to the time and to this country.

Historically, there is thought to be a difference in the ideas which predominate over successive epochs, and there are data for marking the genius of the Classic, of the Romantic, and now of the Reflective or Philosophical age. With the views I have intimated of the oneness or the identity of the mind through all individuals, I do not much dwell on these differences. In fact, I believe each individual passes through all three. The boy is a Greek;

the youth, romantic; the adult, reflective. I deny not, however, that a revolution in the leading idea may be distinctly enough traced.

Our age is bewailed as the age of Introversion. Must that needs be evil? We, it seems, are critical; we are embarrassed with second thoughts; we cannot enjoy any thing for hankering to know whereof the pleasure consists; we are lined with eyes; we see with our feet; the time is infected with Hamlet's unhappiness,—

> Sicklied o'er with the pale cast of thought.

It is so bad then? Sight is the last thing to be pitied. Would we be blind? Do we fear lest we should outsee nature and God, and drink truly dry? I look upon the discontent of the literary class as a mere announcement of the fact that they find themselves not in the state of mind of their fathers, and regret the coming state as untried; as a boy dreads the water before he has learned that he can swim. If there is any period one would desire to be born in, is it not the age of Revolution; when the old and the new stand side by side and admit of being compared; when the energies of all men are searched by fear and by hope; when the historic glories of the old can be compensated by the rich possibilities of the new era? This time, like all times, is a very good one, if we but know what to do with it.

I read with some joy of the auspicious signs of the coming days, as they glimmer already through poetry and art, through philosophy and science, through church and state.

One of these signs is the fact that the same movement which effected the elevation of what was called the lowest class in the state, assumed in literature a very marked and as benign an aspect. Instead of the sublime and beautiful, the near, the low, the common, was explored and poetized. That which had been negligently trodden under foot by those who were harnessing and provisioning themselves for long journeys into far countries, is suddenly found to be richer than all foreign parts. The literature of the poor, the feelings of the child, the philosophy of the street, the meaning of household life are the topics of the time. It is a great stride. It is a sign,—is it not? of new vigor when the extremities are made active, when currents of warm life run into the hands and the feet. I ask not for the great, the remote, the romantic; what is doing in Italy or Arabia; what is Greek art, or Provençal minstrelsy; I embrace the common, I explore and sit at the feet of the familiar, the low. Give me insight into to-day, and you may have the antique and future worlds. What would we really know the meaning of? The meal in the firkin; the milk in the pan; the ballad in the street; the news of the boat; the glance of the eye; the form and the gait of the body; —show me the ultimate reason of these matters; show me the sublime presence of the highest spiritual cause lurking, as always it does lurk, in these suburbs and extremities of Nature; let me see every trifle bristling with the polarity that ranges it instantly on an eternal law; and the shop, the plow, and the ledger referred to the like cause by which light undulates and poets sing;—and the world lies no longer a dull miscellany and lumber-room, but has form and order; there is no trifle, there is no puzzle, but one design unites and animates the farthest pinnacle and the lowest trench.

This idea has inspired the genius of Goldsmith, Burns, Cowper, and, in a newer time, of Goethe, Wordsworth, and Carlyle. This idea they have differently followed and with various success. In contrast with their writing, the style of Pope, of Johnson, of Gibbon, looks cold and pedantic. This writing is blood-warm. Man is surprised to find that things near are not less beautiful and wondrous than things remote. The near explains the far. The drop is a small ocean. A man is related to all nature. This perception of the worth of the vulgar is fruitful in discoveries. Goethe, in this very thing the most modern of the moderns, has shown us, as none ever did, the genius of the ancients.

There is one man of genius, who has done much for this philosophy of life, whose literary value has never yet been rightly estimated;—I mean Emanuel Swedenborg. The most imaginative of men, yet writing with the precision of a mathematician, he endeavored to ingraft a purely philosophical Ethics on the popular Christianity of his time. Such an attempt, of course, must have difficulty, which no genius could surmount. But he saw and showed the connection between nature and the affections of the soul. He pierced the emblematic or spiritual character of the visible, audible, tangible world. Especially did his shade-loving muse hover over and interpret the lower parts of nature; he showed the mysterious bond that allies moral evil to the foul material forms, and has given in epical parables a theory of insanity, of beasts, of unclean and fearful things.

Another sign of our times, also marked by an analogous political movement, is the new importance given to the single person. Everything that tends to *insulate the individual*—to surround him with barriers of natural respect, so that each man shall feel the world as his, and man shall treat with man as a sovereign state with a sovereign state—tends to true union as well as greatness. "I learned," said the melancholy Pestalozzi, "that no man in God's wide earth is either willing or able to help any other man." *Help must come from the bosom alone.* The scholar is that man who must take up into himself all the ability of the time, all the contributions of the past, all the hopes of the future. He must be an university of knowledges. If there be one lesson more than another which should pierce his ear, it is, The world is nothing, the man is all; in yourself is the law of all nature, and you know not yet how a globule of sap ascends; in yourself slumbers the whole of Reason; it is for you to know all; it is for you to dare all; Mr. President and Gentlemen, this confidence in the unsearched might of man belongs, by all motives, by all prophecy, by all preparation, to the American Scholar. We have listened too long to the courtly muses of Europe. The spirit of the American freeman is already suspected to be timid, imitative, tame. Public and private avarice make the air we breathe thick and fat. The scholar is decent, indolent, complaisant. See already the tragic consequence. The mind of this country, taught to aim at low objects, eats upon itself. There is no work for any but the decorous and the complaisant. Young men of the fairest promise, who begin life upon our shores, inflated by the mountain winds, shined upon by all the stars of God, find the earth below not in unison with these, but are hindered from action by the disgust which the principles on which business is managed inspire, and turn drudges, or die of disgust, some of them suicides. What is the remedy? They did not yet see, and thousands of young men as hopeful now crowding to the barriers for the career do not yet see, that if the single man plant himself indomitably on his instincts, and there abide, the huge world will come round to him. Patience,—patience; with the shades of all the good and great for company; and for solace the perspective of your own infinite life; and for work the study and the communication of principles, the making those instincts prevalent, the conversion of the world. Is it not the chief disgrace in the world, not to be an unit;—not to be reckoned one character;—not to yield that peculiar fruit which each man was created to bear, but to be reckoned in the gross, in the hundred, or the thousand, of the party, the section, to which we belong; and our opinion predicted geographically, as the north, or the south? Not so, brothers and friends,—please God, ours shall not be so. We will walk on our own feet; we will work with our own hands; we will speak our own minds. The study of letters shall be no longer a name for pity, for doubt, and for sensual indulgence. The dread of man and the love of man shall be a wall of defense and a wreath of joy around all. A nation of men will for the first time exist, because each believes himself inspired by the Divine Soul which also inspires all men.

CIVILIZATION AND PROGRESS[1]

ARCHIBALD HENDERSON

[Archibald Henderson was born at Salisbury, North Carolina, in 1877. After taking degrees from the university of that state and from Chicago University, he studied in England and on the continent. He joined the faculty of The University of North Carolina in 1898 and is now head of the department of mathematics. Besides a number of books in his professional field he has written works on the drama and on various aspects of American life.]

TODAY the mightiest revolution of history is under way. "It has," says Raymond Fosdick, "completely changed the whole complexion of human life. It has fundamentally altered our daily habits; it has not only modified our environment, but has thoroughly revolutionized it; it has split the anciently established order into a thousand fragments. Since the days of Assyria and Babylon—indeed since the days of our neolithic forefathers—nothing has occurred which has so completely and in so short a time changed the method and manner of living of the human race, as the mechanical revolution of the nineteenth century." So miraculous have been the achievements of science that Charles M. Schwab said only the other day that the miracles related in the Bible were hardly more astonishing than those revealed by science in the last quarter of

[1] From *The Virginia Quarterly Review*, April, 1925. Reprinted by permission of the editor and the author. In the selection as printed here a few paragraphs are omitted.

a century. In his characteristic way, Bernard Shaw says in the preface to his great play, "Saint Joan": "The mediæval doctors of divinity who did not pretend to settle how many angels could dance on the point of a needle cut a very poor figure as far as romantic credulity is concerned beside the modern physicists who have settled to the billionth of a millimeter every movement and position in the dance of the electrons. . . . Why the men who believe in electrons should regard themselves as less credulous than the men who believed in angels is not apparent to me. . . . In the Middle Ages people believed that the earth was flat, for which they had at least the evidence of their senses; we believe it to be round, not because as many as one per cent of us could give the physical reasons for so quaint a belief, but because modern science has convinced us that nothing that is obvious is true, and that everything that is magical, improbable, extraordinary, gigantic, microscopic, heartless or outrageous is scientific."

The real marvel of contemporary science is not merely that it predicts miracles: it brings them to pass. When Hertz more than half a century ago discovered that electromagnetic waves were propagated with the speed of light, he gave the prophetic clue to the marvels of wireless telegraphy, etheric conduction, and the radio. The civilized world is to-day one vast complex of the most sensitive transmitters and coherers; and the cobwebs of antennæ spun by the scientist upon tenuous towers of steel flung up against the sky bring to our ears, as we sit in comfortable drawing-rooms, the voice of the explorer lost in arctic wilds, the mellifluous notes of the great opera singer, news of the marvelous discovery of the buried tomb of an ancient Egyptian King, the latest message to his people of the President of this mighty republic. With new meaning we re-voice the thrilling words of Whittier evoked by the laying of the Atlantic cable: "Round the world—the thought of all is the thought of one." Multitudinous messages from the dim remote flock in upon our thrilled and enraptured senses; and the dream of a collective consciousness of mankind is brought within reach of human realization. The political, social, and ethical consequences of this new discovery are truly incalculable. The barriers of insularity and provincialism are at last transgressed; and the voice of the humblest citizen can reach the ears of mankind. The sociologist has been studying painstakingly for years how the other half lives; to-day, with but a fraction of the effort, we can learn how the other half thinks.

"The opportunity for a hundred millions to think together, feel together, and to act as a single corporate irresistible force," comments Faunce, "is something new in the history of mankind, something that surpasses all the dreams of science or education or religion. Has then the millennium arrived? Shall the golden age be ushered in by the microphone? Alas, no mechanism can usher in any millennium, and no material device can establish the Kingdom of God. The broadcasting station will send out our message of brotherhood, or hiss out our hatred, with equal efficiency. The Greeks had none of our devices, but they built the Parthenon and carved the Hermes—things utterly beyond us now. They had no microphone, but they heard the voice of Sophocles. They never heard the hum of the aeroplane, but they listened to the 'surge and thunder of the Odyssey.' "

When we come to examine the meaning of "progress" and analyze the nature of "civilization," we are dismayed to discover that science, which has procured us such marvels as I have described, has brought innumerable evils in its turn. The civilization which rests upon scientific discovery is rapidly breeding toxins which minister to its own destruction. A revolution in human affairs comparable in importance to the scientific revolution of to-day was the industrial revolution of the nineteenth century. Industry came to be organized upon a monumental scale; and an endless stream of humble workers, men, women, and children, were relentlessly fed into the insatiable maws of huge factories and giant plants. The sun of the day of individual Art and Craft showed a rapid declension; and the bulk of mechanical labor was transferred from man to the machine. The laborer was displaced from the pedestal of craftsmanship to the level of the automaton. Population swarmed to the neighborhood of great factories and industrial plants; and losing that salutary contact with nature and the vernal wood which assures the physical and spiritual health of mankind, millions of men, women and children were pent up in insanitary dwellings, toiling feverishly to keep going the intricate and pitiless monsters of modern mechanism. So powerful in their imaginative appeal are these great Juggernauts of iron and steel that Henry Adams, in his remarkable autobiography, thus describes his awed and worshipful emotions in the presence of a dynamo: "To Adams the dynamo became a symbol of infinity. As he grew accustomed to the great gallery of machines, he began to feel the . . . dynamo as a moral force, much as the early Christians felt the Cross. The planet itself seemed less impressive, in its old-fashioned, deliberate, annual or daily revolution, than this huge wheel, revolving within arm's length at some vertiginous speed, and barely murmuring—scarcely humming an audible warning to stand a hair's-breadth further for respect of power —while it would not awake the baby lying close against its frame. Before the end one began to pray to it; inherited instinct taught the natural expression of man before silent and infinite force."

The lesson of God's word is that frivolity and degeneracy had set in when the Children of Israel set up a golden image and fell down and worshipped it.

> And it came to pass—as soon as he came nigh unto the camp, that he saw the calf and the dancing; and Moses' anger waxed hot, and he cast the tables out of his hands, and brake them beneath the mount.
>
> And he took the calf which they had made, and burnt it in the fire, and ground it to powder. . . .

Have we of the twentieth century substituted the Iron Horse for the Golden Calf? Where is the Moses of the New Dispensation? In his "Erewhon" Samuel Butler depicts the industrial workers arising in their might and destroying the machines which had turned them into mere automata. To-day the Indian apostle, Mahatma Gandhi, preaches against the tyranny of the machine which has destroyed the ancient arts of India; and pleads for a return to the spinning wheel, to Nature, and the simple life. In his remarkable essay, "Civilization: Its Cause and Cure," Edward Carpenter likens modern civilization to a disease because of the break-up of its unity, its entirety, with Man as the central, controlling force. To-day, the Machine, not Man, he points out, is the central instrument of civilization, under the control of corporate wealth; and Man is the slave of the Machine. In the true civilization of the future, as he paints it, the machines will not be refused; but they will have to be brought into subjection.

"Our locomotives, machinery, telegraphic and postal systems; our houses, furniture, clothes, books, our fearful and wonderful cookery, strong drink, tea, tobacco; our medical and surgical appliances; high-faluting sciences and philosophies, and all other engines hitherto of human bewilderment, have simply to be reduced to abject subjection to the real man. All those appliances, and a thousand other such as we hardly dream of, will come in to perfect his power and increase his freedom; but they will not be the objects of a mere fetish-worship as now. Man will use them, instead of their using him. His real life will lie in a region far beyond them. But in thus for a moment denying and 'mastering' the products of Civilization, will he for the first time discover their true value, and reap from them an enjoyment unknown before."

One of the most remarkable plays of our time—a true symbol of this era of machine civilization—is the drama "R. U. R." by the young Czechoslovakian, Karel Capek. The initials stand for "Rossum's Universal Robots"—for young Rossum has at last succeeded in making the Robot: mechanically more perfect than human beings, with an enormously developed intelligence, but with no soul. The words "Robot" and "Robotize," I would have you note, have already been incorporated in the English language—so powerful was the imaginative appeal to the modern consciousness of this artistic depiction of the despiritizing of contemporary man by the force of scientific invention in the hands of a ruthless and rapacious capitalism. The effect of this new invention, we are told in the play, is to usher in a new civilization in which all work will be done by living machines and the enslavement of man to matter will cease. But after a time, so many Robots were manufactured that people became superfluous; and in time the human race was wholly superseded by Robots.

Surely it is not fanciful to see in the dominance of the machine to-day the Robotization of mankind. You and I are Robots to a greater or less extent—doing each day an enormous amount of mechanical and routine work, which requires little thought, no originality—merely efficiency and machine-like accuracy. In the days of the Middle Ages, in the golden era of the Crafts and the Guilds, a workman was an artist, who made every part of a mechanism—whether it were a clock or a tapestry, a *Cloisonné* vase or a Damascus blade. To-day we are the victims of quantity production; and our works, both of art so-called and of utility, are "assembled products." A workman in a Ford factory does not make a Ford car; he makes over and over again, to the destruction of all scientific initiative and craft instinct, the self-same part. The real menace to mankind to-day is the menace of the machine. For it tends to make man himself a mere automaton, a machine. The curse of civilization,—and in especial of American civilization—is the tendency to the standardization of the human product. We are all being run into a mold; and turned out as "finished products"—thinking alike, believing alike, acting alike, looking alike—the wooden toys of a huge American Noah's

Ark. Our civilization is the goose-step march of the Wooden Soldiers to the tune of the national anthem; "Yes, we have no ideas; we have no ideas to-day." . . .

In face of the startling defects and manifold weaknesses of our civilization, we must recognize that the most urgent subject for the scientific study of the future is not merely matter but Man. In the study of matter, from the universe to the tiny atom, science has made almost incalculable progress; but, as Robinson says, "the knowledge of man, of the springs of his conduct, of his relation to his fellowmen, singly or in groups, and the felicitous regulation of human intercourse in the interest of harmony and fairness, have made no such advance." The so-called sciences of ethics and jurisprudence and economics and politics and government—as Count Korzybski has pointed out in his *Manhood of Humanity*—have not kept pace with the rapid progress of science in its study of matter; and "it is because of their lagging that the world has come to be in so great distress."

Is, then, civilization a disease, as Edward Carpenter would have us believe? Is, then, human progress a delusion—as Dean Inge, the "gloomy Dean" of St. Paul's, would almost have us acknowledge? Are we witnessing to-day the reddening sunset of Western culture—as Oswald Spengler dourly affirms in his *Der Untergang des Abendlandes?* Must we, then, scrap the mighty machines of applied science in order to recover the joyousness of Shakespeare, the majesty of Milton, the cosmism of Dante, the craftsmanship of Mediæval Guild, the art-instinct of the Middle Age, the austerity of Rome, the breadth of Greece, the faith of ancient Israel?

I have no counsels of perfection for man's guidance—

self-confidence far greater than mine would shrink from such a task. But I would venture, not without timidity, to suggest for consideration some thoughts which promise creative betterment for the future.

First, we cannot, if we would, undo the work of science and invention. We cannot now escape the complexities of modern living; but we can refuse to be crushed in the intricate mechanism of this Frankenstein monster. We must not heed the pagan call of Carpenter to gather on the high tops to "celebrate with naked dances the glory of the human form and the great procession of the stars"; but we may, we must, once again seek the benignant, all-healing balm of Nature; resolutely revolt against the strangle-hold of the city and the tyranny of the machine; and fling off the modern curse of the Robot. We must heed, not the challenge to revolt of Marx, of Spencer, of Lenin, but the appeal of Pastor Wagner, of John Ruskin, of Lyof Tolstoy, for simplified living, love of humanity, and the primitive innocence of religious faith.

Second, we cannot, if we would—and in view of the rapacious appetite of 110,000,000 people who must be satisfied, we would not if we could—change the processes and policy of standardization and quantity production in business, in industry, in manufacture. But we can, we must, revolt against the standardization of thought and the quantity production of the moron which threaten the future of this still tentative experiment in democracy. We must raise the banner of revolt against the provincial doctrine of pioneer democracies that any man is fit for any task, which breeds a yokel contempt for scientific knowledge, refined culture, and expert literary skill.

America has been called the melting pot of races; but we must not permit democracy to become a mere melting pot of second-hand ideas, a smelter furnace of pseudo-science, jazz music, freak art, half-baked theories of government and all the cheap vagaries and wild delusions of religious bolshevism. Unswerving fidelity to principle, unshaken faith in the doctrines of the founders of the republic, singleness of purpose, the courage of conviction, and the will to free, various and untrammelled thinking—these we must have, and for these we must forever fight. . . .

Le Bon and Wallas have warned us of the dangers of the mob mind; and we must jealously preserve our individuality and guard our independence against the mass-consciousness of the moron, the sub-man, the hysteriac, and the crank. All the wiles of political buncombe, the glamour of partisan hokum, must not blind us to the greatness of our Washingtons and our Wilsons, our Roosevelts and our Eliots, our Michelsons and our Millikans, our Adamses and our Lees.

Third, and lastly, we must not lose sight of the fact that we of today are the posterity of the past, the ancestry of the future. In science—the communion of human thought; in art—the communion of human feeling; and in their fellowship we must look for the harmonious and creative instruments of a great civilization. Professor Einstein recently remarked to me that after a certain high level of scientific evolution is reached, science and art both become merged into esthetics, plasticity, and form. "Man seeks to form a simplified synoptical view of the world," he said in a memorable address, "in a manner conformable to his own nature, in order to overcome the world of experience by replacing it, to a certain degree, by this picture. This is what the painter does, as also the poet, the speculative philosopher, and the research scientist, each in his own way. He transfers the center of his emotional existence into this picture, in order to find a sure haven of peace, one such as is not offered in the narrow limits of turbulent personal experience." Tolstoy has raised the perennial query, *What is Art?* and he has given a noble answer to his self-set query consonant with the higher spirit of the age. "Art," he says, "knows the true ideal of our times, and tends towards it" —and this he defines as "art transmitting the simplest feelings of common life, but such as are accessible to all men in the whole world—the art of common life—the art of a people—universal art."

But beside the communion of thought—which is science; and the communion of feeling—which is art; there is that still greater communion, the communion of spirit—which is religion. When Joan of Arc was deserted by fortune and betrayed by her earthly friends, she turned in pure faith to those divine voices from on high—with which she shared the communion of saints. Harassed by the confusing clamors of civilization, Emerson set his face homeward with the cry:

> What are they all in their high conceit,
> When man in the bush with God may meet?

Says that honestest of contemporary critics, Dean Inge: "There may be in progress a storage of beneficent forces which we cannot see. . . . The source of all good is like an inexhaustible river; the Creator pours forth new treasures of goodness, truth, and beauty for all who will love them and take them. . . . Our half-real world is the factory of souls, in which we are tried as in a furnace." May we, then, find courage and confidence in this message of William Blake:

> Joy and woe are woven fine.
> A clothing for the soul divine;
> Under every grief and pine
> Runs a joy with silken twine.
> It is right it should be so;
> Man was made for joy and woe;
> And when this we rightly know
> Safely through the world we go.

PULVIS ET UMBRA[1]

Robert Louis Stevenson

[For biographical sketch, see page 89]

WE look for some reward of our endeavors and are disappointed; not success, not happiness, not even peace of conscience, crowns our ineffectual efforts to do well. Our frailties are invincible, our virtues barren; the battle goes sore against us to the going down of the sun. The canting moralist tells us of right and wrong; and we look abroad, even on the face of our small earth, and find them change with every climate, and no country where some action is not honored for a virtue and none where it is not branded for a vice; and we look in our experience, and find no vital congruity in the wisest rules, but at the best a municipal fitness. It is not strange if we are tempted to despair of good. We ask too much. Our religions and moralities have been trimmed to flatter us, till they are all emasculate and sentimentalized, and only please and weaken. Truth is of a rougher strain. In the harsh face of life, faith can read a bracing gospel. The human race is a thing more ancient than the ten commandments; and the bones and revolutions of the Kosmos, in whose joints we are but moss and fungus, more ancient still.

[1] From *Memories and Portraits.* Reprinted by permission of Charles Scribner's Sons.

I

Of the Kosmos in the last resort, science reports many doubtful things and all of them appalling. There seems no substance to this solid globe on which we stamp: nothing but symbols and ratios. Symbols and ratios carry us and bring us forth and beat us down; gravity that swings the incommensurable suns and worlds through space, is but a figment varying inversely as the squares of distances; and the suns and worlds themselves, imponderable figures of abstraction, NH_3 and H_2O. Consideration dares not dwell upon this view; that way madness lies; science carries us into zones of speculation, where there is no habitable city for the mind of man.

But take the Kosmos with a grosser faith, as our senses give it us. We behold space sown with rotatory islands, suns and worlds and the shards and wrecks of systems: some, like the sun, still blazing; some rotting, like the earth; others, like the moon, stable in desolation. All of these we take to be made of something we call matter: a thing which no analysis can help us to conceive; to whose incredible properties no familiarity can reconcile our minds. This stuff, when not purified by the lustration of fire, rots uncleanly into something we call life; seized through all its atoms with a pediculous malady; swelling in tumors that become independent, sometimes even (by an abhorrent prodigy) locomotory; one splitting into millions, millions cohering into one, used as we are to it, yet strikes us with occasional disgust, and the profusion of worms in a piece of ancient turf, or the air of a marsh darkened with insects, will sometimes check our breathing so that we aspire for cleaner places. But none is clean:

the moving sand is infected with lice; the pure spring, where it bursts out of the mountain, is a mere issue of worms; even in the hard rock the crystal is forming.

In two main shapes this eruption covers the countenance of the earth: the animal and the vegetable: one in some degree the inversion of the other: the second rooted to the spot; the first coming detached out of its natal mud, and scurrying abroad with the myriad feet of insects or towering into the heavens on the wings of birds: a thing so inconceivable that, if it be well considered, the heart stops. To what passes with the anchored vermin, we have little clue: doubtless they have their joys and sorrows, their delights and killing agonies: it appears not how. But of the locomotory, to which we ourselves belong, we can tell more. These share with us a thousand miracles: the miracles of sight, of hearing, of the projection of sound, things that bridge space; the miracles of memory and reason, by which the present is conceived, and when it is gone, its image kept living in the brains of man and brute; the miracle of reproduction, with its imperious desires and staggering consequences. And to put the last touch upon this mountain mass of the revolting and the inconceivable, all these prey upon each other, lives tearing other lives in pieces, cramming them inside themselves, and by that summary process, growing fat: the vegetarian, the whale, perhaps the tree, not less than the lion of the desert; for the vegetarian is only the eater of the dumb.

Meanwhile our rotary island loaded with predatory life, and more drenched with blood, both animal and vegetable, than ever mutinied ship, scuds through space with unimaginable speed, and turns alternate cheeks to the reverberation of a blazing world, ninety million miles away.

II

What a monstrous specter is this man, the disease of the agglutinated dust, lifting alternate feet or lying drugged with slumber; killing, feeding, growing, bringing forth small copies of himself; grown upon with hair like grass, fitted with eyes that move and glitter in his face; a thing to set children screaming;—and yet looked at nearlier, known as his fellows know him, how surprising are his attributes! Poor soul, here for so little, cast among so many hardships, filled with desires so incommensurate and so inconsistent, savagely surrounded, savagely descended, irremediably condemned to prey upon his fellow lives: who should have blamed him had he been of a piece with his destiny and a being merely barbarous? And we look and behold him instead filled with imperfect virtues: infinitely childish, often admirably valiant, often touchingly kind; sitting down, amidst his momentary life, to debate of right and wrong and the attributes of the deity; rising up to do battle for an egg or die for an idea; singling out his friends and his mate with cordial affection; bringing forth in pain, rearing with long-suffering solicitude, his young. To touch the heart of his mystery, we find in him one thought, strange to the point of lunacy: the thought of duty; the thought of something owing to himself, to his neighbor, to his God: an ideal of decency, to which he would rise if it were possible; a limit of shame, below which, if it be possible, he will not stoop. The design in most men is one of conformity; here and there, in picked natures, it transcends itself and soars on the other side, arming martyrs with independence; but in all, in their degrees, it is a bosom thought:—Not in man alone, for we trace it in dogs and cats whom we know fairly well, and doubtless some similar point of honor sways the elephant, the oyster, and the louse, of whom we know so little:—But in man, at least, it sways with so complete an empire that merely selfish things come second, even with the selfish: that appetites are starved, fears are conquered, pains supported; that almost the dullest shrinks from the reproof of a glance, although it were a child's; and all but the most cowardly stand amid the risks of war; and the more notable, having strongly conceived an act as due to their ideal, affront and embrace death. Strange enough if, with their singular origin and perverted practice, they think they are to be rewarded in some future life: stranger still, if they are persuaded of the contrary, and think this blow, which they solicit, will strike them senseless for eternity. I shall be reminded what a tragedy of misconception and misconduct man at large presents: of organized injustice, cowardly violence and treacherous crime; and of the damning imperfections of the best. They cannot be too darkly drawn. Man is indeed marked for failure in his efforts to do right. But where the best consistently miscarry, how tenfold more remarkable that all should continue to strive; and surely we should find it both touching and inspiriting, that in a field from which success is banished, our race should not cease to labor.

If the first view of this creature, stalking in his rotatory isle, be a thing to shake the courage of the stoutest, on this nearer sight he startles us with an admiring wonder. It matters not where we look, under what climate we observe him, in what stage of society, in what depth of ignorance, burthened with what erroneous morality; by campfires in Assiniboia, the snow powdering his shoulders, the wind plucking his blanket, as he sits, passing the ceremonial calumet and uttering his grave opinions like a Roman senator; in ships at sea, a man inured to hardship and vile pleasures, his brightest hope a fiddle in a tavern and a bedizened trull who sells herself to rob him, and he for all that simple, innocent, cheerful, kindly like a child, constant to toil, brave to drown, for others; in the slums of cities, moving among indifferent millions to mechanical employments, without hope of change in the future, with scarce a pleasure in the present, and yet true to his virtues, honest up to his lights, kind to his neighbors, tempted perhaps in vain by the bright gin-palace, perhaps long-suffering with the drunken wife that ruins him; in India (a woman this time) kneeling with broken cries and streaming tears as she drowns her child in the sacred river; in the brothel, the discard of society, living mainly on strong drink, fed with affronts, a fool, a thief, the comrade of thieves, and even here keeping the point of honor and the touch of pity, often repaying the world's scorn with service, often standing firm upon a scruple, and at a certain cost, rejecting riches: everywhere some virtue cherished or affected, everywhere some decency of thought and carriage, everywhere the ensign of man's ineffectual goodness:—ah! if I could show you this! if I could show you these men and women, all the world over, in every stage of history, under every abuse of terror, under every circumstance of failure, without hope, without help, without thanks, still obscurely fighting the lost fight of virtue, still clinging, in the brothel or on the scaffold, to some rag of honor, the poor jewel of their souls! They may seek to escape, and yet they cannot; it is not alone their privilege and glory, but their doom; they are condemned to some nobility; all their lives long, the desire of good is at their heels, the implacable hunter.

Of all earth's meteors, here at least is the most strange and consoling: that this ennobled lemur, this hair-crowned bubble of the dust, this inheritor of a few years and sorrows, should yet deny himself his rare delights, and add to his frequent pains, and live for an ideal, however misconceived. Nor can we stop with man. A new doctrine, received with screams a little while ago by canting moralists, and still not properly worked into the body of our thoughts, lights us a step farther into the heart of this rough but noble universe. For nowadays the pride of man denies in vain his kinship with the original dust. He stands no longer like a thing apart. Close at his heels we see the dog, prince of another genus: and in him too, we see dumbly testified the same cultus of an unattainable ideal, the same constancy in failure. Does it stop with the dog? We look at our feet where the ground is blackened with the swarming ant: a creature so small, so far from us in the hierachy of brutes, that we can scarce trace and scarce comprehend his doings; and here also, in his ordered polities and rigorous justice, we see confessed the law of duty and the fact of individual sin. Does it stop, then, with the ant? Rather this desire of well-doing and this doom of frailty run through all the grades of life: rather is this earth, from the frosty top of Everest to the next margin of the internal fire, one stage of ineffectual virtues and one temple of pious tears and perseverance. The whole creation groaneth and travaileth together. It is the common and the godlike law of life. The browsers, the biters, the barkers, the hairy coats of field and forest, the squirrel in the oak, the thousand-footed creeper in the dust, as they share with us the gift of life, share with us the love of an ideal: strive like us—like us are tempted to grow weary of the struggle—to do well; like us receive at times unmerited refreshment, visitings of support, returns of courage; and are condemned like us to be crucified between that double law of the members and the will. Are they like us, I wonder, in the timid hope of some reward, some sugar with the drug? do they, too, stand aghast at unrewarded virtues, at the sufferings of those whom, in our partiality, we take to be just, and the prosperity of such as, in our blindness, we call wicked? It may be, and yet God knows what they should look for. Even while they look, even while they repent, the foot of man treads them by thousands in the dust, the yelping hounds burst upon their trail, the bullet speeds, the knives are heating in the den of the vivisectionist; or the dew falls, and the generation of a day is blotted out. For these are creatures, compared with whom our weakness is strength, our ignorance wisdom, our brief span eternity.

And as we dwell, we living things, in our isle of terror and under the imminent hand of death, God forbid it should be man the erected, the reasoner, the wise in his own eyes—God forbid it should be man that wearies in well-doing, that despairs of unrewarded effort, or utters the language of complaint. Let it be enough for faith, that the whole creation groans in mortal frailty, strives with unconquerable constancy: surely not all in vain.

MAN AND THE RACE[1]

GEORGE EDWARD WOODBERRY

[For biographical sketch, see page 132]

IT belongs to a highly developed race to become, in a true sense, aristocratic—a treasury of its best in practical and spiritual types, and then to disappear in the surrounding tides of men. So Athens dissolved like a pearl in the cup of the Mediterranean, and Rome in the cup of Europe, and Judæa in the cup of the Universal Communion. Though death is the law of all life, man touches this earthen fact with the wand of the spirit, and transforms it into the law of sacrifice. Man has won no victory over his environment so sublime as this, finding in his mortal sentence the true choice of the soul and in the road out of Paradise the open highway of eternal life. Races die; but the ideal of sacrifice as the highest race-destiny has seldom occurred to men, though it has been suggested both by devout Jews and by devout Irishmen as the divinely appointed organic law of the Hebrew and the Celt. In the general view of men the extinction of a race partakes of the unreasoning finality of nature.

The vital flow of life has this in common with disease—that it is self-limited; the fever runs its course, and burns away. "All thoughts, all passions, all delights,"

[1] From *The Torch*, copyrighted and published by Harcourt, Brace and Co. Reprinted by permission of the publishers.

have this history. In the large arcs of social being, movements of the human spirit, however embracing and profound, obey the same law of the limitation of specific energy. Revolution, reforms, re-births exhaust their fuel, and go out. Races are only greater units of man; for a race, as for an individual, there is a time to die; and that time, as history discloses it, is the moment of perfection. This is the largest fact in the moral order of the world; it is the center of providence in history. In the life of the human spirit the death of the best of its achieving elements, in the moment of their consummation, is as the fading of the flower of the field or the annual fall of the leaves of the forest in the natural world; and unless this be a sacrificial death, it were wantonness and waste like the deaths of nature; but man and his works are supernatural, and raised above nature by an imperishable relation which they contain. Race-history is a perpetual celebration of the Mass. The Cross initials every page with its broad gold, and he whose eye misses that letter has lost the clue to the meaning. I do not refer to the self-devotion of individuals, the sacred lives of the race. I speak of the involuntary element in the life of nations, or what seems such on the vast scale of social life. Always some great culture is dying to enrich the soil of new harvests, some civilization is crumbling to rubbish to be the hill of a more beautiful city, some race is spending itself that a lower and barbarous world may inherit its stored treasure-house. Although no race may consciously devote itself to the higher ends of mankind, it is the prerogative of its men of genius so to devote it; nor is any nation truly great which is not so dedicated by its warriors and statesmen, its saints and heroes, its thinkers and dreamers. A nation's poets are its true owners; and by the stroke of the pen they convey the title-deeds of its real possessions to strangers and aliens.

This dedication of the energy of a race by its men of genius to the higher ends of mankind is the sap of all the world. The spiritual life of mankind spreads, the spiritual unity of mankind grows, by this age-long surrender of privilege and power into the hands of the world's new men, and the leavening of the mass by the best that has anywhere arisen in it, which is thus brought about. The absorption of aristocracies in democracies, the dissolution of the nobler product in inferior environments, the salutary death of cultures, civilizations, breeds of men, is the strict line on which history, drawing the sundered parts of the earth slowly together, moves to that great consummation when the best that has at any time been in the world shall be the portion of every man born into it. If the old English blood, which here on this soil gave birth to a nation, spread civilization through it, and cast the orbit of its starry course in time, is destined to be thus absorbed and lost in the nation which it has formed, we should be proud and happy in such a fate; for this is to wear the seal of God's election in history. Nay, if the aristocracy of the whole white race is so to melt in a world of the colored races of the earth, I for one should only rejoice in such a divine triumph of the sacrificial idea in history; for it would mean the humanization of mankind.

Unless this principle is strongly grasped, unless there be an imperishable relation in man and his works which they contain, and which, though it has other phases, here appears in this eternal salvage stored up in a slowly perfecting race, history through its length and breadth is a spectacle to appall and terrify the reason. The perpetual flux of time—

> Sceptres, tiaras, swords, and chains, and tomes
> Of reasoned wrong, glozed on by ignorance,—

is a mere catastrophe of blood and error unless its mighty subverting and dismaying changes are related to something which does not pass away with dethroned gods, abandoned empires, and repealed codes of law and morals. But in the extinction of religions, in imperial revolutions, in the bloody conflict of ideas, there is one thing found stable; it is the mind itself, growing through ages. That which in its continuity we call the human spirit, abides. Men, tribes, states disappear, but the race-mind endures. A conception of the world and an emotional response thereto constitute the life of the race-mind, and fill its consciousness with ideas and feelings, but in these there is no element of chance, contingency or frailty; they are master-ideas, master-emotions, clothed with the power of a long reign over men, and imposing themselves upon each new generation almost with the yoke of necessity. What I designate as the race-mind—the sole thing permanent in history—is this potentiality of thought and feeling, in any age, realizing itself in states of mind and habits of action long established in the race, deeply inherited, and slowly modified. The race-mind is the epitome of the past. It contains all human energy, knowledge, experience, that survives. It is the resultant of millions of lives whose earthly power it stores in one deathless force.

This race-mind is simply formed. Life presents certain permanent aspects in the environment, which generate ways of behavior thereto, normal and general among men. The world is a multiplicity, a harvest-field, a battle-ground; and thence arise through human contact ways of numbering, or mathematics, ways of tillage, or agriculture, ways of fighting, or military tactics and strategy, and these are incorporated in individuals as habits of life. The craftsman has the mind of his craft. Life also presents certain other permanent internal aptitudes in the soul, whence arises the mind of the artist, the inventor, the poet. But this cast of mind of the mathematician or of the painter is rather a phase of individual life. In the larger unit of the race, environment and aptitude working together in the historic life of ages develop ideas, moods and energies characteristic of the race in which they occur. In the sphere of ideas, freedom is indissolubly linked with the English, righteousness with the Hebrew; in the temperamental sphere, a signal instance is the Celtic genius—mystery, twilight, supernatural fantasy, lamentation, tragic disaster—or the Greek genius, definiteness, proportioned beauty, ordered science, philosophic principle; and, in the sphere of energy, land and gold hunger, and that strange soul-hunger—hunger to possess the souls of men—which is at the root of all propagandism, have been motive powers in many races.

Thus, in one part or another of time and place, and from causes within and without, the race, coming to its best, flowers in some creative hope, ripens in some shaping thought, glows in some resistless enthusiasm. Each of these in its own time holds an age in its grasp. They seize on men and shape them in multitudes to their will, as the wind drives the locusts; make men hideous ascetics, send them on forlorn voyages, devote them to the block and the stake, make Argonauts, Crusaders, Lollards of them, fill Europe in one age with a riot of revolution and in the next with the camps of tyrannic power. These ideas, moods, energies have mysterious potency; they seem to possess an independent being; though, like all the phenomena of life-energy they are self-limited, the period of their growth, culmination, and decline extends through generations and centuries; they seem less the brood of man's mind than higher powers that feed on men. They are surrounded by a cloud of witnesses—fanatics, martyrs, dupes; they doom whole peoples to glory or shame; in the undying battle of the soul they are the choosers of the slain. Though they proceed from the human spirit, they rule it; and in life they are the spiritual presences which are most closely unveiled to the apprehension, devotion, and love of men.

The race-mind building itself from immemorial time out of this mystery of thought and passion, as generation after generation kneels and fights and fades, takes unerringly the best that anywhere comes to be in the world, holds to it with the cling of fate, and lets all else fall to oblivion; out of this best it has made, and still fashions, that enduring world of idea and emotion into which we are born as truly as into the natural world. It has a marvelous economy.

> One accent of the Holy Ghost
> The heedless world has never lost.

Egypt, India, Greece and Rome, Italy, the English, France, America, the Turk, the Persian, the Russian, the

Japanese, the Chinese, the Negro feed its pure tradition of what excellence is possible to the race-mind, and has grown habitual in its being; and, as in the old myth, it destroys its parent, abolishing all these differences of climate, epoch and skull. The race-mind unifies the race which it preserves; that is its irresistible line of advance. It wipes out the barriers of time, language and country. It undoes the mischief of Babel, and restores to mankind one tongue in which all things can be understood by all men. It fuses the Bibles of all nations in one wisdom and one practice. It knocks off the tribal fetters of caste and creed; and, substituting thought for blood as the bond of the world, it slowly liberates that free soul, which is one in all men and common to all mankind. To free the soul in the individual life, and to accomplish the unity of mankind—that is its work.

To share in this work is the peculiar and characteristic office of literature. This fusion of the nations of the earth, this substitution of the thought-tie for the blood-tie, this enfranchisement of the soul, is its chief function; for literature is the organ of the race-mind. That is why literature is immortal. Though man's inheritance is bequeathed in many ways—the size and shape of the skull, the physical predisposition of the body, oral tradition, monumental and artistic works, institutions—civilization ever depends in an increasing degree upon literature both for expression and tradition; and whatever other forms the race-mind may mold itself into, literature is its most universal and comprehensive form. That is why literature is the great conservator of society. It shares in the life of the race-mind, partakes of its nature, as language does of thought, corresponds to it accurately, duplicates it, is its other-self. It is through literature mainly that we know the race-mind, and come to possess it; for though the term may seem abstract, the thing is real. Men of genius are great in proportion as they share in it, and national literatures are great in proportion as they embody and express it. Brunetière, the present critic of France, has recently announced a new literary formula. He declares that there is a European literature, not the combined group of national literatures, but a single literature common to European civilization, and that national literatures in their periods of culmination, are great in proportion as they coincide for the time being with this common literature, feed it, and, one after another taking the lead, create it. The declaration is a gleam of self-consciousness in the unity of Europe. How slowly the parts of a nation recognize the integrity of their territory and the community of their interests is one of the constant lessons of history; the Greek confederation, the work of Alfred or of Bismarck, our own experience in the Revolutionary period illustrate it; so the unity of Europe is still half-obscure and dark, though Catholicism, the Renaissance, the Reformation, the Revolution in turn flashed this unity forth, struggling to realize itself in the common civilization. The literature of Europe is the expression of this common genius—the best that man has dreamed or thought or done, has found or been, in Europe—now more brilliant in one capital, now in another as the life ebbs from state to state, and is renewed; for, though it fail here or there, it never ceases. This is the burning of the race-mind, now bright along the Seine, the Rhine, and the Thames, as once by the Ganges and the Tiber. The true unity of literature, however, does not lie in the literature of Europe or of India or of antiquity, or in any one manifestation, but in that world-literature which is the organ of the race-mind in its entire breadth and wholeness. The new French formula is a brilliant application, novel, striking and arresting, of the old and familiar idea that civilization in its evolution in history is a single process, continuous, advancing, and integral, of which nations and ages are only the successive phases. The life of the spirit in mankind is one and universal, burns with the same fires, moves to the same issues, joins in a single history; it is the race-mind realizing itself cumulatively in time, and mainly through the inheriting power of great literature.

I have developed this conception of the race-mind at some length because it is a primary idea. The nature of literature, and the perspective and interaction of particular literatures, are best comprehended in its light. I emphasize it. The world-literature, national literatures, individual men of genius, are what they are by virtue of sharing in the race-mind, appropriating it and identifying themselves with it; and what is true of them, on the great scale and in a high degree, is true also of every man who is born into the world. A man is a man by participating in the race-mind. Education is merely the process by which he enters it, avails himself of it, absorbs it. In the things of material civilization this is plain. All the callings of men, arts, crafts, trades, sciences, professions, the entire round of practical life, have a body of knowledge and method of work which are like gospel and ritual to them; apprentice, journeyman, and master are the stages of their career; and if anything be added, from life to life, it is on a basis of ascertained fact, or orthodox doctrine and fixed practice. I suppose technical education is most uniform, and by definiteness of aim and economy of method is most efficient; and in the professions as well as in the arts and crafts competition places so high a premium on knowledge and skill that the mastery of all the past can teach is compulsory in a high degree. Similarly, in society, the material unities such as those which commerce, manufacturing, banking establish and spread, are soonest evident and most readily accepted; so true is this that the peace of the world is rather a matter of finance than of Christianity. These practical activities and the interests that spring out of them lie in the sphere of material civilization; but the race-mind, positive, enduring and beneficent as it is in that sphere, is there parcelled out and individualized, and gives a particular and almost private character to man and classes of men, and it seeks a material good. There is another and spiritual sphere in which the soul which is one and the same in all men comes to self-knowledge, has its training, and achieves its mastery of the world. Essential, universal manhood is found only here; for it is here that the race-mind, by participation in which a man is a man, enfranchises the soul and gives to it the citizenship of the world. Education in the things of the spirit is often vague in aim and may seem wasteful in method, and it is not supported by the thrust and impetus of physical need and worldly hope; but it exists in all men in some measure, for no one born in our civilization is left so savage, no savage born in the wild is left so primitive but that he holds a mental attitude, however obscure, toward nature, man, and God, and has some discipline, however initial, in beauty, love, and religion. These things lie in the sphere of the soul.

It is, nevertheless, true that the greatest inequalities of condition exist here, and not in that part of life where good is measured by the things of fortune. The difference between the outcast and the millionaire is as nothing to that between the saint and the criminal, the fool and the knower, the boor and the poet. It is a blessing in our civilization, and one worthy of the hand of Providence, that if in material things justice be a laggard and disparities of condition be hard to remedy, the roads to church and school are public highways, free to all. This charter of free education in the life of the soul, which is the supreme opportunity of an American life, is an open door to the treasury of man's spirit. There whosoever will shall open the book of all the world, and read and ponder, and shall enter the common mind of man which is there contained and avail of its wisdom and absorb its energies into his own and become one with it in insight, power, and hope, and ere he is aware shall find himself mingling with the wisest, the holiest, the loveliest, as their comrade and peer. He shall have poet and sage to sup with him, and their meal shall be the bread of life.

What, then, is the position of the youth—of any man whose infinite life lies before him—at his entrance on this education, on this attempt to become one with the mind of the race? and, to neglect the material side of life, what is the process by which he begins to live in the spirit, and not as one new-born, but even in his youth sharing in the wisdom and disciplined power of a soul that has lived through all human ages—the soul of mankind? We forget the beginnings of life; we forget first sensation, first action, and the unknown magic by which, as the nautilus builds its shell, we built out of these early elements this world of the impalpable blue walls, the ocean and prairie floors, and star-sown space, each one of us for ourselves. There is a thought, which I suppose is a commonplace and may be half-trivial, but it is one that took hold of me in boyhood with great tenacity, and stirred the sense of strangeness and marvel in life; the idea that all I knew or should ever know was through something that had touched my body. The ether-wave envelopes us as the ocean, and in that small surface of contact is the sphere of sensibility—of light, sound, and the rest—out of which arises the world which each one of us perceives. It seems a fantastic conception, but it is a true one. For me the idea seemed to shrink the world to the dark envelope of my own body. It served, however, to initiate me in the broader conception that the soul is the center, and that life—the world—radiates from it into the enclosing infinite. Wordsworth, you remember, in his famous image of our infancy presents the matter differently; for him the infant began with the infinite, and boy and man lived in an ever narrowing world, a contracting prison, like that fabled one of the Inquisition, and in the end life became a thing common and finite:

> Heaven lies about us in our infancy!
> Shades of the prison-house begin to close
>   Upon the growing boy,
> But he beholds the light, and whence it flows,
>   He sees it in his joy:
>
> . . . .
>
> At length the man perceives it die away,
> And fade into the light of common day.

This was never my own conception, nor do I think it is natural to many men. On the contrary, life is an expansion. The sense of the larger world comes first, perhaps, in those unremembered years when the sky ceases to be an inverted bowl, and lifts off from the earth. The experience is fixed for me by another half-childish memory, the familiar verses of Tom Hood in which he describes his early home. You will recall the almost nursery rhymes:

> I remember, I remember
> The fir-trees dark and high;
> I used to think their slender tops
> Were close against the sky;
> It was a childish ignorance,
> But now 'tis little joy
> To know I'm farther off from Heaven
> Than when I was a boy.

Sentiment in the place of philosophy, the thought is the same as Wordsworth's, but the image is natural and true. The noblest image, however, that sets forth the spread of the world, is in that famous sonnet by an obscure poet, Blanco White, describing the first time that the sun went down in Paradise:

> Mysterious night! when our first parent knew
> Thee from report divine, and heard thy name,
> Did he not tremble for this lovely frame,
> This glorious canopy of light and blue?
> Yet, 'neath the curtain of translucent dew,
> Bathed in the rays of the great setting flame,
> Hesperus with the host of heaven came,
> And lo! creation widened in man's view.

The theory of Copernicus and the voyage of Columbus are the great historical moments of such change in the thoughts of men. As travel thus discloses the amplitude of the planet and science fills the infinite of space for the learning mind, history in its turn peoples the "dark background and abysm of time." But more marvelous than the unveiling of time and space, is that last revelation which unlocks the inward world of idea and emotion, and gives solidity of life as by a third dimension. It is this world which is the realm of imaginative literature; scarcely by any other interpreter shall a man come into knowledge of it with any adequacy; and here the subject draws to a head, for it is by the operation of literature in this regard that the race-mind takes possession of the world.

We are plunged at birth *in medias res,* as the phrase is, into the midst of things—into a world already old, of old ideas, old feelings, old experience, that has drunk to the lees the wisdom of the preacher of Ecclesiastes, and renews in millions of lives the life that has been lived a million times; a world of custom and usage, of immemorial habits, of causes prejudged, of insoluble problems, of philosophies and orthodoxies and things established; and yet, too, a world of the undiscovered. The youth awakes in this world, intellectually, in literature; and since the literature of the last age is that on which the new generation is formed, he now first comes in contact with the large life of mankind in the literature of the last century. It is an extraordinary miscellaneous literature, varied and copious in matter, full of conflicting ideas, cardinal truths, and hazardous guesses; and for the young mind the problem of orientation—that is of finding itself, of knowing the true East, is difficult. Literature, too, has an electric stimulation, and in the first onrush of the intellectual life brings that well-known storm and stress which is the true awakening; with eager and delighted surprise the soul feels fresh sensibilities and unsuspected energies rise in its being. It is a time of shocks, discoveries, experiences that change the face of the world. Reading the poets, the youth finds new dynamos in himself. A new truth unseals a new faculty in him; a new writer unlooses a new force in him; he becomes, like Briareus, hundred-handed, like Shakespeare, myriad-minded. So like a miracle is the discovery of the power of life.

Let me illustrate the experience in the given case—the literature of the nineteenth century. It will all fall under three heads: the world of nature's frame, the world of man's action, the world of God's being. Nature is, in the first instance, a spectacle. One may see the common sights of earth, and still have seen little. The young eye requires to be trained in what to see, what to choose to see out of the vague whole, and so to see his true self reflected there in another form, for in the same landscape the farmer, the military engineer, the painter see each a different picture. Burns teaches the young heart to see nature realistically, definitely, in hard outline, and always in association with human life—and the presence of animals friendly and serviceable to man, the life of the farm, is a dominant note in the scene. Byron guides the eye to elemental grandeur in the storm and in the massiveness of Alp and ocean. Shelley brings out color and atmosphere and evokes the luminous spirit from every star and dew-drop and dying wave. Tennyson makes nature and artist's easel where from poem to poem glows the frescoing of the walls of life. Thus changing from page to page the youth sees nature with Burns as a man who sympathizes with human toil, with Byron as a man who would mate with the tempest, with Shelley as a man of almost spiritualized senses, with Tennyson as a man of artistic luxury. Again, nature is an order, a law in matter, such as science conceives her; and this phase appears inceptively in *Queen Mab* and explicitly in *In Memoriam*, and many a minor poem of Tennyson, not the less great because minor in his work, in which alone the scientific spirit of the age has found utterance equal to its own sublimity. Yet, again, nature is a symbol, an expression of truth itself in another medium than thought; and so, in minute ways, Burns moralized the *Mountain Daisy*, and Wordsworth the *Small Celandine;* and, on the grand scale, Shelley mythologized nature in vast oracular figures of man's faith, hope, and destiny. And again, nature is a molding influence so close to human life as to be a spiritual presence about and within it. This last feeling of the participation of nature in life is so fundamental that no master of song is without it; but, in this group, Wordsworth is preëminent as its exponent, with such directness, certainty, and power did he seize and express it. What he saw in his dalesmen was what the mountains had made them; what he told in *Tintern Abbey* was nature making of him; what he sang in his lyric of ideal womanhood was such an intimacy of nature with woman's being that it was scarcely to be divided from her spirit. The power which fashions us from birth, sustains the vital force of the body, and feeds its growing functions, seems to exceed the blind and mute region of matter, and feeding the senses with color, music, and delight shapes the soul itself and guides it, and supports and consoles the child it has created in mortality. I do not overstate Wordsworth's sense of this truth; and it is a truth that twines about the roots of all poetry like a river of life. It explains to the growing boy something in his own history, and he goes on in the paths he has begun to follow, it may be with touches of vague mystery but with an expectant, receptive, and responsive heart. In regard to nature, then, the youth's life under the favor of these poets appreciates her in at least these four ways, artistically, scientifically, symbolically, and spiritually, and begins to fix in molds of his own spirit that miracle of change, the Protean being of matter.

To turn to the world of man's life, the simplest gain from contact with this literature of which I am speaking is in the education of the historic sense. Romance discovered history, and seeking adventure and thriving in what is sought, made that great find, the Middle Ages, which the previous time looked on much as we regard the civilization of China with mingled ignorance and contempt. It found also the Gael and the Northmen, and many an outlying region, many a buried tract of time. In Scott's novels characteristically, but also in countless others, in the rescued and revived ballads of England and the North, and in the renewed forms of Greek imagination, the historic sense is strongly drawn on, and no reader can escape its culture, for the place of history and its inspirational power in literature is fundamental in the spirit of the nineteenth century. But what most arrests the young heart, in this world of man's life, is those ideas which we sum up as the Revolution, and the principle of democracy which is primary in the literature of the last age. There the three great words—liberty, fraternity, and equality—and the theory that in Shelley was so burning an enthusiasm and in Byron so passionate a force, are still aflame; and the new feeling toward man which was implicit in democracy is deeply planted in that aspect of fraternity which appears in the interest in the common lot, and in that aspect of liberty which appears in the sense of the dignity of the individual. Burns, Scott, Dickens illustrate the one; Byron, Shelley, and Carlyle the other. The literature of the great watchwords, the literature of the life of the humble classes, the literature of the rebellious individual will—the latter flashing out many a wild career and exploding many a startling theory of how life is to be lived—are the very core and substance of the time. The application of ideas to life in the large, of which Rousseau was so cardinal an example, opens an endless field in a century so rich in discovery, so active in intellect, and so plastic in morals; and here one may wander at will. Here is matter for a lifetime. But without particularizing, it is plain how variously, how profoundly and vividly through this literature the mind is exercised in the human world, takes on the color, picturesqueness, and movement of history, builds up the democratic social faith and develops the energy of individual freedom, and becomes a place for a career of great ideas.

There remains the world of God's being, or to vary the phrase in sympathy with the mode of approach characteristic of the nineteenth century, the world in which God is. It may be broadly stated that the notion of what used to be called an absentee God, a far-off Ruler overseeing by modes analogous to human administration the affairs of earth as a distant province, finds no place in this literature of the last age. The note of thought is rather of the intimacy of God with his creation and with the soul of man. God is known in two ways; as an idea in the intellect and as an experience in the emotions; and in poetry the two modes blend, and often blur where they blend. Their habitual expression in the great poets of the age is in pantheistic forms, but this is rather a matter of form than of substance. The immanence of the divine is the root-idea; in Wordsworth it is an immanence of sublime power, seized through communion with nature; in Shelley, who was more profoundly human, it is an immanence of transcendent love, seized through his sense of the destiny of the universe that carries in its bosom the glory of life; in Tennyson, in whom the sense of a veiled intellect was more deep, it is an immanence of mystery in both the outer and the inner world. In other parts of the field, God is also conceived in history, and there immanent as Providence. His immanence in the individual—a matter dark to any thought—is most explicitly set forth by Emerson. It is perhaps generally considered that in the literature of the nineteenth century there is a large sceptical and atheistic element; but this is an error. Genius by its own nature has no part in the spirit that denies; it is positive, affirms and creates. Its apparent denials will be found to be partial, and affect fragments of a dead past only; its denials are, in reality, higher and more universal affirmations. If Wordsworth appears to put nature in the place of God, or Shelley love, or Keats beauty, they only affirm that phrase of the divine which is nighest to their own apprehension, affection, and delight. Their experience of the divine governs and blends with their intellectual theory, sometimes, as I have said, with a blur of thought. Each one's experience in these things is for himself alone, and private; the ways of the Spirit no man knows; but it is manifest that for the opening mind, whether of youth or of older years, the sense of eternity, however delicate, subtle, and silent is its realm, is fed nobly, sweetly, and happily, by these poets in whom the spirit of man crying for expression unlocks the secrecy of its relations to the infinite.

Such is the nature of the contact of the mind with literature by means of which it enters on its race inheritance of idea and emotion, takes possession of the stored results, clothes itself with energies whose springs are in the earliest distance of time, and builds up anew for itself the whole and various world as it has come to be known by man in his age-long experience. The illustration I have employed minimizes the constancy, the completeness, the vastness of the process; for it takes no account of other disciplines of religious tradition and practice, of oral transmission, and of such universal and intimate formative powers as mere language. But it will be found on analysis that all of these depend, in the man, on literature in the broad sense; and, in the education of the soul in the higher life, the awakening, the revealing and upbuilding force lies, I am persuaded, in the peculiar charge of literature in which the race-mind has stamped an image of itself.

It is obvious that what I have advanced brings the principle of authority into a cardinal place in life, and clothes tradition with great power. It might seem that the individual in becoming one with the race-mind has only to endue himself with the past as with a garment, to take its mold with the patience of clay, and to be in the issue a recast of the past, thinking old thoughts, feeling old emotions, doing old actions, in preëstablished ways. But this is to misconceive the process by which the individual effects this union; he does not take the impress of the race-mind as the wax receives the imprint of the seal. This union is an act of life, a process of energy, joy and growth, of self-expression; here learning is living, and there is no other way to know the doctrine than to do its will; so the race-mind is not copied, but is perpetually re-born in men, and the world which each one of us thus builds for himself out of his preferred capacities, memories, and desires—our farmer's, engineer's, painter's world, as I have said—is his own original and unique world. There is none like it, none. Originality consists in this re-birth of the world in the young soul. This world, nevertheless, the world of each of us, is not one of wilfulness, fantasy, and caprice; if, on the other hand, it is such stuff as dreams are made of, on the other it is the stuff of necessity. It has a consistency, a law and fate, of its own, which supports, wields, and sustains it. Authority is no more than the recognition of and obedience to this underlying principle of being, whose will is disclosed to us in man's life so far as that life in its wholeness falls within our view; in knowledge of this will all wisdom consists, of its action in us all experience is woven, and in union with it all private judgment is confirmed. Authority, truly interpreted, is only another phase of that identity of the soul in all men by virtue of which society exists, and especially that intellectual state arises, that state which used to be called the republic of letters and which is the institution of the race-mind to be the center, the home and hope of civilization in all ages—that state where the unity of mankind is accomplished in the spiritual unities of science, art, and love.

To sum up these suggestions which I have thought it

desirable to offer in order that the point of view taken in these lectures might, perhaps, be plain, I conceive of history as a single process in which through century after century in race after race the soul of man proceeds in a progressive comprehension of the universe and evolution of its own humanity, and passes on to each new generation its accumulated knowledge and developed energies, in their totality and without loss, at the acme of achievement. I conceive of this inheriting and bequeathing power as having its life and action in the race-mind. I conceive of literature as an organ of the race-mind, and of education as the process by which the individual enters into the race-mind, becomes more and more man, and in the spiritual life mainly by means of literature. I conceive of the body of men who thus live and work in the soul as constituting the intellectual state, that republic of letters, in which the race-mind reaches, from age to age, its maximum of knowledge and power, in men of genius and those whose lives they illumine, move and direct; the unity of mankind is the ideal of this state, and the freeing of the soul which takes place in it is its means. I conceive of the progressive life of this state, in civilization after civilization, as a perpetual death of the best, in culture after culture, for the good of the lower, a continuing sacrifice, in the history of humanity, of man for mankind. And from this mystery, though to some it may seem only the recourse of intellectual despair, I pluck a confident faith in that imperishable relation which man and his works contain, and which though known only in the continuity of the race-mind, I am compelled to believe, has eternal reality.

A WORLD OF OPPORTUNITY[1]

CHARLES MILLS GAYLEY

[For biographical sketch, see page 37]

THE world was never better worth preparing for. The panorama unrolled before the mind was never more gorgeous:—a new renaissance revealing reaches unimagined; prophesying splendor unimaginable; unveiling mysteries of time and space and natural law and human potency.

Archæology uncovers with a spade the world of Ariadne and of Minos, of Agamemnon and of Priam. Where Jason launched the Argo, paintings are unearthed that antedate Apelles. Mummied crocodiles disgorge their papyri: and we read the administrative record of the Ptolemies. Bacchylides breaks the silence of centuries: himself Menander mounts the stage, and in no borrowed Roman sock; and Aristotle reappears to shed fresh light upon the constitution of the Athenians.

History availing herself of cognate sciences deciphers documents and conditions anew; and the vision of the past is reinterpreted in terms of social and economic actuality. Emigrations and conquests become a modern tale of commerce and industrial stress. Cæsar and Agrippina, Cromwell and Marie Antoinette, are all to read again; and the Bard of Venusia acquires a new

[1] Reprinted from *Idols* by permission of the author and of Doubleday, Page and Company, publishers.

and startling modernity as the literary advance agent of a plutocratic wine firm. As in a "glass prospective" literature is viewed; and kaleidoscopic transformations of *gest* and ballad, epic and drama, cross-sections of the crypt of fiction, dazzle the eye of critic and philologist and poet.

With golden keys of psychology, history and philology, the anthropologist unlocks the mind of primitive man. The student of the holier things invades the Temple itself; and from day to day the sacramental doors swing back on age-long galleries of worship.

Taking fresh heart of ethics, economics wears a new and most seductive smile. No longer the minimizing of material cost, but the maximizing of vital value, she regards. She seeks the psychic income, the margin of leisure for the soul, the margin of health for the body: the greatest of national assets—the true wealth of nations. To the modern problems of social and political theory and of jurisprudence, of municipal and national and colonial administration, a similar fascination of beneficent discovery attracts; and to that development of international politics which aims at constitutional law rather than the substantive private law of nations.

Geology multiplies her æons, and astronomy her glittering fields. "Hills peep o'er hills, and Alps on Alps" of new discovered cause "arise." "The idea of the electron has broken the frame work of the old physics to pieces, has revived ancient atomistic hypotheses, and made of them principles," and radio-activity "has opened to the explorer a New America full of wealth yet unknown." The science of the law of celestial movements has given birth to the science of the substance of celestial bodies; and, with astro-physics, we study more narrowly than ever our one star, and its outcasts, the planets. We wonderingly contemplate the transport of matter from star to star—and from planet to planet, maybe, of life.

Geology has given birth to physiography. We pass from inorganic to organic, and probe the interaction of physical environment and animate nature. In evolutionary science they are saying that new species leap into being at a wave of the wand of mutation; and the war between Mendelism and Darwinism wages. The knighthood of the Quest of Life enrolls in the order of psychic mystery or the order of mechanism, and presses on. Though neither win to the Grail, each wins nearer to its law. By the delicate ministrations of surgery, life is prolonged. Immunization lifts ever higher her red cross.

Engineering advances, agriculture advances, commerce expands. We compass the earth, we swim the seas, we ride the air. Our voices pierce the intervals of space, and our thoughts the unplumbed waves of ether. And from her watch-tower scrutinizing all—science, pure and applied, history and art, mechanism and spirit, teleology, evolution—the science of sciences, Divine Philosophy rounds out her calm survey. Never more tempting, more vital, the problem than that which she faces now; the problem of the fundamental character of personality. "In the light of all this evolution or mutation, what is God?" she asks. "Is he, too, but a cosmic process in which we assist; or an eternal standard of perfection against which we measure ourselves and in terms of which we strive?"

ATTAINMENT[1]

MADISON CAWEIN

On the heights of Great Endeavor,—
Where Attainment looms forever,—
Toiling upward, ceasing never,
Climb the fateful Centuries:
Up the difficult dark places,
Joy and anguish in their faces,
On they strive, the living races,
And the dead that no one sees.

Shape by shape with brow uplifted,
One by one where night is rifted,
Pass the victors, many gifted,
Where the heaven opens wide;
While below them fallen or seated,
Mummy-like, or shadow-sheeted,
Stretch the lines of the defeated,—
Scattered on the mountain side.

And each victor, passing wanly,
Gazes on that Presence lonely,
With moving eyes where only
Grow the dreams for which men die:
Grow the dreams, the far, ethereal,
That on earth assume material

[1] Reprinted by permission of Small, Maynard & Company.

Attributes, and, vast, imperial,
Rear their battlements on high.

Kingdoms, marble-templed, towered,
Where the arts, the many-dowered,—
That for centuries have flowered,
Trampled under War's wild heel,—
Lift immortal heads and golden,
Blossoms of the times called olden,
Soul-alluring, earth-withholden,
Universal in appeal.

As they enter—high and lowly,—
On the hush these words fall slowly:—
"Ye who kept your purpose holy,
Never dreamed your cause was vain,
Look!—Behold, through time abating,
How the long, sad days of waiting,
Striving, starving, hoping, hating,
Helped your spirit to attain.

"For to all who dream, aspire,
Marry effort to desire,
On the cosmic heights, in fire,
Beaconing, my form appears:—
I am marvel, I am morning!—
Beauty in man's heart and warning!—
On my face none looks with scorning,
And no soul attains who fears."